# WHAT IS A NATION?
# AND OTHER POLITICAL WRITINGS

COLUMBIA STUDIES IN POLITICAL THOUGHT /
POLITICAL HISTORY

COLUMBIA STUDIES IN POLITICAL THOUGHT /
POLITICAL HISTORY

*Dick Howard, General Editor*

Columbia Studies in Political Thought / Political History is a series dedicated to exploring the possibilities for democratic initiative and the revitalization of politics in the wake of the exhaustion of twentieth-century ideological "isms." By taking a historical approach to the politics of ideas about power, governance, and the just society, this series seeks to foster and illuminate new political spaces for human action and choice.

Pierre Rosanvallon, *Democracy Past and Future*, edited by Samuel Moyn (2006)

Claude Lefort, *Complications: Communism and the Dilemmas of Democracy*,
translated by Julian Bourg (2007)

Benjamin R. Barber, *The Truth of Power: Intellectual Affairs in the
Clinton White House* (2008)

Andrew Arato, *Constitution Making Under Occupation: The Politics of
Imposed Revolution in Iraq* (2009)

Dick Howard, *The Primacy of the Political: A History of Political Thought from the Greeks
to the French and American Revolution* (2010)

Paul W. Kahn, *Political Theology: Four New Chapters on the Concept of Sovereignty* (2011)

Stephen Eric Bronner, *Socialism Unbound: Principles, Practices, and Prospects* (2011)

David William Bates, *States of War: Enlightenment Origins of the Political* (2011)

Warren Breckman, *Adventures of the Symbolic: Post-Marxism and Radical Democracy* (2013)

Martin Breaugh, *The Plebeian Experience: A Discontinuous History of Political Freedom*,
translated by Lazer Lederhendler (2013)

Dieter Grimm, *Sovereignty: The Origin and Future of a Political and Legal Concept*,
translated by Belinda Cooper (2015)

Frank Palmeri, *State of Nature, Stages of Society: Enlightenment Conjectural History
and Modern Social Discourse* (2016)

Elías José Palti, *An Archaeology of the Political: Regimes of Power from
the Seventeenth Century to the Present* (2017)

Zvi Ben-Dor Benite, Stefanos Geroulanos, and Nicole Jerr, eds.,
*The Scaffolding of Sovereignty: Global and Aesthetic Perspectives on
the History of a Concept* (2017)

Ute Tellmann, *Life and Money: The Genealogy of the Liberal Economy
and the Displacement of Politics* (2017)

# WHAT IS A NATION?
# AND OTHER
# POLITICAL WRITINGS

———

ERNEST RENAN

———

TRANSLATED AND EDITED BY
M. F. N. GIGLIOLI

Columbia University Press
*New York*

Columbia University Press
*Publishers Since 1893*
New York    Chichester, West Sussex
cup.columbia.edu

Library of Congress Cataloging-in-Publication Data
Names: Renan, Ernest, 1823–1892, author.
Title: What is a nation? : and other political writings / Ernest Renan ;
translated and edited by M.F.N. Giglioli.
Other titles: Qu'est-ce qu'une nation? English
Description: New York : Columbia University Press, 2018. |
Series: Columbia studies in political thought / political history |
Includes bibliographical references and index.
Identifiers: LCCN 2018002846 (print) | LCCN 2018018856 (e-book) |
ISBN 9780231547147 (e-book) | ISBN 9780231174305 (cloth : alk. paper)
Subjects: LCSH: Nation-state. | Nationalism.
Classification: LCC JC311 (e-book) | LCC JC311 .R35313 2018 (print) |
DDC 320.1—dc23
LC record available at https://lccn.loc.gov/2018002846

# CONTENTS

# ACKNOWLEDGMENTS

Part of the research for this project was made possible by support from the Fondation Maison des sciences de l'homme, the European Commission's Action Marie Curie COFUND program, and CEVIPOF (Centre de recherches politiques de Sciences Po) in Paris.

I wish to thank Larry Wolff, Edward Berenson, Samuel Moyn, Aurelian Craiutu, Ezra Suleiman, Lucien Jaume, Perrine Simon-Nahum, Pascal Perrineau, Odile Gaultier-Voituriez, Michel Wieviorka, Benedicte Rastier, Vincent Martigny, Nadia Marzouki, Linda Boukhris, Giuseppe Ballacci, Isacco Turina, Michelle Cheyne, Caterina Zanfi, Joe Paff, Robert Priest, Sandro Dal Lago, Wendy Lochner, Dick Howard, Pier Paolo Giglioli, Ann Hagman Frye, Ilaria Giglioli, and Daisy Cockburn.

MFNG
Petrolia, Calif.
June 2017

# SERIES EDITOR'S FOREWORD

Readers familiar with the series "Political Thought / Political History" may be surprised to encounter this carefully selected and historically annotated edition of the *political* writings of a nineteenth-century French academic scholar known today, if at all, for his 1882 definition of the nation as "an everyday plebiscite." Others may have encountered the author's name, if not much of his work, through its denunciation in Edward Said's account of what he criticized as "orientalism" in a book bearing that title (Said 1978). But the erudition of Ernest Renan's voluminous historical and philological work remains buried on the shelves of academic libraries. A few will have heard about the debates that resulted from publication of his rationalist reconstruction of the *Life of Jesus* (1863) the year after he was removed from his position at the Collège de France as a result of pressure from the Catholic Church. But those who know of that book are more aware of the scandal aroused by it than of the fact that it was one of eight volumes of Renan's *History of Christianity*. Given this contemporary context, M. F. N. Giglioli's presentation of Renan's political thought in his own words as being worthy of our attention echoes well the larger theme of this series as it was summarized in the editor's foreword to Claude Lefort's *Complications* (2007): "no political thought without history; no history without political thought."

Reading Renan as political today is complicated; the plethoric work of the scholar is a bit pedantic and certainly dated. Giglioli presents it under the credo that heads up this volume as an epigraph: "Although knowledge of the present is less instructive than that of the past, the present is also one face of reality; it is worthy of study." How does this faith in knowledge unearthed from the past comport with Renan's apparently voluntarist definition of the nation? How does it relate to that domain that defines the political?

Giglioli offers one thread for an interpretation when he points out that, although Renan left the seminary (and lost his faith) at the age of twenty-two, he immediately set to work on a book titled *The Future of Science*, which he did not publish until 1890, two years before his death. (Giglioli adds that Renan retained the oratorical style of the religious novice in that book.) But the "science" to which Renan devoted his mature faith was neither the rank positivism of Comte nor the flat utilitarianism of Mill; it was, one might say, an idealist science, a faith in *spiritual* progress that is also *rational*. Thus, to remain with the brief text that is his most familiar work for contemporary readers, Renan insists (through an exhaustive accumulation of historical examples) that a nation cannot be defined by empirical facts such as race or language, religion or geography, or functional needs; he insists that a nation is a "moral consciousness." As such, a nation may perish if citizens withdraw or abandon their active faith in it. Indeed, he notes, eventually "Europe" will no doubt come to replace present-day nations (although Renan neither affirms its necessity nor insists that this represents a desirable future). In the meantime, as underlined by Giglioli's epigraph, the present remains "worthy of study."

Renan does not propose a systematic political theory; Giglioli situates Renan's quite French variant of liberalism in the "antipolitical ethos" of the nineteenth century (in which he includes Nietzsche). From this perspective, Renan combines, in an unsteady methodical approach bolstered by dense historical retrospective, what might be called an "idealist positivism," which believes firmly in the progress of the human spirit, with a "spiritualist voluntarism," which can never be certain of the stability of its advances. From this perspective, the aristocracy of mind that began to replace the aristocracy of birth in 1789 was a tentative and tenuous advance into the tumultuous nineteenth century, in which it would be repeatedly threatened, recanted, and again regained. This idealist (but not idealistic) faith in humanity's spiritual progress was moral before it was political; it was not metaphysical; in the text republished here, it was above all public, civic, and cultural and certainly not the simple faith of the historical pedant for whom knowledge of the past was more "instructive" than understanding of the present. From this perspective, although he was neither a friend of emerging industrialism nor a supporter of egalitarian democracy, Renan's political writings can be read nonetheless as standing on the side of progress insofar as they challenge their positivist or utilitarian interpretations by treating them as an object for "study."

The book series "Political Thought / Political History" is not the collective expression of its different and diverse authors, who cannot be assumed to have shared in a predefined project. Still less is it the product of the editor's global vision.[1] The task of the editor, expressed in a brief foreword like this one, is to suggest a conceptual framework that binds together unique works of thought. The framework appears and is developed as the series grows and thickens. In the case of Renan, it appears that the challenge he tries to meet is to maintain the unsteady, always uncertain, and regularly challenged relation between an idealistic positivism constantly alert to (i.e., "studying") the possibilities present but latent in the interstices of social relations and a spiritualist voluntarism actively engaged with an ideal (e.g., the "nation") that continues to exist precisely because it is always just beyond reach. Political essays do not resolve this tension; they explore its history without shying from polemic in order to preserve the challenge of critical rationality.

Dick Howard
September 5, 2017

# INTRODUCTION

*Bien que la connaissance du présent soit moins instructive que celle du passé, le présent est aussi une des faces de la réalité; il mérite d'être étudié.*[1]

—ERNEST RENAN, QUESTIONS CONTEMPORAINES *(1858)*

Joseph Ernest Renan was born in Tréguier, in the Côtes-du-Nord department of Brittany, on February 28, 1823.[2] Renan's worldview was enduringly influenced by his upbringing in his native province: Brittany, with its Celtic heritage, its diffuse piety, its tradition of resistance to Parisian centralization, provided him with his first cultural and political models.[3] He was the youngest of the three children of Philibert Renan and Magdelaine Féger. His father, a captain in the merchant marine, was lost at sea when Ernest was five, leaving the family in difficult economic conditions. The boy, however, soon demonstrated exceptional intellectual promise, and in 1838, through the intercession of his sister Henriette (1811–1861), managed to secure a scholarship in the Catholic seminary of Saint-Nicolas-du-Chardonnet in Paris, then run by the Abbé Félix Dupanloup. Renan's ecclesiastical education, begun in Brittany, lasted nearly a decade.

The first great crisis of Renan's life coincided with the loss of his religious faith, which culminated in 1845 with the abandonment of his seminary studies. While Renan's separation from Catholicism paralleled a broader wave of mass dechristianization throughout Europe in the nineteenth century, what is remarkable about his case is the degree to which his working habits, writing style, and even presentation of self (in Erving Goffman's sense[4]) bore the influence of the seminary ethos of his formative years throughout his life. The ideal of the man of letters, of the savant that Renan was to preach and embody during his career appeared strikingly similar to a secularized cleric, a high priest of the cult of scientific truth and learning. Thus, while his separation from the church freed him from conformity to metaphysical dogma, his habitus retained its seminarian discipline.

A national political trauma quickly followed Renan's existential crisis. In February 1848, the July Monarchy of the Orléans king Louis-Philippe was overthrown by popular protests, and France was plunged into half a decade of political convulsions, resulting ultimately in the proclamation of the empire of Napoleon III. The demise of the Orléanist regime posed a broader historical and philosophical dilemma for French liberalism (v. infra), but for a young scholar of twenty-four, fresh from his break with Christianity, it provided a catalyst for the expression of some of his most deeply felt ideas. Faced with the open class warfare of the June 1848 days, the erosion of the new republican institutions, the opportunism of the Catholic party, Renan responded with his first major text, *L'avenir de la science*. Kept unpublished until the very end of Renan's life, but in a sense providing a program for his entire intellectual career, *L'avenir de la science* sets forth the ideal of unbounded development of knowledge as man's highest calling, to which all other political and social goals must be subordinated. The resulting position is a curious hybrid, allying the rhetoric of the era of progress (reminiscent of J. S. Mill's *The Present Age*) with a much more ancient, indeed premodern, and decidedly anti-utilitarian ideology of intellectual exceptionalism. The practical implementation of such a stance, beyond its claims to social centrality, was anti-political, a commitment to the disinterested pursuit of knowledge far from the vain commotions of the day.[5]

Having abandoned the microcosm of ecclesiastical learning institutions, Renan was faced with the problem of securing material resources to support his scholarly lifestyle. In the cultural conditions of mid-nineteenth-century France, only the state could replace the church in the role of patron. In this arrangement lay the main dilemma of Renan's position, for the independence of the scholar found its limit in the tolerance of the state's cultural policy makers.

One of the earliest experiences of this contrast occurred in the context of Renan's mission to Italy. The government that financed Renan's archaeological expedition (October 1849–June 1850) was not only engaged in a severe crackdown on freedom of speech domestically but was also intervening militarily in the Italian peninsula to crush Mazzini's republican experiment in Rome and restore the pope to his throne. Renan's journey to Italy was therefore significant in three respects: It gave Renan his first field experience, an invaluable addition to his theoretical erudition. Furthermore, it placed him in contact with social and intellectual conditions, such as those of southern Italy, wholly outside the pale of modern progress, thus alerting Renan to the spatial limits of the modern society he had extolled in *L'avenir de la science* and providing a first dimension to his developing orientalism.[6] Finally, it exposed him to a geopolitical context in which his scholarly independence and neutrality, his role as a bystander, could appear questionable.

Shortly after Renan's return to Paris, the Second Republic succumbed to the ambitions of its president, Louis-Napoléon Bonaparte. For the young liberal intellectuals of Renan's generation, the shock of the loss of political freedoms was severe. However, once it appeared that the new regime was secure and unchallenged, the dilemma of ideological opposition or constructive criticism became pressing. Renan was characteristic of a certain stratum of bourgeois intelligentsia in adopting a line of principled resistance mixed with practical accommodation toward the December coup and the regime that sprung from it. Excluded from direct involvement in the machinery of government, liberal opinion under the Second Empire focused on broader cultural struggles—chiefly, in the fight against Catholic reaction and obscurantism. Until 1869, when a thaw in the regime made Renan believe he might be destined to a wider political role, his main political engagement was his confrontation with the various cultural institutions of the French state, and the cause of his struggles and polemics was the defense of free thought against religious encroachment. These continued exchanges acquainted Renan with the internal dynamics and competing political influences within the structure of Napoleonic power and, in particular, with the opposing court factions of the reactionary Empress Eugénie and the relatively broader-minded Prince Jérôme Napoléon. Hence, Renan attempted to navigate the shifting politics of personal favor of the Second Empire, aided by his social proximity to decision-making circles in the world of Parisian salons. At the same time, the capital offered Renan the opportunity to consort with some of the most distinguished and free-spirited literary personalities of the age, as in the celebrated *dîners Magny*, where he was a constant presence alongside Gustave Flaubert, Charles Augustin de Sainte-Beuve, George Sand, the Goncourt brothers, Théophile Gautier, and Hippolyte Taine. Indeed, it is possible to note a parallelism between Renan's career under the Second Empire and Taine's: barred from recognition in the traditional French intellectual institutions (university, Académie française, etc.) because of their heterodox political views, both liberal writers became increasingly central to the broader Parisian cultural scene of the 1850s and 1860s.

Renan's ambivalent relation with the Napoleonic regime is apparent in two major events of his life in the early 1860s: the mission to the Levant and the Collège de France controversy.

The mission to Lebanon, Syria, and Palestine (October 1860–October 1861) was a major landmark for Renan's scholarly pursuits, offering him invaluable firsthand knowledge of the physical setting for his investigations into the origins of Christianity. At the same time, it was strongly encouraged by, and highly beneficial to, the regime. France was intervening militarily in the Levant as part of its geopolitical involvement in the "Eastern Question." At the time of Renan's mission, six thousand French troops and a naval squadron were present in the area to protect Eastern Christians against the great Druze revolt in the Ottoman Empire. The possibility to add cultural luster to a power-politics enterprise was extremely welcome in Parisian governmental circles. Therefore, Renan's firsthand experience of the East was indissolubly linked with the workings of European imperialism.

While the archaeological mission of 1861 showed Renan at his most collaborative with the aims of the Second Empire, the controversy surrounding his appointment to the chair of Hebrew philology of the Collège de France and his immediate suspension from it following his inaugural lecture illustrate the chasm that separated them. Appointments to the Collège de France always bore a political significance, given traditional governmental involvement in cultural policy. While Renan's scholarly qualifications were beyond question, the scandal of his freethinking positions (in his lecture he denied, in passing, the divinity of Jesus), issuing from a chair that Catholic opinion considered tantamount to one of biblical exegesis, proved enormous.[7] What followed was a textbook polemic on free speech and education: Renan refused to retract his statements or accept any of the accommodations envisaged by the authorities, and he let himself become a very public victim of Catholic-inspired censorship.

The mid-1860s saw the explosion of Renan's public notoriety, thanks to the publication of the *Vie de Jésus* (1863), which became an international best seller.[8] They were, however, years of political quiescence and isolation for Renan. Even his involvement in Émile Ollivier's project of liberalization of the Empire, culminating in Renan's unsuccessful run for parliament in the 1869 elections, was fleeting. The great crisis of 1870–1871, on the contrary, was a turning point for Renan's life and political engagement. France's defeat by Otto von Bismarck was the close of an era: it spelled the end of French ascendancy in Europe and the explosion of the contradictions of its developmental model. The Paris Commune was but the consequence of the failures of the Empire. At the same time, especially for the Germanophile Renan, it signified the demise of the ideal of a Goethian Germany; in its place arose the strange and troubling hybrid of ancien régime mentality and modern technological/organizational prowess represented by Prussia.

Faced with this completely novel scenario, Renan conceived of political and intellectual engagement in current affairs as a form of civic duty. His *Réforme intellectuelle et morale* (1871) was a blueprint for rescuing France from the abyss of defeat and civil war, a setting out of the necessary reforms for a future revanche. This work contributed to the process of reflection on the creation of a ruling class for a country without a loyal aristocracy, which was to receive practical application in a series of contemporary institution-building projects, such as the creation by Émile Boutmy of the École libre de sciences politiques, the forerunner of Sciences Po. Renan's endeavors of these years were also an effort at broader political education, a negotiation of the role of the liberal heritage in the new France, at a time in which the country's constitutional form was still in dispute.

Renan was a late and measured convert to republicanism. Throughout the 1870s, he opposed the religious conservatism of the *ordre moral* and became progressively convinced of the practical unfeasibility of a monarchical restoration. However, it was only as a consequence of President MacMahon's attempt in May 1877 unlawfully to impose a monarchist government on what had become a republican-dominated parliament that Renan perceived the Republic's solid roots in the country and the unavoidability of its triumph. His theoretical evolution proceeded apace: his play *Caliban* (1878)[9] charts the possibility of channeling popular passions within democratic institutions that still guarantee the freedom and independence of science. Meanwhile, his principled opposition to the Empire on religious policy and the aura of victimhood from the Collège de France controversy afforded Renan political capital with the republicans. His *Réforme* could come to be seen (with a few exceptions, such as his positions on suffrage and centralization) as a list of liberal constraints whose respect would guarantee liberals' support for republican nation building. After all, he shared with the republican founding fathers a secular demopedic ideal.[10] Similarly, they agreed on the necessary role of nationalism in the wider acceptance of a democratic order. Hence, despite some remaining areas of ambiguity, Renan could be associated to the pantheon of intellectual leading lights of the conservative Republic and to its politics of *opportunisme*.[11]

Reinstated by the government in his chair at the Collège de France and duly elected to the Académie française in 1878, Renan in his last years multiplied his interventions in public debate and contributed preemptively to his memorialization.[12] At the time of his death, which came to him in his office of the Collège on October 2, 1892, he was considered one of the greatest French intellectuals of the age.

## RENAN AND FRENCH LIBERALISM

English contemporaries of Renan experienced, in the course of their lifetime, one political regime and three sovereigns. French political life in this period differed considerably from the stability, consensus, and gradual, orderly broadening of the political system that characterized the Victorian era in Britain. Similarly, the tradition of French liberalism in the nineteenth century exhibited certain aspects that differentiated it markedly from its Anglo-Saxon counterpart.[13] In order to understand Renan's personal contribution to the history of liberal thought, it is therefore necessary to keep in mind the special path of French political history and the specific issues with which French liberals were confronted.

To attempt a periodization, it could be claimed that Renan belongs to a third generation of liberal thought in France. Much historiographical attention[14] has been devoted to the two preceding generations, that of the *idéologues* under the Napoleonic Consulate and Empire and that of the doctrinaires of the Restoration and the July Monarchy. A history of classical liberalism in France could plausibly begin with the great antiauthoritarian works of Benjamin Constant, denouncing the slide from Jacobin radicalism into military dictatorship,[15] and end with the last works of Alexis de Tocqueville after the fall of the Second Republic.[16] With respect to such a canon, Ernest Renan would belong to a postclassical phase, a "silver age," of French liberalism that attained political consciousness with the Revolution of 1848 and the coup d'état of December 1851. His generation was the last in French history to face an authoritarian regime in peacetime. Following the fall of Louis-Napoléon's empire, it was also confronted with the historical task of transferring the liberal heritage of the Enlightenment and of the Revolution of 1789 into the institutional structures and ideology of the Third Republic, the first stable non-monarchical regime in the history of France.

Certain structural challenges peculiar to the French political system affected the positions of French liberal thinkers, both in the early decades of the century and in midcentury and beyond. Among these particularities, three specifically stand out: France's statist tradition, the relationship with the Revolution of 1789, and colonial expansion.

The double French tradition of administrative centralization in Paris and government intervention in the economy was an enduring one. Despite the fact that perhaps the greatest of French liberals, Tocqueville, had offered a timely diagnosis of the long time horizon of the phenomenon, liberals, even when in government, found it difficult to reverse. Doctrinaire commitment to local self-government and free markets was often overruled by political expediency. Social instability made centralization and interventionism appear indispensable, but it was also heightened by overreliance on the state—a vicious circle. Oppositional voices in favor of market liberalization, such as Frédéric Bastiat's, were marginalized. Hence, French liberalism, on the whole, could hardly conceive of laissez-faire, beyond rhetorical commitment, as an actionable governmental policy: there were scarcely any French Cobdenites of note.[17]

More than economic policy or the vertical separation of powers, the main task with which French liberals saw themselves confronted was one of historical reconciliation. The highest-order political issue France faced in the nineteenth century was the need to bridge the *gouffre de la Révolution*: to resolve the central ideological cleavage left by 1789 and its aftermath. In this debate, liberals strove to preserve the heritage of the moderate phase of the Revolution (such as the Declaration of the Rights of Man and the rationalization of the legal system), while eschewing Jacobin and democratic radicalism. It would be possible to develop a summary periodization of the entire arc of liberal thought in France by describing successive attempts to tackle the revolutionary heritage, its historiography and political theory, beginning with Benjamin Constant's work on representation[18] and reaching to François Furet.[19] A key position in this debate, however, at least in the nineteenth century, was occupied by the Catholic Church[20]: the revolutionary–anti-revolutionary split was also, in large measure, a split between piety and secularism that had its roots in the dechristianization campaigns of the Jacobins and the alliance of throne and altar during the Restoration. Hence, church-state relations acquired a political centrality in French liberal thought that had no true equivalent in British liberalism of the time.

The third distinctive element of French liberalism was its approach to colonial expansion. Whereas the British Empire was the result of a series of accretions, in many cases effected by private actors such as the East India Company, in France, colonialism was a state matter from the outset. The second French colonial empire, founded in 1830 with the conquest of Algiers, began as a prestige policy of the ailing Bourbon monarchy; successive regimes turned to overseas expansion for popularity more than for commercial advantage. Liberal thinkers in France shared in European liberalism's general support for imperialism and overseas expansion,[21] but their reasons for doing so were different from their English counterparts, especially with regards to geopolitical balance-of-power considerations.[22] A further complication concerned the role of Catholic missionaries in French colonialism and, by extension, the identity of the civilization in whose name the enterprise was being conducted.[23]

These high-level structural challenges engendered a form of liberalism with very distinctive characteristics. The most salient clustered around the opposition of liberty and equality or, in other words, the defense of property and "quality" in society.[24] Indeed, the class aspect was particularly prevalent in nineteenth-century French liberal thought. In its intellectual confrontation with the various strains of utopian socialism, French liberalism did not disdain to don the mantle of defender of civilization against the rising egalitarian tide, whose violent symptoms could be seen in the recurrent popular uprisings in Paris. This need for social resistance against the eruption of chaos, one of the by-products of industrial development, could also be articulated, in comparative historical terms, as a specter of the barbarian "Other" besieging modern European civilization. In this attitude, which combines domestic social control with Eurocentrism, lie the origins of the cultural preoccupation with decadence of the end of the century.

The suffrage question was an extension of liberal concerns about the trampling of property rights. It has been argued that universal suffrage was conceptually the most radical innovation of nineteenth-century politics, even with respect to radically redistributive economic claims.[25] Nevertheless, French liberalism was more than hesitant on the matter precisely because it took political and economic egalitarianism to be indivisible. Hence, to avoid the uncontrollable escalation in material demands that had characterized previous experiments with popular government, French liberal theorists devised and debated the relative merits of a variety of systems for the limitation of suffrage and their normative justification. The goal was to guarantee the rule of the civilized elite in the absence of traditional social deference, while allowing mechanisms for the progressive co-optation of wider strata into the representative system. This elitist worldview found a confirmation of sorts under the Second Empire: the regime's populist use of universal suffrage, in order to avoid radicalism, necessarily entailed heavy manipulation and official interference with the electoral process. For universal suffrage not to lead to socialism, it could not be allowed to be free and fair.

The transition to Louis-Napoléon's regime was the last in a line of political transformations in an era of instability for France. The problem of the permanence of liberal values in the face of the cycle of revolutions was significant, especially because political personnel had become so thoroughly divided among competing dynastic loyalties. Liberal theorists were therefore confronted with the transferability of their principles from one political dispensation to the next. This was theorized in the context

of a broader defense of moderation and the rule of law beyond the metaphysical abstractions of the question of sovereignty and the harsh realities of the struggle for power.[26] Furthermore, the cycle of regime changes
was contextualized, from the viewpoint of the philosophy of history, as
the necessarily indirect path progress takes—a view that could lead to
ironic detachment and tranquil faith in long-run outcomes, even in the
face of apparently disastrous setbacks. More generally, the transience of
regimes, even liberal-led ones such as the July Monarchy, induced an attitude focused on policy results rather than process: liberals could coexist
with a regime that would guarantee liberal rights efficiently, even if they
were excluded from active political life in a system in which public careers
were not fundamentally open to talents. Such, after a fashion, was the
status quo under the Second Empire, in a sociological context of vested
interests splintered by the clash of legitimisms, but also of outward peace
and economic prosperity.

On this basis, French liberal thought in the nineteenth century enter-
tained an uneasy relation with republicanism. Strongly anti-socialist,
elitist, suspicious of democracy, having learned from experience the sep-
arability of liberal rights from popular sovereignty, liberalism was separated from republicanism in France above all by a skepticism regarding
the advantageousness of forcible political change. Fear of reaction and
obscurantism was more than matched by distaste for radicalism and the
revolutionary tradition.


## RENAN'S POLITICAL THOUGHT

Renan was not a systematic political thinker. His positions, varying with
mood, occasion, and pragmatic intent, were not free from internal contradiction. This is not to say, however, that his worldview lacked any consistency. Renan's political thought is not a closed, organic whole, but in its
open-ended and adaptable manifestations, several general, stable features
may be discerned.

Foremost, Renan's commitment to liberalism was never in doubt
throughout his public career. However, beyond a generic allegiance to the
normative value of freedom, such a label requires qualification in order

to identify a real-life political position. Renan's liberalism was intimately allied with the idea of progress, so much so that for him liberalism was *the* political form of modernity itself. However, his notion of progress[27] is distant from other nineteenth-century formulations, such as the Comtian or the utilitarian one: it pertains exclusively to the sphere of knowledge and the development of the human spirit. In other words, Renan's principle is idealist and entertains a wholly instrumental relation with material conditions in the economic, technological, or, for that matter, political fields. As an intellectual principle, it is also entirely compatible with an elitist attitude toward social organization: beyond the equal respect due to all human lives as such, Renan sees little of independent normative value in the concept of equality. Indeed, by developing an ideal-type of nobility defined on the basis of virtue and cultivation, he appears to believe that social stratification is not only inevitable and justifiable but also beneficial per se. However, although his anti-materialist stance, indeed his sovereign disdain toward all economic matters, separated him from more progressive versions of nineteenth-century liberalism, his idealism is not a conservatism. What set him apart from it was the merely instrumental value he was prepared to grant to tradition, together with the frankly iconoclastic extremes to which he pushed pure speculation, especially in matters of religious belief. Nonetheless, there are some elements of commonality with the type of skeptical traditionalism embodied in the twentieth century by Michael Oakeshott.

With regard to his general philosophy of history, Renan's view of progress lent his tone, when discussing current political events and specific power struggles, a certain dispassionate detachment and light irony; this historicist response to the vagaries of politics and the impermanence of institutions drew on the classical trope of the wheel of fortune, as described by Boethius. Renan's tone most closely resembles the characterization that Hayden White has offered[28] of a later liberal theorist, Benedetto Croce. Seen from a different angle, Renan was sufficiently secure in the immanent logic of progress (as he conceived it) to have a fairly open attitude toward different political and institutional configurations, an attitude, what is more, that very rarely required personal involvement and engagement. Renan, in other words, can be associated with the "anti-political" ethos of many European intellectuals in the nineteenth century.[29] Therefore, his interventions in the public sphere tended to take the shape of incidental by-products of his scholarly pursuits. The only major exception was his direct confrontation with the crisis of 1870–1871, when Renan believed he was witnessing a change of major historical significance, warranting a greater-than-contemplative response.

Until the Prussian crisis, Renan was known in the political sphere essentially for his positions in two closely related policy areas: education and church-state relations. In the former, consistent with his principles, Renan voiced an anti-utilitarian defense of education. Inasmuch as knowledge is a personal and social good in itself, freedom of inquiry becomes a nonnegotiable requirement under any circumstance, and the role of politics becomes to protect the development of science. Renan is aware of the broader integrative role of education in society, but his writings on the matter are disproportionately skewed toward the needs of higher education and research (thus, never wholly shedding the appearance of being pleas *pro domo sua*).

This attitude, in turn, was at least in part shaped by his lifelong confrontation with the Catholic Church and its institutions. His position on church-state relations was always militant, to a certain extent *malgré soi*. Ever since the scandal of his abandonment of the seminary, Renan was at pains to de-emphasize the polemical side of his relation with revealed religion and its followers. In this sense, he represents the rhetorical opposite of Voltaire in the tradition of French anticlericalism: after all, he was separated from the irreverence of the Enlightenment by the weighty historical experience of the Revolution, from the Civil Constitution of the Clergy to Jacobin deism. However, no amount of serenity, bonhomie, and finesse could mask the heart of Renan's political position. His stated goal of separating the historical significance of the church's ethical message from its real-world political influence ultimately amounted to advocating freedom *from* religion, at least for the knowledge elite. The fact that Renan still saw a (subaltern) role for the church in promoting popular devotion in the interests of social control did little to ingratiate him with the Catholic hierarchy and with Catholic public opinion. Beyond its polemical impact, however, Renan's position may be seen as part of a broader intellectual transition from the philological approach to the study of religion of the 1830s and 1840s to the more sociological preoccupations of the fin de siècle.[30]

The fall of the Second Empire erased the institutional preconditions of Renan's anti-political stance, as well as heralding a fundamental shift in the European status quo. Renan attempted to provide a theoretical solution to the void of social authority into which political instability had plunged France. The problem of the formation of the ruling class transcended a mere question of education or institutional engineering and presented itself to Renan under the guise of the broader issue of moral regeneration, or the necessity for a secular ethics of duty. Seen in this light, Renan's proposed solution, a sort of paternalist utopia with drastically curtailed popular participation, is comparatively less interesting than his perception of the dawning crisis of legitimacy in European politics as a whole in the era of transition to a society of masses.[31] In any case, it is worth noting how, even at his most committed, and in the middle of what amounted to a rescue of the state by civil society, Renan conceived of his public role, and that of intellectuals more generally, in very limited terms. Far from succumbing to the philosopher-king temptation, Renan maintained his goal of the independence of the learned from political power and only aspired to indirect influence.[32] His position is most definitely at odds with the model of French public intellectual born of the Dreyfus affair.[33]

With regard to the aftermath of the Prussian crisis, three further elements of Renan's political thought should be noted. The first relates to suffrage and the social question. Renan's rearguard opposition to universal suffrage was perhaps colored by his personal setback of 1869, but mainly drew on the abuses of the Second Empire and the perceived excesses of the Commune. He couched it in the classic philosophical tropes on the rule of the ignorant rabble. At the same time, he perceived the importance of the clash of material interests and was not unsympathetic to the aspirations for material betterment of the masses. Furthermore, Renan, like others in the fin de siècle, understood the problem of coordination between domestic political struggles and international competition among states—namely, the lack of solidarity of the masses with the state's power and prestige goals.

This problem of collective identification, raised at the level of the nation, needed to be resolved at the level of the nation. The second element in Renan's political thought to germinate in 1870 was his theory of nationality. It cannot be overemphasized to what extent this best-known part of Renan's political thought was shaped in the shadow of the loss of Alsace-Lorraine. Indeed, absent such a pressing political necessity, it is hard to fathom how

Renan would have reached what, in fact, amounted to a rather comprehensive refutation of his previous scholarly positions. Adopting a voluntarist theory of nationality to protest the German annexations required the abandonment—or, at the very least, the marginalization—of the categories of race, ethnicity, and national character on which much of his historiographical work rested.[34] In a way, by underlining the political irrelevance of historical-anthropological categories of analysis and the impermanence of scientific results, Renan was subtly undermining his own authoritativeness as an intellectual in the public sphere.[35] Moreover, by stressing the importance of historical oblivion in the formation of national identity, Renan emphasized the challenges of preserving it in a modern age, characterized by the refinement and diffusion of historical scholarship that tended to make complete oblivion impossible. Nonetheless, the feeling of nationality was seen as indispensable, also to address the aforementioned crisis of legitimacy: for Renan, the viability of the Republic in France ultimately hung on its ability to foster a nondivisive sense of national belonging.

How separate Renan's theory of nationality was from the rest of his scholarship, how indistinguishable his "everyday plebiscite" from a democratic legitimation by consent, can be seen by comparison with his views on colonialism, European expansionism, and transcultural dialogue. On these topics, an essentialist view of civilizations inexorably drove the international division of labor. Renan's thought may be associated with a tradition of cultural explanations for political regimes and socioeconomic development in French thought that runs from Montesquieu to Gobineau to Durkheim. Its specific identity was provided by a theory of the influence of different languages on the development of speculative thought and of science, whose most notable formulation was Renan's theory of the Semitic races. This is perhaps the part of Renan's legacy with the most problematic implications for modern readers.[36] It provided a significant contribution to the construction of the worldview of European imperialism (which Renan supported wholeheartedly, also in the interests of defusing social tensions in the metropole). Indeed, when applied to colonial settings, his voluntarist theory of nationality is extremely favorable to settlers, exclusively focused as it is on political communities, with no regard to issues of prior occupation of land.

Most disturbing to our sensibilities in Renan's position on relations with native peoples is his unapologetic enrollment of science (here, in a very material sense, as weapons technology) as a bulwark against a return of barbarism: science placing "force in the service of reason" thus became a slogan for civilization out of the barrel of a gun. Hence, despite the opportunities afforded by the process of secularization to achieve reconciliation with religious minorities (such as the Jews) within the metropole, Renan's political thought conceived of modernity exclusively in Eurocentric terms. Or, to be more precise, Renan perceived the two social effects of science, the development of industry in the technological sphere and the furtherance of secularism in the cultural one, as inseparable and as the distinctive characteristic of European civilization.

This leads us to the third element of note in Renan's thought to emerge from the *crise allemande de la pensée française*.[37] The unification of Germany through war and conquest had essentially altered the status quo of Europe. Renan had the lucidity to perceive immediately that what was at stake greatly exceeded the curtailment of France's role by the appearance of a new, rising state; indeed, the capacity of the European balance of power to function in its traditional manner had been fundamentally called into question. An era of international relations characterized by the spread of liberal ideas throughout the continent had come to a close. Faced with this new scenario, Renan sensed that a European federation was the only horizon of possibility for the transcendence of Franco-German antagonism. On the basis of this essentially negative stance, Renan has been made to fill the role of one of the intellectual forefathers of the project of European union. Inasmuch as it is understood that his position was speculative, intellectualist, and somewhat of an obiter dictum, Renan may be grouped with the likes of the Abbé de Saint-Pierre in conceiving of the future unity of Europe by analogy to the unity of the Republic of Letters. But Renan can more plausibly be understood as a "good European" in the sense Nietzsche gave to the label.[38] Hence, his reaction to the birth of the Second Reich demonstrated foresight essentially because he perceived the risks to which the European state system would henceforth be exposed, threatening traditional European pluralism. In this sphere, as in others, Renan identified the challenges with which European thought would grapple in the age of crisis of the early twentieth century.

## RENAN'S LITERARY STYLE

In the experience of his contemporaries, the impression left by Renan's ideas could hardly be dissociated from that left by his prose style. Renan was one of the great French literary figures of his day, a fact that influenced the reception of his ideas and his political strategies in the public sphere. The rhythm and richness of his sentences, which may at times sound verbose to a modern sensibility, appeared melodic and supremely elegant to the coeval ear, as attested by many distinguished witnesses, from Flaubert to Sainte-Beuve.

Renan employed a variety of literary genres for political expression, from the pamphlet to the conference, from the book review to the open letter, depending on the different stages of his intellectual career and his growing weight in the cultural field. With respect to the entirety of his production, his political writings represent a small and tangential subset, far from the center of his scholarly activity on the history of early Christianity. Nonetheless, it is precisely the circumstantial nature of many of his political writings (a characteristic he himself defended eloquently in others[39]) that constituted the main appeal of his style of political commentary. According to Sainte-Beuve,[40] Renan had become the undisputed master of a new literary genre, the *article de revue*, or journal article, in which the scholar's learning was employed with a light touch and a lively, discursive voice to illuminate questions of current interest. In its effort to make the results and insights of scholarship available to a broader, nonspecialist public, this type of literary production was, in a way, following an Enlightenment tradition of diffusion of knowledge; it also shared with it a tendency to pursue political goals through the adoption of a literary style suitable to winning the hearts and minds of a well-defined, influential social group. To grasp the nuances of the text, however, this refined intellectual *divertissement* demands of the modern reader both a fine-grained knowledge of the French political situation of the time and an appreciation of the humanist culture steeped in classical antiquity and European history on which Renan draws so heavily.

From a formal standpoint, Renan's critical distance and lightly ironic detachment from political controversy find expression in a very supple prose, characterized by a discursive tone, a richness of broader cultural references, a plurality of voices linked by occasionally fanciful transitions. Renan's *medietas*, however, did not exclude lyrical moods or a more general aesthetic penchant for intensity,[41] indeed a fascination with the sublime, most readily apparent in his famous virtuoso piece, *Prière sur l'Acropole* (1876).

Renan's "perspectivism," his claim to appreciate all sides of an argument as the privilege of the detached scholar, was particularly grating for his adversaries. They saw his custom of prudence, the constant hedging of positions, as a subtle form of hypocrisy. Indeed, to his critics, Renan appeared to employ against the church Catholicism's own rhetoric of moderation, adding insult to injury. Whatever its virtues and its shortcomings as a polemical weapon, Renan's style marked an era in French prose, and *renanisme* became a distinctive mode of essay writing into the fin de siècle.

## RECEPTION

During his lifetime, Renan was an intensely controversial figure, at the heart of some of the most divisive intellectual and political debates of the age. Public attitudes toward him remained sharply contrasted after his death, as well: on three occasions (1894, 1905, 1923), his detractors managed to avoid his ultimate civic consecration, the transferal of his ashes to the Pantheon. However, the lack of unanimity in assessing Renan's legacy was not due to the fact that he was too exclusively associated with the partisans of one faction; his thought was appropriated and his authority invoked from many different points along the ideological spectrum.

Renan was, undoubtedly, one of the patron saints of the bourgeois republic. As such, he was fully incorporated into the hegemonic topography: streets and squares throughout the country were named after him, along with lycées and even a navy ship (which, fittingly enough, saw service in the eastern Mediterranean during World War I and the Greek-Turkish War). His co-optation by the republicans was not a foregone conclusion: after all, statesmen such as Guizot, who shared Renan's elitist liberalism, were considered hopeless reactionaries after 1870. The key difference, apart from the credibility afforded Renan as a victim of the

Second Empire's persecution of free thought, was that his meritocracy, focused as it was on the field of pure science, lacked the obvious class connotations of the doctrinaires.[42] Therefore, he was duly claimed as an intellectual forerunner when the republican regime, under Combes, opted to move decisively against the clergy and the congregations to effect the separation of church and state. The anecdote related to the government's erection of a commemorative statue in Renan's hometown of Tréguier in 1903, and the rioting by a right-wing mob that followed, pertains to this political battle.

Renan's influence was felt within the Catholic Church as well, especially with regard to the movement of theological Modernism. Alfred Loisy, perhaps the Modernists' most learned and radical biblical scholar, had attended Renan's courses of Hebrew at the Collège de France.[43]

While Renan was a recognized champion of secularism even beyond Third Republic France,[44] the ambiguities of his thought were also exploited, in a different vein, by antisystem movements. A paradigmatic case was the appropriation of Renan's criticism of centralization that Action française attempted in its anti-Jacobin polemics. Charles Maurras's neo-royalist movement was particularly attracted by some of Renan's more somber moods of denunciation (in the *Réforme*, for instance) of the materialistic bourgeoisie for its lack of national devotion, compared to the historical function of the crown. Furthermore, Renan's Celtic identity and defense of provincial traditions against republican universalism created cultural common ground with Maurras's worldview. More generally, the Revolutionary Right[45] in fin-de-siècle France adopted Renan as an authoritative critic of republican zealotry in attempting to "nationalize" the political culture of the French Revolution, leading to a reopening of the great cleavage of 1789 and, consequently, to an international weakening of the country.

Another voice on the antisystem Right at the turn of the century, Maurice Barrès, had close links with Renan. His politics of aesthetic preeminence sought to draw on Renan's authoritativeness: the early Barrès[46] aimed to secure for himself, in Renan's image, the position of the detached intellectual and celebrated prose stylist as an external standard of legitimacy to be reinvested in the political realm.

On the opposite side of the political spectrum, Georges Sorel[47] mobilized Renan's thought and, in particular, his historiographical method

in the context of his polemics against the Third Republic of the victorious Dreyfusards and in favor of his heterodox brand of Marxism and
direct-action syndicalism. Many further lines of political and intellectual
filiation can be traced in the Belle Epoque and beyond, from Paul Bour-
get's *Essais de psychologie* to Anatole France, Albert Thibaudet, and the
young Raymond Aron.[48]

One of the most enduring contributions of Renan to political debate
had to do with intellectual and moral reform. Though the formula was
originally Quinet's,[49] Renan's book popularized the idea, which then
recurs as a leitmotif throughout the following generation, both on the
Right and on the Left, all the way to Antonio Gramsci's engagement with
the concept in the early 1930s.[50] The idea of reform, initially employed to
identify a "Catholic gap" in social development and adaptation to modern
society,[51] then expanded to include the problem of mass secularization in
Europe, focuses on the necessity for a fundamental change in social attitudes above and beyond institutional engineering. Renan's foregrounding
of this theme in 1871 was prescient: for the next seventy years, European
political thought would attempt to come to grips with this need for reform
and this crisis of legitimacy.


## CONTEMPORARY RELEVANCE

Renan was a central figure in the "postclassical" phase of French liberal
thought in the second half of the nineteenth century. The comparative
obscurity into which he has fallen among the English-speaking public has
hampered the development of a more comprehensive understanding of
the transition from the age of Tocqueville and John Stuart Mill to the "new
liberalisms" of the early twentieth century and beyond. Renan's political thought, however, is not of mere historical interest. Issues of lifelong
importance for him remain at the forefront of public life today, and some
of his suggestions and perspectives allow us to view contemporary debates
in novel, productive ways. Similarly, Renan has remained a controversial
thinker; his ideas have fueled passionate contemporary polemics. To limit
discussion to the most politically salient topics, Renan's thought today
appears especially relevant for issues of public morality and the formation

of the ruling class, the shaping of public education and civic culture, and the role of organized religion in society and public institutions.

The themes of the *Réforme*—namely, the search for a new structuring of a society that has cast off its traditional institutions and is effectively rudderless in the face of a competitive and menacing international environment—have lost none of their timeliness. Indeed, in the various nation-building processes attempted in developing countries in the second half of the past century, for instance, the question presented itself in stark form. In the face of the overly mechanistic reliance on institutional engineering often promoted by external advisers and international organizations, the importance of the moralization of public life, especially in the case of corruption, has increasingly become apparent. Significant strands of contemporary political thought[52] have similarly explored the need for elements of social cohesion beyond collective self-interest correctly understood. Contemporary political actors ignore at their peril the close relation Renan draws between this issue and the legitimating role of educational institutions in the selection of the elite.

Renan's ideas on educational organization are especially poignant in France, given the long time frame of debates on centralism and secularization (there were, for instance, mass demonstrations into the 1980s in favor of the freedom of private confessional education). His early critique of republican meritocracy,[53] though, can be applied more broadly to separate-track higher-education systems. However, perhaps the most interesting part of his reflections on education concerns the relation with popular religious beliefs. From our point of view, at the opposite end of the trajectory of modern "disenchantment of the world" and in the face of religious revival, Renan's arguments in defense of the freedom of scientific enquiry are still obviously relevant, though they are given a new dimension in the context of multiculturalism.[54]

While the liberal reform of the Catholic Church without the intervention of the state has—at least to a certain degree—taken place with the Second Vatican Council, a century after Renan invoked it, arguably the most pressing contemporary concern is the relation among different religious faiths within the state and, specifically, the integration of Islam within the institutions of liberal democracy. This problem has a bearing both on Renan's ideas regarding intercultural dialogue and on his views of progress and adaptability of traditional worldviews to modernity. In this regard, however, a fundamental challenge has been raised against the ideological preconditions of Renan's position. Edward Said used Renan's case as one of the paradigmatic examples of orientalism in nineteenth-century European intellectual life.[55] Said's accusations were not entirely novel (Aimé Césaire had already voiced a similar critique in 1950),[56] but the controversy they generated was much broader in scope, within the context of continued involvement of Western powers in Middle Eastern politics and the ideological backing of purportedly neutral scientific experts.

Similar, though less immediately politically charged, was Renan's role in the renewal of nationalism studies in the early 1980s:[57] the "Nation" lecture, perhaps the only Renan text to be durably included in the canon of classic social-scientific thought in English-speaking institutions, was reread by Benedict Anderson with a special emphasis on the notion of sacrifice and oblivion, thus to highlight the dynamics of domination inherent in the voluntarist conception of nationalism.[58]

Both Said's and Anderson's critiques contain indubitable elements of truth, and both highlight how Renan's thought included motifs that could be—and have been—exploited for political purposes far from the modern trajectory of liberalism. In particular, in both cases Renan falls under the long shadow of racialist thought in France, from Henri de Boulainvilliers to Georges Vacher de Lapouge, whether in imperialist or class racist guise.[59] Without aspiring to resolve complex interpretation debates, the present edition pursues the more modest goal of placing the readership in a position to reach its own opinion, not only through Renan's words but also through a critical apparatus aimed at retrieving the personal, cultural, and political contexts that made certain positions acceptable, unremarkable, commonplace, or, on the contrary, deeply contentious in their original setting.

## THE PRESENT ANTHOLOGY

In illustrating the criteria that have directed the choice of texts for this anthology, we should begin with what has been excluded. The present volume does not contain any excerpt from the works to which Renan

owed the admiration of his contemporaries and his enduring reputation as a specialist scholar. His philological, historical, and philosophical work, notably including his monumental treatment of the origins of
Christianity, falls outside the bounds of this project. Such a choice contains a significant degree of arbitrariness; indeed, it may be argued that
embedded in Renan's scholarly writings are anthropological claims that
represent the most politically controversial part of his thought for a contemporary audience. In particular, critical attention has been focused on
Renan's characterization of Semitism and on the function this plays in his
teleological accounts of progress and civilization.[60] Without wishing to
prejudge the issue, and in the hope that the entirety of Renan's corpus will
soon be reissued in English, the present anthology adopts a definition of
politics more in keeping with Renan's own (as evinced in this introduction's epigraph): a topical discussion of current public events, an engaged
account of the present.

It should be added that this volume is not conceived as a comprehensive collection of Renan's writings on politics; rather, it is a representative
anthology of his specifically political texts. Moreover, attention has been
paid to the availability in English of Renan's texts with a bearing on politics; hence, no passages from *L'avenir de la science* or *Caliban* have been
included, since late-nineteenth-century translations of these works,[61] no
longer covered by copyright, have recently been reissued.

The texts assembled herein are representative along several spectrums.
Chronologically, they cover most of Renan's writing life, from his earliest
forays into the public sphere to some of his last interventions. In terms of
the choice of literary means and public context, the selection offers a sense
of the variety of Renan's production: pamphlets, newspaper articles, open
letters, public speeches. In terms of the notoriety of the texts, some of
his most celebrated compositions are juxtaposed to much less circulated
pieces.

———— ∞ ————

"On Clerical Liberalism," an article that appeared in 1848 in the journal
*La liberté de penser*, presents Renan's fears that the Revolution would be
exploited by the Catholic Church to reverse the tolerant approach to religion and science of the freethinking July Monarchy. An early, polemical

text, making somewhat questionable use of its primary sources, it presents a style Renan himself later considered too militant and aggressive.

"Mr. de Sacy and the Liberal Tradition" (originally, "L'école libérale, ses principes et ses tendances" in *Revue des deux Mondes*) states Renan's belief in the need for an aristocracy of the mind to replace the aristocracy of birth that the Revolution of 1789 had destroyed. Its occasion was the review of an anthology of articles by Samuel Ustazade Silvestre de Sacy (1801–1879), a liberal publicist, man of letters, and director of the Mazarin Library, who was elected to the Académie française in 1854. In it, Renan draws an idealized portrait of the engaged intellectual, while at the same time subtly criticizing an earlier generation of French liberal political thought. The article is a notable statement of Renan's anti-utilitarianism.

"The Philosophy of Contemporary History," also first published in *Revue des deux Mondes*, is an extended review of the memoirs of François Guizot, the foremost political personality of the Orléanist era. The text offers the most articulate expression of Renan's political position under the Second Empire, focusing on the defense of liberal freedoms and the preoccupation for the excesses of universal suffrage. It is also notable for its antitechnocratic sentiment, as a reflection on the shortcomings of the doctrinaires in office.

"The Role of the Family and the State in Education" is a speech that issued from Renan's unsuccessful run for a parliamentary seat in the Seine-et-Marne in 1869. It discusses the role of public education, a key issue for the liberal opposition to the Second Empire. The speech is notable chiefly for its clever deployment of a traditional argument of the French Catholic clergy against the centralizing, Jacobin tradition of government—namely, the defense of freedom of conscience—in order to uphold the role of the family vis-à-vis religious institutions in the molding of the child's basic personality, while maintaining the preeminence of the state in formal education.

"Constitutional Monarchy in France," which appeared in *Revue des deux Mondes* on November 1, 1869, was a postmortem for Renan's electoral campaign. It restates the author's belief in a temperate system of government that mediates between central authority and universal suffrage. Furthermore, it interprets the bellicose nature of the Second Empire as an attempt to garner, through foreign policy adventures, the legitimacy that the dynasty lacks at home, an inherently unstable equilibrium.

Particularly interesting is Renan's insight regarding the extent to which industrialization has increased the need for public order, tranquility, and discipline—and, consequently, increased the destructiveness of revolutions. This existential need for order in industrial societies also prefigures the appeal of authoritarian solutions to political chaos.

"The War Between France and Germany" was an article in *Revue des deux Mondes* that appeared on September 15, 1870, shortly after the defeat at Sedan and the fall of the Second Empire. The themes of the article foreshadow the argument in "Intellectual and Moral Reform," calling for a period of national reflection and frank self-criticism. At the same time, Renan does not see the possibility for a lasting peace in Europe without transcending nationalism and creating a "federal pact" among its three leading nations, England, Germany, and France.

The first of the "Two Letters to Mr. Strauss," prompted by a public appeal by David Friedrich Strauss (the German biblical scholar and author of the seminal *Das Leben Jesu* [1835], later the target of one of Nietzsche's *Untimely Meditations*), appeared in the *Journal des débats* the day after "The War Between France and Germany." The second letter, a rejoinder to Strauss's reply, was written after the experience of the Commune and published in the *Journal des débats* in December 1871. It is one of the most extreme examples of Renan's biting sarcasm as a controversialist.

The longest and perhaps most important text first translated here, "Intellectual and Moral Reform of France," is a pamphlet expressing Renan's beliefs on the causes and possible remedies of French social and political decadence in the wake of the defeat of 1870 and the Paris Commune. It stresses the importance of discipline and national education and invites France to learn from its conqueror. In many ways the most conservative statement of Renan's political beliefs, it nonetheless enjoyed a remarkable posterity among political thinkers far removed from its stated positions. In its tone and organization, it is a curious blend of medical metaphors and a rhetoric of palingenesis reminiscent of the ancient Hebrew prophets.

"What Is a Nation?", undoubtedly Renan's most widely known political composition, was originally a lecture held at the Sorbonne in 1882; it illustrates his voluntarist theory of nationalism. The answer to the title's question, the definition of a nation, is reached through a process of elimination, by critiquing alternative grounds for political community. From a contemporary perspective, one of the most striking aspects of the argument is how speedily Renan dismisses the hypothesis of community of interests as the driving force of national allegiance.

"Islam and Science" was an article published in two parts in the *Journal des débats*, drawing on a public lecture originally delivered at the Sorbon-ne. This is one of the most accessible expressions of Renan's intellectual orientalism in its relation to his liberal political convictions. Of particular interest is his exchange of views with Jamāl al-Dīn al-Afghānī (ca. 1839–1897), one of the fathers of the Islamist renaissance in the second half of the nineteenth century, whose position is subjected to a sort of anthropological reductionism. More generally, Renan's argument showcases all the advantages and drawbacks of a critique of Islamic fundamentalism based on the European liberal historicist tradition.

The final text of the anthology, "Original Unity and Gradual Separation of Judaism and Christianity," was an 1883 lecture at the Society for Jewish Studies, which had recently been founded by Baron Rothschild. This text highlights the role Renan set for himself in public debate in the context of the growing anti-Semitism then prevalent in France, stressing the intimate link between Judaism and liberalism.

Throughout his career, Renan remained loyal to the same Parisian publishing house, Lévy Frères, headed by Michel Lévy and subsequently by his brother Calmann. Many of his writings that had originally appeared in scholarly journals or in the press were then published by Lévy Frères in book form. The original texts on which this translation is based derive from such edited volumes. Specifically, "Du libéralisme clérical" and "Philosophie de l'histoire contemporaine" (chapters 1 and 3 in this anthology) appeared in *Questions contemporaines* (1868); "M. de Sacy et l'école libérale" (chapter 2), in *Essais de morale et de critique* (1859); "La part de la famille et de l'État dans l'Éducation" (chapter 4), in a brochure of the same title, published in 1869; "La Monarchie constitutionnelle en France," "La guerre entre la France et l'Allemagne," "Lettre & Nouvelle lettre à M. Strauss," and "La réforme intellectuelle et morale de la France" (chapters 5–8), in *La réforme intellectuelle et morale*, 3rd ed. (1872); "Qu'est-ce qu'une nation?," "L'Islamisme et la science," and

"Identité originelle et séparation graduelle du judaïsme et du christianisme" (chapters 9–11), in *Discours et conférences* (1887).

Other editions of the original texts consulted include the version of
*Réforme intellectuelle et morale* edited by P. E. Charvet for Cambridge
University Press (1950) and the one by Mona Ozouf for Perrin (1992),
*L'islam et la science: avec la réponse d'Al-Afghânî* (Montpellier, France:
L'Archange Minotaure, 2005), as well as Renan's collected works in ten
volumes edited by H. Psichari (1947–1961). With the exception of
chapters 9 and 10,[62] none of these works have previously been available in
English, to the best of my knowledge.

The present translation has endeavored to render the complexity and
orotundity of the original prose, eschewing stylistic anachronisms in the
simplification of sentence structure and vocabulary. Hence, the division
in sections and paragraphs respects the original, and punctuation has
only marginally been altered. The repetitions that characterize Renan's
style have similarly been preserved.

Renan's French is, for the most part, extremely clear and precise, allowing for uniform rendering of terms. A few difficulties in translation nonetheless arise. Some are inherent in French lexical characteristics, such
as the double meaning, subjective and objective, of *droit*; the notorious
polysemy of the terms *esprit* and *génie*; or the specific use of *former* in
pedagogical contexts. Other difficulties derive from specific historical
and institutional references: the storied notion of *honnêteté*, *fonction* with
regard to public service, *laisser-aller* with regard to ideology, *légitimité* to
identify the cause of the Bourbons, the metaphorical and analogical uses
of *conscience* and *mouvement*, the term *politique* as a noun designating
a person. The intricacies related to the word *race* in nineteenth-century
French thought have been alluded to above. As for the oft-recurrent term
*science*, occasionally rendered as "knowledge," in Renan it typically designates the field of the *Geisteswissenschaften*. The conventions Renan followed with respect to gendering have been preserved (or extended, as in
the complicated case of the term *patrie*), even though they may clash with
modern sensibilities: the sole exception is with regard to countries, which
have not been personified.

The version of foreign names most common in English (e.g., Tamerlane, Averroes) has been adopted when possible. Renan's many scriptural
citations have been rendered by means of the King James Bible: its literary

prestige and recognizability for an English-speaking public trumped philological or historical considerations. A series of passages from Jacques-Bénigne Bossuet's *Politique tirée des propres paroles de l'écriture sainte* in chapter 1 are from Patrick Riley's translation for Cambridge University Press's Texts in the History of Political Thought series (1990), in the interests of providing the reader with easy cross-reference to the standard edition of this work in English. The translation of a few verses of Statius's *Silvae* in chapter 5 is by D. R. Shackleton Bailey and Christopher A. Parrott (Loeb/Harvard University Press, 2015). The translation of two verses from Vergil's *Aeneid* in notes to chapters 5 and 8 are from John Dryden's classic version. All other translations are my own.

—— ∝∝ ——

Note to the text: Renan's own notes are displayed throughout as footnotes and marked with symbols on each page (*, †, ‡, §, and so forth). The editor's notes are gathered at the back of the book and numbered consecutively within each chapter.

M. F. N. Giglioli

# CHRONOLOGY

| Date | Events in Ernest Renan's life | Political, diplomatic, and military events | Cultural events |
|------|-------------------------------|--------------------------------------------|-----------------|
| 1823 | Born in Tréguier, Brittany (February 28) | | |
| 1828 | Death at sea of Renan's father | | |
| 1830 | | France conquers Algiers; beginning of the second French colonial empire | |
| | | July: Following three days of street fighting in Paris, the Bourbon monarchy is overthrown; Louis-Philippe of Orléans becomes king of the French | |
| 1831 | | Defeat of Polish uprising against Russian rule | Death of Georg Wilhelm Friedrich Hegel |
| | | | John Stuart Mill publishes "The Spirit of the Age" in *The Examiner* |

*(continued)*

| Date | Events in Ernest Renan's life | Political, diplomatic, and military events | Cultural events |
|------|-------------------------------|--------------------------------------------|-----------------|
| 1835 | | | Alexis de Tocqueville publishes the first volume of *De la démocratie en Amérique* |
| | | | David Friedrich Strauss publishes *Das Leben Jesu* |
| 1837 | | Victoria becomes queen of the United Kingdom | |
| 1838 | Entry into seminary; beginning of religious education | | |
| 1840 | | Treaty of London ends the second Egyptian-Ottoman War: France excluded from role in Eastern Question in "diplomatic Waterloo" | Alexis de Tocqueville publishes the second volume of *De la démocratie en Amérique* |
| 1841 | | | Thomas Carlyle, *On Heroes, Hero-Worship, and the Heroic in History* |
| 1842 | | | Augustin Thierry, *Considérations sur l'histoire de France* |
| | | | Jules Michelet, *Histoire de France* |
| 1845 | Crisis of faith; abandonment of ecclesiastical career | | |
| 1846 | | Giovanni Maria Mastai Ferretti is elected pope as Pius IX | |
| 1847 | Wins the Prix Volney with essay on the history of Semitic languages | François Guizot becomes prime minister of France | |
| 1848 | | February: Louis-Philippe toppled by street protests in Paris; Second Republic proclaimed | Karl Marx and Friedrich Engels, *Manifest der Kommunistischen Partei* |
| | | June: suppression of working-class uprising in Paris | |

| Date | Events in Ernest Renan's life | Political, diplomatic, and military events | Cultural events |
|------|-------------------------------|--------------------------------------------|-----------------|
| 1849 | Associated with the mission for the discovery of ancient manuscripts in Italian libraries: visits Rome, Florence, Padua, Venice | French troops suppress Giuseppe Mazzini's Roman Republic and restore the pope to his throne | |
| 1851 | | December: Louis-Napoléon Bonaparte, president of the Republic, carries out a coup and establishes the Second Empire | Edgar Quinet, *Les révolutions d'Italie* |
| 1852 | Presents his doctoral thesis on Averroes | | |
| 1853 | | | Jules Michelet, *Histoire de la révolution française* |
| 1855 | | | Arthur de Gobineau, *Essai sur l'inégalité des races humaines* |
| 1856 | Is admitted to the Académie des inscriptions et belles-lettres; marries Cornélie Schaeffer | End of the Crimean War (peace of Paris) | Alexis de Tocqueville, *L'Ancien Régime et la Révolution* |
| 1857 | | | Gustave Flaubert on trial for obscenity for *Madame Bovary* |
| 1859 | Publishes *Essais de morale et de critique* | Italian War of Independence: France fights alongside the Kingdom of Sardinia against Austria | John Stuart Mill, *On Liberty* |
| | | | Charles Darwin, *On the Origin of Species* |
| 1860 | Archaeological mission in the Levant (Lebanon, Syria, Galilee, Palestine) | Annexation of Nice and Savoy to France | Jacob Burckhardt, *Die Kultur der Renaissance in Italien* |
| | | French intervention in Lebanon in defense of the Christian Maronite community | |

(*continued*)

*(Continued)*

| Date | Events in Ernest Renan's life | Political, diplomatic, and military events | Cultural events |
|------|-------------------------------|---------------------------------------------|-----------------|
| 1861 | His sister Henriette dies of fever in Amschit, Lebanon | | John Stuart Mill, *Considerations on Representative Government* |
| 1862 | Named to the Collège de France, but his course is suspended after the initial lecture | Otto von Bismarck becomes minister-president of Prussia | |
| 1863 | Publishes *La vie de Jésus*, first of the seven volumes of his *Origines du Christianisme* | Uprising in Poland against Russian rule | John Stuart Mill, *Utilitarianism* |
| 1864 | | Pope Pius IX promulgates the *Syllabus* | |
| 1865 | New trip to the Levant (Egypt, Asia Minor, Greece); in Athens, composes *Prière sur l'Acropole* | | |
| 1866 | | Prussia defeats the Austrian Empire at Sadowa (Königgrätz), dissolves the German Confederation, and creates a new North German Confederation under its hegemony | |
| 1867 | | Mexican expedition ends in disaster; emperor Maximilian is executed. French volunteers defeat Giuseppe Garibaldi at Mentana, thwarting his attempt to capture Rome | Karl Marx publishes the first volume of *Das Kapital* |
| 1868 | Publishes *Questions contemporaines* | | |
| 1869 | Unsuccessfully stands for parliament in Meaux (Seine-et-Marne) | | Matthew Arnold, *Culture and Anarchy*. John Stuart Mill, *The Subjection of Women* |

| Date | Events in Ernest Renan's life | Political, diplomatic, and military events | Cultural events |
|------|-------------------------------|--------------------------------------------|-----------------|
| 1870 | In Norway with Prince Napoléon when war erupts; remains in Paris during the siege | Vatican Council: Papal infallibility proclaimed<br><br>Franco-Prussian War declared in July; defeat of the French at the siege of Sedan; the emperor is made a prisoner; proclamation of the Republic in Paris (September); Prussian siege of the capital<br><br>The Kingdom of Italy occupies Rome and puts an end to the secular power of the papacy | |
| 1871 | April: one month after the proclamation of the Commune, retires to Versailles<br><br>Publishes *La Réforme intellectuelle et morale de la France* | Proclamation of the German Empire in Versailles<br><br>March: proclamation of the Paris Commune<br><br>May: Commune is crushed with tens of thousands of casualties in the *semaine sanglante* ("bloody week")<br><br>Peace of Frankfurt with Germany: France cedes Alsace and part of Lorraine to the Second Reich | |
| 1872 | | Anti-Catholic *Kulturkampf* policy intensifies in Germany | |
| 1876 | Publishes *Dialogues et fragments philosophiques* | | Friedrich Nietzsche, *Unzeitgemässe Betrachtungen* (contains "David Strauss: der Bekenner und der Schriftsteller") |

(*continued*)

| Date | Events in Ernest Renan's life | Political, diplomatic, and military events | Cultural events |
|---|---|---|---|
| 1877 | | May: failure of President MacMahon's attempt to impose a cabinet against the wishes of the republican parliamentary majority | |
| 1878 | Elected to the Académie française; composes *Caliban* (later collected in *Drames philosophiques*) | Death of Pope Pius IX<br><br>Vincenzo Luigi Pecci is elected pope as Leo XIII | |
| 1881 | | Tunisia becomes a French protectorate<br>Léon Gambetta's *Grand Ministère: la République des Républicains* | |
| 1882 | Delivers the conference *Qu'est-ce qu'une nation?* at the Sorbonne | | |
| 1883 | Publishes *Souvenirs d'enfance et de jeunesse* | | |
| 1887 | Publishes a collection of *Discours et conférences*; begins publication of the five-volume *Histoire du peuple d'Israël* | | |
| 1888 | | Death of Wilhelm I, emperor of Germany | Maurice Barrès, *Huit jours chez Monsieur Renan* |
| 1890 | Publishes *L'avenir de la science, pensées de 1848* | Otto von Bismarck falls from power | |
| 1892 | Dies in Paris (October 2) | Franco-Russian alliance: end of France's diplomatic isolation | |

# WHAT IS A NATION?
## AND OTHER POLITICAL WRITINGS

# 1

## ON CLERICAL LIBERALISM
## (*DU LIBÉRALISME CLÉRICAL*, 1848)

**N**othing allows us better to understand the irresistible energy of the movement of ideas than the force with which humanity drags along with it the very people who presented themselves as its most dangerous adversaries and attempted most boldly to block it. It looks like a storm, sweeping backward those who attempt to stand up to it. The regressive parties, who believe they are denied their rights if humanity achieves its own and breaks free of the yoke with which one aimed to restrain it, soon come around to presenting themselves as the persecuted ones and demanding the benefit of the liberty they had so sharply opposed, when it was against their interests. A great step has been taken the day things come to the point where the enemies of progress appeal to the principles that overthrew them, and find it in their interest for matters to be brought to their ultimate conclusions. One should not put too much faith in this tactical liberalism; however, the principles at least have been admitted, and it is pleasing to see these sacred rights proclaimed and invoked by the men who had at first rejected them most offensively.

Already, during the last years of the previous regime, the most absolute party, the one that feels oppressed if it is not dominating, led a vehement controversy against the representatives of liberal ideas while speaking of nothing but freedom. But this about-face was nothing compared to the events we have been witnessing for the past few months. Monks transformed into fiery democrats, former allies of the nobility turned more

republican than the Third Estate, priests blessing the tree[1] they have so
often cursed, and calling tyrannical the government they had originally
called anarchic: here are the miracles that this year has reserved for us. In
fact, let us go back to 1830.[2] What fury! What cries of impiety, of sacrilege!
And against what? Was it against the mistakes that in the past few years
rendered the struggles of the July fighters pointless? Was it that the believers predicted the harm that in certain respects this dynasty would cause
France? Ah, no doubt, had they known that one day state religion would
be reborn, that one day freedom of thought would be sacrificed to a disastrous pact with the party that calls itself religious, their fury would have
been mollified, and even had they not granted the newcomer the heartfelt
affection one could only feel for the first-born son of the Church,[3] they
would nevertheless not have hurled as many anathemas at him. Why then
such violence? Because power was at first too liberal, or rather was forced
to be so; because it overthrew a cherished regime, for which they had high
hopes; because they no longer could expect the holy alliance of throne
and altar.

Let us come to 1848. How times have changed! With what good grace
they submit to the circumstances! With what alacrity they turn democrat,
while laughing in secret at democracy! With what harshness they excori-
ate a government that after all was less exceptionable than the one of the
Restoration, for which they have nothing but sympathy! Is the Revolution
of 1848, by any chance, any more by divine right than the one of 1830?
Were the July fighters any less rebels than the February[4] ones? If the toil
of the former came to naught through the selfishness of politicians, was it
the fighters' fault? Well, how did the clergy treat them? As rebels, as insurgents. The prayers of the Church have been refused them or accorded
grudgingly. At heart, one damned them as having died in the sin of rebellion. Several priests, in order to find an excuse for the official ceremonies,
claimed that by praying for the deceased of July, it had not been specified
which deceased were meant, and that one could focus one's intent on the
Swiss guards[5] and the other victims of the royal cause.

After that, can one really be serious in turning the February dead
into heroes and martyrs? Do not believe it. It is nothing but rancor and
self-interested calculation. The clergy's rancor lasts long: eighteen years,
and eighteen years of blandishments, had not softened them. The king[6] of
August 9 was still a usurper, and God knows after how many generations

and in exchange for how many concessions his dynasty would have been legitimated. February satisfies the Catholics, because February eases their ill will against the man who had supplanted the king God cherished; because February, they believe, will smooth the path for the son of David, that beloved Jehoash, who will come to repair the evils of revolutions and bring back the "beauty of ancient times."

Let us consider, in good faith, whether this liberalism can be serious; let us consult the precedents, which for the Church are a binding rule, to determine if such principles are ancient within it. The embarrassment of a clergyman, who, in the middle of his democratic protestations, was confronted with a much less republican passage drawn from his previous writings, has been mocked. Does the Church as a whole, when it turns liberal, not stand exposed to a similar rebuttal?

Let us first of all posit that the Church can never separate itself from its past, that to disown one of its acts is, for it, tantamount to self-destruction: *sint ut sunt, aut non sint*[7] will always be the motto of the orthodox. I recognize that this is an unfortunate position, anomalous, I dare say, within humanity. Philosophy never being more than a formulation of truth, more or less advanced, but always incomplete, the thinker never envisages either an absolute retraction or an unwavering immobility. He wishes to lend himself to the successive modifications brought about by time, without ever breaking with the past, but without being its slave; he wishes that, without disowning the symbols he has loved, he could explain them in new ways and show the portion of ill-defined truth they contained. Such is the method of philosophy. If a philosopher surpasses himself and wears out several systems, this has nothing contradictory to it: it does him honor. But things are not the same for orthodoxy. Since its pretention is that it was created on the first attempt and all at once, it places itself by this very fact outside progress; it becomes rigid, brittle, inflexible, and while philosophy is always contemporary to humanity, religion one day becomes old-fashioned; because it is immutable, and humanity changes. It is not that the Church has not changed under duress like everything else. But it denies it; it lies to history, it distorts all critical faculties to prove that its current state is similar to its primitive one, and it is obliged to do so in order to remain orthodox.

The past being the insurmountable law of the Church, if its past precludes liberalism, if it cannot adopt the modern ideas in politics without disowning its previous decisions, it will be proven that the orthodox do not have the right to speak of freedom, and that, if they do speak of it, they are hypocrites and heretics.

Four articles condense the entire charter of modern liberties: (i) The existence of the nation as a moral personality with rights as well as responsibilities. (ii) The participation of all in government, to different degrees. (iii) Universal religious toleration. (iv) Unlimited freedom of thought, and consequently of speech and of the press, in the speculative domain. Let us see what the Church can accept in this program.

I

The treatises of theology and ecclesiastical philosophy* concur in denouncing the principle of the sovereignty of the people.† The "theory of the social contract," which, though quite faulty if considered as a historical hypothesis, remains the basis of modern politics, is a heresy in the eyes of the theologians. The divine right of the powers that be is a proposition the orthodox doctors prove through scripture, and, as their exegesis does not deny itself contradictions, an abundance of texts present themselves: "By me kings reign"‡—"Submit yourselves to every ordinance of man for the

---

* The Scholastics of the Middle Ages professed much more liberal a doctrine. But that was an echo of the writings of Aristotle and the ancient philosophers in them.

† This is how Mr. Frayssinous described it: "theory as absurd as it is seditious, which flatters the multitude only to lead it astray, and praises its rights only to induce it to violate all its duties. Even to the most superficial of inquiries, it will appear that the words *people* and *sovereign* do not fit together anymore than *light* and *darkness*, etc." (*Conférence sur l'union de la religion et de la société*). One of the most peculiar monuments of the political doctrines of the Church is the bull by Pius VII against the Carbonari (September 13, 1821), who are condemned because they teach "that it is permissible to rouse rebellions, to despoil of their power kings and those who command, to which they give the injurious title of tyrants." The bull excommunicates them, together with anyone who reads their books and does not denounce them to the bishop as soon as he has knowledge of them (*L'Ami de la religion et du Roi*, October 10, 1821).

‡ Proverbs 8:15. These words, in the mouth of divine wisdom, are very simple. But here we are discussing the sense theologians have thought they saw in them.

Lord's sake: whether it be to the king, as supreme; Or unto governors, as unto them that are sent by him . . . For so is the will of God"*—"Let every soul be subject unto the higher powers. For there is no power but of God: the powers that be are ordained of God. Whosoever therefore resisteth the power, resisteth the ordinance of God: and they that resist shall receive to themselves damnation. . . . For he is the minister of God . . . Wherefore ye must needs be subject, not only for wrath, but also for conscience sake. . . . for they are God's ministers, attending continually upon this very thing"†8 The Church Fathers are not lacking: "We do not attribute the power to confer kingdoms and empires to anyone but the true God,"9 says Saint Augustine.‡ God preserve me from lacking critical faculties to the point of giving Saint Peter, Saint Paul, and Saint Augustine the character of absolutists on the basis of a few isolated texts. One would have as much evidence to make Jesus Christ into a revolutionary. I relate the arguments of the theologians to show what the generally established opinion among them is. The theory of divine right begins to be formulated explicitly in the age of Constantine.10 The Church Fathers, and especially Lactantius,11 never desist from illustrating to the emperors the advantage Christianity offers them, by guaranteeing them subjects who never rebel.§

One has long gained the habit of saying that the Gospel contains principles of political liberty, and this trite phrase is repeated complacently. One would be entirely at a loss if one had to quote even a single passage of the Gospel containing the smallest kernel of the political system adopted by modern nations. The admiration all elevated minds profess for this sublime book should not go as far as finding within it what it does not contain. The principle of the Gospel is the moral and religious idea, the improvement and purification of the inner man. Without doubt, the respect of humanity that such a doctrine inspires could not fail to introduce worthier manners in politics. But it is by way of consequence that such a happy result has come to pass. The only political passage one may cite from the Gospel is an expression of superior

---

* 1 Peter 2:13.

† Romans 13:1–7.

‡ *De civitate Dei*, book V, 21.

§ Cf. Edward Gibbon, *History of the Decline and Fall of the Roman Empire*, chap. XX.

indifference: "Render therefore unto Caesar the things which are Caesar's; and unto God the things that are God's."* [12]

And, in point of fact, is it from Christianity that liberal ideas have directly sprung? Was it Christianity that made the Revolution? Since the beginning of modern times, has traditional Christianity not attempted to stifle all the aspirations of western Europe? Have not the Catholic writers who have felt obliged to be consistent been the most hostile to political progress? It is the modern spirit, nurtured no doubt in part by Christianity, but freed from Christianity, that produced all the great emancipation movements. Orthodoxy at first cursed these movements; then, when it saw that it was impossible to stop the torrent and that humanity kept going without worrying overmuch about leaving it behind, it started running after its disloyal pupil, showering it with attention, claiming it had desired such an outcome all along and that it was owed much gratitude for it.

If you want to appraise this "latter day" liberalism in its veritable form, read the orthodox authors who wrote freely and before the "misery of the times" forced them to offer concessions. Take, for example, the *Politique tirée des propres paroles de l'écriture sainte*[13] by Bossuet. Do you know what politics this Father of the Church, this great exegete of the Catholics, draws from Scripture? Here is the summary in his own words:

> The best form of government is monarchical government, hereditary from male to male and eldest to eldest.

Bossuet adds,

> Hence, France, where the succession is regulated in this manner, can glory in having the best possible State constitution, and the most in conformity with that which God himself has established. All of which taken together shows both the wisdom of our ancestors, and the particular protection of God over this kingdom.†—God establishes kings as his ministers, and reigns through them over the peoples.—The person of kings is sacred.‡—Royal authority is absolute. The prince need account to no one for what

---

* Matthew 22:21.
† Book II, art. 1.
‡ Book III, art. 2.

he ordains.*[14]—The sole defense of individuals against the public power must be their innocence.—One must obey princes like justice itself. They are gods, and share in some way in divine independence.—The prince can correct himself when he knows he has erred, but against his authority there can be no remedy except his authority.—Only God can judge the judgments and persons of princes.—There is no coactive force against the prince.—In the State, only the prince is armed.—The people must fear the prince, but the prince must only fear doing evil.—The fear of upsetting pushed too far degenerates into criminal weakness.— The prince must make himself feared by the great and small.—Royal authority must be invincible.—Firmness is an essential characteristic in royalty.†—Majesty is the image of the greatness of God in a prince. (There follows a parallel between God and the prince‡).—One must serve the State as the prince understands it; for in him resides the reason which guides the State.§—Obey passively.**—Subjects have nothing to oppose to the violence of princes but respectful remonstrances without mutiny or murmurings, and prayers for their conversion.††—Never a rebellion whatever the reason.‡‡

The majority of these axioms are the titles of as many chapters, each of which is proved in the style of a theology proposition, with a great wealth of biblical citations. Bossuet, after all, does nothing but summarize orthodox politics, and there is no Catholic who, in secret, would not agree that this would be the best of regimes, if such a regime were still possible. In fact, insofar as man is considered naturally evil, insofar as repression sums up morality, repression is also the last word of politics. The sternest regime, the most capable of mastering the passions, is the best. The

---

\*    "For he doeth whatsoever pleaseth him. Where the word of a king is, there is power: and who may say unto him, What doest thou?" (Ecclesiastes 8:3, 4). [In Latin in the original.]

†    Book IV.

‡    Book V, art. 4.

§    Book VI, art. 1.

**    Book VI, art. 2.

††    Book VI, art. 2, 6th proposition. "Is to suffer all from legitimate authority without a murmur," he says elsewhere, "not akin to fighting for it?" (*Sermon sur l'unité de l'Église*, first point).

‡‡    *Polit.*, Book VI, art. 2 and 3.

politics that is always concerned, like Mr. de Maistre[15] is, with atonement, with crime inherent to man and predating his birth, with incurable evil in human nature, can hardly acclaim that which serves progress. A formidable justice system, torture, soldiers, an executioner: these are the true means of government, and the famous publicist, in dreaming this nightmare and smugly settling on it, was simply being consistent with his orthodoxy. Since in this system one thing alone is necessary, to save souls whatever the price and whatever the means, one must prefer over all others the government that commands man most energetically, that is best at making society resemble a severely ordered monastery in which all freedom is vigorously directed toward good and in which evil is rendered necessarily impossible.

The legitimacy of legal opposition, when the rights of the nation go unrecognized, is the consequence of national sovereignty. But all orthodox moral treatises consider it a crime without qualification or explanation. Read, for instance, Bossuet's *Cinquième avertissement* and his *Défense de l'histoire des variations,** dedicated to confuting the letters of Jurieu.[16] The minister had supported the theory of the sovereignty of the people, of implicit pacts, and of the right the nation has to change the constitution.† This seemed to Bossuet quite simply "a doctrine liable to rouse all States. Do parents," he added, "need to reach a pact with their children in order to oblige them to obey?"‡

---

\* Also see *Hist. des variations*, book X, §§ 25ff., and de Maistre, *Du Pape*, book II, chap. II.

† He was the first to utter the exaggerated principle that "the people have no need for reason to validate their acts."

‡ "I have vindicated," he says, by way of summing up,

> the rights of kings and all sovereign powers; for they would all equally be under attack if it were true, as it is claimed, that the people dominate everywhere, and that the popular State, which is the worse of all, is the foundation of all States. I have responded to the authorities of Scripture that are brandished against them. They are considerable; and each time God speaks, or his decrees are appealed to, one must respond. As for the frivolous argumentations employed by the speculative philosophers to determine the rights of the powers that govern the universe, their own majesty is defense enough; and one should simply despise these worthless political theorists who, without knowledge of the world of public affairs, think they can subject the thrones of kings to the laws they erect among their books, or dictate in their schools.

Here is the true point. If the sovereign possesses his state legitimately, as a property he obtained from God, to dispossess him of it is both an injustice and a sacrilege. This peculiar idea of legitimacy by divine right, which plays such a large role in the history of modern nations, and which does not appear in ancient history, outside of the Jews, was developed among us under clerical influence. The clergy, having borrowed from Hebrew theocracy the anointment of kings, turned them into "Christs of the Lord," and gave their inviolability a religious sanction. Royalty hence became a sort of sacrament inscribing a separate "character," a separate "order"; and in fact several ceremonies of the anointment were copied from priestly ordination.*

Therefore, far from advancing the emancipation of peoples, the Church, it must be said, delayed it. Such emancipation could only take place once the people had preliminarily emancipated themselves from the Church. Without doubt ecclesiastical authority, and especially the papacy, was often, in the first half of the Middle Ages, a protection against the barbarism of the age. The maxims of humaneness that the Church has always professed, except for the cases when it was in danger, the possibility of appealing in the face of conquest and brutality to a spiritual power were an immense benefaction in a time when force reigned absolute. But, while the Church typically supported the oppressed, it never attempted to assert their freedom or to awaken in them a consciousness of their rights. The services it rendered resemble modern constitutions the way the individual alms of yesteryear resembled the organized establishments of public charity; a host of partial ills were staved off, but the root of evil remained. Everything was precarious, and depended on the goodwill of an individual. The Church practiced political charity; it did not establish political right.

II

The theory of national sovereignty entails as a consequence government through national representation, which can admit of different forms and

---

* The ignorant understood the matter on this basis. In Brittany, I have heard simple folk claim that Louis-Philippe, not having been anointed, had no more right to exercise kingship than a nonordained priest had to perform sacerdotal functions.

degrees, but is not complete except when each citizen, by means of election, has his[17] part in the government. Now, one would be incapable of expressing how much the Church has always disapproved of this government of the nation by the nation. In fact, the Church has always prided itself on realizing, in its own constitution, the ideal government. Now, each century of the history of the Church shows it chasing further and further from its bosom anything that appeared to resemble popular representation. What form did the government of the Church approximate more and more? The least democratic form, the one in which ranks are separated by the most insurmountable barrier, by which I mean a sacred, indelible character. Hierarchy is the basis of the entire Catholic system: it is "by faith," as the theologians say.* Whereas originally the Church was a gathering of believers governing themselves, the Church nowadays is divided into governors and governed, and the former have taken for themselves all the rights the people enjoyed under the primitive constitution. Originally, the judgment on doctrine was shared among all: the modern system formally excludes laymen, who now go to church exclusively to listen. Originally, the apostolic mission derived from each person's conscience, or from the vote of the faithful assembled: nowadays, the hierarchy has assumed the sole right of bestowing it.† And even then, if only one could say that something of the primitive fraternity that united the cooperators of the Gospel had been conserved in this directive senate! Far from it, the ranks have been deeply divided within the clergy. The priest, who Saint Jerome clearly declared to be the equal of the bishop,‡[18] has become by divine right his subordinate. The priest has been successively excluded from the councils and from any participation in episcopal jurisdiction; it has become rash to say that the second-order clergy forms the necessary counsel of the bishop, and that he cannot make any decision on faith or discipline without its involvement. Was the equality of

---

\*   *Concil. Trident.*, sess. XXIII, can. 4, 6, 7, 8.

†   *Concil. Trident.*, sess. XXIII, can. 7.

‡   "Priest and bishop are the same, and before sects appeared at the instigation of Satan, within the religion the churches were governed by the collective wisdom of the priests." [In Latin in the original.] One must read the entire following passage (in chap. I Epist. ad Tit.). On the primitive identity of the πρεσβύτερος and the ἐπίσκοπος, see Phil. I, 1, and the observation of Theodoret on this passage.

bishops preserved any better? No; it has become a common subjection to a single head. I know agreement is not unanimous on this, and that certain churches have preserved some maxims that are less removed from the ancient spirit. According to Gallican doctrine, the Church is a sort of representative monarchy, in which infallibility and government only reside in the union of the head and the limbs. But this depends on the fact that, on a host of theological questions, historical criticism and the modern decisions of the Church are in contradiction. The Gallicans triumph when they appeal to events of ancient times; but they have nothing to answer when their adversaries confront them with more modern decisions, which they themselves are obliged to admit as irrefutably authoritative. What can they say, for instance, about texts such as this one from the Council of Florence:[19] "We determine that the full power of shepherding and governing the universal Church was handed down by Christ to the Roman Pontiff through the Blessed Peter,"[20] and this other from the Second Council of Lyon:[21] "The Roman Church holds supreme and entire primacy over the universal Catholic Church,"[22] and this other from the Council of Trent:[23] "The popes, because of the supreme power they inherited over the entire Church"?*[24] Can one express absolute monarchy in clearer terms, and is not the narrowest opinion here, as always, the most orthodox?

It is interesting to study throughout the history of the Church this constant march from the most perfect democracy, which was the regime of most of the primitive churches, to episcopal oligarchy, and, from there, to papal monarchy, to see how the central authority, once constituted, severely repressed any attempt to reclaim expired rights. The Councils of Constance and Basel,[25] which attempted to establish a sort of parliamentary regime for the Church, failed completely. The Council of Trent, at the outset, also expressed very hostile intentions toward papal omnipotence, intentions that the cold hand of authority, to speak like Mr. de Maistre, subsequently came to stem.† But nothing shows the aversion of the Church for anything resembling a popular regime more openly than the way in which it responded, on the one hand, to the attempts of the

---

\*     *Concil. Trident.*, sess. XIV, chap. 7.

†     Cf. Leopold von Ranke, *Histoire de la papauté au XVIe et XVIIe siècle*, vol. II, init.

Jansenists[26] to restore ancient discipline to the Church, and on the other, to the Constitution of 1791,[27] which was simply the resumption of the Jansenist attempt. The fundamental idea of the Constitution of 1791 was to adapt the government of the Church to the system of modern states, thence bringing it back to its original form. The principles of this famous act were to give the bishop a permanent council formed by his clergy,* and to establish elections on the broadest and most liberal bases.† How did the orthodoxy respond to it? By the condemnations of the Sorbonne, by papal briefs, by the hierarchy's definitions as schismatic and subversive. Antiquity was rather more liberal, when it declared election as being by divine tradition and divine right.

III

People often recommend tolerance to the Church, without asking themselves whether it can grant it. This is the thorny point in all controversies, the one on which a categorical reply can never be obtained. Because, in fact, the Church has never been tolerant; it will never be, it cannot be, and the orthodox admit it fairly willingly, in the moments in which they relinquish all timidity. But here, as in a host of other cases, they have one doctrine for those who are not scandalized by anything, and another doctrine that can be presented to outsiders. First of all, do not ask of the Catholic that interior tolerance that is not skepticism, but critical faculty: the Catholic condemns it as evil and impossible. In fact, as soon as one admits any religious doctrine as absolutely and exclusively true, it becomes impossible to admit that another doctrine also has its part of truth. Any absolute doctrine is, by its essence itself, intolerant. Orthodoxy thus will never have that high philosophical impartiality that weighs and appraises all opinions coolly. Now, this interior tolerance is the necessary condition for exterior tolerance, the one that makes goodwill between dissenting parties possible, and that, in politics, grants both the same rights.

---

\*     Title I, art. 14.
†     Title II in its entirety.

In the eyes of the orthodox, indeed, the heterodox is guilty. Since the orthodox is obliged to maintain that true belief is of all clear things the clearest, error in religion can only derive, in his opinion, from crass ignorance or resolute bad faith. The most charitable sentiment of the orthodox for the misbeliever is pity. If he cannot assume involuntary ignorance (and in such a manifest matter, involuntary ignorance seems almost a chimerical hypothesis to him),* the believer is obliged to condemn anyone who does not think like him. Now, one is quite close to burning in this world the people one burns in the next. Besides, since wholesome belief is, according to the viewpoint of the orthodox, the greatest good to which all the rest must be sacrificed, and since the prince, as they say, may and must dare all for the well-being of his subjects, the prince acts as a father in separating the wheat from the chaff and burning the latter.†[28] The *compelle intrare*[29] is legitimated by its results. Willing, forced, what does it matter? Save the truth first and foremost and at whatever price! Thus do the theologians unanimously grant the prince the power to demand the "external profession" of the recognized religion, and the Council of Trent pronounces an anathema against those who argue that one may not bring back by means of temporal punishments those who no longer accept at an older age the promises made on their behalf when they were baptized.‡ This is, after all, perfectly logical. It is wrong to press the Catholics on this point; one should not demand of them what they cannot give. Ask them, ultimately, to give up orthodoxy, but do not ask them to remain orthodox and suffer heterodoxy. This for them is a question of being or not being Catholic.

---

\* Mr. Frayssinous, answering questions he had been asked on the salvation of heretics, and attempting to broaden Catholic doctrine as much as possible, recognizes that error in good faith must be considered as the exception. The general maxim "Outside the Church there is no salvation" also presupposes it.

† It is well known that the Inquisition had a text to present its pyres as a divine institution: "If a man abide not in me, he is cast forth as a branch, and is withered; and men gather them, and cast them into the fire, AND THEY ARE BURNED." (John 15:6) [In Latin in the original.]

‡ "Si quis dixerit . . . parvulos baptizatos, cum adoleverint, interrogandos esse an ratum habere velint quod patrini eorum nomine, dum baptizarentur, polliciti sunt, et ubi se nolle responderint, suo esse arbitrio relinquendos, nec alia interim poena ad christianam vitam cogendos, nisi ut ab Eucharistiae aliorumque sacramentorum perceptione arceantur, donec resipiscant, anathema sit" (*Concil. Trident.*, sess. VII, *De bapt.*, can. 14).

Therefore, any time the Church will be in the position to persecute without danger, it will do so, and it will be consistent by persecuting. Nothing matters in comparison with the one thing necessary, saving souls. If by sacrificing one thousand corrupt souls it is possible to save even one, orthodoxy will find the sacrifice sufficiently offset. If by burning people in this world one can save them, or others, from being burned for eternity, a meritorious act has been accomplished. I am not inventing this; I am merely relaying the arguments one finds everywhere among the truly orthodox authors to justify the Inquisition and measures of a similar type.

No rights matter in the eye of the true believer faced with the supreme necessity of preserving the faith. The rights of the family, for instance; assuredly, the Church has invoked them often these past years against state schooling. To remove the youth from public education, which was not to its liking, the Church insisted with an impatient liberalism on the rights of the family to the child. But do you know how that same Church respected these rights, when it was in power? It established in practice, if not as a general principle, the right to abduct children from their family, when it was not an orthodox one: "The child," says Canon law,* "must not remain with those people who may be suspected of plotting against its salvation or its life"[30]—"We order," says the Fourth Council of Toledo (633),† "that the baptized children of Jews, so as not to be swept away by the errors of their parents, be separated from relations with them, and that they be assigned to monasteries or to Christian men, so that they may progress in morals and in faith."[31] Several theologians grant the prince the right to have the children of Jews and infidels baptized by force, and the reason they allege for it is evident: the prince has the right to prevent the father from assassinating his son: now, by detaining him in unbelief, the father does even worse than assassinating. All, at the very least, agree that the child won over to orthodoxy, by whatever means of capture, is no longer subject to his parents; that the children of slaves, if the master consents, and the children of those who, having embraced orthodoxy, have returned to heresy, may be baptized by force; that the consent of a single parent is sufficient, and that in the event of the conversion of one of them, the infant child must follow the faithful party. After all, the rigorous exigencies of the Church with regard to the children of mixed marriages are well known,

---

*    *Decretales Gregorii*, book III, title XXXIII, *De convers. infid.*, chap. 2.
†    Fourth Council of Toledo, can. 60.

whereas equity would require that the division were according to gender, as the Protestant sects admit. Finally, the Church had nothing but praise for the acts that intruded on the freedom of families with which Louis XIV[32] preceded and bolstered his revocation of the Edict[33] of Nantes.* The Church, when it could, thus caused the state to violate the rights of the family on religious education. And yet these rights are much more sacred as concerns religion than as concerns education. The state must have some power on the intellectual and moral education of its members; it has no influence on religion. Religion, indeed, is essentially a thing of tradition. "Our forefathers worshipped thus:" this is its best, or, better said, its only reason for existence. All conversions are evil; for all conversions attribute an absolute value to relative and debatable forms of worship. Birth must govern religions; reason alone must govern individual opinions.

IV

If orthodoxy is obliged to show its sternness against any belief that departs from wholesome theological doctrine, what will it do against the freethinker, who places himself outside any religious doctrine? The greatest mercy it can afford him would be to treat him as a heretic. Indeed, the Church hardly distinguished between the two: the Inquisition was the common remedy it employed against both the freedom to believe and the freedom to think.

I know that within the Church there is a more liberal party that condemns these barbarous measures. But this is one of the mitigations that scarcely consistent minds have introduced on several points of Catholic doctrine and discipline that had become too shocking to modern sensibilities. With regard to these attenuations, serious orthodoxy follows a tactic in accordance with its general character. It is careful to avoid accepting them; but it is content that there be naive scholars to put forth superficial explanations with which laypeople are satisfied. Convinced in advance

---

* The task of the *Nouvelles catholiques* was to offer a sanctuary against paternal influence to young Protestant girls who had been brought over to Catholicism willingly or by force. When the reformed churches allowed themselves similar acts, the Catholics appealed to liberty!

that the objections against their faith are faulty, Catholics often devise faulty rebuttals, knowing full well what they are worth. This derives from that supreme disdain for those who doubt or do not believe, which lies at the base of theological controversies. To save the fundamental thesis, they are accommodating with the rest. The theologian, always considering himself as possessing a superior science that simple folk cannot understand, treats his adversaries the way a mathematician treats the public to which he is obliged to explain a problem with transcendental numbers. The mathematician, in such a case, allows himself many twists in the proof that he knows are not exact, but that he finds appropriate to his audience. The theologian, considering the layperson incapable of grasping the true reasons of the truth, is quite content with seeing him clasp certain solutions that satisfy his ignorance and of which he, the theologian, clearly perceives the fragility.

To return to the Inquisition, the orthodox fairly readily allow it to be said that it was an abuse, that it was not the work of the Church, which therefore has no interest in defending this odious tribunal. They allow it to be said, but they know very well that it cannot be believed. And, indeed, it is not true: the Inquisition is the logical consequence of the entire orthodox system; it is the summation of the mentality of the Church; the Church, when it can, will bring back the Inquisition, and if it does not, it is because it cannot.

To substantiate this claim I need only direct the reader to a peculiar pamphlet by an Italian theologian, the canon Muzzarelli,* who dedicated a long and erudite dissertation† to proving that the Church Fathers, the Councils, and the universal discipline of the Church are favorable to the Inquisition; that the Inquisition is in the spirit itself of the Gospel (wrong: but certainly in the spirit of the Church), and that only unbelievers can be hostile to it.

This is no doubt a sad thesis, but unfortunately a very true thesis. Indeed, what can the orthodox reply to the Councils that established and approved the Inquisition and to the Church Fathers and bishops who

---

* Muzzarelli was the most authoritative theologian in Rome under the reign of Pius VII and the close adviser of this pope.

† It may be read in partial translation following volume V of the *Histoire générale de l'Église* by Baron Henrion.

recommended and practiced inquisitorial measures? Father Lacordaire[34] admits that since Constantine, that is to say since the Church has wielded some power within the state, the Church has always called on public authority for the preservation of the faith, and this, he says, is completely natural, religion being the first good of the peoples.* The Christian emperors were, for the most part, intolerant, at the instigation of the bishops.† Constantine intervened directly in the Donatist controversy.‡ A host of individual Councils—Aquileia (381), Milan, under Saint Ambrose[35] (389), the fifth in Carthage (400), Milevum (416)—besought the civil power's aid against the heretics. Dioscorus of Alexandria,[36] having been condemned by the general Council of Chalcedon (451), was punished, by order of the Council, with secular penalties. The Third Council of Orléans (538), the sixth of Toledo (638), and that of Toulouse (1119) foreshadowed the Inquisition. Pope Innocent III, the Councils of Toulouse (1229), Arles (1234), Narbonne (1235), Béziers (1246), and Albi (1254) progressively completed the organization of this redoubtable institution. Two ecumenical Councils have strongly approved it. The Council of Vienne dispatched inquisitors, enjoined bishops to aid them, prescribed, with the greatest care, the security measures of prisons, the trustworthiness of guards, their watchfulness, and their secrecy. The words of the Fourth Lateran Council are cause for shuddering:

> Let secular authorities, . . . be advised and urged and if necessary be compelled by ecclesiastical censure, . . . to take publicly an oath . . . to expel from the lands subject to their jurisdiction all heretics designated by the church. . . . If however a temporal lord, required and instructed by the church, neglects to cleanse his territory of this heretical filth,

---

\*   *Mémoire pour le rétablissement en France de l'ordre des frères prêcheurs*, prefacing his *Vie de saint Dominique*, pp. 136 and ff. (3rd ed., 1844).

†   It can be interesting to learn Bossuet's feelings on this point. Here are some further axioms drawn from his *Politique*: "A prince should use his authority to destroy false religions in his State" (book VII, art. 3, prop. 9). "Those who do not accept the prince using rigor in matters of religion fall into an impious error." Having described the conduct of Christian princes, he adds: "The Church thanked them for these laws." The prince, again according to Bossuet, is the executor of the law of God; he must mind the religious education of his peoples, ensure the feast-days are sanctified, punish blasphemers (book VII, art. 4, 5, and ff.).

‡   See Fleury, *Hist. eccl.*, book X, no. 10 and ff.

he shall be bound with the bond of excommunication by the metropol-
itan and other bishops of the province. If he refuses to give satisfaction
within a year, this shall be reported to the supreme pontiff so that he may
then declare his vassals absolved from their fealty to him and make the
land available for occupation by Catholics so that these may, after they
have expelled the heretics, possess it unopposed and preserve it in the
purity of the faith—saving the right of the suzerain provided that he
makes no difficulty in the matter and puts no impediment in the way. . . .
Catholics who take the cross . . . shall enjoy the same indulgence . . . as is
granted to those who go to . . . the Holy Land. Moreover, we determine
to subject to excommunication believers who receive, defend or support
heretics. We strictly ordain that if any such person . . . refuses to render
satisfaction within a year, then by the law itself he shall be branded as
infamous and not be admitted to public offices or councils or to elect
others to the same or to give testimony. He shall be intestable, that is
he shall not have the freedom to make a will nor shall he succeed to an
inheritance. Moreover nobody shall be compelled to answer to him on
any business whatsoever, but he may be compelled to answer to them. If
he is a judge, sentences pronounced by him shall have no force and cases
may not be brought before him; if an advocate, he may not be allowed to
defend anyone; if a notary, documents drawn up by him shall be worthless . . .; and in similar matters we order the same to be observed.[*]

The measures prescribed for the search for heretics correspond to
these fearful penalties.[†] Catholics, when one talks to them about these
persecutions, reply that the Church has never spilt blood, that the secular
princes are alone responsible for such cruelties.[‡] Why do they not add that
the Church forced the princes into such cruelties under the most terrible

---

[*]   *Conc. Later. IV*, can. 3.

[†]   A pious historian of the Church adds to the description of these facts the following
      reflection: "The Church at that time possessed these rights and this authority, for it
      employed them freely, and it still maintains them, although it considers it need not use
      them now as before." *Need* in such a case means "can." (Baron Henrion's *Histoire générale
      de l'Église*, vol. V, p. 263).

[‡]   This is the reply of Mr. de Maistre, in his *Lettre à un gentilhomme russe sur l'inquisition
      espagnole*, and of Mr. Lacordaire, in the above-cited work. The truly orthodox, on the
      contrary, openly recognize the unmediated power of the Church.

penalties, that they were excommunicated, deposed, treated like heretics if they did not obey?

We fear we would be accumulating superfluous evidence if we quoted a great number of passages to demonstrate to the orthodox that their fore-fathers in the faith were zealous inquisitors. Saint Augustine is among those one is most startled to find at the forefront of the list. After having initially opposed such measures of severity, he was one of the fiercest in imposing them on the Donatists.* "Well then! said Petilian forcefully, per-haps the service of God demands that you assassinate us with your own hands! You are mistaken, evildoers; God does not have executioners for ministers." Augustine answered:

> Why would the pious man not oust the impious by means of the estab-lished powers, and the just man the unjust? . . . The only thing we must examine is whether you were in the right or in the wrong in separating yourselves from the universal communion. For if we find that you have acted impiously in separating yourselves, you should not be surprised if God will not be lacking ministers to scourge you: in this case, you suffer persecution not from us, but, as it is written, from your own acts.†

> Parmenian, he says elsewhere, dares complain about Constantine's order to send to the camp, that is to execution, the Donatists who, having been found guilty by ecclesiastical judges, were not able to prove what they said in front of him . . . What injustice can there be in the penalties suffered, as punishment for their sins and by order of authority, by those whom God warns by the present judgment and this retribution to avoid the eternal fire? Let them prove first that they are neither heretics nor schismatics, and only then complain of being punished unjustly.

These coercive measures were already quite common in episcopal jurisdiction.‡[37] Hilary of Poitiers[38] and Saint Jerome hardly prove any less

---

* See Fleury, *Hist. eccl.*, book XXIII, no. 39 and ff.

† *Contra litt. Petil.*, book II, no. 42, 43.

‡ "You extracted the confession of such horrid crimes . . . by beating them with rods, a mode of correction used by schoolmasters, and by parents themselves, and often also by bishops in the sentences awarded by them." (S. Aug., Epist. 159 [aliis 133]). [In Latin in the original.]

rigorous. Saint Gregory the pope[39] continuously calls upon the governors and exarchs to strike and exile the heretics.* Saint Leo[40] acted the same way, and having discovered some Manichaeans in Rome, turned them over to the secular arm.† The universal practice of the Church, in short, proves that it believed it possessed such a right; and, in effect, the Council of Constance, in one of the sessions everyone considers ecumenical, condemned the proposition of Jan Hus[41] that the ecclesiastical power does not have the right to make recourse to the secular power to support its censures.‡ What can the orthodox theologian answer to this? Can he still maintain that the Inquisition is an abuse, a political institution? If the Inquisition has been the universal practice of the Church, is the theologian not obliged to recognize that the Church possessed the rights such practices presuppose, and to admit that, if the Church does not now make use of this right, it is simply doing us a favor?

Freedom of thought is associated with the right to express one's thought freely, both through speech and through the press. It is interesting to see how the Church has respected this liberty, the most necessary of all, for it alone is sufficient to win and preserve the rest. It may be remembered that, in a recent circumstance,§ a people being reborn to political life requested from the most liberal of popes this primary need of modern nations, and their request was answered by a decree of the Lateran Council.** The reply was peremptory. A host of acts of the Roman Church, numerous papal bulls, institutions clad in the sanction of the universal Church are the negation of the right of free issuance of ideas. Read, for instance, the regulations made by order of the Council of Trent concerning the Index. It is impossible to imagine a better-devised design for stifling the freedom of thought. It is not merely the works relative to theology and scripture that are subjected to the most tyrannical obstacles: all the books of heresiarchs, whatever the subject, are prohibited; the condemnation *in odium auctoris*[42]

---

\* Book I, epistle 74; book IV, epistles 7 and 34.

† Fleury, *Hist. eccl.*, book XXVI, no. 54.

‡ Fleury, *Hist. eccl.*, book CIII, no. 74.

§ This is an allusion to an incident from the early days of Pope Pius IX.

\*\* It was mistakenly believed to be the Second Lateran Council against Arnold of Brescia (Labbe, *Concil.*, vol. X, col. 999 and ff.). Actually it was the Lateran Council under Leo X (sess. X), whose decrees on the matter were invoked by the Council of Trent (sess. IV).

is already established in principle;* the most severe penalties are reserved for offenders. The subsequent regulations of the pope and the Holy Office completed this system of oppression. The most harmless books, or the ones whose knowledge is the most indispensable, for example Descartes and Malebranche,[43] were placed on the Index. Reading them was prohibited, under threat of excommunication, to everyone, even to bishops, except to inquisitors and those who obtained permission to read them by declaring their formal and predetermined intent to refute them. The theologians, with their ordinary scrupulousness, even make a point of remarking that excommunication strikes those who simply skim the book with their eyes, without pronouncing the words, or those who would have it read to them by others. The single churches strengthened these regulations even further. Obliviousness has greatly simplified the duties of the faithful in this matter: many people doubtless do not know that they have fallen into excommunication in the diocese of Paris by having in their home the *Provinciales* of Pascal.[44]

It will perhaps be objected that I have considered orthodoxy only on its dark and severe side, that there exists a more obliging Catholicism that has learned how to come to terms with the necessities of the times and throw a veil over unduly hard truths. I know this; but of all systems, that one is the least consistent. I can conceive of the orthodox, I can conceive of the unbelievers, but not of the neo-Catholics. Only the profound ignorance of biblical exegesis and theology in which France, outside the clergy, finds itself could generate a school so superficial and full of contradictions. It is among the Church Fathers, among the Councils that true Christianity must be sought, and not among minds both feeble and frivolous, who have altered the Christian doctrine by softening it, without making it more acceptable.

Might one say that the times have changed, that the Church no longer intends to do what it once did? Thus, it is only so as to serve its cause better that it renounces its rights. If it allows us liberty, it is because it would be too difficult to repress our deviancies. We are abandoned to the hardness of our heart; we are allowed to breathe, because they cannot

---

\*    *Conc. Trid.*, sess. IV and XVIII, and the rules *De libris prohibitis* carried by the Council and approved by the constitution *Dominici* on March 24, 1564 (Labbe, *Conc.*, vol. XIV, col. 950 and ff.).

choke us.* Freedom is a favor they grant us, alms they give us with a sigh. We do not want it on this basis; freedom is our right, not a concession we want to owe to evil times: it is our right to speak our mind with no other control than public reason. You cannot generously give what already belongs to us!

And why, I pray thee, would repression be less necessary now than before? Would it be that in your eyes opposition to Catholicism is less dangerous nowadays? Without a doubt you do not believe that. Therefore, it is because you cannot do otherwise. You are moderate, because it would be dangerous for you to be violent. It is not tolerance to suffer one's enemies, when lacking the force to fetter them or burn them.

Tell us honestly: if you were the masters, what would you do? Would you invite thought to open its wings in complete freedom? Would you deliver yourselves without a breastplate to the blows of criticism? No; you would entrench yourselves behind the cloud of a "self-evident" revelation; you would raise the old idol of respect; you would call your enemies voluntarily blind, debasers of public conscience; you would be consistent and attempt to root them out at all costs. You would act, in short, the way you did under the Restoration, the way you do each time an obliging power agrees to lend you a hand, to be repaid in kind. Speak no longer of liberty, of tolerance; pronounce no longer these sacred words of our profession of faith; in order to make use of them, you are obliged to distort them. Your tolerance is an extorted gift; if you were strong enough, you would revoke it: we are in no way thankful for it.

Let the Church therefore remain what it is, and admit its doctrines. Its sincerity will be recognized. It will be greeted with the benevolence one has for historic remnants; it will be respected like those dotards who are excused for not accepting new ideas, for missing the past, and even for becoming the acrimonious and disagreeable censors of the present. Let the Church surround itself with the whiff of veneration that attaches itself

---

* Here, for instance, is the Catholics' theory on the Edict of Nantes and the repeal of that edict: Henry IV had to carry it, they say, because he could not do otherwise (and they destroy the entire character of this prince in order to prove that, as a fervent Catholic, he granted nothing to heresy except grudgingly). Louis XIV was obliged to repeal it because he was strong enough to do so. Power has always been the measure of the Church's tolerance.

to old things, but let it not attempt to remake itself following the fashion of the day. Let it keep its old banners, innocent old trinkets that only produce a smile; but let it not attempt to take up this new flag that conflicts with its outmoded habits. A dotard is not ridiculous if he keeps the garb of his time; he is if he dons a red bonnet and assumes a youthful air that contrasts with his senility.

# 2

## MR. DE SACY AND THE LIBERAL TRADITION
## (*M. DE SACY ET L'ÉCOLE LIBÉRALE*, 1858)

Gentlemanliness is the veritable aristocracy of our age; it does not need to be protected, for, although some attempt to fake it, they never manage to usurp it. Nobility always ends up being associated with the qualities that in certain decisive epochs caused the salvation of humanity. The privileged class, born out of feudalism, that had up until the Revolution of 1789 constituted the Germanic establishment in France, reaped, after more than a thousand years, the benefit of the great revolution that replaced the administrative despotism of the Roman Empire with what seemed like barbarism, but was in fact individual and local independence. I often imagine that the new nobility of the future will likewise be composed of those who, in one form or another, will have resisted the harmful tendencies of our time, by which I mean this general abasement of character that makes man accept everything, by detaching him from what strengthens political consciousness—this vulgar materialism under the influence of which the world would become as a vast field of stocks that a gust of wind sways all together: a fateful condition that, in my view, is liable to lead society, not to ruin (this word could not be employed with reference to humankind as a whole), but to a violent reaction of individual forces against shameful laziness and resigned inertia.

It is significant, and one may already consider this as one of the most important results of the first half of our century, that the moral resistance I have described can be found especially among men who devote themselves to the life of the mind. The ancient social classes did their part; none however may claim the honor of a more specially effective protestation. The Revolution has smashed all social aggregate and all solidarity in our country so thoroughly that it could not have been otherwise, and in any case it is not only in our own time that the government's administrative action encounters among us more assistance from individuals than from the different orders of the state. Intellectuals are the true nobility of our history. The French knighthood, at least since the Valois succession, produced nothing but the facile qualities of bravery, frivolousness, and elegance, which allowed it to play such a brilliant role in the world. All too often it lacked seriousness and morality; it forgot the fundamental function of an aristocracy: the defense of its rights, which in many senses were the rights of all, against royalty. Especially from the seventeenth century onward, all the duties of the nobility collapsed into a single one: to serve the king. All well and good, no doubt, but not enough. The French nobility failed in its other obligation, which consists in representing the privileges of individuals, in limiting power, in preserving modern times from the exaggerated notion of the state that ruined ancient societies. It only conceived of its privileges as a superiority over the bourgeoisie; its prerogatives were, for it, the source of disdain and not true pride, a reason for servility and impertinence much more than a duty to fulfill. Hence this attitude, both vapid and ponderously hidebound, frivolous and set in its ways, which has shaped the character of the French nobility; hence this internal vice that prevented it from being the origin of a free government and turned it, once such a government was established without it, into the most resolute adversary of the regime of which it should have been the founder and the supporter.

Whence, then, came the resistance that so often in our history, despite the absence of regular institutions, has set a limit to power? Where did the king of France encounter the sole force that obliged him to reckon with public opinion? Among the people of intellect. One could show that during almost the entire Middle Ages the cleric and, I dare say, the expert in public law led the hand of royalty, even when the latter appeared the most rebellious to such inspirations. The only period of actual tyranny that France has traversed could only come about following the preliminary liquidation of the people of intellect. The Terror, by decapitating France, was the true cause of the unprecedented lowering of character that marked the last years of the eighteenth century and the first of the nineteenth. Undoubtedly, if the generations of 1789 and 1792 had not been decimated by the axe or distorted by exile, if so many eminent representatives of the eighteenth century—who in the normal course of things should have continued their existence into the nineteenth and presided over the founding of the new society—had survived the Revolution, what followed would not have been possible. No comparison should be drawn in this matter between the years we are living through and the first ones of our century. The society that was the immediate product of the Revolution was servile because all intellectual aristocracy had disappeared, because the most serious exercise of thought at that time was reduced to some translations of Horace and some Latin verse. This is not the state of our times. Intellect has survived its apparent defeat: the means of doing without it have not been found, and it does not appear that, despite airy promises, anyone has yet discovered the secret of being liked without talent or being followed without heart.

In the middle of this uniform plane that equality has created around us, a sole fortress has thus remained standing, that of intellect. Literature is often blamed for the penchant that draws it toward the regions of politics, and it is rightly blamed, if by politics one intends the frivolous restlessness of a vulgar ambition. A superior man applying his faculties to the petty management of affairs or to administrative detail is indeed committing a sacrilege and an impropriety: the practice of life demands qualities completely different from speculation; high aspirations and deep views are of little use in an order of things in which what is humble and down-to-earth has a thousand times more chances of succeeding than what is nobly conceived and felt. But that literature must limit itself to a game of intellect with no application to the social questions that are debated in our time is a base notion, which demeans both politics and literature, and whose effect would be to lead us back to the grammarians of antiquity. If literature is serious, it implies a system on matters divine and human; politics, on its side, presupposes established ideas on the goal of societies, and consequently a philosophy. Hence literature and science can no longer be something harmless, administratively regulated, like performances or public amusements. Truly beautiful works cannot be ordered; the man capable of thinking for himself will never accept a yoke that requires of those who bear it mediocrity as its first precondition. The attempt of an official literature will always fail when faced with the double impossibility of bestowing originality on those who lack it and imposing obedience on those who do have it.

|

"I admit it sincerely," says Mr. de Sacy, at the beginning of the interesting collection that lends me the occasion for these reflections.*

> I have not changed. Whether it be a virtue or a fault, I have remained the same. Far from shaking my convictions, reflection, age, and experience have strengthened them. I am a liberal as I was thirty years ago. I believe in law and justice as I believed in them in my most tender youth. I am happy once again to take up this principle of liberty, deferred in politics by the times and the circumstances, in literature, philosophy, and all that pertains to conscience and pure thought. It is what we attempt to do in the *Journal des débats*.[1] With different nuances of taste and opinion, it is the spirit that unites us all; it is also, I hope, the spirit one will encounter in each line of the critical and literary articles that constitute these two volumes.

Indeed, it is the glory of the liberal school, and the best response it can offer to unjust disparagement, that it found itself, following the catastrophe that seemed to prove it wrong, in the very same state as when the leadership of the world belonged to it.[2] I will soon state with which reservations one must, in my opinion, accept the principles of this school; but there is one praise it cannot be refused: it possesses serious conviction, which does not let itself be repelled by setbacks, superior to success, persistent in hope against all hope. We shall not examine whether the resistance it offered to contemporary weaknesses could have been, I will not say more sincere, but more effective. Perhaps, unaccustomed as it was to reckon with other obstacles apart from those of its conscience, it did not always

---

\*   *Variétés littéraires, morales et historiques*, by Samuel Ustazade Silvestre de Sacy, of the Académie française; 2 vol., Paris, 1858.

employ, as Mr. Guizot[3] claimed on a solemn occasion, all the liberty it possessed. It never being in the interest of the state to push matters to the extreme, individuals have many advantages against it, when they are both prudent and resolved not to yield; but it is quite simple for moderate men, who conceive of liberty as a right of those who are worthy of it, and not as a privilege of the bold, to be shyer than others when they are obliged to be their own censors. This constraint, in any case, produces excellent literary results: it seems that the ennoblement of the publicist dates from the moment in which he could say everything only on condition that he say it well. Once, one barely deigned to grant a position in literature to the man devoted to the harsh toil of writing for the day; now, the Académie française,[4] gifted with such a delicate tact for discerning and following each movement of public opinion, has admitted in its midst a man who has only ever written newspaper articles, and clearly states he will never write anything other. It was thought that the rapid improvisations of the daily press could not have the solidity of studied works; it was believed that our old academic language was not appropriate to the busy eloquence of a positive century: now here is a book composed of newspaper articles, and this book, whatever opinion may be held on the substance of the ideas, is perhaps the one which in our own day best calls to mind the language of the century to which the title of "classical" has been awarded. The ephemeral occasion often produces writings that are not: Bossuet, Bayle, Voltaire hardly composed a work without being provoked to it by a contemporary occurrence; the most beautiful books of antiquity were in their time writings of circumstance. I would go even further: we are only completely safe from sounding declamatory when necessity obliges us to write or speak, and when we can say to ourselves that it is not by our own choice that we are making bold to involve the public with ourselves and our thoughts.

Of the two sorts of characters into which the world is divided, the ones shaping their opinion through the specific and analytical observation of each object, the others through a sort of general reason and faith in the righteousness of their instinct, the second is most decidedly the one to which Mr. de Sacy belongs. He is neither a historian, nor a philosopher, nor a theologian, nor a critic, nor a politician: he is an honest man demanding of his right and sound judgment alone opinions on all the issues that others seek to resolve through science or philosophy.

The historian will protest against his judgments, the poet will protest, the philosopher will protest, and often rightly so; but general common sense has its rights as well, as long as it is not intolerant and does not attempt to limit great originality. Thus it appears in Mr. de Sacy: the prejudices of this appealing writer are not those of a narrow mind that refuses to accept what upsets its habits and remains impervious to anything it does not understand; they are, if I dare say, the agreements an honest heart concludes with itself not to observe what cannot contribute to make it better. The truly narrow mind does not notice its smallness; it believes the world limited to the horizon it embraces; because of this it irritates us, like all pretentious and futile things; but here the limit is perceived and willed, the prejudices are aware of themselves and do not attempt to impose themselves on others. Such prejudices, deriving neither from laziness nor coercion, are the precondition for a host of excellent qualities necessary for the good of the world. The strength of society can only be obtained at the price of a certain number of principles accepted on faith, and that do not await a rational proof to become established.

Before examining what such a mind can produce, when applied to the types of intellectual work whose essence consists precisely in keeping many things under one's gaze at the same time, and embracing different worlds in a broad and lively sympathy, one must see it applied to its natural element, which is morality. I will perhaps have a few qualifications to offer to the verdicts of Mr. de Sacy the literary critic or Mr. de Sacy the historian; I cannot but applaud without reservation the opinions of Mr. de Sacy the moralist. It is neither the range, nor the depth, nor the curiosity of mind that makes the honest man: systematic obstinacy, so prejudicial in all the branches of pure speculation, is conversely the precondition itself of practical wisdom and its most secure basis.

A charming quality, which I would term the taste for the antique in all things, lends the ethical writings of Mr. de Sacy a suaveness that has rarely been equaled, and holds the secret of that exquisite tone, a blend of refinement and affability, which imparts to the whole book so delicious a perfume of ancientness. Hence, the author rises almost to poetry, although such a word is not precisely appropriate to describe his ordinary gifts. Poetry and morality are in fact two different things; but they both presuppose that man is not the being of a day, with no tie to the infinity that precedes him, with no responsibility toward the infinity that follows him.

I admit, it would be impossible for me to reside or even to travel with pleasure in a country without archives or antiquities. The interest and beauty
of things depend on the stamp of the man who trod, loved, suffered there.
A small town in Umbria, with its Etruscan walls, its Roman ruins, its
medieval towers, its Renaissance pavilions, its jesuitic churches of the seventeenth century, will always have more charm than our endlessly rebuilt
cities, where the past seems to have remained standing, not as a right,
but as a favor and as a theatrical backdrop. The plaster that removes the
traces of time and the level that makes the old foundations of human life
disappear are the natural enemies of all poetry. Gentlemanliness, likewise,
is what is least suitable to improvisation: it is the product of generations.
No abstract principle, whether philosophical or religious, has the power
to create an honest man. So-and-so boasts that he did not begin to have
any integrity until the day he converted. Ah! What an illusion, and how I
would distrust such a man, if I did not believe he was slandering himself
by a rhetorical figure and for the needs of his cause! Many things, and
many excellent things in the sphere of the mind, are young in the world;
but such is not the case in the sphere of morality: here nothing remains to
be invented or discovered. In ethics, what is ancient is true; because what
is ancient is honor; what is ancient is freedom.

It is after all not without reason that Mr. de Sacy loves the past: he only
knew it through the best of its traditions. The illustrious Silvestre de Sacy,[5]
the father of our publicist, belonged to that society for which the term
Jansenist[6] was less the sign of a dogmatic dissidence than the symptom of
a vocation of gravity and of austere religion. The most charming pages of
Mr. de Sacy's book are, in my opinion, those he devoted to the memory
of this venerable world in which he spent his youth, and of which he is
among us the last survivor. Talking of two respectable booksellers dear to
bibliophiles,* he says,

> How well they represented that old bourgeoisie of Paris, grown rich by
> an honorable commerce, these families who transmitted the same pro-
> fession from father to son like a nobility, with the often black and smoky
> shop of the ancestor and the ancient signboard, a coat of arms as worthy
> as any! What earnest and gracious affability burst forth in their greeting!

---

\*   Messrs. de Bure.

What an air of candor and perfect loyalty was traced on their faces! The good old times radiated from them in their entirety. No pretentiousness, no haughtiness; not a whiff in their manners of the lowliness of profit or the pride of a fortune acquired. They were contented, inasmuch as one can be in this world, by the gentle and peaceable uniformity of their lives, by a union that not a single day belied, by the happiness they spread around them. . . . Ah! If those were indeed the good people of yesteryear, I avow that yesteryear was better than today. Is family spirit, alas!, among the feudal relics we have suppressed? . . . I do not know if it is because I am becoming old myself, but it seems to me that the men I knew in my youth possessed an originality of physiognomy and a zest of character one no longer finds today. I saw all the old Académie des Inscriptions.[7] Without wishing to wrong anyone, one could hardly compose a similar one now, I believe so at least. May God and the new Académie pardon me if I am mistaken! What is certain, is that the Springs and Summers were more beautiful in those times than they are today. Whoever says the contrary is lying. Why would scholars not be affected by the universal decadence?

I owe it to the new Académie des inscriptions to protest gently; but how charming this idyll of the rue Hautefeuille and the rue Serpente is (Alas! Do they still exist?), and how I resent the need for a straight line that destroys around us every passing day the image of these ancient customs! In reading this delightful page, how well I see our old colleagues relive, Silvestre de Sacy, Lanjuinais, Anquetil-Duperron, Camus, Larcher, du Theil, Villoison, Saint-Croix, Daunou, and many others who sixty years ago rescued these studies from oblivion! We understand more, perhaps, we are subtler philologists, more sensitive critics. Since science has been pacified like all else, we are at pains to understand their conflicts, their rigidity, their rivalries, their assurance in their opinion; but at the same time what vigor! What firmness! What self-esteem! What austerity of character! How they hated! How they loved! They had many a prejudice; but who knows if we should not envy them for it? They followed a severe religion, but never a narrow religion. The sectarian spirit, which they often carried in their faith, had great advantages itself, the members of a dissident sect almost always being individually superior to the believers of the great established churches, simply by the fact that belief for them is the result of a choice and requires a personal effort of reason.

It is in one of these learned and patriarchal houses, embellished only by the austere poetry of duty, that one must search for Mr. de Sacy's origins. So sensitive a taste for the work of the mind, so solid and constant an education, so finely maintained a hue of religion amid diverse pitfalls, and in which the advantages of skepticism and the good aspects of faith are so happily combined, so sincere and yet so free a piety, collaborating with anything outside it that aspires to the same goal by other ways, all these qualities, which are so little of our time—how to find an explanation for them, if not in the studious habits of an elite church, which, instead of demanding the blind obedience of its believers, made it their duty to think for themselves? These inflexible Christians were far from imagining the theory (so convenient for laziness) invented in our time, according to which the believer, leaving the responsibility of determining dogma to whom it may concern, is dispensed from the effort of absorbing it by reflection. They loved books and read a lot; they even copied them, and in some of these strict families the youth had no more agreeable pastime than transcribing from cover to cover the writings of Saint-Cyran[8] and Father Quesnel.[9] The habit laypeople often had of reciting their breviary, by completing each hour a circle—varied in its monotony—of prayers, hymns, pious readings, placed a salutary obstacle to the vulgarity and permissiveness that have since invaded the mores. One studied antiquity in the fashion of Le Beau,[10] history in the fashion of Rollin.[11] By seriousness, integrity, and reading the Ancients one reached the same liberal principles that the philosophy of the century attained by a completely opposite route. A general tinge of sadness compensated for great poetry, whose sense the age generally lacked. It was not the irritating sadness that only leads to powerlessness and is one of the banes of our century: it was the fruitful sadness that stems from a serious conception of human destiny, like the *Melencolia* of Albrecht Dürer;[12] mistress and maker of great things. The moral levity of our time is due in large part to the fact that life has become too easy and too carefree, and without a doubt if the ideal of materialist well-being to which some reformers aspire came to be realized, the world, deprived of the spur of suffering, would lose one of the means that have contributed most to making an intelligent and moral being out of man.

The layman who occupies himself with theology in Catholic countries seems so singular a phenomenon that many people could not but be surprised to see a man involved in our everyday struggles publish a *Spiritual Library* and attempt to rescue ascetic literature from the discredit into which it has fallen. Others have felt that the taste for these sorts of works implies a level of commitment that exceeds the average amount of faith assigned to our time. This is a double error caused by the lack of familiarity our century has with religious matters. It is true that Christian piety in the age of theological dogmatism presupposed an established faith; but it no longer presupposes it because religion has abandoned the sphere of disputation in order to find refuge in the calm region of sentiment. Besides, we owe thanks to Mr. de Sacy from another point of view for having rescued the taste for spiritual readings. These readings had very positive effects, in particular on women. The readings drew them away from frivolous or too constantly vulgar cares; they held the place that was later usurped by a dull and immoral literature. By giving religion an individual basis, these readings sheltered them from this degrading pliancy, this moral abdication, inevitable effects of an unreflecting devotion. One of the most characteristic traits of the new school that has, much to the detriment of solid piety, assumed the direction of consciences is precisely its inability to create any ascetic literature worth mentioning. It only knows how to insult and contend. Where is its Tauler?[13] Where its Henry Suso?[14] The healthy doctrines of the spiritual life have also disappeared, leaving a large void in the pure souls to which they furnished an infinite amount of consolation.

I am concerned with the moralist and not the critic here; I am to investigate, not the truth of such-and-such a belief, but its effects on character and taste. Now, one cannot deny that religion, depending on the manner in which it is accepted, exerts a completely different influence on the intellectual and moral development of the individual. The faith that appears at first glance the most irreconcilable with a free development elevates, betters, and fortifies man, as soon as it is the product of a conviction acquired by the exercise of reason. On the contrary, the faith that is apparently the most broad-minded crushes and shrinks those who submit to it, when it is accepted as an official yoke emanating from an external authority. The past few centuries have often been intolerant and unenlightened in their belief; but never, before our day, had anyone dreamed of proclaiming the principle that religion has as its goal to dispense us from reflecting on divine matters, on our destiny, or on our duties. Having placed civil and political man in administrative tutelage, it was only natural that the same occur with consciences, and that everyone become accustomed to seeing dogmas, like laws, arrive fully formed from an infallible center, without the need to understand or discuss them.

So pronounced a taste for the past necessarily led Mr. de Sacy to be stern with the present. Mr. de Sacy is a pessimist, and he is surely right to be. There are times when optimism involuntarily arouses suspicion of some pettiness of intellect or baseness of heart in those who profess it. Here, however, an explanation is necessary. While agreeing with Mr. de Sacy on the serious dangers caused to modern society by the loss of so many solid qualities that made up the force of the old world, I differ from him slightly on the manner of appraising the intellectual movement of our time. I believe that no century has pushed its gaze as far as ours into the true theory of the universe and of humanity; I think there is more depth of intellect, more refinement, more true philosophy, and even more moral sensitivity in a few thousand of our contemporaries than in all of the past centuries combined; but this rich culture, to which, in my opinion, no age has anything comparable, is outside the times and has little influence on them. A crass materialism, valuing things only in view of their immediate utility, tends more and more to take charge of humanity, and to cast into the shadows what only serves to satisfy the taste for beauty or pure curiosity. Household cares, which the societies of yore hardly worried about, have become important affairs, and the manly pursuits of our fathers have given way to humbler concerns. Adopt the language of whichever religion or philosophy you will, man is here below for an ideal, transcendent aim, superior to pleasure and to interests. Does material progress assist in bringing us nearer to this aim? Has the world, since its transformation, become as a whole more intelligent, more honest, more mindful of liberty, more sensitive to beautiful things? This is the issue. One may believe in progress without sharing that dangerous optimism that observes without shame the humiliation of the intellect, when this humiliation appears favorable to certain improvements. Were they as indisputable as some of them are problematic, these improvements would always, in the eyes of liberal people, be a poor compensation for the loss of the only things that render human life desirable and give it meaning and value.

Certainly, material progress should not be despised, and between two societies that are equally intelligent and decent, one of which presented a rich blossoming of external civilization, while the other was denied such an advantage, the first should be preferred without hesitation. Simply put, what should not be accepted is for material progress to be considered a compensation for moral decadence. The most certain sign of the weakening of a society is this indifference for noble struggles, which causes the great political issues to appear secondary with respect to issues of industry and administration. All despotisms have been based on persuading society that they would take care of its business better than it would itself. Every people thus has in its history a moment of temptation in which the seducer tells it, while displaying the goods of the world, "I will give you all this, if you will worship me."

Let us not overgenerously lend past centuries a moral force that always was the purview of a small number of people. Virtue decreases or increases in humanity depending on whether the imperceptible aristocracy in which the store of human nobility resides does or does not encounter an environment in which to live and propagate. Now, one cannot deny that the great development of industry, by levying an enormous tax on those who are not manufacturers, that is to say on those one would have once termed nobles, in a certain fashion obliges the world to conform. A fateful law of modern society tends ever increasingly to force all to exploit the aptitudes or capital allotted to them, and renders the life of those who do not produce anything with a monetary value impossible. Some supporters of the modern system admit this consequence, and recognize that industry will not cease to be prejudicial to certain classes until everyone is in his own way industrial. Who can fail to see that the effect of such a state of affairs, if brought to the extreme (which, I recognize, will never occur), would be to render our planet uninhabitable for those whose duty is precisely not to sacrifice their inner freedom for material advantage? Would you turn the artist into a manufacturer, producing statues or paintings following the express or implied specifications of the buyer? Is this tantamount to eliminating great art, evidently less lucrative than that which panders to frivolity and bad taste? Would you turn a scholar into a manufacturer producing works for the public? But in scientific matters, the more a work is meritorious, the fewer readers it is destined to have. Abel,[15] one of the greatest mathematicians of our century, who was at the same time an accomplished man, died in poverty. Therefore, it is evident that, for many of the most excellent products of humanity, there is an infinite disproportion between the value of the work and what it will fetch, or, better stated, the value of the work is inversely proportional to what it will fetch. Consequently, a society in which independent life becomes more and more difficult, and in which the nonproducer is crushed by those who produce following the public's demands must end in a great degradation of all that is noble or, in other terms, unproductive. The Middle Ages pushed the sense of this truth to the point of paradox by making mendicancy a virtue and determining that the man devoted to spiritual duties was to live off alms. At least it was a recognition that there exist in the world things that are priceless, that intellect does not represent any material value whatsoever, and that with regard to the services rendered to the soul no remuneration can pass for a salary. The church, with much tact, has maintained the same principle: it does not accept ever being paid; it always claims to be poor. Even if it owned the universe, it would still say that in the order of material things it only wishes for what Saint Paul requested, *victum et vestitum*.[16]

The ever-expanding power of man over matter is an obvious good, and we must applaud the progress our century has attained in this direction; but such progress is of truly first-rate value only if, by placing man above the obstacles with which nature confronts him, it aids in expediting the accomplishment of his ideal mission. A beautiful thought, a noble feeling, an act of virtue make man into the king of creation much better than the ability instantaneously to deliver his orders and desires to the end of the world. This royalty is in our soul: the ascetic in the deserts of the Thebaid,[17] the contemplative on the peaks of the Himalaya, slaves to nature in so many respects, were much more its sovereigns and interpreters in spirit than the materialist who upends the surface of the globe without understanding the divine meaning of life. Their sadness, full of philosophy and charm, was worth more than our vulgar joys, and their ravings honor human nature more than so many ostensibly reasonable existences that have been filled only with the calculations of interest or the insignificant struggles of self-conceit.

Therefore, Mr. de Sacy is right to complain about the disappearance of a host of excellent things that no longer find a place in our society. These not being the kind of things that are needed daily, their absence goes unremarked; but in time one will notice the enormous void they have left in the world by their loss. The same mistake our century commits in the theory of education, by refusing to see that above specialized knowledge, which alone has positive applications, there is a general culture that has no purpose except to educate moral and intellectual man, it also commits in social theory. Anything that escapes the bounds of its utilitarian categories appears like a luxury or an ornament to it. Certainly, one may not miss the aristocratic gentleman: this term implied a quality of birth, and distinguished men in our day are recruited from all ranks in roughly the same proportion; but we do strongly miss the *honest man*, in the sense in which the seventeenth century employed the term, I mean to say the man free from the narrow views of all professions, having neither the manners nor the frame of mind of any class. Each specialty of labor most often carries with it particular habits, and to thrive properly within it, it is even proper to have what is called *the sense of one's station*. Now, nobility consists in having none of these limits; distinction cannot be represented in the world except by people who have no station. It is not fair for such people to be rich, for they provide society no service that can be valued in money; but it is fair that they be the aristocracy, in the very limited sense one is henceforth permitted to give this word, so that the general movement of human affairs may conserve its dignity, and the different ways of tackling life, of which people devoted to special functions or views cannot properly understand the legitimacy, may be represented freely.

I believe that anything delicate and long term will suffer in the near future from the excessively narrow basis that the reformers of modern society have given it. Nothing lasting centuries is possible any longer. Anything that requires two or three hundred years to reach its maturity has the time to see in the course of its existence the world change its master and its plan ten times. The imminent demise of poetry in humanity is due to the same causes. Poetry resides entirely in the soul and the moral sentiment; now, the tendency of our age is precisely to replace the moral agents with material agents in all things. The most insignificant object, the most vulgar fabric, for instance, became almost a human and moral thing, when hundreds of living beings had breathed, felt, suffered perhaps between each of its wefts, when the spinner alternately raising and lowering her spindle, the weaver pushing the shuttle in a more or less hurried rhythm, had contributed to it, interweaving their labor with their thoughts, their conversations, their songs. Today an iron machine, with no soul, no beauty, has replaced all this. The old machines, marvelously appropriate to man, had achieved with time a veritable organic unity and perfect harmony; but the modern machine, angular, without elegance or proportion, is condemned never to become a human limb. It humiliates and stultifies those who serve it, instead of being, as the erstwhile tool was, an auxiliary and a friend for them.

Man is not a divine being except by the soul: if he manages to attain intellectual and moral perfection in some measure, the goal of his existence is achieved. Nothing that can serve toward this sublime aim is without interest; but it is a grave mistake to believe that material improvements that do not lead to the progress of the mind and morality have any value in and of themselves. Exterior things have value only through the human feelings to which they correspond. The most ordinary garden today contains splendid flowers that only the royal greenhouses once held. What does it matter if the wildflowers, such as God has made them, spoke better to the heart of man and awoke in him a more delicate sense of nature? Women in our day can adorn themselves in a way only queens once could; what does it matter if they are neither more beautiful nor more amiable? The means of pleasure have been refined in a thousand ways and have infinitely multiplied; what does it matter if tedium and loathing poison them, if the hardship of our fathers was happier and more joyful? Have the advances in intelligence been in proportion with the advances in industry? With regards to the taste for beautiful things, are we worthy of the generation that preceded us and produced the brilliant and lively movement in which we still live? Is education steered in a more liberal direction? Have characters gained much in strength and magnanimity? Does one find in the men of modern times more dignity, nobility, intellectual culture, respect for their own opinions, fortitude against the seductions of wealth and power? I shall not attempt to answer; I shall only say that this is all progress can consist in. Until such progress is made, it will be scant comfort for well-born souls only to receive, in exchange for the virtues of the past, an increase in well-being that does not make them happier, and an assurance of repose that does not make them better.

II

Does this essentially conservative instinct of beautiful and good things, which makes such an excellent moralist of Mr. de Sacy, have equally good effects on his literary and historical judgment? Here I hesitate to answer. The moralist, proceeding by the spontaneous feeling of what he believes is best, and the critic, proceeding by independent research and without pre-conceived notions, are necessarily led to differ on many points. The moralist never hesitates in his judgments, for they ensue in him from a choice made once and for all, the reasons for which he has found in his cast of mind much more than in an impartial exam long in the balance. The critic always hesitates, because the infinite variety of the world appears to him in its complexity, and he cannot cheerfully resign himself to shut his eyes to entire sides of reality. The moralist does not have much curiosity, because for him there is little to discover: to his eyes, the measure of goodness and beauty has been realized in a few masterworks that will never be equaled. The critic always searches, for a new element added to his knowledge modifies in part the body of his opinions: he thinks that the most correct judgment cannot substitute for what the positive documents alone can teach us; hence any discovery or any ingenious way of interpreting already-known facts is an event for him. The moralist only appreciates fully mature writers and works in their completed form. The critic prefers origins and what is in the process of being made, because for him everything is a document and a clue of the secret laws that preside over the developments of the mind. The moralist appreciates what is ancient, but not what is very ancient; for in primitive creations there is an earnestness of tone that disrupts his thoughtful habits. The critic searches for the primitive in everything: if he knew of something more ancient than the Vedas[18] or the Bible, that would be his literary devotion. Greece itself seems very recent to him; he is tempted to recognize that the Egyptian priests were right, that the Greeks were nothing but inconsequential and spiritual children, who spoiled an older antiquity for us. The moralist and the critic agree on one point only, but this point takes the place of the whole: it is the love of goodness and truth, and consequently of liberty, the precondition of both. Character draws men together much more than intellect, and the greatest differences of opinion are nothing compared with the moral sympathy that ensues from shared hopes and shared aspirations.

Mr. de Sacy's criticism is a criticism of personal preferences. The literature of the seventeenth century for modern times, Latin literature in antiquity, these, I believe, are the two literary monuments on which his choice fell. He says:

> I must confess that in literature my tastes are exclusive. Never having had the time to read as much as I would have liked, I have only read excellent books; I have constantly reread them. There is a host of books, very good no doubt in their genre, that everyone knows but whose acquaintance I will never make. It is a misfortune, perhaps; but despite myself, and by an instinct I do not master, my hand of its own accord seeks out in a library the books that children already know by heart.

Tastes cannot be argued about, and one must recognize how exquisite Mr. de Sacy's is. Here however I will allow myself to be slightly more archaic than him. I love the Middle Ages, I love remote antiquity. I prefer the *dies irae*[19] to the hymns of Santeul,[20] the poetics that inspired the romance of the Round Table to that of Boileau,[21] and even the mystics of the thirteenth century to those of Port-Royal.[22] Beauty, like goodness, must be searched for in the past; but one should not stop halfway: one must reach back beyond any rhetoric; the primitive alone is true, and it alone has the right to bind us.

One cannot deny the seventeenth century the special gift that makes literatures *classical*, I mean a certain combination of perfection in form, and measure (I was about to say mediocrity) in thought, thanks to which a literature becomes the adornment of all memories and the appanage of the schools; but the limits appropriate for schools must not be imposed on the human spirit. Just because such a literature is the obligatory instrument of any education and nobody can avoid saying of it *puero mihi profuit olim*,[23] that is not a reason to attribute an exclusive character of excellence and beauty to it. I cannot grant this exclusive character to the writings of the seventeenth century in particular, whatever their lasting and solid qualities. Foreign nations, except those that have no literary originality whatsoever, do not understand the extraordinary attraction the works of this time have for us, and see them as nothing but a *tertiary* literature,

if I dare say so, an echo of Latin literature, itself an echo of Greek literature. The Germans, so broad and eclectic in their taste, who have toiled
with such passion to elucidate the minutest details of Italian literature,
of Spanish literature, of our Provençal Middle Ages, hardly ever dwell
on our Great Century, and are at pains to see its interest. They are much
mistaken, according to me; but their negligence is due to quite a serious
cause. This literature is too exclusively French: it will suffer somewhat,
I fear, from the coming of a criticism whose fatherland is the human spirit,
and whose characteristic is not to have exclusive preferences. Its title of
classical will not be disputed; it will be left in charge of the schools, where
it alone can offer an appropriate nourishment to the youth; the curious
will read it, like they read everything, as a document toward the history
of a memorable age; writers will seek in it the secret of expressing in our
language even the thoughts that were initially foreign to it. But I fear it will
not remain in its entirety the sole reading of men of taste, I doubt that
distinguished characters of all times will continue to have recourse to it to
raise themselves up, to console themselves, to shed light on their destinies. We have surpassed the intellectual state in which this literature was
produced; we see a thousand things that the keenest men of the seventeenth
century did not see: the stock of knowledge on which they lived is to our
eyes incomplete and inexact. It will be difficult for the favor of [the section
of] the public that reads not in order to satisfy its conscience, but following
an intimate need, to remain tied indefinitely to books from which there is
little to learn about the problems that preoccupy us, in which our moral
and religious sense is often offended, and in which we constantly find mistakes, even while admiring the genius of those who made them.

In history, I am equally tempted to find Mr. de Sacy insufficiently attentive to origins. Loyal to his literary system, Mr. de Sacy fears that the discussion of facts and the diversity of opinions will harm the beautiful style
of history; he finds that it would be easiest to pick a system according
to one's taste, and follow it on its word. "I will quietly confess," he says,
"that, seeing the formidable aspect of those piles of in-folios that clog the
entrance to our history, I have more than once felt ready to curse erudition and lament that we did not coarsely keep to our Trojan origin and our
good King Francus,[24] son of Hector and founder of French monarchy." He
barely forgives the most eloquent historians of our time for being both
scholars and critics; he would like an agreed version, on which rhetorical

and moralistic historians, the Livys and Plutarchs, could freely expatiate. The seventeenth century (the great Benedictine school excepted) indeed considered history in this guise; but this is one of the points on which it is hardest for us to follow the classical tradition. History, for us, is the immediate view of the past: now, only the discussion and interpretation of documents can bring about this intuition. I will certainly scandalize Mr. de Sacy; but, if I were given the choice between the notes of an original historian and his completely redacted text, I would prefer the notes. I would give all of Livy's fine prose for some of the documents he was consulting and sometimes altered in such a strange fashion. A collection of letters, of dispatches, of expense accounts, of charters, of inscriptions speaks much more to me than the clearest of narratives. I do not even think one can acquire a clear notion of history, of its limits and of the degree of confidence one should have in its different orders of investigation, without the habit of handling the original documents.

Liberalism, having the pretention of being grounded in the principles of reason alone, ordinarily believes it does not need traditions. This is its mistake. Says Mr. de Sacy:

> We are done, I hope, with the Gauls and the Franks. Whether our freedom comes from the Teutons or not ultimately matters little to us. The child is born; he is big and strong. If today a Boulainvilliers[25] lay claim to the rights of conquest in the name of his Frankish ancestors, we would reply that in 1789 and in 1830 the vanquished, the Romans, the serfs, took their revenge, and that in turn they are the conquerors and the victors.

Well! no; neither 1789 nor 1830 had as much importance, in the establishment of freedom, as a fact emanating from the barbarians a thousand years ago would now have, such as a great charter extorted by rebellious barons, a humiliation inflicted on invading royalty, a firm resistance of the towns in defense of their institutions. If Gaul, in place of its instincts of equality and uniformity, had had a touch of provincial or municipal spirit; if strong individualities, like the cities of Italy or the Germanic guilds, had had the chance to form on our soil; if Lyon, Rouen, Marseilles had had their *carroccio*,[26] symbol of the independence of the city, administrative centralization would have been prevented; Philip the Fair,[27] Louis XI,[28] Richelieu,[29] Louis XIV[30] would have been thwarted; the Revolution would have been neither possible nor necessary. The error of the liberal school is to have believed too sincerely that it is easy to create freedom through reflection, and not to have seen that an institution is not stable unless it has historical roots. Ruled by an idea quite similar to the one that has governed China for centuries, I mean that false opinion according to which the best society is the one rationally organized for its own greater good, it forgot that the respect of individuals and of existing rights is as far above the happiness of all as a moral interest trumps a purely worldly interest. It failed to see that all its efforts could result only in a good administration, but never in liberty, because liberty derives from a right that precedes and is superior to that of the state, and not from an improvised declaration or a more or less skillfully deduced philosophical argument.

Of the two systems of politics that will always divide the world among them, one based on abstract right, the other on previous possession, France, land of logic and generous ideas, always preferred the former. Who would dare to criticize it, since it owes the splendor of its history and the sympathy of mankind to this glorious shortcoming? But such is the elusive nature of all that concerns societies: the nation that in perfect sincerity wished to work for the liberty of mankind, precisely because of this found it impossible to establish its own. Serfs buying their liberty penny by penny and arriving after centuries of effort, not at a condition of equality with their masters, but of coexistence with them, have found themselves in modern times to be freer than the nation that, since the Middle Ages, proclaimed the rights of man.* Purchased liberty or liberty wrung inch by inch has been more lasting than liberty by nature. Believing we were establishing abstract right, we established servitude, while the grand barons of England, hardly generous, hardly enlightened, but intractable when it came to their privileges, have by defending them established true liberty.

On almost all points that concern the organization of civil society, the liberal school thus appears to me to have seen the goal to be reached much better than the means of reaching it. Eliminating the privileges of

---

* The curious decree of Louis X is well known: "Since, according to the right of nature everyone must be free [franc], . . . we, considering that our kingdom is termed the Realm of the Franks, and wishing the thing to be truly in accordance with the name, by the deliberation of our grand council, have ordained and ordain . . ."

individuals and bodies, it could not envisage the various social functions
except as attributions of the state. Power being exercised solely by civil
servants in such a system, and these civil servants neither owning their
post, nor consequently having any possibility for resistance, it is clear to
see the degree of tyranny to which one could be led. Certainly, if there is
something that is theoretically absurd, it is the venality of judicial functions, by virtue of which certain individuals bought and sold the right to
judge. Nonetheless one can grasp how a judge possessing his office, thus
placed above any desire and any expectation, might offer more guarantees
than a civil servant judge, who is consequently dependent on those who
confer the posts. The same may be said of executive power. The feudal
conception, according to which the king owned his crown by the right of
the sword, as his subject owned his privileges against him, is the opposite
of reason. If on the contrary there is a logical conception, it is sovereignty
envisaged as a delegation from society. History proves that the former
notion, as absurd as it is, produced the best political condition the world
has known, and that the superiority of modern civilization over those of
antiquity is due to the fact that kingship among us has for centuries been
nothing but a large sharecropping arrangement, only ever requiring that
dues be discharged as established by good customs or agreed upon by
the estates.

To see in its true light this great law of the philosophy of history,
which logic certainly would not have revealed, it is China especially that
one must study. China offers the philosophy of history the marvelously
instructive spectacle of another humanity developing practically without
contact with that of Europe and western Asia, and following its trajectory
with a rigor our much more complicated societies could not suggest. Now,
China has realized since the remotest antiquity the type of rational society based on equality, on competitive examinations, on an enlightened
administration. The *Zhou Li*,[31] a sort of imperial almanac of the age of the
Zhou,* in the twelfth century before our era, surpasses anything the most
bureaucratic of modern states have attempted in this respect. The emperor
and the feudatory princes are restrained by rituals and censorship, the
employees at all levels by hierarchical dependence and a perpetual system

---

\*   See the translation that the late Mr. Édouard Biot made of it (Paris, 1851) and the work of
the same scholar on the *Histoire de l'instruction publique en Chine* (Paris, 1847).

of inspection, the people by education that the state alone has the right to impart. The entire system rests on a single idea, that the state alone is charged with providing for the good of all.* Imagine the Académie des sciences morales et politiques[32] and the Académie française transformed into ministries, the former governing the affairs of the intellect, the latter the mores, and you will have a rather fair sketch of China's intellectual and political constitution. The ideal of those who dream of an administrative regulation of the intellect has long been realized there.† When the Jesuits demonstrated to Qianlong[33] the errors of the sanctioned astronomy, the emperor refused to let them be corrected, because such a reform would have proved the classical books wrong and required the introduction of new words. What has resulted from this organization, apparently so reasonable, in fact so baneful? A condition of decrepitude without equal in history, in which an empire of 150 million men waits for a few thousand barbarians to supply it with masters and renovators. What happened during the invasion of the Roman Empire by the Germanic mobs will happen for China. All states that sacrifice the moral interests and free initiative of individuals for the sake of comfort go against the goal they aim for: a small number of forceful men, coming from outside or from within, will then be sufficient to topple a country indifferent to everything save its repose, to obtain its acclaim, and thus establish once more the true nobility, which is the nobility of moral strength and of the will.

"Whatever infatuation one claims nowadays for barbarism or barbarians, it must be recognized," says Mr. de Sacy, "that our civilization is Roman, our centralization is Roman, our laws and our letters are Roman; the Roman character has ultimately conquered the barbarian character!" This is quite true. The whole secret of our history lies in the struggle of the Gallo-Roman character against the Germanic character (what Mr. de Sacy calls *barbarian*), the Gauls abhorring the divided sovereignty that constituted feudalism, and always wishing to return to the egalitarian administration of the empire, not the one of the first Caesars, still imbued with a certain aristocratic character, but rather the one of the time of Diocletian,[34] which has always remained the ideal of our country. The French Revolution and what followed are the last act of the struggle

---

*     Mr. Mohl, *Journal asiatique*, August 1851.

†     See Mr. Bazin's report on the Academy of Beijing (*Journal asiatique*, January 1858).

between the Gallic character and the Germanic character, ending with the definitive victory of the former. Many Germanic elements entered into the beginnings of the Revolution, I know, and gave the movements of those first years a truly liberal appearance; but they disappeared in the struggle, and left the Gallic character rule alone; the latter, from the Convention[35] to 1815, gave free rein to its taste for unitary administration and its dislike for all independence. This is when reason of state, first proclaimed by the jurists of Philip the Fair, definitively overcomes the noble principle of the Middle Ages, which only admitted the rights of individuals. I am not of those who consider the Middle Ages an ideal epoch of morality and happiness; it seems to me, however, that the liberal school maligns it somewhat. The Middle Ages was a dreadful epoch only in its second half, when the church became persecutory and the feudatories bloodthirsty. Hitherto there were long centuries during which the feudatories were truly patriarchal and the church maternal. I believe that, from the eighth to the twelfth century, the Christian countries that were sheltered from the incursions of the Saracens and the Normans lived rather happily.

I would not insist on these historical subtleties, had the errors of conduct of the liberal school not stemmed almost entirely from its incomplete and sometimes deficient philosophy of history. An error concerning the Carolingian revolution, the beginnings of feudalism, the thirteenth century, or Philip the Fair are not as innocuous as Mr. de Sacy believes. One always bears the consequences of the principle from which one proceeds. Issuing from the abstract idea of a rational sovereignty exercised for the greater good of the nation, the liberal party could not envisage itself as a simple caretaker charged with protecting the rights of all and developing the initiative of everyone. By intrinsic necessity, it was led to govern too much. It saw correctly that a society, to flourish, must be very strong; but it was mistaken in believing that the means of strengthening a society was to govern it a lot. Despite innumerable precautionary measures, the order it had established and supported, not without glory, fell by the most incredible surprise of which history has preserved the memory. I do not wish to render the liberal party responsible for a situation it did not bring about. A fateful principle ruled it: the Revolution, to which it was linked, could produce administrators, but not bodies. The principle that creates institutions, namely conquest and personal right, was the very principle it undertook to eliminate.

The organization of public education seems to me the most suitable example to illustrate the serious consequences of the principle adopted by the liberal school, and to show how this principle is by its nature liable to turn against those who established it. England, Germany, and formerly France had provided for the interests of knowledge and education by means of rich corporations that were nearly independent from the civil power. The new France, following its custom, resolved the same problem through administration. Each year, every city in France receives from an office of the rue de Grenelle[36] some men the city does not know, who are tasked with raising its children according to certain regulations, in whose making the city had no part. "All activities relative to meals, recreation, perambulation, sleep," says the regulation of 1802, "will be carried out by company. . . . In each lycée there will be a library of fifteen hundred volumes; all libraries will contain the same works; no work shall be allowed there without the authorization of the Minister of the Interior." This creation has been considered the finest of the age, and I would happily concur, if it were proven to me that the men in charge of applying such regulations would always be men of broad, refined, distinguished character, who understand with sensitivity the problems of education and of the government of intellects; but, honestly, can one have such a certainty? Now, if we can admit the possibility that such an administration were to fall into the hands of men who do not possess all the qualities listed above, consider the consequences. The interests dearest to the mind, the entire literary, scientific, philosophic, even religious movement would be exposed to a dominion all the more dangerous the more the administrative machine employed to wield it is perfected.

Let us thus cease to believe that the Revolution of 1789 dispenses us from penetrating deeper into the past of mankind. As important as this event is, it produces in us an optical illusion, much as the last chain of mountains always limits our view, and hides the much higher mountains that lie beyond. The Revolution attracts us first of all by the pride of its bearing, and by that great passionate aspect that all stories that take place in the streets have. Long it dazzled me: I was well aware of the intellectual mediocrity and the meager education of its actors; but I persisted in lending to their work a great political scope. Later, I recognized that with very few exceptions the men of this time were as unsophisticated in politics as in history and philosophy. Seeing few things at once, they failed to realize how human society is a complicated machine, how its conditions of existence and magnificence are due to imperceptible nuances. They completely lacked a thorough knowledge of history: a certain emphasis in poor taste troubled their brains and put them in that state of intoxication peculiar to the French character, in which great things are often accomplished, but which renders any forecasting of the future and any far-reaching political views whatsoever impossible.

Are these reasons to despair and to consider the liberal development of France as withered in its bloom? Certainly not; they are reasons to redouble our seriousness so as to compensate by our efforts for the advantages our fathers did not transmit to us. In politics as in morality, the true duties are the everyday ones. Only feeble souls fashion their opinions on the basis of their probable success in the future. I would almost say that the future does not matter for the honest man, since to devote oneself to beautiful and good things it is not necessary to reckon they are destined to prevail. If some class in French society has not fulfilled the task that seemed reserved for it, one can only conclude that its place is ripe for the taking. All nations pass through history carrying with them an essential vice that saps them, just as each of us presents at birth the principle of the disease that, barring accidents, will carry him off; but a host of mishaps constantly deflects events from the course they would have followed if they had obeyed a necessary inclination. The revolutions of Athenian democracy are still today the talk of the world, yet from its first day this democracy was beset with a radical flaw. The Roman Empire had within it, from the time of Augustus, the seeds of its dissolution; nonetheless, it lived for four or five centuries with its wound, and in its slow agony it passed through the century of the Antonines.[37] The great deficiency France carries in its heart must not further forbid us from entertaining extended hopes and constant efforts.

Certainly, if a single race and a single dominion stretched over modern Europe, if the Christian nations formed a unitary world, analogous to the *orbis romanus*,[38] decadence would be inevitable, because there would be no element of regeneration outside this closed circle. But the principle of diversity and of individual vitality that created an invincible obstacle in Europe to any universal dominion will be the salvation of modern society. A divided civilization has resources unknown to a unitary civilization. The Roman Empire perished because it did not have a counterweight;

but if next to the Empire there had been strongly organized Teutons and Slavs, the Empire, forced to reckon with the obstacles and the freedom of without, would have followed a completely different course: despotism, indeed, cannot endure but on one condition, that all lands that surround it be in unison with it. There is the reason for hope. The Stoic[39] was right to envelop himself in his cloak and despair of virtue; for there was no egress from the iron circle in which he lived, and to the end of the world then inhabitable he would have found the odious centurion, the representative of his merciless fatherland. A hundred times in history the highest and most delicate thought has perished; a hundred times the righteous cause was wrong, and I am persuaded that the authors of the noblest efforts that humanity has attempted in order to ascend to goodness will forever remain mingled in the summary worship of the unknown saints. This was due to the fact that, in past centuries, the power of the mind was bound within narrow confines. Since the beginning of modern times, human consciousness has expanded immensely. Dignity of character and nobility no longer have as their only recompense the sympathy of a small number of beautiful souls, who are always friends of the vanquished. Symmachus[40] no longer launches his defense of the dead gods into the void, and Boethius[41] no longer writes his *Consolation of Philosophy* in prison.

# 3

## THE PHILOSOPHY OF CONTEMPORARY HISTORY (*PHILOSOPHIE DE L'HISTOIRE CONTEMPORAINE*, 1859)

I t is practically an obligation for the man who has held in his hand the great affairs of his country to justify before posterity the principles that directed his actions and the set of opinions he brought into government. Few statesmen have failed to do so, and there are no documents more valuable for history than these sorts of confessions in which the actors themselves come to narrate in front of a calmer and more disinterested public the facts whose true character could initially escape it in the heat of passion. The eminent historian who in our day demonstrated with such brilliance what education and talent applied to the direction of human affairs can and cannot accomplish could elude such a duty even less than others; but in accepting it Mr. Guizot[1] deviated from the example of his illustrious predecessors on an essential point.* Ordinarily, it is after the death of the author, or at least once he has clearly admitted that his political career is over, that such writings see the light. It is believed that this forestalls most of the motives that skew judgments of contemporary history, and, by making impartiality simpler for the reader, makes candor easier for the writer. This time, to the contrary, it is in the midst of very energetic activity that the statesman whose cast of

---

* *Mémoires pour servir à l'histoire de mon temps*, by François Guizot; vol. I and II, 1858–1859. Paris, Michel Lévy Frères.

mind and character have had the most decisive influence on his country comes to set forth his opinions on the struggles in which he took part. It is not from the grave, as is customary, but from a retirement from which no hope is banished, that we hear the voice that must teach us the thoughts and doctrines whose consequences have weighed so heavily on the lives of us all.

One perceives right away how much this circumstance, apparently insignificant, must mark a difference between the *Mémoires* of Mr. Guizot and those left to us by most statesmen. All confessions made before the time when one can admit without fear that one has sinned cannot but resemble a justification. As distant as Mr. Guizot may be from the vulgar enthusiasms to which the men who draw their dignity from without are invariably prone, he, like anyone who is truly ambitious (this word is a compliment when ambition is justified), does not recognize fate's right to decree exiles without return. For him, public matters can no longer be an adornment; but they can always be an object of high concern. The causes he defended, attacked, jeopardized vie for victory, and on such a victory depends the definitive judgment that people will agree to pass on his role and his influence. It is enough to say that more than once in his *Mémoires*, the preoccupation with the future must have weighed on the explanation of the past. Politics hardly entails the lofty impartiality of history; the claim to infallibility, so wounding in the eyes of the critic, is simply an obligatory response to the hypocritical peevishness of the opposing parties. The candid admission of a mistake would only excite a prideful pity among the jealously vain or the presumptuously mediocre, and if someone dared tell these blind detractors, "He that is without sin among you, let him first cast a stone,"[2] a throng of lunatics would boldly close in to stone him.

The success of Mr. Guizot's book would in any case excuse him, were he to require an excuse for the bold plan he has devised to be the one to furnish history with the evidence on which he wants to be judged. Nowhere has the series of political principles that guided him for twenty-five years shown itself with such consequence and such clarity. The liberal spirit, the moderation, the respect for different opinions, the severe and lofty serenity that waft through the whole book are the best response to so many regrettable misunderstandings that the levity of the crowd established and the pride of Mr. Guizot would not stoop to rectify. The style of the *Mémoires* has its faults; as a writer, Mr. Guizot has never worried about perfection. He did not receive from heaven the lively, deep, animated expression of Mr. Sainte-Beuve,[3] nor the richness, the vigor, the dynamism of Mr. Michelet.[4] It is definitely not the winged style, the lovely abandon that accepts no other slips of the pen than those it actually intended, this charming weave of a fabric sewn with gold and silk the secret of which a learned and airy muse seems to have revealed to Mr. Cousin.[5] It is not the austere correctness, the high notion of the rigor of the French language, the assiduous study of the old models that cause the solidity of the style of Mr. de Sacy.[6] One can be an eminent writer and not possess those qualities. Without speaking of authors such as Chateaubriand,[7] such as Maistre,[8] who shone by their passion and imagination, but who never reached a complete notion of French prose, of its timbre, of its harmonious and manly range, among our first-rate prose writers, such as Lamennais[9] or Augustin Thierry,[10] how many have kept themselves to this inflexible tenor of style, the product of a perpetual attention and of the sacred trembling that causes the sheet of paper destined to become irrevocable to be retained for hours and days? I dare say that such an effort would be jarring in certain works, where any literary afterthought is out of place. Mr. Guizot's expression, while hardly disciplined, has that touch of sobriety, of strength, and of measure that suits great affairs. A general tone of reserve and discretion lends the book much nobility. Of all the writers of our time, Mr. Guizot is the freest from a certain coquettishness of bad taste, which has become quite common ever since our ideas of personal dignity and of suitability were weakened; nobody less than him has become familiar with the public or encouraged the public to become familiar with him. This merit, I know, is scarcely appreciated in France. Reserve, timidity, respect for oneself and others, ordinary signs of serious and distinguished natures: all are taken for pride among us. I have heard people treat this dignified and severe coldness of Mr. Guizot's as a flaw and regret that he does not try harder to make himself beloved. As for me, I commend him for it: ordinarily, one does not make oneself beloved by the crowd except by one's quirks or one's vices. The statesman has confessions, not gossip to make; those whose duties place them in contact with the public must show themselves to it as abstractions only.

I

Let us set aside the vulgar precautions to which one must have recourse when one wishes to speak without injury of the false intellect that thinks itself impeccable. At the height at which Mr. Guizot has placed himself, praise and blame lose all personal connotations, because the man who has come to represent one of the great causes that carve up the world between them is only guilty of the fateful law condemning any theory of being only partially legitimate. The critical faculty is never more at ease than with those whom glory has thus consecrated, and whose only fault is not to have resolved the insoluble problem mankind will eternally present to those who wish to understand or govern it. It is as superficial to reproach statesmen for the shortcomings or the transience of their accomplishments as it would be to reproach Leibnitz or Hegel for not having said the last word on man, the world, and God. Each philosophical and political system is a great prejudice that must be judged not inasmuch as it represents absolute truth and right, but inasmuch as it holds a more or less lofty position in the moral order. All that is great is legitimate after its own fashion; mediocrity alone has no place in the kingdom of God. It is time to abandon this almost invariably petty critique that, believing it holds the key to truth, reproaches men of talent or of genius for not having attained what, since the beginnings of human thought, legions of the presumptuous thought they grasped without their pretenses ever being justified.

The first two volumes of the *Mémoires* published by Mr. Guizot run from 1814 to 1832. We are duty bound to limit ourselves strictly to the years treated thus far by the illustrious historian, and to await the explanations he will provide regarding the epoch in which his role became central. I do not have a firm opinion on the complicated debates that filled the last ten years of the parliamentary regime in France; others would be much better judges than I of the rivals of these passionate struggles and would appreciate the justice or injustice of so many contradictory accusations. After all, I do not conceal it, while I recognize the purpose of the internecine wars of parliamentary government, I hardly have a taste for the details of these fights. In the field of strategy, only the result affects me. Political history is not the history of parties, in the same way the history of the human spirit is not the history of literary coteries.

Above the parties, there are these great movements that fill the history of all times, but for the past seventy years have taken the name and the shape of revolutions. This is the object that, in contemporary history, must hold the attention of the philosopher and the observer.

Of the two great revolutions that Mr. Guizot includes in his narrative, the first, among all the events of our history, is the most appropriate to stimulate a reflection on the nature of modern societies and their constitutive laws. The Restoration, the absolute negation of the French Revolution, nevertheless applies the latter's best tenets; apparently illiberal, it establishes liberty among us; a foreign product, it ushers in a period of political awakening and public spirit; often represented by men of a mediocre span of intellect, it begins the true intellectual development of France in the nineteenth century, and remains an age dear to those who think. To understand so strange a phenomenon, one must fully realize the historical necessities that determined the return of the House of Bourbon. One must especially rise to a general appreciation of the facts that establish so profound a difference between modern civilization and the dazzling but invariably ephemeral developments of antiquity.

In my view, this difference consists in a fundamental point whose consequences stretch to the entire social order, by which I mean a completely opposite manner of conceiving of government. The ancient state, whether it took the form of monarchy as in the Orient, or of republic as in Greece, or of military principality as in the time of the Roman Empire, is always absolute. One began with the idea that the community is omnipotent over those who compose it, that there is no legitimate resistance to the state, that the individual has no right to develop except according to the law of the state. Liberty for antiquity was hardly distinguished from national independence: in truth, one was not freer in Sparta than in Persepolis. "Law" was no doubt better than the will of the "great king;" but it was not less tyrannical, in the sense that it meddled in a host of matters that, according to our ideas, only concern the individual. Each state of antiquity, thus having a very narrow and very exclusive organic principle, moved quickly through the different stages of life: decadence inexorably followed on splendor; hegemonies and dynasties replaced one another according to rules that in a sense were calculable, and the ancient world itself, as a whole, ultimately collapsed. A phenomenon such as that of modern civilization, carrying within itself the seeds of indefinite progress, or such as that of France, maintaining for eight hundred years the same dynasty, always very powerful despite periods of setbacks, is unexampled among the states of antiquity.

The Germanic race, by destroying the framework of the Roman Empire, accomplished the greatest political revolution of the history of the world. It was the victory of the individual over the state. The empire, by its administrative despotism, had so weakened the civilized world that an imperceptible minority was sufficient to topple it; a fistful of courageous adventurers rendered it the service of conquering it. The character of the Germanic peoples was the most absolute individualism: the idea of the "state" was completely foreign to them; among them, everything rested on free commitments, on "loyalty," on the temporary league of individuals associated for a shared task. The final development of this social principle was feudalism. When somebody gives us a good history of the origins of French nobility, it will be seen that each center of feudal families corresponds to a center of Germanic colonization, and that most of the truly ancient families of France date back to an establishment of the Carolingian era. In fact, the character of feudalism is the Germanic character in its purest form. The free man owes the king only what he has pledged himself to; he is freed from his duties, if the king does not observe his own; he alone is the judge on this last point, and, if he is not satisfied with his sovereign, he can wage war on him honorably. Joinville[11] is without doubt the model of knightly loyalty; moreover, it is known what personal affection he had for Saint Louis;[12] nonetheless, hear him:

> One day it came to pass that a sergeant of the King laid his hands on a knight of my troop. I went to the King to complain, and told him that, if he did not render justice unto me, I would leave his service, because his sergeants struck knights. He rendered justice unto me, and justice was such, following the customs of the land, that the sergeant came to my lodgings barefoot and in breeches, an unsheathed sword in his hand, he knelt in front of the knight and said to him: "Sire, I beg your pardon for laying my hands on you, and I bring you this sword for you to cut my hand off, if you so desire." And I entreated the knight to pardon him, and so he did.

Can one conceive of a general of Constantine[13] or Theodosius[14] writing the emperor that due to some personal dissatisfactions he had decided to abandon the service of the state?

I do not wish to ignore the role Christianity played in this revolution by the progress it promoted in general morality and by the sense of respect for the dignity of man that all of its dogmas exude. One cannot claim, nonetheless, that political liberty is its work; it appears, rather, that at times it was prejudicial to it. Having developed in opposition to the idolatry of the state, which was the character itself of the empire, for three centuries Christianity definitely was the protestation of conscience against the official yoke; but at no point in the course of the heroic struggle it carried out does one see a political idea emerge. Beginning in the fourth century, the era of its intimate alliance with Roman despotism, it displays a marked preference for absolute powers, when they consent to become persecutors on its behalf. During the first age of the Germanic invasion, and even under Charlemagne, the activity of the clergy, civilizing in one sense, corrupting in another, deployed entirely in favor of Roman ideas: it is the bishops who provided the Germanic chieftains with ideas of sovereignty that had not even occurred to them. The papacy, beginning with Gregory VII,[15] served liberty, it is true, by preventing the establishment of excessively powerful secular sovereignties; but it acted on the basis of a principle of universal centralization that, in its domain, was quite tyrannical, and would have become much more so, if the Roman pontiffs had been able to become the true leaders of Christendom and to bring about the sort of Christian caliphate to which they aspired.

The particular nature of royalty that was to come of this fecund chaos is easily recognizable. It had to be, it was in fact, first of all, strictly hereditary. The law of succession in the Orient and in the Roman Empire had never been rigorously defined. Thanks to the almost superstitious cult of heredity, modern civilization was shielded from that regime of misadventures that once or twice has given the world some years of happiness, but that, through the mistrust, the hesitations, the rivalries it brings in its train, constantly features murder, treason, and drowns society in a torrent of blood. Royalty was, secondly, the consequence of a personal right and, as it were, an extension of property. The sovereignty of the people established the old republics and the old despotisms. In this new political order, such a sovereignty is out of the question. The Middle Ages (I exclude the Peripatetic Scholastics, who copied Aristotle without worrying about the true constitution of the states of their time) had no notion of the nation conceived as a source of power. The king is the owner of his crown, and if he is deprived of it without just cause he is offended in his rights. Thirdly, royalty happens to be bound by charters or by freely consented obligations, to perform which the king may be forced by war, by the refusal of taxation and of military service. Fourthly and finally, it is quite limited: the king concerns himself with significantly fewer matters than the ancient despot; his court is of little importance; he has only a small budget or none at all; he allows true republics, the church, the universities, religious orders, towns, corporations of all sorts freely to exist around him. All wield privileges and customs against him that the sovereign dare not encroach upon. The honest Charles V[16] died with a heavy conscience for having raised taxes to which the estates had not consented and for having kept permanent armies. The evident necessity of the times did not suffice to reassure him on the legitimacy of these acts, which the entire Middle Ages saw as offending to the principles of Christian right.

No less important a consequence of the transformation of Europe affected by the races we commonly call barbarian was its division into a certain number of strongly constituted states, whose rivalries have doomed all dreams of universal monarchy. Mr. Gervinus[17] has quite rightly compared the constitution of Christian Europe to that checkerboard of small states that ancient Greece displayed, small states whose alliances changed constantly and among which only passing hegemonies ever managed to form. Uniformity is despotism, and conversely complete and lasting despotism is only possible with universal monarchy, since the Christian republic could not accept that one of its members completely infringe the rules of the whole. The division of Europe has thus become the guarantee of its freedom: it is this division that made the Reformation, Philosophy possible; it is what will destroy all old-style tyrannies, and shield the modern world from the inevitable ruin destined for societies that have no counterweight.

The entire superiority of modern states, all their reasons to have hope for the future can be summarized, in my opinion, in these two points: first, a divided Europe, which has reached a condition of stable equilibrium; second, an organization of kingship that keeps executive power out of all contention, that blocks unregulated ambitions, that eliminates both the passing tyrannies of the republican countries (such as Greece, or Italy in the Middle Ages) and the praetorian caesarism of the Roman age. The king does not hinder any legitimate development of human activity.

Not only has he no power over private property, but it is only through a misuse of a barbaric age that he concerns himself with religion; what little tolerance there was in the Middle Ages was, in the end, bestowed by royalty. This entrusting of the continuity of the nation once and for all into the hands of a family sequestered, after a fashion, for the benefit of the community, this method of taking sovereignty away from the people in order to mortgage it on an entailed estate, is assuredly the opposite of the rational theory of the organization of society. Nonetheless, states of marvelous solidity sprang from it. Whereas the ancient tyrant succumbed to the first shortcoming or the first setback, the king of France could be a man as despicable as Louis XV, he could be reduced to as low a station as Charles VII, without anyone questioning his rights, his patrimony, or the mission he fulfilled.

Only England, I know, has fully developed the type of government we have sketched here; only there has feudalism borne its fruit, which is the parliamentary regime and the separation of powers. Ever since Philip the Fair,[18] the king of France, by preferring to depend on legal experts (representatives of the Roman principle), has waged a fierce war against local sovereignties and provincial liberties, and attempted to establish a very different kind of sovereignty from that of Saint Louis. In the sixteenth century, the Renaissance caused an even more marked return, in politics as in all else, to the ideas of antiquity. The publicists of that time, mostly Italians or under the influence of Italy, revive, whether in republican or absolutist form, the principles of the state after the Greek and Roman fashion: some dream of democratic utopias based on an abstract conception of man; others, true corruptors of princes, become the promoters of the great idolatry of their time, I mean the adoration without reservations of powerful sovereigns. France in particular, following its taste for uniformity and the theocratic tendency that Catholicism brings in its wake, ultimately produces the strangest phenomenon of modern times, the monarchy of Louis XIV,[19] an imitation after a fashion of the Sassanid or Mongol ideal, which must be considered an occurrence contrary to nature in Christian Europe. The Middle Ages would have excommunicated him, this Oriental despot, this anti-Christian king, who proclaimed himself sole proprietor of his kingdom, disposed of souls as much as of bodies, and eliminated all rights before the boundless pride that the feeling of his identification with the state inspired in him.

THE PHILOSOPHY OF CONTEMPORARY HISTORY 59

But, once the notion of the state is unleashed, it cannot be relied upon. The aberration of Louis XIV entails the French Revolution as an immediate consequence. The pure conception of antiquity prevails again. The state becomes an absolute sovereign again. People allow themselves to believe that a nation must be happy so long as it has a good legal code. They wish first of all to establish a just state, without realizing that they are destroying liberty, carrying out a social revolution and not a political revolution, setting the framework for a despotism similar to that of the Caesars of ancient Rome. The modern world would have reverted to ancient errors, and liberty would have been lost forever, if the movement that was sweeping France toward the despotic conception of the state had become universal. But the French Revolution was not a general occurrence: it placed France in a fatefully hostile situation with respect to the other powers of Europe. The countries in which the Germanic element predominated, and for which France's administrative and military regime was insufferable, set a vigorous reaction in motion. In claiming their independence, they led France back to the pure notion of royalty, from which it had departed centuries previously, and which, it must be said, was in no way in agreement with some of its most secret instincts.

These are the origins of the Restoration, and in these origins one may easily discern the principle of its shortcomings and its advantages. It was a return to a regime that suits European states best, but an unintelligent return and unpleasant to France, always dominated by its ideas of the sovereignty of the people, by its military tastes. It was a civil and in many ways a liberal government, but despite itself and despite France. It had nothing military about it; it was the result of foreign pressure, legitimate in its principle, for the European republic possesses, like the United States of America, albeit to a lesser degree, the right of amphictyony;[20] but it did not grasp that, once the age of heroic deeds has passed for a great country, there is but one way of comforting it in the widowhood of glory, namely the noble domestic activity, the dispatch-box struggles, the religious controversies, the literary sects, the awakening of intellects. It could not live without the constitution,[21] because, as Mr. Guizot admirably puts it: "For the House of Bourbon and its partisans, absolute power is impossible: with them, France needs to be free; it only accepts their government if it can keep an eye and a hand on it." Unfortunately, neither Louis XVIII[22] nor those who surrounded him fully understood the nature of this great pact; "the constitution was presented as a pure royal concession, rather than proclaiming what it truly was, a peace treaty after a long war, a series of new articles added by mutual agreement to the pact of ancient union between the nation and the king."

It was especially among the class that surrounded the throne that error was widespread and that all the true notions of the preconditions of moderate royalty were ignored. It is essential for modern states, which have derived from feudalism, to have an aristocracy, a remainder of formerly sovereign families, whose role consists in limiting royalty and preventing the exaggerated development of the idea of the state. French nobility has always lacked this vocation. Dazzling and inconstant, it can be seen, since the fourteenth century, to have placed its glory in appearing with splendor at court; "to serve the king" always was its supreme duty: enormous error that warped our history and was the origin of our ills! If it is only a question of "serving," there is no need for nobles. Louis XI[23] used his valets, the Oriental despots their slaves; that is consistent. Aristocracy is a precondition of liberty, because it gives the king natural-born servants; because independence of character, the most solid of all, is rare, it is worthwhile that there be an independence of position, so that not all of those who reach high office will have been obliged to follow those regrettable paths along which everyone leaves a part of their self-esteem, if not a part of their honor. But if the born servants of the king are themselves the most devoted instruments of absolute power, one can see how the odiousness of privilege in all its force will be added to the abasement inseparable from despotism. The Orient is governed by servants, but at least these servants do not form a separate caste. The exaggerated importance of the court in ancient France entailed a veritable perversion of ideas. For the nobility, Versailles was the tomb of all virtue. Thus, one can say without injustice that the nobility has been the true guilty party of our history: it did not establish freedom; by its lack of aptitude for governmental matters and its impertinence toward the Third Estate it rendered impossible or useless the Estates General, from which, according to the true analogies of modern history, the constitutional regime of our country should have emerged. It left the role of the opposition to the *parlements*,[24] whose nature was in no way political, and whose intervention in state affairs in general was awkward, hardly enlightened, and lacking all legitimacy.

With a few fine exceptions, the nobility of the Restoration was no wiser than that of the old order. Far from helping the development of a parliamentary life, in which it would have had the finest of roles, by a strange reversal it was seen to deny or attenuate with all its might the liberal consequences of the constitution, and to be more royalist than the king. Such were its ignorance with respect to general history and its blindness regarding its true duties that most of its members imagined that the natural mission of a nobility was to uphold absolute power. They preferred a servitude of which they were the agents over freedoms they would have shared with the other orders of the nation. The right to humiliate the bourgeoisie was almost the only one they seemed to care about. Their alliance with the clergy, legitimate enough in a time in which the high clergy of France was in some sense, by the way in which benefices were distributed, a member of the nobility, became senseless since the clergy had lost all political character and had begun to be recruited from among the popular classes. The deplorable tradition of the seventeenth and eighteenth centuries, Louis XIV and his prevaricating splendor went to everyone's head. One wanted to be of the king's religion, without considering that, if the king is free to have the opinion he chooses in religion and in literature, his activity in these sorts of matters must limit itself to what is appropriate to the first private citizen of the realm and not exceed in any way the limits of a completely private propaganda.

The nobility was not, I know, the only one to be guilty of those reminiscences of the past that so deeply troubled the establishment of a new order. The nation followed its tendency, which is to prefer good administration and social equality to liberty. Class issues, always so fatal to political issues, took on an exaggerated importance. The true liberal is hardly troubled at all that there be above him an aristocracy, even a dismissive one, as long as this aristocracy allows him to work without obstacles at what he conceives as his right. In his view, there is only one solid equality—that is, equality before duty—the man of genius, the nobleman, the peasant, all raising themselves up by the same means, which is virtue. The liberals of the time of the Restoration were far from understanding this abnegation. Hence, bothersome alliances with the partisans of fallen regimes, among which the new youth found, I imagine, hardly any distinction or character. Mr. Béranger, in particular, created a very evil combination, in which the bourgeois spirit, vulgar materialism, the taste for despotism, as long as it took on national appearances, all united. The most regrettable was that the malcontents, rather than fighting against royalty with legal weapons, attempted to overthrow the established order by means of conspiracies. These attacks against the principle of government led the government in turn to commit a serious mistake. It mistook the repression of seditious acts, which in itself has nothing illiberal about it, with laws destructive of liberty, which are always catastrophic and unjust, because they hardly reach the truly guilty, and limit the rights of all in order to prevent the error of a few.

This uncompromising disposition of the nation was, it must be recognized, the cause of many of the errors whose responsibility has been attributed to the Restoration government. The lack of ability of some of the men it placed at the head of governmental affairs was only a problem as a consequence of France's administrative character, and because we have become accustomed in our country to demanding from our governments more than they can deliver. As for me, I would see no inconvenience in having the high offices of the state occupied by well-educated and passably superficial gentlemen, but under one condition: that they only discharge their duties in a summary fashion. If the gentleman simply lets himself be guided by his general instinct as a man of the world, he will pose less of a threat to freedom than the professional administrator or the parvenu; but it is clear that, if the gentleman stoops to create petty problems and wishes to impose his prejudices on everyone, he remains well below the administrator, who, along with his mediocre traits, is at least able and serious. Neither the government nor public opinion understood these nuances. The liberals began with the idea, quite widespread among us, that positions are owed to merit, and that the man of talent has a sort of natural right to be a civil servant of his country, when in fact the man of talent only has one right (and this right is common to all): to develop freely, that is to say not to encounter the government as a jealous rival that oppresses him and is an unfair competitor. The government, on the other hand, had the mad pretention of molding intellects in its own image. Why did the harmless Charles X,[25] who, three or four centuries ago, would have been what one called a "good king," become so unpopular? Why did his small flaws, his narrow-minded devotion, his frivolousness, his somewhat puerile taste for etiquette, his tendency to surround himself with superficial characters, become public misfortunes? Alas! Because he was asked to accomplish a task superior to the forces of a man of genius, I mean to administer thirty million citizens for their greater good. Mr. de Polignac[26] assuredly was the last of men to whom to turn in order to resolve such a problem. If one turns government into an issue of universal management of the character of a nation, one must be consistent and apply the Chinese system all the way; prefects and ministers, I say, must issue from public competitions and through a system of examinations. There is a glaring contradiction in wishing that a government of gentlemen, foreign by their condition to any specialized knowledge, be at the same time a government of administrators and mandarins.

Such is, in my opinion, the explanation of this peculiar age, worthy at the same time of so much praise and of such severe blame. It failed in its essential duty, which was to establish liberty. The Restoration forgot that, not being national, it was obliged to be liberal; but it did have the good fortune of being weak. The core of gentlemanliness that was in its nature forbade it the learned tyranny that, blocking even the possibility of an opposition, has no need to make recourse to acts of violence. It was loyal toward its enemies, in the sense that it fought them, often it crushed them with its weight, but it never anticipated them by disarming them. The greatest glory of governments is in what they allow to be done. Harsh and at times odious in the detail of its actions, the Restoration will be absolved by the future, thanks to this constellation of distinguished men who developed without it and despite it, but whose development it was neither strong enough nor adroit enough to block. One will forget the shared antipathy they had for it while being thankful for the fact that it did not smother them. By a strange twist of fate, it will be complimented for having let its enemies mature, and it will benefit from what it could not prevent.

Such is also the origin of the peculiar position of the Legitimist party and of the strange contradiction on the basis of which this party represents in our midst at one and the same time what is most excellent and most blameworthy: on one hand, the resistance against the brutality of facts in the name of a principle, the disinterested attachment to an apparently sterile abstraction; on the other, the inanity of its views and ideas, the systematic refusal to submit to the most uncontroversial results of the modern mind. I hasten to say that whoever is loyal to an opinion renders a service to the human race by shielding the world from this carelessness, worse than barbarism, that delivers it to the whim of any passing wind. Nothing is as valuable as the sincere Legitimist, who holds, against all hope and apparently against all reason, to his obstinate cult of ancient rights; but if this obstinacy is nothing but perseverance in a historical error, if it is to despotism and not to the king that one is loyal, to the extent that the simple semblance of absolute power is sufficient to obtain conversions one had declared impossible on the altar of liberty, the Legitimist party is without question the greatest obstacle to the destinies of our country. Certainly, it would be better if a nation stretched patience and reason to the point of enduring the harshest trials for the pure love of law; but such a heroism will always be rare: our country in particular hardly understands that it is sometimes useful to sacrifice the spirit for the letter, and that it is better for the sick to heal slowly and painfully according to principle, rather than hide the illness by the workings of a deceptive empiricism.

II

The resistance to the coup d'état of July was, from the point of view of constitutional law, perfectly legitimate. The decrees[27] infringed the fundamental pact of the state. Only the narrow and subtle mind of Charles X and his counselors could see in article 14 a pretext for such a measure. Never should one posit that a pact has been drafted in such a way as to make it illusory. Now, such would have been the case, if the author of the constitution had inserted an article in it that would have allowed the constitution itself to be suspended in peacetime and without provocation on the part of the nation. The king and his counselors were so conscious of this that they prepared for this deplorable act the way one prepares for an ambush. To put it in practice they felt obliged to call upon survivors of another world, men amnestied in advance because of their lack of foresight and thought. In the fanatic party, the efforts made to blind oneself and excite oneself to bold deeds were barely hidden.* "What one calls a coup d'état, said the avowed mouthpieces of the cabinet, is something

---

* Guizot, vol. I, p. 351.

social and honest, when the king acts in the general interest of the people, even were he to appear to act against the laws."

Charles X's situation, therefore, was that of a king of the Middle Ages, who violated the laws of his kingdom, despoiled his great vassals, abolished the rights of the good cities, that of a King John, for example, who tore up the Magna Charta he had issued. All the casuists of the Middle Ages agree that at this point resistance is legitimate, for, by violating the pact, the king ceases to be king and is nothing more than a tyrant. "In this case," Saint Thomas says energetically, "it is the tyrant that is seditious."*

But if resistance was legitimate, up to what point was it appropriate to push it? Ultimately, the situation was not as novel as is ordinarily believed. Says Mr. Guizot:

> More than once, nations have had to fight, not only by means of laws, but by force, to maintain or recover their rights. In Germany, in Spain, in England, before the reign of Charles I, in France up to the mid-seventeenth century, the political bodies and the people have often resisted the king, even by arms, without feeling obliged or feeling they had the right to change the dynasty of their princes or the form of their government. Resistance, insurrection itself had their restraint and their limit, both in the condition of society, and in men's conscience and common sense; the future of society as a whole was not constantly being risked. Nowadays and among us, all the great political conflicts are turned into questions of life and death; peoples and parties, in their blind abandon, immediately seek the last extremities; resistance suddenly transforms itself into insurrection and insurrection into revolution. All storms become deluges.

In other terms, the conflict should have been a resistance, not a revolution. Certainly, it is difficult from a distance to trace limits for that daring impetus of a people to whom the powers themselves, by violating the law, had given the signal for anarchy; but the arbitrariness of revolutions is as fatal as that of kings, the actions of a roused people must be subjected to a severe exam like those of government. The first moment in which it appears that resistance should have ceased was when, on

---

\* "Perturbatio hujus regiminis (tyrannici) non habet rationem seditionis. . . . Magis autem tyrannus seditiosus est" (*Summa*, II$^a$ II$^{ae}$, q. LXII, art. 2).

July 30, Mr. de Sussy brought back to parliament from Saint Cloud the withdrawal of the decrees and the composition of a new cabinet. Several times did Englishmen thus accept the recanting of their delinquent kings, and benefited from it. It would be important to realize what happened at that decisive hour. Unfortunately, the record of the meeting is quite incomplete and does not bear an official character. It suggests that the suspicion of parliament regarding these concessions rested on very serious grounds. Mr. Guizot's narrative,* confirmed by several witnesses, also shows that the king, by withdrawing his imprudent provocation, was not acting with perfect uprightness. It is difficult, therefore, to blame the precautions parliament took in this circumstance.

But, after the abdication of Charles X and the clear designation of a successor against whom no avowed reason for repulsion was extant, was the continuation of the divorce with the eldest branch legitimate and appropriate? I do not think so. A long regency beginning with the triumph of liberal ideas offered an occasion the like of which rarely presents itself in the life of nations to establish a parliamentary regime. The English, while confining their treacherous King John to the Isle of Wight, were careful to choose as his successor his young son Henry III. Apart from a small number of wise men, whose conscience must be in my opinion marvelously at ease,† everyone incurred a mistake that is a very common one in our country, I mean an outsized preoccupation about the personal qualities of the head of state. Induced to error by a deceiving analogy, which has many people repeat that France has only been great under great sovereigns, public opinion among us often allows itself to believe that the nation is only worth as much as its sovereign. The minorities, the regencies, excellent moments for the development of the constitutional regime, are disastrous moments in France. We want a king who governs us. From the fact that a given family appears to us worthier of reigning, we conclude that it is the legitimate one, as if power were a reward or the prize of a competition. We do not consider that a dynastic line tempered by time, nourished by the thought of its traditional honors, shielded by the sense

---

*    Vol. II, pp. 8–9.

†    The record of the session of July 30 mentions only one intervention in this respect: "Mr. Villemain declares that, peering into his conscience, he is unable to find the conviction that the right to change dynasty has been entrusted to him by his constituents."

of its own majesty from the restlessness that new dynasties escape with difficulty, is better at sequestering power than a young, active dynastic line, which is obliged to make its way in the world. We forget that royalty is a trust that must be transmitted, like all other hereditary matters, by birth, that this is a simple question of family registry, not of merit, and that to bring issues of popularity and ability into consideration in the case of the succession to the throne is to attribute to the person of the king an importance he must not have except under absolute monarchies.

God forefend that I become the accomplice of the sad Legitimist party, which has had the privilege of rendering the rule of law odious, and whose hand you cannot shake except after you have stated that you take it for something other than what it believes it is! I do not misestimate the reservations imposed on the theorist in the case of an age in which, through the fault of both the rulers and the ruled, revolution has seemed to foil the best-advised solutions at will. This is merely a question of regrets, and certainly such a feeling is permissible in the face of the fateful divorce that has made a utopia out of right, and has reduced wise men themselves to expedients. The responsibility for this fateful alternative must be borne first of all by the power that brought it about. The liberal opposition, on the other hand, ignored some of the preconditions of modern royalty. It harbored in its ranks very diverse elements, old military men incapable of political ideas, sectarians, onlookers. The people, to whose courageous intervention it had been necessary to resort, were quite incapable of that degree of refined abnegation that leads the philosopher to prefer abstract right, even when it has the most distressing consequences, over revolution that immediately realizes its desires. The average of public opinion was too superficial to sacrifice the palpable good of the moment to metaphysical truths, and to resist the urge, apparently so legitimate, to do what one thinks is best. How many lessons are necessary for a country to come to the understanding that only general principles are lasting, and that without them the most ingenious arrangements are ultimately adventures and risks!

One can see first of all the serious consequences that the infringement of the laws of inheritance committed by the July Revolution entailed for the dynasty that emerged from this revolution. The King Louis-Philippe,[28] despite his rare qualities, his admirable common sense, his lofty and philosophical humaneness, constantly had to struggle with the delicate position in which his origins placed him. Wavering between an elected king and a legitimate king, he was led by necessity to take indecisive steps, from which his dignity suffered. I will not say he did not keep his promises: he had made none; but one can say that the situation had made them for him. It is certain that he lent himself first to the idea of a completely popular origin; later, he clearly saw the radical contradiction implied in the idea of an elected king, and he subscribed to another theory. However, that was an actual betrayal of the principle that had made him king. To establish a dynasty is to abstract a family, to oppose it to the nation as an independent, but limited, force. Royalty does not issue from an Hôtel de Ville.[29] Those one has called "comrades" and "dear compatriots" never become subjects. We do not make the king, he is bestowed upon us. The enlightened and skillful prince, charged with so hard a task by the vagaries of our revolutions rather than his own choice, never escaped this fateful dilemma: weak when he was loyal to his origins, galling when he was not, he permitted to be pried from him like concessions the acts that the public opinion from which he had received his investiture demanded as rights, because he was only too aware that the deference to which he consented as an elected king humiliated him as a legitimate king.

The French character was, if truth be told, the first culprit in this imprudent attempt, which, with the pretext of making royalty popular, in truth removed its liberal temperament. One of France's flaws is to desire its sovereigns to be in intimate relations with it. It loves to touch those who lead it; it wants to sense the person in them, and is not wounded by this type of familiarity of a superior with an inferior that so resembles impertinence. The king, conceived as a sort of neutral person on whom one imposes the abdication of his own personality for the benefit of all, is for us the least understandable thing in the world. It is easy to see how unfavorable such a frame of mind is to the constitutional regime. I know of no king of England who, according to this way of judging, would have been appreciated in France. Constitutional royalty, in fact, is not a position well suited to developing great talents and acquiring a brilliant renown. One of the advantages of this royalty is precisely that it is not very enviable. Here, the sovereign is the sacrificed figure; he does not act, he does not write, he has no regular *cursus honorum*, no career. The qualities he must possess are those the wise value above all, but the crowd cannot appreciate. The very ambitious, in such a state of affairs, would much rather be ministers than king.

The republican king, a sort of leader of the people in arms, that Mr. de La Fayette[30] imagined, had nothing in common with this noble and pacific image of the ancient king who, if he had dared show himself on the barricades, would have seemed, I imagine, a vision from feudal times.

Of all those who attempted to offer a theory for a situation whose misfortune was precisely that it fell outside of theory, Mr. Guizot was without question the one to deploy the most ingenious acuteness. His system gradually became that of the king himself. Says Mr. Guizot:

> The King immediately determined that my way of understanding and presenting the revolution that had recently placed him on the throne was the most monarchical and the best suited to establish a government. He did not adopt it openly or fully: he had too many people to mollify to act thus; but he expressed his appreciation to me, and clearly let me understand that we understood each other.

According to this theory, the King Louis-Philippe was wrong to seek a popular consecration at the hôtel de ville: no one had made him king, and he owed no one gratitude; he inherited directly from the title of the Restoration, and had to continue its traditions. Says Mr. Guizot:

> Obliged by violence violently to break with the eldest branch of our royal House, we appealed to the youngest branch to preserve the monarchy whilst defending our freedoms. We did not choose a king; we dealt with a prince we found next to the throne, and who alone could guarantee our public rights and preserve us from revolutions, by ascending to it. The recourse to popular suffrage would have given the reformed monarchy precisely the character we were anxious to exclude from it; it would have replaced necessity and contract with election. . . . I was always tempted to smile when I heard the King Louis-Philippe referred to as "the king of our choice," as if, in 1830, we had had to choose, and as if the duke of Orléans had not been the only and necessary option. . . . I revealed the duke of Orléans for what he in fact was, a prince of royal blood luckily found near the broken throne, and that necessity had made into a king.

Mr. Guizot is perfectly right to reject election and the appeal to popular suffrage as the means of establishing royalty; what issues from popular suffrage has an entirely different name. The elected leader or the representative of the sovereignty of the people will always be too strong to accept the modest role of moderate royalty. Mr. de La Fayette, mistaking his noble accolade for an investiture, was as gravely wrong as the Senate of 1814, filled with the ideas of the imperial school, when it declared Louis XVIII recalled by the "will of the nation." Only one thing identifies the king, it is his birth: merit and the will of the people are weak bases for it. Only one thing confers his prerogative, it is his accession, implying the recognition of the constitutional rights of the nation. But who can fail to see that, to remain consistent with such a way of conceiving of royalty, it was not acceptable to compromise on heredity? The Legitimist party, to which Mr. Guizot appears to me to attribute too little historical importance in general, remained as a fateful protestation that had a decisive weight in due time. The appeal to the people changed hands, and became the weapon of those who considered that their will had not been interpreted exactly.

To justify the bold act by which the rights of the eldest branch of the House of Bourbon were transferred to the youngest branch, Mr. Guizot invokes necessity. This necessity was real, and was amply sufficient to absolve those who submitted to it; but such a principle implied serious consequences. The root of all these dynastic disruptions is necessity. The advantage of hereditary royalty is precisely to avoid these dangerous conjunctions of circumstances in which a man can present himself as the only one capable of saving the country. If it was in order to appease the triumphant revolution and out of respect for public opinion that one felt obliged to break with the fundamental laws of the State, does one not perceive what principle of impermanence was thus introduced into the new regime? And let it not be said that these are speculative theories, appropriate to the casuists of politics, theories that the man of action, attentive only to the needs of the moment, must despise. Abstract principles, apparently without application in the world, are ultimately the greatest realities, because they contain the logic and the reason of facts. Time, I know, has remedies for all wounds: rights have begun by being facts, and, in a country in which events had been less subject to rigorous consequentiality than in our own, it is not doubtful that the most desirable regime would have been consecrated by its duration, a clear sign of the national will. Duration, unfortunately, is quite fickle by nature. An exemplary moderation, marvels of ability, noble devotions did not manage to save a government, legal without fault, that struggled against a wrong it was not guilty of. Its honesty itself was but another cause of weakness in a situation that could not be saved except by boldness. The greatest mistake reticent people can make is to place themselves in positions that require for success flaws they do not possess. If Louis-Philippe had been a tyrant, he would have perhaps lasted. Honest as he was, he thought himself obliged to withdraw in the face of even the most equivocal manifestation of national will: this is the fateful condition of peoples that call their dynasty into question, or rather, the crime of the dynasties that oblige nations to doubt them!

The accession of a prince who, in many respects, can only be compared to the exemplary Charles V, inaugurated in issues of constitutional law the dangerous regime of approximation, tore apart the pact of unity of the nation, accustomed the French to answer with a superficial smile when one talks of issues of principle with them, and implanted the opinion that characters, treaties, constitutions, all oaths in a word should be respected only inasmuch as one is not strong enough to contravene them.

III

With this wound at its heart, how did the government of the King Louis-Philippe face the numerous difficulties that assailed it from its first days? This is what we now aim to investigate. Let us say it out loud, so as not to be unjust with an accomplished family and eminent men: this government gave France the eighteen best years our country and humanity perhaps ever experienced. It is enough to defend it against those who have an interest in believing that it was only weak and ignoble; it is not enough for the philosopher who, considering the impact of events on a long-term scale, has become accustomed to judging the facts of history only on the basis of their definitive influence on the progress of human morality and civilization.

Loyal to his theory of the origin of the rights of the King Louis-Philippe, Mr. Guizot summarizes in a word the way in which he understood the duties of the government that issued from the July Revolution: two parties contended for the direction of the country, the party of movement (which elsewhere Mr. Guizot calls the party of permissiveness) and that of resistance; the latter party had to be that of the king and his ministers. In putting this theory into practice, Mr. Guizot was simply following the line he had always preferred. On November 23, 1829, Mr. de La Fayette wrote to Mr. Dupont (de l'Eure): "Mr. Guizot is more monarchical and less democratic than you and I, I think, but he loves freedom. He knows much, expresses himself with talent; he has high-mindedness, character, and integrity. With a doctrinaire administration, he would halt before we would; up to there, all ministerial projects will find in him a skillful over-seer in the liberal interest."* After the July Revolution he was what he had promised to be before, and, seeing as public opinion then followed enthu-siasms that were often disorderly, he thought that in general the duty of a statesman had to be to resist public opinion.

I hardly want to engage in a detailed criticism of conduct dominated by imperious necessities. Nonetheless, I confess that the formula that the skillful theorist of the July Revolution assigns to the politics of the new dynasty appears to me to imply a certain confusion of ideas. The tendency to overgovern and revolution are not two opposite things; they often go together: it is liberty that is the opposite of both one and the other. Certainly, permissiveness is always bad. All disorder, violence, attacks on others' rights must be pitilessly repressed. Offenses against people and property are no more allowed in one period than in another. Blood spilled to prevent the least offensive breach of the law is not to be regretted. However, from this to the general principle of resistance to public opin-ion, which Mr. Guizot appears at times to offer as the summation of his politics, there is much distance. A government should neither system-atically resist public opinion nor follow it blindly; it should protect the rights and liberty of all. I do not understand why one agrees to be called the party of movement or the party of resistance; these two words must be set aside. Speak to us of rights and liberty, and there will be no misun-derstanding, because in the face of these words the ideas of resistance and revolution disappear or at least lose their odious and subversive meaning.

Certainly, there are cases in which the government has the right and the responsibility to resist public opinion, even when it is not doubtful that this opinion is that of the majority. It is indeed public opinion that,

---

* *Mémoires* of General La Fayette, vol. VI, p. 341.

over a century and a half, has urged the government to so many actions, now of perfidious, now of cruel intolerance against the reformed religion. The government that revoked the Edict of Nantes[31] and ordered the *dragonnades*[32] was no less guilty for it. The search for popularity is the sign of a second-rate sovereign or statesman. An accomplished prince, who fulfills his duties with discretion, coolness, reserve, not trespassing on the liberty of anyone, having no personal views, not attempting to make himself loved except in his intimacy, not using his position to make people personally dependent on him—such a prince, I say, would be only moderately popular. Nonetheless, the statesman should not feel obliged never to give in to public opinion in order to escape its tyranny. I know what austere appeal there is for strong natures to defy impotent mediocrity and provoke the ire of fools. There are people for whom the sweetness of being loved does not come near to the sweetness of being hated. The displeasure of superficial minds being a sure sign by which the wise are distinguished, haughty souls believe they can see in unpopularity a negative proof of their moral worth. Mr. Guizot has excessively relished this pleasure, against which the highest philosophy does not always warn us. He has abandoned himself to the dangerous joy of letting one's disdain be felt. Public opinion is a monarch after its own fashion, but not an absolute monarch: it must be confronted, when one believes it is necessary to do so, but all the while respecting it and finding in public opinion itself the necessary grounds for attacking it.

In sum, government is neither a machine for resistance nor a machine for progress. It is a neutral power, charged, like the *podestà* of Italian cities,[33] with maintaining the freedom of the struggle, not with weighing in the balance in favor of one of the parties. When public opinion obliges the government to act in the sense in which it desires, it commits an injustice, for it obliges a power that was supposed to play the role of an umpire and a conciliator to encourage a direction to the detriment of all others; it crushes its adversary by invoking against it a formidable assistant, which soon will become its own master. France, which does not have enough faith in freedom and believes too readily that ideas assert themselves by means other than the natural progress of intellects, often falls into this error. Imagining that progress operates from without and that the good can be decreed, it is satisfied when it has planted its gardens of Adonis; it trusts the sun to make its flowers without roots bloom: it does not see that the only desirable progress consists in the betterment of souls, the strengthening of characters, and the elevation of intellects.

How the conditions themselves of the July government made it difficult for it to assume that almost self-effacing role, without which there can hardly be a solid royalty or true liberty! And first of all the new regime was and could not but be the government of one class. In a society in which all privileges, all special rights, all intermediary bodies have been destroyed, the only distinguishing feature that remains to constitute a college of notables is wealth, whose measure is the levy of taxes. Such a system evidently had to bring about what Mr. Guizot rather aptly terms a "bourgeois Toryism." Instead of representing rights, the government could only represent interests. Materialism in politics produces the same effects as in ethics; it can inspire neither sacrifice nor, consequently, loyalty. The bourgeois Tory conceived by Mr. Guizot is too ruled by his interests to become a truly political man. One will claim perhaps that his interests, when correctly understood, by making him appreciate the need for stability will act as a substitute for principles and will provide a strong attachment to his party: this is not the case. Far from suggesting firmness, his interests will lead him to be always in agreement with the strongest. Hence the fateful type that has issued from our revolutions, the man of order as he is called, prepared to suffer anything, even what he loathes, this eternal Fouché,[34] with his honest perfidies, lying out of conscientiousness, and, no matter who won, always a winner. At times one hesitates to be too severe with him, one can argue that, ordinarily, a fairly correct sense of the needs of the moment has guided him: he has betrayed all governments, he has not betrayed France; but, I am mistaken, he has betrayed it by inaugurating the reign of selfishness, of cowardliness, and of this disastrous belief that the good citizen will resign himself to anything to save what he considers the sole thing necessary, the interests of his class and the apparent order of the state.

The Gospel correctly said: "Whosoever will save his life shall lose it."[35] Self-interest cannot create anything, because, horrified by great deeds and heroic devotions, it brings about a condition of weakness and corruption in which a determined minority is sufficient to topple the established powers. The day that follows these sorts of surprises, the conservative mind is in a way the accomplice of the transgressors of the law, because, letting itself be led astray by an erroneous calculation and not indulging in chivalry, it finds it to be more beneficial to accept illegality than to fight it. Thus, by wishing for calm at any price, it loses precisely what it wished to acquire by sacrificing its honor and its pride.

Bourgeois Toryism does not create stability; it does not create liberty either. This reproach is not aimed at the esteemed statesmen who employed so much talent and eloquence to introduce liberal customs among us. No finer and stronger pages on the rights of the press than those one encounters here and there in the book itself that forms the object of our study* have been written. Unfortunately, the need for security, which constitutes the first instinct of societies based on self-interest, provided a formidable counterweight to these lofty theories. More impressed by the abuse than by the right, the practical men, in their outbursts of "ardent selfishness," to use an excellent expression of Mr. Guizot's, demanded repressive measures against what frightened them. Two months after the July Revolution, the two articles 291 and 294 of the Criminal Code were declared perfectly valid; they were thus worded:

> No association of more than twenty people whose goal is to meet every day, or on certain designated days, to engage in religious, literary, political or other pursuits will be permitted to form without the authorization of the government, and subject to the conditions the public authorities will choose to impose on the society.—All individuals who, without the permission of the municipal authorities, grant or allow the use of their home, in whole or in part, for the meeting of the members of an association, even if the association is authorized, or for the performance of acts of worship, shall be punished with a fine of 16 to 200 francs.

I do not wish to deny that such legislation was necessary; I only wish to point out the peculiarity of a people that destroy a dynasty to defend liberty and, a few days later, are led to give themselves such chains. I do not think that any nation of antiquity or of the Middle Ages ever knew so tyrannical a law. Imagine such a law in the past: neither the Academy, nor the Lycaeum, nor the Stoà,[36] nor Christianity, nor the Reformation would have been possible, because these great movements have entailed without exception meetings of more than twenty people. That article, applied over

---

*   Vol. I, pp. 50, 176, 282, 408ff.

half a century, would be sufficient to snuff out any intellectual or religious initiative in a society. Mr. Dupin demanded at least the rights of religious freedom, but went unheeded; the principle was admitted that nobody has the right to communicate his thought to his fellow creatures without the permission of the authorities, and that, unless one is salaried by the government, one cannot have anything good to say to the public.

How could it happen that the day after a liberal revolution such a measure could be taken by strongly liberal men? The first cause of such legislation must undoubtedly be sought in the regrettable tendency popular associations among us have to transform themselves into government committees. The club is the most legitimate thing in the world, as long as it remains a meeting in which good or bad ideas are developed: it is a crime as soon as it aspires to be a power within the state. But the friends of order did not stop at this essential distinction. What they called for was "for all these meetings that were troubling public tranquility and blocking commercial operations to be brought to a halt." Freedom bore the costs of suffering industry, and to rescue the business of a few industrialists it was considered a quite simple affair to declare a vast curfew over society. Imagine the peal of laughter that would have greeted the request of merchants in Florence or Pisa to abolish public life because it was detrimental to their commerce. We are excessively subject to the tyranny of these sorts of interests, fully respectable as they are. The state is not required to concern itself with private wealth: industry is owed freedom; but one should not sacrifice that of others to it. Strange sight! It was the Garde Nationale that, on its own initiative and without troubling to determine whether it had such a right, invaded the clubs, booed the orators (quite ridiculous in fact, I am sure), and accompanied the exit of those in attendance with jeers. The education of liberty was so little advanced, that a body formed with the purpose of defending order committed an action twenty times more seditious than those it wished to prevent, in order to give satisfaction to its fears.

I have insisted on this example, for there is no other that illustrates so completely the fateful reciprocity of error that exists between popular upheaval on the one hand, always prone to weigh illegally on the state, and on the other the exaggerated forcefulness that makes the conservative party believe that all movements of public opinion must be prevented as a danger. Conspiracies and secret societies almost always come about

as a response to a transgressed freedom. England does not have conspirators, because it has *meetings*.[37] The meeting, one will say, is the club, and
the club is anarchy. The club is anarchy in the state of affairs in which,
to obtain what one desires, it is necessary to topple power and replace
it with oneself. The club will be useful or harmless when the legal paths
of propaganda and resistance will be available to all. Open on all sides
of the social volcano some partial escape valves, and you will avoid the
explosions that shake the world. Waiting is insufferable for the oppressed
minority that sees no hope in front of it; it is almost sweet, when you can
believe you are sure to triumph in due time by the force of public opinion.
Everything is poison without liberty: order itself, without it, is but a lie.
Seventeen years after the suppression of the last of the clubs issued from
the July Revolution, a miserable child's play, a banquet[38] that should have
been allowed to proceed on the sole condition that it not block the public
thoroughfare, sufficed to annihilate the product of so much noble work,
and to open an abyss whose depth we are still far from having glimpsed.

Thus, conservatives fought revolution by exquisitely revolutionary
means. They became violent in the name of order, seditious for the sake of
moderation. They strengthened the principle from which all the troubles
of modern times have sprung, this suspicion of liberty that leads governments to see what is done without them as being done against them, to
bar the way to lawful proselytism, and to claim the right to direct public
opinion. In such a political condition, what may the man devoted with
some energy to the doctrine he has adopted, whether true or false, do?
One thing only: attempt to take over the government, to make the idea he
could not serve by the pacific means of discussion triumph by force. In
this way, everything becomes a question of state. The humblest ambition
is obliged to take on a political shape. A machine of terrifying power, and
compared with which individual efforts are but an atom, has been created; any man, rather than fight for his opinion with his isolated forces,
will necessarily attempt to gain control of the formidable lever by means
of which anyone at all can lift the world. Saint Paul, nowadays, should
consider becoming a minister or a tribune; Luther and Calvin would be
obliged to become conspirators.

All the criticism one has the right to direct at those who steered
the government that issued from the July Revolution in its first years
thus comes down to one word: they loved liberty, but they did not fully

understand its preconditions. The Revolution and the Empire, which had not been able to create any political institution, had created a peculiarly extensive and complicated public administration. The Restoration on the whole preserved the imperial administration, while tempering it with a system of personal connections and exceptions, which was better than equality in subjection, but which only really benefited the nobility. The liberals saw these limits as abuses, and the July Revolution was a pure and simple return to the imperial administration. No one understood that they were attempting to establish liberty by strengthening the most serious of obstacles that lay in the path of liberty. As Mr. Guizot says quite correctly:

> Where public administration is free like politics, when local affairs are handled and decided by local authorities or influences, and await neither their impulse nor their solution from the central power, which only intervenes inasmuch as the general affairs of the State absolutely require it, in England and in the United States of America, in Holland and in Belgium, for example, the representative regime easily coexists with an administrative regime that only depends on it on important and rare occasions. But, when the higher power is charged both with governing by means of freedom and with administering by means of centralization, when it has to fight at the summit over the great affairs of the State, and at the same time settle everywhere, under its own responsibility, almost all the affairs of the country, two serious drawbacks soon burst forth: either the central power, absorbed by the concerns of general affairs and by its own defense, neglects local affairs and allows them to fall into disarray and torpor, or it links them closely to general affairs, it has them serve its own interests, and then the entire administration, from the hamlet to the palace, is nothing more than a means of government in the hands of the political parties that contend for power.

What is strange is that the party that believed itself to be the most liberal was the most inclined to commit this misdeed. Mr. Guizot was at first as free from it as the circumstances allowed. "Search for men who think and act by themselves," he wrote on September 14, 1830, as minister of the interior, to Mr. Amédée Thierry, prefect of the Haute-Saône. "The first requirement for this country is that on all matters independent opinions and influences develop. The centralization of minds is worse than that of affairs."

These excellent principles were hardly followed. The state was charged with many more functions in January 1848 than in June 1830. The growth of the budget during those eighteen years proves it; now, all growth in the budget corresponds to some loss of liberty. It would be supremely unjust to compare the type of tyranny that sprung from our administrative advances with the brutal tyrannies that have left a bloody memory in history. The tortures and torments of the past compared with the apparent gentleness of our legislation would lead to believe at first glance that a golden age has followed on an iron age. One may not realize that the characteristic of an administrative regime is to prevent what the ancient regimes punished; its gentleness is hardly praiseworthy, I will almost say it is detrimental, because, by imposing wisdom preventively, it renders any initiative impossible. The press in the eighteenth century was subjected to a legislation apparently more severe than that of our time, because the death penalty appeared in it, yet Voltaire passed through the loose net of censorship. The first edition of the *Spirit of the Laws* could not be printed in France; but in eighteen months there were twenty-two clandestine editions of it. Nowadays, a pamphlet from Holland would be seized at the first post house. The expansion of public services, by placing interests dear to all in the hands of the state, has made society as a whole dependent on the government. Under such a regime, everybody needs the state at some point, and whoever places himself outside the official order is, like a helot, deprived of his natural rights. In this way, an aristocracy of civil servants is formed, with most of the drawbacks of the ancient nobility, and none of the advantages.

In its dream of a republican royalty, the liberal school of 1830 rather than establishing a limited royalty in fact governed more than anyone. Rather than diminishing royalty, all contributed at every possible opportunity to augment it. The true liberal conduct would have been to give back to the individual the full power to exercise his activity for better or for worse within the limits in which the rights of others were not infringed, to allow corporations, associations, meetings of all kinds to be established, thus to create among men ties separate from those of the state. A completely opposite path was followed: the great reproach the opposition leveled at the government was that it did not do enough, that is to say evidently that it did not govern enough. It was thought that liberty was being saved by contesting the king's right to rule on his own and by attempting to transport full sovereignty to the council of ministers: a fairly sterile debate, for I am rather uninterested in who governs me if I am excessively governed. Certainly, parliamentary guarantees are indispensable, because without them all governments are led by the force of events to encroach upon what does not concern them; but what matters above all is that those who govern, whoever they are, remain within the limits prescribed by the rights of all. In politics, freedom is the goal that must never be sacrificed, and to which everything must be subordinated.

In truth, the liberal opposition, by urging France farther and farther along the path of government, simply followed the tradition of the Revolution, much as the Revolution simply followed the bad example of royalty of the past two centuries. An eminent publicist,[39] for whom enlightened France is in mourning, has shown, in the finest book of political and historical philosophy to have been published in these past years, that freedom is not exactly in France's tradition. One can admit this without siding with those who think there is no way to establish it among us. The true patriot is not the one who tries to discover the weak side of his country in order to flatter it. Let us refrain from the fatal reasoning that leads the arrogant to be proud of their defects and to do nothing to acquire the opposite virtues. If France so far has sinned through the absence of freedom, it is by freedom that one must attempt to cure it. The true cause of revolution is the conception of the state that has been produced by the combined action of Richelieu,[40] Louis XIV, the Republic,* and the Empire. We will not exit the age of revolutions without reforming this idea: now, one cannot reform the exaggerated idea of the state except by correcting it with freedom. Conflict and unrest are as old as humanity; what characterizes our century are these sudden and complete about-faces that make it so that no government falls only partially. The edifice that once rested on a large number of stays, several of which could weaken at once without causing its collapse, now rests on only one point; an attack at its base is

---

\* It is worth observing that this rebuke should not fall on the superior men who prepared the Revolution or even began it: Montesquieu, Turgot, first-rate and truly liberal politicians. It falls on the revolutionary school proper, which was related especially with Rousseau and who gave the French Revolution its definitive character, that is to say, its tendency toward abstract organization, without taking into account either previous rights or freedom.

sufficient to bring down the colossus whose head has been inordinately enlarged. Paris is not guilty, as is often repeated, of this instability. The revolutionary character of Paris could be destroyed without destroying the revolution. The revolution will stop the day in which the excessively strong governments the French Revolution has created are diminished and divided, the day in which one ceases to consider public works, public education, religion, the arts, literature, science, commerce, and industry as branches of public administration. The stability of governments (Mr. de Tocqueville has proven it) is inversely proportional to their power, or, to phrase it better, to the range of their activity. What are the powers of the queen of England, compared with those granted to the heads of our various governments? Nonetheless, which of our governors in the past century has sat on his throne as securely as the queen of England?

And let it not be said that this is an ideal best kept for a remote future, that France still needs a long education to be capable of putting it in practice. If things stand thus, let us abandon all hope. If France is not ripe for liberty, it will never be. Political education is not accomplished through despotism; a people that has long suffered the administrative system plunges ever deeper into it. I harbor no illusions regarding the disadvantages that would initially be caused by a regime that, in order to be beneficial, requires that one be able to await its consequences for a long time; but I believe I can say without paradox that the ill that derives from freedom is better in a sense than the good that derives from the administrative regime. The good is not the good unless it comes from the conscience of individuals; the good imposed from the outside leads, in the long run, to the greatest ill, which for a nation is lethargy, vulgar materialism, the absence of public opinion, and official incompetence, under the sway of which nothing is hated and nothing is loved. The creation of a power provided with the right to make everyone agree, to remove, as one says, the causes of division among citizens, seems at first glance a precious benefaction. It has only one disadvantage, that after fifty years it will have exhausted the nation a hundred times more than a series of civil and religious wars would have. These wars, as appalling as they would be, ordinarily rendered the people more serious and energetic. Public administration, on the contrary, destroys souls' resilience by subjecting them to continuous tutelage. Only the clergy so far has been able to preserve some privileges in the face of this invading force, somewhat like one saw, in the waning days of the Western Empire, the bishops remain standing in the middle of a society killed by administration; but, although the clergy is a good assistant in the struggle against despotism, because all despotism is necessarily obliged to fall out with the spiritual power, it must be admitted that in general this body is almost exclusively concerned with its own independence. After all, Catholicism, by accustoming men to devolve to others a host of concerns, such as the education of children, public charity, and the direction of one's own conscience, in general presents serious dangers for freedom.

Thus from all sides one comes to see freedom as the solution par excellence and as the remedy to almost all the ills of our time. Many people have grown accustomed to believe, on the authority of a few sectarians, that freedom is only appropriate to the ages in which, since no one is certain of possessing truth, no opinion has the right to reject the others completely. This is a serious mistake. Freedom is the basis of a lasting society at all times. Indeed, on one hand truth can only be demonstrated to free listeners; on the other, the possibility of doing evil is the essential precondition of the good. The modern world cannot escape the fate of ancient civilizations except by granting everyone the full right to set to work their God-given talent in their own way. The dignity of man depends on his responsibility. May all have their destiny in their own hands; may society beware that by preventing evil it at the same time makes the good impossible. Even if we were obliged once more to pay the price of barbarism for liberty, many think it would not be dearly bought; for only liberty offers individuals a reason to live, and it alone prevents nations from dying.

The *Mémoires* of Mr. Guizot shed much light on the great problems of contemporary history. Mr. Guizot has not reached and will not reach popularity either by his book or by his actions. This dubious reward is reserved among us for qualities and flaws that are not his. France, in meting out glory, considers its preferences much more than cold justice. For it, glory is a national reward, not a judgment of reason. To have a doctrine opposed to its will is almost seditious. France wants to be flattered and wants its defects to be shared; what it forgives least is for someone to have been wiser than it was. The frivolous poet, docile echo of the errors of the crowd, was its idol; the austere thinker who attempted to rise above the prejudices of his time and his country incurred the most serious of reproaches, that of not being "national." Guilty of having left to chance only what he could not shield from it, and of having thought of the future in a country that at times turns prudence into a state crime, Mr. Guizot (and I suppose he is proud of it) must hardly appear a man of his time to those for whom patriotism consists in not foreseeing anything. His *Mémoires* are an eloquent appeal to the tribunal of impartial opinion against these false judgments. During the eighteen years they cover so far, the mistakes of Mr. Guizot were most often those of the dominant opinion or of fate. The following books will narrate the mistakes that were his own. Perhaps we will see at least that they came as a consequence of the necessities of the situation, and that his adversaries were often as guilty of them as he was.

# 4

## THE ROLE OF THE FAMILY AND THE STATE IN EDUCATION (*LA PART DE LA FAMILLE ET DE L'ÉTAT DANS L'ÉDUCATION*, 1869)[1]

Ladies and Gentlemen,

You have just heard some noble, excellent words, stated with high authority. I subscribe to them completely. I believe, as does our honorable and illustrious president,* that the question of education is a question of life and death for modern societies, a question on which the future hangs. Our mind, gentlemen, is set on this point. We will never retreat from the philosophical principle that every man has the right to enlightenment. We have confidence that enlightenment is beneficent, and that if it sometimes presents dangers, it is the only remedy to these dangers. If those who do not believe in the reality of duty and who conceive of morality as an illusion preach the bleak thesis of the necessary bruti-fication of a part of the human species, so be it; but, for those of us who believe that morality is an absolute truth, such a doctrine is inadmissible. Whatever the price, and whatever the consequences, *may there be more enlightenment!* This is our motto; we will never abandon it.

Many people, and occasionally good people, entertain scruples, I know. They are alarmed by the progress that, in our day, leads consciousness into areas of humanity that up to now had remained closed to it. "There are," they say, "in human labor certain humble functions to which the

---

* Mr. Carnot, representative in the Corps législatif.

educated and cultivated man will never consent to submit. The dawning of consciousness is always more or less accompanied by revolt; the diffusion of education will render wholly impossible order, hierarchy, and the acceptance of authority, without which humanity has hitherto been unable to live." This, gentlemen, is very bad reasoning, and, I would venture to say, very impious. It is the reason that has been used, for centuries, to maintain slavery. "The world," one argued, "has lowly necessities that a free man will never undertake; hence, slavery is necessary." Slavery has disappeared, and the world has not collapsed on this count. Ignorance will disappear, and the world will not collapse. The reasoning I rebut proceeds from a false and vulgar doctrine: that education serves only for the practical use one makes of it; hence, he who, because of his social position, does not need to be appreciated for his cultured spirit has no need for such culture. Literature, according to this way of seeing things, is of use only to the man of letters, scientific knowledge to the expert, good manners and an air of distinction only to the man of the world. The poor must be ignorant, for education and knowledge would be useless to them. Blasphemy, gentlemen! To seek a cultivated intellect [*la culture de l'esprit*] and a cultivated soul is a duty for all men. They are no simple ornaments; they are matters as sacred as religion. If a cultivated intellect were but a frivolous thing, "the least vain of the vanities," as Bossuet[2] put it, one could maintain that it is not for everyone, in the same way as luxury is not for everyone. But if a cultivated intellect is what is holy par excellence, nobody must be excluded from it. One has never dared to say, at least in a Christian country, that religion is something reserved for a minority, that the poor and humble should be chased out of the church. Well, gentlemen, education and the cultivation of the soul are our religion. We do not have the right to chase anyone away from them. To condemn a man a priori not to receive an education is to declare that he does not have a soul, that he is not of the children of God and of Light. This is the very definition of impiety. I join the honorable Mr. Carnot[3] in declaring a war unto the death against it.

The specific question I must discuss before you, gentlemen, is one of the most difficult among those relative to this delicate matter of public education. I set out to discuss the reciprocal rights of the family and of the state in a child's education. This problem has given rise to the most divergent solutions. It concerns the most basic principles of the theory of society, principles to which I must ask you, first of all, to direct your utmost attention.

With the exception of extremely rare cases, gentlemen, man is born in society, that is to say that from the outset, and without him choosing to do so, he belongs to groups of which he is a natural-born member. The family, the town or the neighborhood, the county, the district or the province, the state, the church or whatever other religious association, are all groups I would term natural, in the sense that all of us belong to them by birth, and share in their advantages and responsibilities. Establishing the correct equilibrium between the opposing rights of these different groups is the great question of human affairs. Nowhere is this endeavor more difficult than in the case of education. In all other parts of civil government, the subject, the member of the state is considered to be adult, free, responsible, capable of reasoning and discernment. In the case of education, however, the subject, the child, is under tutelage, incapable of making his own decisions. The choice of his teacher, a choice he does not participate in, will decide his life. His life, in other words, will be completely different depending on whether his father, his mother, his native town, the state to which he belongs, or the religious confession in which he chanced to be born take charge of his education. In such matters experiments are conducted on live subjects, on souls, and on underage souls, if I may say so, on which the law is obliged to take a decisive stance.

In fact, gentlemen, man is an essentially educable creature. The gifts each of us is born with are worth next to nothing if society does not step in to develop them and direct their use. Animals are also susceptible, to a certain extent, to an expansion of their aptitudes through education; it is, however, but a small matter, and in any case only humanity, as Herder[4] has said, has the possibility to capitalize upon its discoveries, to add new acquisitions to the older ones, so that each of us is the heir of an immense sum of abnegation, sacrifices, experiments, and reflections, which constitute our patrimony, establish our link with the past and the future. No philosophy is more superficial than that which, taking man to be an egoistic and limited creature, expects to account for him and trace his duties outside the society of which he is a part. One might as soon consider the bee in abstraction from the hive, and maintain that it builds its cell on its own. Humanity is a whole in which all parts are in solidarity with each other. We all have ancestors. A friend of freedom who suffered for it centuries ago has conquered the right for us to conduct our thoughts freely; we owe a fatherland, a free and civil existence to a long series of honorable and obscure generations. It is education, gentlemen, education at all levels that gives us possession of this treasure of reason and science, ever increasing, which we have received from the past and will entrust to the future. This treasure belongs to the society that bestows it. In what form, by what hands, and with what guarantees should it be bestowed?

A principle on which all good intellects of our day seem to be in agreement is that we should charge society, by which I mean the town, the province, the state, only with those things that isolated or associated individuals cannot freely accomplish. Indeed, in the future social progress will consist in transferring a great mass of matters from the category of state affairs to that of free affairs, left to private initiative. Religion, for instance, was once an affair of state; it is no longer, and tends to become ever more a matter of free choice. May we conceive of a society where public education could similarly be considered a free affair, one that concerns only the individual and the family, a society where there would be no public education administration, where the state and the town would not meddle with the choice of school a father sends his son to any more than with the brand of clothes he provides for him, a society where all would select a professor, or a doctor, according to the opinion they form of their abilities, without worrying whether they held state certifications? Undoubtedly, such a society is conceivable; the moment such an absence of legislation were possible, an immense intellectual and moral progress would have been attained. This moment, however, is far removed. Not one country in the world, and free America least of all, believes it is possible simply to leave the care of public education to the solicitude of private individuals. It cannot be doubted that the application of such a system would cause, in the present state of affairs, a deplorable reduction in the number of those who receive an education, and would miserably lower its level. Hence, gentlemen, we will not discuss a utopia that will perhaps one day become a reality, the utopia of a completely free education, I mean to say one in which neither the state nor the county nor the district nor the town would meddle, either to fund it or to oversee it. We will instead seek to determine how, in the current state of our societies, it is possible, in this matter, to balance the interest of the state with the sacred rights of the family and the individual.

The further we reach into the past, gentlemen, the more strongly we find the rights of the state over the education of the child to be stated, and even exaggerated. In those small and seductive Greek societies that appear to us as a touchstone in the panorama of history, education was an affair of state, in the same way as religion. Education was regulated down to its slightest details; everyone practiced the same physical exercises, learned the same songs, participated in the same religious ceremonies, underwent the same initiations. To effect any changes was a crime punishable by death: "to corrupt the youth," that is to say to lead them away from state education, was a capital crime (as Socrates testifies). And this regimen, which would feel insufferable to us, was seductive then; for the world was young, and the city-state offered so much life and so much joy that one pardoned all its injustices, all its tyrannies. A beautiful bas-relief, discovered in Athens by Mr. Beulé[5], at the foot of the Acropolis, shows us a war dance of ephebes, a pyrrhic: there they are, sword in hand, going through the steps with an astonishing unity and individuality combined; a muse presides over their exercises and directs them. One senses in all this a unity of life that we can no longer imagine. It is all quite simple. The ancient city-state, gentlemen, was in reality a family: everyone in it was of the same blood. The conflicts that in our time divide the family, the church, and the state did not exist then. Our ideas on the separation of church and state, on free schools and public schools, made no sense then. The city-state was at the same time family, church, and state.

Such an organization, I repeat, was only possible in very small republics, founded on the nobility of the race. In large states, a similar dominion exercised over matters of the soul would have been an insufferable tyranny. Let us be clear as to what constituted liberty in these ancient Greek city-states. Liberty was the independence of the city-state, not the independence of the individual, the right of the individual to develop following his fancy, independently of the spirit of the city-state. The individual who wished to develop in this fashion emigrated; he would set out to colonize, or else he would seek asylum in some large state, a kingdom where the bases of intellectual and moral culture were not as constricting. There was probably more freedom, in the modern sense of the term, in Persia than in Sparta, and it was indeed the tyrannical aspect of this ancient discipline that propelled the world in the direction of the great empires, such as the Roman Empire, where people of all sorts were mixed without distinction of race and blood.

———— ∞∞∞ ————

The Roman Empire, gentlemen, sadly neglected public education, and certainly this was one of the causes of its weakness. I am convinced that, if the three emperors that succeeded each other from Nerva[6] to Marcus Aurelius[7] had directed their attention in this direction in a more sustained manner, the rapid decadence of this great machine would have been avoided. Christianity did what the Empire had not been able to do. Through a thousand persecutions, despite vexatious laws made expressly to hamper the private associations of citizens, Christianity gave rise to the era of the great free initiatives, of the great associations outside the state. It took charge of man more intimately than anything had before. The church in a sense revived the Greek city-state, and created a microcosm where man found reasons to behave well and reasons to love, in the midst of the icy cold of an egoistic society. Beginning with the triumph of Christianity in the fourth century, the state and the city renounce almost all rights over education, the church alone is entrusted with it; and notice, gentlemen, how dangerous it is in human affairs to follow a single direction exclusively: this association of souls, which raised the level of human morality so much, debased the human intellect [*l'esprit humain*] to complete nothingness for six or seven centuries. Recall what the sixth, seventh, eighth, ninth, and tenth centuries were like: a long slumber during which humanity forgot any learned tradition of antiquity and fully relapsed into barbarism.

The reawakening occurred in France; it occurred in Paris, at the time when Paris was most completely and most legitimately at the heart of Europe, under Philip Augustus,[8] around 1200, or I should say under Louis the Younger[9] and Suger,[10] in the age of Abelard.[11] At that time something wholly extraordinary was founded, namely the University of Paris, soon imitated throughout western Europe. The University of Paris, which begins to appear around 1200, is, I maintain, something wholly new and original. It sprang from the church, from the parvis of Notre-Dame, and it always remained to a greater or lesser extent under the often jealous surveillance of the church, so that, at the time of the Revolution, the degrees of the University of Paris were still granted by the chancellor of Notre-Dame. But a new power that was waxing then, the king of France, took the university under his protection and removed it to a considerable extent from ecclesiastical jurisdiction. The king of France, in proclaiming the University of Paris his first-born daughter, in reality emancipated education, and created the great regime of teaching guilds, partially independent from the state and possessing significant wealth independently from the state, which obtained such good results, and still obtains them in Germany and England. The Protestant Reformation completed the emancipation of the universities in the countries that adopted it, and gave to the church schools a rank they had not previously enjoyed, almost on a par with the church itself. In the Catholic countries, on the other hand, the importance that the Jesuit order obtained diminished the universities, and gave education a very questionable direction, in my opinion. But let us come to our own time, and to the system that after much trial and error from the National Assembly of 1789 to our day seems to have become a part of our customs, and that one may consider a sort of covenant established, after long debate, to satisfy equally legitimate expectations.

What characterizes all the works of the French Revolution, gentlemen, is the exaggeration of the idea of the state. Led by a powerful enthusiasm rather than ruled by a sense of reality, the men of that time believed it to be possible, in our great modern nations, to return to the idea of the ancient citizen, who lived only for the state. It was a noble error. Without doubt, modern man has a fatherland, and for the fatherland he will be able, if needs be, to equal the most commended acts of ancient heroism; but this fatherland cannot be a narrow mold, a kind of military order like Sparta and the republics of antiquity. Our modern states are too large for it. The fatherland, according to us, is a free society that all love because they find therein the means of developing their individuality, but that must not hinder anyone. The French Revolution did not understand this sufficiently, or, rather, it forgot it, for its original views on education were admirable. Almost all the remonstrances [*cahiers*, i.e., *Cahiers de doléances*] to the Estates General (the real program of the Revolution) insisted both on the creation of a general system of public education and on the proclamation of the freedom to teach. That is how things stood. One is struck with how upstanding and sound these first instincts of the Revolution were.

The plan of Mr. de Talleyrand,[12] read during the sessions of September 10 and 11, 1791, in the Constituent Assembly, is the most remarkable theory of public education ever proposed in our country. The role of liberty in it is quite large. It is already less so in the plan presented by Condorcet[13] to the Legislative Assembly, on April 20, 1792. A certain sectarian rigidity, which certainly has its grandeur, begins to obscure the necessities of real life. It is much worse in the Convention: Sparta is the universal dream. The child, according to the ideas often proclaimed during these times, must be removed from his family to be brought up according to the views of the state; parents (the true teachers, gentlemen, never forget it!) are held in suspicion. It was a strange, feverish state; the most contradictory ideas appeared. In the midst of these dreams, it is a happy surprise to see the terrible assembly at one point proclaim "the freedom to teach." This expression was nothing but a passing flash. The plans of the Directory and the Consulate strayed in the direction of an education imparted in principle by the state alone. Teaching became first a function of the state, then the work of a corporation completely dependent on the state. The organization of public education of 1802 and the Imperial University of 1806 are founded on this principle. The education of this period is wholly military, every school is a regiment divided into companies, with sergeants and corporals; everything takes place at drum's pace; the goal is much more to train soldiers than men. Man's interiority is completely disregarded. The role afforded to religion and morality is almost nonexistent. Certainly, religion is a part of the curriculum; it is allotted its class hours and exercises, but it is an official religion, a regimental religion, something like a military Mass, where one performs the exercise and hears nothing but the sound of guns and orders. There was no trace of true religion and true morality, the kind one draws from a family tradition, from a mother's lessons, from the dreamy pastimes of a free youth. Hence, the tinge of aridity, brutality, and narrow-mindedness that characterizes the age. Only the small seminaries, tolerated, but strictly limited, offered an escape from this oppression; there the poetic soul of a Lamartine[14] could be formed. Recall the first moment of anger of this great poet against

> these geometric men, who alone were allowed to speak then, and who crushed us, the young, with the insolent tyranny of their triumph, thinking they had caused to wither forever in us what they had in fact managed

to blight and kill in themselves, the whole moral, divine, melodious part of human thought. Nothing can depict, for those who did not experience it, the haughty barrenness of that age.

I will not recount the struggles that followed, which belong entirely to contemporary history. Suffice it to say that a sort of concordat seems to have been reached between those who wish the state to be the only teacher and those who would entrust education entirely to private enterprise. In this new system, gentlemen, the state plays the role of the champion, the chief promoter of education: it sustains pecuniary expenses for its sake, as do the towns. Society, ultimately, takes an active interest in a matter that it perceives as being of great importance to it, but it does not force anyone. It does not punish the father guilty of not educating his son. The father who does not want anything to do with public schools has others from which to choose. I will not examine if this ideal is actually put into practice; in particular, I will not explore whether the state applies to the direction of public education the solid and liberal spirit that would be proper to such a subject. I only concern myself with the general system. As for me, such a system has my endorsement, for it balances reasonably well, were it to be faithfully implemented, the rights of the family and the rights of the state.

It is in fact clear, gentlemen, that a system of education analogous to that of Greek antiquity, a uniform system, compulsory for all, that removes the child from the family, submitting him to a discipline that might offend the conscience of the father—such a system, I say, is in our day and age absolutely impossible. Rather than being an educational mechanism, it would be a mechanism of brutification, stupidity, and ignorance. The ideas of the age of the Revolution (with the exception of Talleyrand's project) and especially Napoleon the First's university were struck in this regard by a fatal flaw. Read the regulation of studies from 1802: "All activities related to meals, recreation, excursions, sleep shall be organized by company . . . There shall be in each lycée a library with 1,500 volumes; all libraries shall contain the same works. No other work shall be placed therein without the authorization of the Minister of the Interior."

This is what Mr. Thiers[15] calls "perhaps the most beautiful creation of the reign of Napoleon." We beg to differ. This uniformity of education, this bureaucratic attitude [*esprit officiel*] would be the intellectual death of a nation. No, this is in no way our ideal. The state must uphold a standard, not impose one. Even with regards to the question of whether the state should declare a certain *minimum* level of instruction compulsory, I hesitate. That there is a moral obligation for the father to provide his son with the necessary education, the education that makes a man a man, is too obvious even to mention. But should such an obligation be written into the law, and associated with a criminal penalty? Well, I repeat, I am hesitant. If a father, or a mother (and this will be a frequent case) undertook to provide or have others provide their child in the home with an education that they believe is best, how will one determine whether such an education is the equivalent of what is furnished in a primary school? Will the child be subjected to an exam? This exam troubles me. Who will administer it? What topics will it cover? Certainly, if practical persons assured me that such a legislation were necessary to break the weight of ignorance that crushes us, I would consent; but I do not think that this is the case. Things stand quite differently with regards to the question of whether elementary education should be free of cost; this is desirable. It is necessary that the father who does not educate his son be inexcusable. May the blame of the public latch onto him—that is right and good! But I wish for nothing more. The true penalty in this respect, as with all things of the moral realm, is to allow through freedom a strong public opinion to form, which will deal severely with the many misdeeds that the law will never reach.

In any case, a key distinction must be made here, a distinction that will allow us to delve more deeply into our subject. Among the many different parts of which man's culture is comprised, some can be furnished by the state, indeed can be well furnished only by it; there are others, however, for which the state is completely incompetent. The moral and intellectual culture of man, in fact, is comprised of two well-distinct parts: on one hand, *schooling*, the acquisition of a certain amount of positive knowledge, which differs according to the vocation and aptitude of the young man; on the other, *education*, the education, I say, that is equally necessary to all of us, the education that makes gentlemen, honorable men, well-brought-up men. It is clear that this second part is the most important one. It is permissible to be ignorant of many things, or even to be ignorant in the absolute sense of the term; it is impermissible to be a man without principles of morality, to be badly brought up. That these two fundamental elements of human culture can be separated, alas, is but too clear! Do you not encounter every day very knowledgeable men devoid of distinction, kindness, sometimes even honesty? Do you not see, on the other hand, excellent people, delicate, distinguished, who are defenseless against all the snares of ignorance and absurdity? It is clear that perfection lies in reuniting the two. Now, of the two, the former, schooling, the state alone can best furnish, but for the latter, education, the state can do little. If you leave schooling to the initiative and choice of individuals, it will be very weak. The dignity of the professor will not be sufficiently safeguarded: the appreciation of his knowledge will be abandoned to arbitrary and superficial judgments. If on the other hand you leave education to the state, it will do what it can, but it will simply produce those great boarding schools, the unfortunate heritage of the Jesuits of the seventeenth and eighteenth centuries, where the child, separated from his family, isolated from the world and from interaction with the other sex, can acquire neither distinction nor tact. I must admit, the more I maintain the primacy of the state in teaching proper, the more I would like to see the state give up its boarding schools: the responsibility is too great, this is a task only the family can perform effectively. Education is respect for what is truly good, great, and beautiful; it is politeness, the charming virtue that stands in for many other virtues; it is tact, which is almost a virtue as well. No professor can teach all this.

Where can the child and the young man learn this purity, this fine quality of conscience, basis of any solid morality, this crowning sentiment that one day will constitute the charm of the grown man? In books, in lessons carefully followed, in rote-learned texts? Certainly not, gentlemen: such things are learned in the atmosphere where one lives, in the social environment in which one is placed; they are learned through the family, not otherwise. Schooling is imparted in class, in a lycée, at school; education is received in the paternal home; the teachers are the mother, the sisters. Recall, gentlemen, the beautiful description by John Chrysostom[16] of his entry into the school of the rhetorician Libanius,[17] in Antioch. Libanius was accustomed to questioning each new student who arrived at his school about his past, his parents, and his country. John, thus questioned, told him that his mother, Anthusa, having been widowed at twenty, refused to remarry in order to devote herself completely to his education. "O Gods of Greece," exclaimed the old rhetorician, "what mothers and what widows among these Christians!" This is the model, gentlemen. Yes, only the profoundly serious and moral woman can tend to the wounds of our time, refashion the education of man, revive the appreciation for the good and the beautiful. To this end, one must take back the child and not entrust him to paid care or be separated from him, except during the hours consecrated to the teaching of classes, or at any age deprive him completely of the company of females. I am to such an extent convinced by these principles that I would like to see introduced among us a custom that exists in other nations, and produces excellent results for them: the schools for the two sexes should be separated as late as possible, school should be common to both for as long as possible, and this common school should be headed by a woman. Man, in the presence of women, has the sentiment of something more fragile, more delicate, more distinguished than himself. This obscure and deep instinct has been the basis of all civilization, man drawing from this sentiment the desire to submit himself, to render service to the more fragile being, to demonstrate his secret sympathy to her through gentle care and politeness. The interaction of man and woman is thus essentially educational. The education of man is impossible without women. The argument, I believe, is that the separation I oppose is enforced in the interests of morality; I am persuaded that it is one of the causes of the lack of respect for women that is regrettably to be encountered in certain youths. German youths certainly have purer customs than our own, and nonetheless their education is much freer, much less barrack-like.

"What you describe," one may reply, "is an impossible ideal. Even in a great city, such a system of education would, given our customs, be extremely difficult. In the small towns, in the countryside, it is impossible; the boarding school is the necessary consequence of the fact that not all families have an educational institution at their doorstep where they can send their children." I realize that I am describing an ideal that, in many cases, will be hard to attain. All I claim is that the boarding school must always be considered a second-best solution. Even in the cases in which the separation of the child from the family is necessary, I would forgo this desperate method as much as possible. Germany, so advanced in terms of education, has scarcely any boarding schools. How do they achieve this? If a family is obliged to separate itself from a child, it places him with relatives, with friends, with pastors, with professors who have with them a dozen pupils or so. At an age in which we believe a child needs to be overseen constantly, they do not hesitate to leave him to his own devices, to give him the responsibility to house himself, to feed himself, to navigate a big city. But if our customs do not permit such arrangements, if the new shape of Paris in particular lends itself as little as possible to this city remaining what it has always been, a city of studies, I would have at least one demand: that boarding schools, if they are necessary, not be administered by the state, that they be private establishments placed under the control of the parents who have the responsibility of choosing among them.

*Responsibility*—a fundamental term, gentlemen, which holds the secret of almost all the moral reforms of our age. An excess of precautions, of preventive measures, appears to be wisdom; it has only one drawback, which is to cut the roots of good and evil at one stroke. The error of our old French habits, in education as in many other matters, was to attempt to diminish responsibility. The parents' aim was to find a good establishment to which they could entrust their child with a clear conscience, so as not to have to worry about him anymore. Well, this is very immoral. Nothing excuses man from his duties, from his responsibility before God. This fashion of placing the child outside the family environment during his education is, I repeat, a heritage of the system introduced by the Jesuits, who have so often misled the ideas of our country with regards to education. What was the tactic of the Jesuits in the sixteenth and seventeenth centuries to attain their goal, which was to gain hold of the education of youth? It was quite simple. They gained an ascendant over the mother, and portrayed for her the terrible weight that the education of her children would place upon her before God. Then they offered a very convenient way to escape this responsibility, that is, to entrust her children to the Order. They explained to her, with all possible precaution, that she did not possess the competence for education, that she must confer this care to the authorized doctors (an enormous error! In such a matter the authorized doctor, gentlemen, is the mother). Entrusted to the best teachers, the child no longer weighed on the conscience of the parents. Alas! The mother, too often flighty, willingly heeded this argument; she herself was perhaps not unhappy to be free of her austere cares. Thus, everyone was content; the mother was free to pursue her pleasures and certain of going to Heaven; the Reverend Father guaranteed it. Hence this fateful separation of mother and child was consummated;

hence was the cruelest wound inflicted on our national customs; hence were these gigantic schools founded, of which the old *collège* Louis-le-Grand[18] (which at the time belonged to the Jesuits) was the first model. The invention was considered admirable; it was disastrous, and we are still suffering its consequences. Woman gave up her noblest task, the one she alone can accomplish. The family, rather than being considered the basis of education, was held to be an obstacle. It was considered suspect; it was kept at a distance as much as possible, and the child was warned against the influence of his parents; his days off from school were presented as days of danger for him. The university itself imitated the Jesuit boarding schools more than it should have, and this regiment-like organization became the fundamental trait of French education. I believe nothing good can come of it. The church, the monastery, the medieval college (which was quite different from our lycées) did in their own way bring up men, and created a more or less complete type of education. Only one institution never could bring up anyone: the barracks. Notice the sad memories our young men often retain of the years that should have been the happiest of their lives. Notice how few derive from this boarding life the solid principles of morality and the deep instincts that put man, so to speak, in the happy position of being incapable of evil. A uniform rule is not able to produce distinguished individual characters. Any friendliness between teacher and students is, in such circumstances, almost impossible.

Who, indeed, is the teacher with whom the boarding school student in a lycée is most often in contact? It is the supervisor, the proctor [*maître d'étude*]. There is much hidden dedication, much honorable abnegation among these respectable teachers. However, I fear it may always prove impossible for the state to train a body of proctors who are equal to the task. This is not the case for professors; only the state, as I have said, will be able to have a body of eminent professors. But for proctors, it is quite the opposite. Condemned to a subaltern role with respect to the professors and the administration, the body of supervisors in state establishments, despite some very honorable exceptions, will always fall short of expectations. Now, such a body, almost insignificant if the state limits itself to its true role, which is to provide schooling in day-schools, becomes more important if the state undertakes the difficult task of raising men in their entirety.

In all things, ladies and gentlemen, let us return to the traditions that an enlightened Christianity and a wholesome philosophy concur in teaching us. The most glorious trait of France is that, better than any other nation, it is capable of perceiving its faults and censuring itself. In this we resemble Athens, where the brighter sort spent their time speaking ill of their city and praising the institutions of Sparta. Let us realize that we would be prolonging the brilliant and spirited society of the past two centuries very poorly if we were to be nothing but flippant. Simply imitating one's ancestors' flaws is to honor them poorly. Let us beware of taking to extremes the risky game that consists in consuming without abatement the living forces of a country, behaving like the Arab horsemen who gallop their steeds up to the edge of the precipice, believing they always have it in their power to stop them.—The world only stands upright thanks to a bit of virtue; ten just individuals often are enough to absolve a guilty society; the more the consciousness of humanity becomes set, the more virtue will be necessary. Egoism, the passionate search for wealth and pleasure are in a position to found nothing at all. Thus, let us all do our duty, gentlemen. We all, in our several ranks, are the guardians of a tradition that is necessary for the continuation of God's work in this world. Assuredly, strange is the situation of man, placed between the imperious dictates of moral conscience and the uncertainties of a destiny that Providence chose to cover with a veil. Let us heed our conscience, and believe in it. If, God forbid!, duty were a trap set for us by a deceiving spirit, it would be a worthy thing to have been fooled thus. But this is not the case: as far as I am concerned, I hold the truths of natural religion to be as certain, in their way, as those of the real world. This is the faith that saves, the faith that allows us to envisage the few days we spend on this earth as something besides senseless revelry; the faith that assures us that all is not in vain in the noble aspirations of our heart; the faith that strengthens us and that, if at times clouds gather on the horizon, shows us, beyond the storm, the joyful fields where humanity, drying its tears, will one day console itself of its sufferings.

# 5

## CONSTITUTIONAL MONARCHY IN FRANCE (*LA MONARCHIE CONSTITUTIONNELLE EN FRANCE*, 1869)

istory is neither an inflexible geometry nor a simple succession of fortuitous incidents. If history were dominated in an absolute fashion by necessity, everything could be predicted; if it were a simple game of passion and fortune, nothing could be predicted. Now, the truth is that human affairs, while they often prove wrong the conjectures of the most sagacious minds, nonetheless lend themselves to calculation. The events that have come to pass contain, if one can distinguish the essential from the superfluous, the general lines of the future. The role of accidents is limited. "The small grain of sand that fell in Cromwell's urethra"[1] was a capital event in the seventeenth century; nonetheless, the philosophy of history of England is independent of such a detail. Health or illness, good or bad disposition of princes, quarrels or reconciliations of significant personages, diplomatic intrigues, alternating vicissitudes of war—the greatest genius is of no use in predicting all this. These types of events take place in a world where reasoning has no application—the personal valet of a sovereign could, with regard to important news, rearrange the ideas of the greatest mind; but these accidents, impossible to predict and to determine a priori, fade away on the whole. The past presents us with a continuous design, in which everything fits and makes sense; the future will judge our time like we judge the past, and will see rigorous consequences where we are often tempted to see nothing more than individual wills and chance encounters.

It is in this spirit that we would like to propose a few observations on the serious events that took place in this year 1869. The philosophy we deploy in this examination will not be that of indifference. We do not exaggerate to ourselves the role of reflection in the conduct of human affairs; however, we do not believe the time has yet come to flee public life and abandon the affairs of this world to intrigue and violence. A rebuke can always be aimed at those who criticize the affairs of their century without having accepted to get involved in them; but those who have done what an honest man can do, those who have said what they think without worrying about being liked or disliked by anyone, can rest completely easy in their conscience. We do not owe our country a betrayal of truth for its sake, a failure of taste or tact for its sake; we do not owe it the following of its whims or conversion to the thesis that finds favor; we owe it to say, quite precisely and without the sacrifice of any nuance, what we believe is the truth.

|

The French Revolution is so extraordinary an event that it must be the starting point for any series of considerations on the affairs of our time. Anything important that happens in France is a direct consequence of this capital occurrence, which has profoundly changed the conditions of life in this country. Like anything great, heroic, bold, like anything that surpasses the common measure of human forces, the French Revolution will for centuries be the subject that people will discuss, that will divide them, that will serve as a pretext to love or hate one other, that will provide the subject matter for plays and novels. In one sense, the French Revolution (the Empire, as I think of it, is part of the same whole) is the glory of France, the French age par excellence; but almost always the nations that have in their history an exceptional fact atone for this fact with long suffering and often pay for it with their national existence. So it was for Judaea, Greece, and Italy. These countries have traversed centuries of humiliation and national death for having created unique products the world lives and profits by. National life is a limited, mediocre, bounded thing. To do something extraordinary, universal, one must tear this narrow network asunder; by this same act, one tears one's fatherland asunder, a fatherland being a set of prejudices and fixed ideas that humanity as a whole could not accept. The nations that created religion, art, science, empire, the church, and the papacy (which are all universal, not national things) were more than nations; they were by that same token less than nations in that they were victims of their work. I think that the Revolution will have similar consequences for France, but less lasting, because the accomplishments of France were less lasting and less universal than those of Judaea, Greece, and Italy. The exact parallel of the current situation of our country seems to me to be Germany in the seventeenth century. Germany in the sixteenth century had accomplished a task of the highest importance for humanity, the Reformation. In the seventeenth it atoned for it by an extreme political debasement. It is likely that in the history of France the nineteenth century will similarly be considered as the expiation of the Revolution. Nations do not depart with impunity from the mean, which is that of practical common sense and viability, any more than individuals do.

If indeed the Revolution created a poetic and sentimental position of the first order for France in the world, it is certain, on the other hand, merely considering the requirements of ordinary politics, that it has committed France to a path filled with eccentricities. The goal France wished to achieve by the Revolution is the one all modern nations pursue: a just, honest, humane society, guaranteeing the rights and freedom of all with the least possible sacrifice of the rights and freedom of each. France today, after spilling torrents of blood, is very far from this goal, whereas England, which did not proceed by revolutions, has almost reached it. France, in other words, presents this strange spectacle of a country belatedly attempting to catch up with the nations it had considered backward, learning from the people to which it had claimed to impart lessons, and striving to achieve by imitation the work in which it believed it was deploying great originality.

The cause of this historical oddity is quite simple. Despite the strange fire animating it, France at the end of the eighteenth century was fairly ignorant of the preconditions for existence of a nation and of humanity. Its prodigious attempt entailed many mistakes; it completely misunderstood the rules of modern liberty. Whether one grieves or rejoices for it, modern liberty is nothing like ancient liberty or that of the republics of the Middle Ages. It is much more real, but much less dazzling. Thucydides

and Machiavelli would not understand it, and yet a subject of Queen
Victoria is a thousand times freer than any citizen of Sparta, Athens,
Venice, or Florence was. No more of these feverish republican agitations,
full of nobility and danger; no more of these cities composed of a refined
people, vibrant and aristocratic; in their place, large stolid masses, where
intelligence is the privilege of a few, but which contribute mightily to
civilization by placing at the disposal of the state, through conscription
and taxation, a wonderful treasure of abnegation, docility, good character.
England sets the model for this way of existing, which is certainly the
one that wears down a nation the least, and preserves its strengths best.
England has reached the most liberal state the world has known so far
by developing its institutions of the Middle Ages, and not by revolution.
Freedom in England does not derive from Cromwell nor from the republicans of 1649; it derives from its entire history, from its equal respect for
the rights of the king, the rights of the lords, the rights of municipalities
and corporations of all kinds. France went in the opposite direction. The
king had long swept aside the rights of the lords and the commons; the
nation swept aside the rights of the king. It proceeded philosophically in
a matter where one must proceed historically: it believed that freedom is
established by the sovereignty of the people and in the name of a central
authority, whereas freedom is only obtained by a succession of small local
victories, by slow reforms. England, not priding itself on any philosophy,
England, which only broke with its tradition for a single moment of passing disorientation followed by a prompt repentance, England, which, in
place of the absolute dogma of the sovereignty of the people, only accepts
the more moderate principle that there is no government without the people or against the people, found itself a thousand times freer than France,
which had so proudly raised the philosophical banner of the rights of
man. The fact is that the sovereignty of the people does not institute constitutional government. The state thus established in the French fashion
is too strong; far from guaranteeing all freedoms, it absorbs all freedoms;
its shape is the Convention[2] or despotism. What was to emerge from the
Revolution could not, ultimately, differ much from the Consulate[3] and the
Empire; what was to emerge from such a conception of society could not
be anything but public administration, a network of prefects, a narrow-
minded civil code, a machine for grasping the nation, a swaddling cloth
in which it would be impossible for it to live and grow. Nothing is more

unjust than the hatred with which the French radical school treats the achievements of Napoleon. The achievements of Napoleon, except for a few errors that were personal to this extraordinary man, were in sum nothing but the revolutionary program executed in its viable parts. Even if Napoleon had not existed, the final constitution of the Republic would not have differed fundamentally from the constitution of the year VIII.

Indeed, what lies at the heart of all French revolutionary efforts is a notion of human society that is quite incorrect in several ways. The original mistake was masked at first by the magnificent outburst of enthusiasm for freedom and right that filled the early years of the Revolution; but once this beautiful fire died out, there remained a social theory, which was dominant under the Directory,[4] the Consulate, and the Empire and deeply marked all the creations of the time.

According to this theory, which can well be described as materialism in politics, society is not something religious or sacred. It has only one goal: for the individuals composing it to enjoy the greatest possible amount of well-being, with no thought of the ideal destiny of mankind. Dare we speak of uplifting, of ennobling human consciousness? It is only a question of pleasing the many, of providing everyone with a kind of vulgar and certainly quite relative happiness, since the noble soul would abhor such happiness and would revolt against the society that claimed to provide it. In the eyes of an enlightened philosophy, society is a great providential occurrence; it is established not by man but by nature itself, so that intellectual and moral life may happen on the surface of our planet. Isolated man has never existed. Human society, the mother of any ideal, is the direct product of the supreme will that desires that goodness, truth, and beauty have beholders in the world. This transcendental function of humanity is not accomplished through the simple coexistence of individuals. Society is a hierarchy. All individuals are noble and sacred, all beings (even animals) have rights; but all beings are not equal, all are members of a large body, parts of an immense organism that fulfills a divine task. The negation of this divine task is the error that French democracy easily commits. Believing that the enjoyment of the individual is the sole goal of society, it is led to disregard the rights of ideas, the primacy of the spirit. Besides, not understanding racial inequality, because in fact ethnographic differences disappeared from its midst from time immemorial, France is led to conceive of a sort of universal mediocrity as social perfection. God save us from dreaming of the resurrection of what is defunct; but without advocating the reconstitution of the nobility, it is quite acceptable to deem the emphasis bestowed on birth to be better in many respects than the emphasis bestowed on wealth; one is no more just than the other, and the only right distinction, which is that of merit and virtue, is more readily found in a society where rank is settled by birth than in a society where wealth alone determines inequality.

Human life would become impossible if men did not grant themselves the right to subject animals to their needs; it would be hardly less impossible if one maintained the abstract notion that considers all men as holding at birth an equal right to wealth and social rank. Such a state of affairs, equitable in appearance, would spell the end of all virtue; it would inevitably entail hatred and war between the sexes, since nature created, within the human species itself, an undeniable difference of roles. The bourgeoisie considers it fair that, after having liquidated hereditary royalty and nobility, one should halt before hereditary wealth. The worker considers it fair that, after having liquidated hereditary wealth, one should halt before the inequalities of gender, and even, if he has but a little sense, before the inequalities of strength and ability. The most exalted utopian considers it fair that, after having liquidated in imagination any inequality among men, one should accept the right of men to employ animals according to their needs. And yet it is no fairer for an individual to be born rich than it is for an individual to be born with social status; the one has obtained his privilege through personal effort no more than the other. One always begins with the idea that nobility had merit as its origin, and, as it is clear that merit is not hereditary, it is easily proven that hereditary nobility is absurd; but this is the eternal French error of distributive justice, which the state should adjudicate. The social purpose of nobility, considered as a publicly beneficial institution, was not to reward merit, but to provoke certain types of merit, to render them possible, even easy. Had it only had the effect of showing that justice should not be sought in the official constitution of society, it would have already achieved something. The slogan "to the worthiest" has few applications in politics.

The French bourgeoisie is deluded in believing it is building a just society by its system of public examinations, special schools, and regular progression. The people will easily show it that poor children are excluded from these examinations, and will maintain that justice will be served only when all the French will be placed at birth in identical conditions. In other words, no society is possible if we push notions of distributive justice with regard to individuals to their extreme conclusions. A nation that would pursue such a program would condemn itself to an incurable weakness. Eliminating heredity, and thereby destroying the family or rendering it optional, it would soon be defeated either by the parts of it that retain the old principles, or by foreign nations that retain these principles. The race that triumphs is always the one where family and property are the most highly organized. Mankind is a mysterious ladder, a series of results proceeding from each other. Hardworking generations of commoners and peasants produce the existence of the honest and thrifty bourgeois, who in turn produces the nobleman, the man exempt from material labor, entirely devoted to disinterested matters. Each in its own rank is the guardian of a tradition that is important for the progress of civilization. There are not two moralities, two sciences, or two educations. There is but one intellectual and moral aggregate, a splendid accomplishment of the human mind, of which everyone except the selfish creates a small part and in which everyone participates to some degree.

Mankind perishes if one does not accept that entire classes must live for the glory and the enjoyment of others. The democrat considers the peasant of the old order, who works for his nobles, loves them, and enjoys the high life others lead by his labor, to be duped. Certainly, this is nonsensical from the perspective of a narrow, withdrawn life, where everything happens behind closed doors, as in our days. In the present state of society, the advantages that one man enjoys over another have become exclusive and personal matters: to rejoice in the pleasure or nobility of others seems an extravagance; but it has not always been thus. When Gubbio or Assisi saw the wedding cavalcade of their young lord pass by, no one was jealous. At that time, everyone participated in the life of all; the poor delighted in the wealth of the rich, the monk in the joys of the worldly, the worldly in the monk's prayers; for all there was art, poetry, religion.

Will the cold considerations of the economist manage to replace all this? Will they be sufficient to curb the arrogance of a democracy sure of itself, which, not having halted before sovereignty, will be more than tempted not to halt before property? Will there be sufficiently eloquent voices to make eighteen-year-old youths accept arguments for old men, to persuade young ardent social classes, who believe in pleasure, and are not yet disillusioned with enjoyment, that it is not possible for all to enjoy, for all to be well educated, polite, even virtuous in the refined sense, but that nonetheless there must exist men of leisure, scholars, well educated, polite, virtuous, in whom and through whom others may delight and taste the ideal? The events will tell. The superiority of the church and the strength that still guarantees its future is that it alone understands this fact and renders it intelligible. The church knows that the best are often the victims of the superiority of the allegedly higher classes; but it also knows that nature intended the life of humanity to occur at several levels. It knows and admits that it is the coarseness of many that produces the education of a single one, it is the sweat of many that permits the noble life of a few; nonetheless, it does not call these privileged or those dispossessed, because for it the task of humanity is indivisible. Abolish this great law, place all individuals on the same plane, with equal rights, without ties of subordination to a common endeavor, and you will have selfishness, mediocrity, isolation, barrenness, the impossibility of living, something like the life of our time—the saddest that ever was led, even for the common man. If you only consider the right of individuals, it is unfair that a man be sacrificed to another; but it is not unfair that all be subject to the superior endeavor being carried out by mankind. It belongs to religion to explain these mysteries and to offer in the ideal world superabundant consolations to all who are sacrificed here below.

This is what the Revolution, as soon as it lost its great sacred intoxication of the early days, did not sufficiently understand. The Revolution was ultimately irreligious and atheist. The society it dreamed of in the sad days following the bout of fever, when it sought to collect itself, is a kind of regiment composed of materialists, in which discipline takes the place of virtue. The completely negative basis that the dry and hard men of the time gave French society can only produce a rogue and rude people; their code, a product of distrust, has as its first principle that everything is assessed in terms of money, that is to say, of pleasure. Jealousy sums up the entire moral theory of these alleged founders of our laws. Now, jealousy institutes equality, not liberty; putting man always on his guard against the encroachments of his fellow man, it prevents sociability between classes. No society without love, without tradition, without respect, without mutual agreeableness. In its false notion of virtue, which it mistakes for the bitter claim of what each sees as his right, the democratic school does not realize that the great virtue of a nation is to withstand traditional inequality. According to this school, the most virtuous race is not the race that practices sacrifice, devotion, idealism in all its forms, but the most turbulent, the one that provokes the most revolutions. One surprises the most intelligent democrats considerably when one tells them that there still are virtuous races in the world, the Lithuanians, for example, the Dithmarsians, the Pomeranians, feudal races, full of vital forces in reserve, who understand duty as Kant does, and for whom the term revolution is meaningless.

The first consequence of this surly and superficial philosophy, which supplanted that of Montesquieu and Turgot[5] too soon, was the abolition of royalty. For minds imbued with a materialistic philosophy, royalty must have seemed an anomaly. Very few people understood in 1792 that the continuity of good things must be safeguarded by institutions that are, if you will, a privilege for some, but that constitute the organs of national life without which certain needs remain unattended. These small fortresses in which society's treasures were kept safe appeared akin to feudal towers. All traditional subordination, all historical pacts, all symbols were denied. Royalty was the first of these pacts, a pact dating back a thousand years, a symbol that the puerile philosophy of history then in vogue could not understand. No nation has ever created more complete a legend than this great Capetian[6] royalty, a kind of religion, born in Saint-Denis, consecrated in Reims by the community of bishops, with its own rites, its liturgy, its holy ampulla, its oriflamme. To each nationality corresponds a dynasty in which the genius and the interests of the nation are embodied; a national consciousness is fixed and firm only once it has contracted an indissoluble marriage with a family that undertakes by contract not to have any interests distinct from those of the nation. Never was this identity as perfect as between the Capetian House and France. It was more than a royalty, it was a priesthood; a priest-king like David, the king of France wears the cope and wields the sword. God enlightens his judgments. The king of England concerns himself but little with justice, he defends his rights against his barons; the emperor of Germany concerns himself even less with it, forever hunting in the mountains of Tyrol as the ball of the world rolls as it will; the king of France, though, is just: surrounded by his counselors and his solemn clerics, with his hand of justice, he resembles Solomon. His coronation, imitated from the kings of

Israel, was something strange and unique. France had created an eighth sacrament,* which was only administered at Reims, the sacrament of royalty. The anointed king performs miracles; he is invested with an "order": he is an ecclesiastical figure of the highest rank. To the pope, who admonishes him in the name of God, he responds by showing his anointment: "I too am of God!" He allows himself unparalleled freedoms with the successor of Peter. Once he had him arrested and declared a heretic; another time, he threatens to have him burnt at the stake; backed by his doctors of the Sorbonne, he sermonizes him, deposes him. Notwithstanding this, his most perfect type is a canonized king, Saint Louis,[7] so pure, so humble, so simple and strong. He has his mystical worshipers; the good Joan of Arc did not distinguish him from Saint Michael and Saint Catherine; this poor girl lived the religion of Reims, to the letter. Incomparable legend! Holy fable! It is the vulgar knife intended to bring down the heads of criminals that is brandished against it! The murder of January 21[8] is, from the point of view of the idealist, the most hideous act of materialism, the most shameful profession of ingratitude and baseness, of commoner vileness and neglect of the past that was ever committed.

Is this to say that the old order—whose memory the new society sought to remove with the particular kind of relentlessness found only in the upstart against the great lord to whom he owes everything—is this to say that this old order was not seriously guilty? Certainly it was: if I were now discussing the general philosophy of our history, I would show that the royalty, the nobility, the clergy, the parliaments, the cities, the universities of the old France had all failed in their duties, and that the revolutionaries of 1793 did nothing but bring to fruition a series of mistakes whose consequences weigh heavily on us. One always atones for one's greatness. France had conceived of its kingship as something unlimited. A king after the English fashion, a kind of stadtholder paid and armed to defend the nation and to hold certain rights, appeared paltry to its eyes. Since the thirteenth century, the king of England, constantly at war with his subjects and bound by charters, is an object of derision for our French poets; he is not powerful enough. French royalty was too sacred; one cannot control the anointed of the Lord; Bossuet[9] was consistent in drawing the

---

* The word *sacrament* is used for the coronation of Reims. *Hist. litt. de la France*, t. XXVI, p. 122.

theory of the king of France from scripture. If the king of England had had that tinge of mysticism, the barons and the towns would have failed to subdue him. French royalty, to produce the brilliant meteor of the reign of Louis XIV,[10] had absorbed all the powers of the nation. The day after the state found itself constituted under a single hand in this powerful unity, it was inevitable that France would take itself as the great king had made it with its all-powerful central government, its freedoms destroyed, and, judging the king superfluous, would treat him as a mold that has grown useless once the statue is cast. Richelieu[11] and Louis XIV were thus the great revolutionaries, the true founders of the Republic. The exact counterpart of the colossal royalty of Louis XIV is the Republic of 1793, with its frightening concentration of powers, incredible monster, the likes of which had never been seen. Examples of republics are not rare in history; but these republics are cities or small confederate states. What is absolutely unprecedented is a centralized republic of thirty million souls. Exposed for four or five years to the vacillations of the drunken man, like a sinking *Great Eastern*,[12] the enormous machine fell back into its natural bed, into the hands of a powerful despot, who at first was capable of organizing the new movement with prodigious skill, but who met the end of all despots. Mad with pride, he drew upon the country that had delivered itself to him the cruelest insult a nation can experience, and caused the return of the dynasty that France had expelled with the worst outrages.

II

The analogy of such a course of events with what happened in England in the seventeenth century is easy to notice. This struck everyone in 1830, when one saw a national movement substitute the legitimate branch of the Bourbons with a collateral branch more willing to take the new needs into account. Louis-Philippe[13] must have seemed a William III,[14] and one had reason to hope that the final consequence of so many convulsions would be the peaceful establishment of a constitutional regime in France. A kind of peace, a bit of tranquility and oblivion penetrated with this consoling thought into our poor troubled French consciousness; everything was pardoned, even the follies and crimes, and one considered oneself the privileged generation, destined to reap the fruit of the mistakes of past generations. This was a great illusion; the most inconceivable surprise in history was successful; a band of lunatics, against whom the constable's stick should have been sufficient, overthrew a dynasty on which the sensible part of the nation had rested all its political faith, all its hopes. To dispatch a theory conceived by the best minds out of the most attractive appearances, one hour of thoughtlessness in some, of weakness in others, sufficed.

What are the reasons for this singular discomfiture? Why did what occurred in England not occur in France? Why did Louis-Philippe not become a William III, glorious founder of a new era in the history of our country? Should one say it was the fault of Louis-Philippe? It would be unfair. Louis-Philippe made some mistakes; but all governments must be allowed to commit some. Whoever took the lead of human affairs on the condition of being infallible and impeccable would not reign a single day. In any case, if Louis-Philippe deserved to be dethroned, William III deserved it much more. What has been most criticized in Louis-Philippe, unpopularity, inability to inspire love, a taste for personal power, lack of concern for external glory, convergence with the Legitimist party to the detriment of the party that had made him king, efforts to reconstitute the royal prerogative, could be criticized all the more in William III. Why then were results so different? Undoubtedly this had to do with the difference of times and countries. Historical operations possible among a serious and lumbering people, full of trust in heredity, with an invincible repugnance to force the last resistance of the sovereign, may be impossible in a time of spiritual levity and argumentative thoughtlessness. Besides, the republican movement of 1649 was infinitely less deep than that of 1792. The English movement of 1649 did not come to constitute an imperial power; Cromwell was not a Napoleon. Lastly, the English republican party did not have a second generation. Crushed by the restoration of the Stuarts,[15] decimated by persecution or seeking refuge in America, it ceased to exert any considerable influence on the affairs of England. In the eighteenth century, England seems to assume the task of atonement by a sort of exaggeration of *loyalism* and orthodoxy for its momentary deviations of the mid-seventeenth century. It took more than a hundred and fifty years for the death of Charles I to cease being an influence on politics, for anyone to dare think freely and not feel obliged to display a wild legitimism. Things would have turned out in much the same way in France, if the royalist reaction of 1796 and 1797[16] had prevailed. Restoration would have taken a much more earnest appearance, and the Republic would have been in the history of France what it is in the history of England, an inconsequential incident. Napoleon, by his genius, and aided by the wonderful resources of France, saved the Revolution, gave it a shape, an organization, an unprecedented military prestige.

The weak and unintelligent Restoration of 1814 could in no way uproot an idea that had lived so deeply within the nation and carried after it an energetic generation. France, under the Restoration and under Louis-Philippe, continued to live off the memories of the Empire and the Republic. The Revolution regained favor. While in England, beginning with the restoration of Charles II and after 1688, the republic was relentlessly cursed, and a man was ill-placed in polite society if he named Charles I without calling him the martyr king, or Cromwell without describing him as a usurper, in France it became the norm to couch histories of the Revolution in an apologetic and admiring tone. It was a serious matter that the father of the new king had taken a considerable part in the Revolution;[17] one became accustomed to considering the new dynasty a compromise with the Revolution, rather than the inheritor by substitution of a legitimacy. A new republican party, linked with some old surviving patriarchs of 1793, managed to regroup. This party, which had played a significant role in July 1830, but had subsequently failed to impose its absolute theoretical ideas, never ceased to lambast the new government. The alteration of 1688 in England had had nothing revolutionary about it, in the sense in which we understand the word; the people did not cause this alteration; it violated no rights, except those of the dethroned king. In our case, on the contrary, 1830 unleashed some anarchic forces and deeply humiliated the Legitimist party. This party, which in some respects contained the most solid and moral parts of the country, waged a cruel war against the new dynasty, whether by its abstention, preventing it from resting on the sole basis that establishes a dynasty, the heavily conservative element, or by its connivance with the republican party. Thus, the government of the House of Orléans could not be seriously established; a puff of wind overthrew it. William III was forgiven everything; Louis-Philippe was forgiven nothing. In England the monarchical principle was strong enough to undergo a transformation; it was not in France. Certainly, if the republican party in

England under William III had had the importance it had in France under Louis-Philippe, if such a party had had the support of the faction of the Stuarts, the constitutional settlement of England would not have lasted. In this case, England benefited from a huge advantage it possesses: its aptitude for colonization. America was the outlet for the republican party; without it, the party would have remained like a virus in the mother country, and would have prevented the constitutional settlement. Nothing that is strong and sincere is lost in the world. These republican exiles were the fathers of those who fought the War of Independence in the late eighteenth century. The revolutionary element in England, instead of being a solvent, thus became a creator; English radicalism, instead of rending the motherland, produced America. If France had been colonizing rather than military, if the bold and enterprising element that elsewhere creates colonies had been capable, among us, of anything other than conspiring and fighting for abstract principles, we would not have had Napoleon; the republican party, driven out by the reaction, would have emigrated around 1798 and would have established far away a New France that, following the norm for colonies, would now doubtless be a separate republic. Unfortunately, our civil discord only led to deportations. Instead of the United States, we had Sinnamary and Lambèse![18] In these sad dwellings, wretched settlers died, escaped like convicts, awaited a new revolution or an amnesty; meanwhile, the motherland continued to mill the formidable problems that had led to their exile, without a shadow of progress.

A major error of historical philosophy contributed at least as much as France's particular taste for theories to distorting the national judgment on this serious issue of forms of government: it was, indeed, the example of America. The republican school was always quoting this example as good and easy to follow. Nothing could be more superficial. It is only natural that colonies accustomed to governing themselves independently should break the bond with the mother country, and that, this bond once broken, they should forgo royalty and provide for their safety by a federal pact. This method of separating oneself from the trunk like a cutting that carries within it the germ of life is the eternal principle of colonization, a principle that is one of the preconditions of the progress of humanity, and of the Aryan race in particular. Virginia and Carolina were republics before the War of Independence. This war changed nothing in the internal constitution of the states; it only cut the cord binding them to

Europe, which had become inconvenient, and replaced it with a federal link. It was not a revolutionary accomplishment; an eminently conservative conception of right, an aristocratic and legal spirit of provincial freedom was at the base of this great movement. Similarly, when Canada and Australia will break the slender link connecting them to England, these countries, accustomed to governing themselves, will continue their own lives, almost without noticing the change. If France had seriously undertaken the colonization of Algeria, Algeria would have the opportunity of becoming a republic ahead of France. Colonies, formed by people who are not at ease in their home country and seek more freedom than they have at home, are always closer to a republic than the mother country, bound by its old habits and prejudices.

Thus did a party continue to live in France that does not allow constitutional monarchy to develop: the radical republican party. The situation in France was by no means that of England; in addition to the right, left, and center, there was an irreconcilable party, a complete repudiation of the existing government, a party that does not tell the government, "Do such a thing, and we are with you," but that rather suggests, "Whatever you do, we will be against you." The republic is in a sense the end state of any human society, but one can conceive of two very different ways of reaching it. To establish the republic through conflict, by destroying all obstacles, is the dream of ardent characters. There is another, gentler and safer path: to preserve the old royal families as precious monuments and ancient memories is not simply an antiquarian fancy; the dynasties thus preserved become infinitely convenient instruments of constitutional government on certain days of crisis. Will the countries that have followed this course, like England, one day reach a perfect republic, without hereditary dynasty and with universal suffrage? It is like asking whether the hyperbole reaches its asymptotes. It hardly matters, since in reality it comes so close to them that the distance is imperceptible to the eye! This is what the French republican party fails to understand. For the form of the republic, it sacrifices its reality. Instead of following a great road, already traced, by making a few detours, it prefers to jump into precipices and crevices. One rarely sees so much honesty together with so little political intelligence and penetration.

The year 1848 exposed the wound, and illustrated to all trained minds the fundamental principle of the philosophy of our history. The Revolution of 1848 was not an effect without a cause (such an assertion would be meaningless), it was an effect completely disproportionate to its apparent cause. The impact was nothing, the damage was immense. What happened in 1848 is what would have happened in England, had William III been swept away by one of those bouts of strong dissatisfaction his government caused. Under such a hypothesis, the history of England would have been turned upside down. In England, the taste of the people for legitimacy and the fear of the republic were sufficiently potent to carry the new dynasty through difficult times. In France, the moral decay of the nation, its lack of faith in royalty, the energy of the republican party sufficed to overthrow a throne whose foundations lacked all solidity. That day, the catastrophic situation in which France has remained since the Revolution was apparent. If the Revolution and the Republic had grown shallower roots in France, the House of Orléans and with it the parliamentary regime would surely have been consolidated; if the republican idea had been dominant, it would, after several actions and reactions, have carried the country and the republic would have been established: neither of these assumptions came to fruition. The republican spirit found itself strong enough to prevent constitutional monarchy from lasting; it was not strong enough to establish the republic. Hence an ambiguous position, bizarre and liable to bring about a sad decadence. What happened in 1848 could happen several times again; let us seek to clarify the secret law and inner reason for this.

When we see a man dying of a cold we do not conclude that colds are fatal diseases, but rather that this man was consumptive. Similarly, the disease the July government died of was so light that it must be admitted that its constitution was very sickly. The trifling agitation of the banquets[19] was one a government must be capable of enduring, on pain of not being able to live. How, with all the appearance of health, did the July government happen to be so weak? Because it did not have what grants good lungs, a strong heart, and solid guts to a government; I mean the serious concurrence of the sturdy parts of the country. The sense of profound humanity that prevented Louis-Philippe from offering battle, while it implied a distrust of his rights, is not sufficient to explain his downfall. The republican party that made the Revolution was an imperceptible minority. In a country in which government had been less centralized, in which public opinion had found itself to be less divided, the majority would have turned back; but the provinces did not yet entertain the notion of resisting a movement coming from Paris; further, while the faction that took part in the movement on February 24, 1848, was insignificant, the number of those who could have defended the defeated dynasty was also quite inconsiderable. The Legitimist party triumphed, and, without erecting barricades, had its revenge that day. The Orléans dynasty had not managed, despite its profound uprightness and its rare honesty, to speak to the heart of the country and to inspire love.

Thus confronted with an action carried out by a turbulent minority, what was France to do? A country that has no universally accepted dynasty is always rather awkward and embarrassed in its actions. France yielded; it accepted the Republic without believing in it, slyly, and quite determined to be unfaithful to it. The occasion did not fail to present itself. The vote of December 10[20] was an evident repudiation of the Republic. The party that had caused the February Revolution was submitted to the law of retaliation. If we may be allowed an unrefined expression: it had played a lousy trick on France, France played a lousy trick on it. It acted like the honest bourgeois who has fallen into the hands of street kids during a day of rioting and has been dressed up by them in the red cap; this worthy man might allow himself to be pushed around for the love of peace, but he would probably harbor some resentment. The surprise of the election replied to the surprise of the riot. Surely the conduct of France would have been more dignified and loyal if, when the Revolution had been announced, it had openly resisted, politely arrested the representatives of the provisional government as they stepped off their stagecoaches, and convened a sort of general council that would have restored the monarchy; but several reasons that are too easily guessed for it to be necessary to spell them out rendered such a conduct impossible at that time; moreover, the nation that is granted universal suffrage always becomes somewhat duplicitous. It holds an all-powerful weapon that allows it to dispense with civil wars. When one is certain the enemy will be obliged to go through a mountain pass that one controls where it will be forced to take fire without returning it, one does not attack. France waited, and in December 1848 it dealt the republican party a fierce blow. If February had proved that France did not care much for the constitutional monarchy of the House of Orléans, the election of December 10 showed that it did not care much for the Republic, either. The political impotence of this great country appeared in full light.

What can be said of what happened next? We do not like coups d'état any more than revolutions; indeed, we do not like revolutions, precisely because they lead to coups. However, one cannot grant the party of 1848 its fundamental claim. This party, in the name of I know not what divine right, arrogates to itself the power it grants no other party, to be capable of binding France: the illegalities that have been committed to break the bonds with which it had enfolded the country are crimes, while its own February Revolution was simply a glorious act. This is unacceptable. Who would suffer the Gracchi complaining of sedition?[21] All they that take the sword shall perish with the sword.[22] If the guns that were trained on Mr. Sauzet[23] and the Duchess of Orléans on February 24, 1848, were innocent, the bayonets that invaded the Lower House on December 2, 1851,[24] were not guilty. In our opinion, each of these acts of violence is a stab to the fatherland, a wound that touches the most essential parts of its constitution, one more step in a maze with no exit, and we have the right to say of all these fatal days:

> May that day fall out of time nor future generations credit it!
> Let us at least keep silence and suffer
> The family reproach to be covered up, buried in darkest night.[25]

### III

The Emperor Napoleon III and the small group of men who share his intimate thoughts provided the government of France with a program that, though not based on history, was not lacking in originality: to hark back to the tradition of the Empire, to profit from its grandiose legend, still so alive among the people, to give voice to popular sentiment in this matter through universal suffrage, to obtain by such suffrage a mandate for the future and inaugurate heredity, to cause a dynastic election, following an idea dear to France;* domestically, personal government by the emperor,

---

\* The idea that election played a role in the origin of the dynasties of France, although historically false, can be found since the end of the thirteenth century. See the romances of *Hugh Capet* and *Baudouin de Sebourg*.

with the appearances of a parliamentary government skillfully reduced to naught; internationally, a brilliant and active role to restore France gradually, by war and diplomacy, to the first-order position it occupied among the nations of Europe sixty years ago and that it had lost since 1814.

For seventeen years, France has let this experiment continue with a patience one might call exemplary, if it were ever good for a nation to practice excessive self-denial when it is a question of its destiny. At what point is the experiment? What results has it produced?

Can it be said first of all that the new Napoleonic House is established, that is to say that it has elicited around it the feelings of affection and personal devotion that are the strength of a dynasty? In this regard, one should harbor no illusions. Selfishness, skepticism, indifference toward rulers, the persuasion that they are owed no gratitude have completely dried up the heart of the country. The matter has become a matter of interest. Public wealth having increased greatly, if the question were framed in these terms, *revolution—no revolution*, the latter would gain an overwhelming majority; but often a country that does not want revolution acts in such a way as to bring it about. In any case, these feelings of tender effusion and loyalty the country once experienced for its kings are out of the question now. Those who have for the Napoleonic dynasty the feelings the royalist of the Restoration had for the royal family are few enough to be counted. There are almost no Napoleonic legitimists; this is a fact of which the government cannot persuade itself enough.

The part of the Emperor Napoleon III's program that concerned military glory and the preponderant role of France had a certain greatness to it, and those who, from the viewpoint of the general interests of civilization, are grateful to the emperor for the Crimean War[26] and the Italian one[27] cannot judge with severity all points of the Second Empire's foreign policy; but it is clear that France is not in tune with such ideas. Put to universal suffrage, the plebiscite *no war* would garner a much stronger majority than *no revolution*. France today is no more heroic than it is sentimental. The dominance of one European nation over the others has become impossible in the present condition of societies. Threatening intentions unwisely expressed on this side of the Rhine (and it was not the government that was guiltiest or clumsiest in this regard) have caused among the Germanic nations an emotion that will abate the day they are reassured regarding the ambitions they could imagine us entertaining. That day the strength of

Prussia within the Germanic body will cease, a strength that has no other reason for existence than the fear of France. That same day the desire for political unity will probably cease, a desire incongruent with the Germanic character and that among the Germans has only ever been a defensive measure, impatiently tolerated, against a highly organized neighbor.

This single variation in the original program of the Emperor Napoleon III would be sufficient to change everything that relates to domestic government. The Emperor Napoleon III never thought he could govern without an elective chamber; simply, he hoped to remain for long, if not forever, in control of elections. This was a calculation that could not be achieved except with perpetual wars, and perpetual victories. Personal government is maintained only on the condition that it always and everywhere have fame and success. How could one expect except in the case of dazzling prosperity that the country would forever place in the ballot box the ballot the administration put in its hand? It was inevitable that one day France would wish to use the powerful weapon it had been left, and take some part of responsibility in its affairs. In politics, one cannot long play with appearances. It was to be expected that the travesty of parliamentary government that the Emperor Napoleon III had always preserved would became a serious reality. The latest elections have transferred this assumption into the sphere of accomplished facts. The elections of May and June 1869 showed that the norm of our society could not be that of Roman Caesarism. Roman Caesarism was also originally a despotism surrounded by republican fictions; despotism killed the fictions; here, on the contrary, the representative fictions have killed despotism. This did not happen under the First Empire, since the method of election to the *Corps législatif* was at the time completely illusory. Nothing proves better than the events of these past months how the ideal of government created by England imposes itself by necessity on all states. It is often said that France is not made for such a government. France has just proven it thinks otherwise; in any case, if this had been true, I would say one should despair of the future of France. The liberal regime is an absolute necessity for all modern nations. Those that cannot accept it will perish. First, the liberal regime will bestow upon the nations that have adopted it an immense superiority over those who cannot submit to it. A nation incapable of freedom of the press, freedom of assembly, and political freedom will certainly be surpassed and defeated by nations that can withstand such freedoms. The latter will always be better informed, more educated, more serious, better governed.

Yet another reason decrees that, if France is condemned to a fatal alternative of anarchy and despotism, its ruin is inevitable. One does not exit anarchy except by means of a large military state, which, in addition to ruining and exhausting the nation, can maintain its influence over the nation only on condition of always being victorious abroad. The domestic regime of military oppression necessarily leads to foreign war; a defeated and humiliated army cannot oppress energetically. However, in the present state of Europe, a nation doomed systematically to wage foreign wars is a doomed nation. This nation will constantly provoke coalitions and invasions against it. This is how the unstable condition of France's domestic government constitutes an international threat for it, and makes it a bellicose nation, although its general opinion is very peaceable. The balance of Europe requires that all nations that compose it have roughly the same political constitution. An *ebrius inter sobrios*[28] cannot be tolerated in this concert. The First Republic was consistent in its propaganda war; it felt that the French Republic could not exist if it were not surrounded by Batavian, Neapolitan, etc. Republics.[29]

From all sides, one thus arrives at the same result: France must enter without delay into the path of representative government. A preliminary question arises here: will the Emperor Napoleon III resign himself to this change of role? Will he change to such an extent a program that for him is not a simple calculation of ambition, but a faith, an enthusiasm, a belief that explains his whole life? Having loved to the point of fanaticism an ideal he considers the only great and noble one, but which France spurned, will he not experience an invincible distaste for the regime of peace, economy, and small ministerial battles, which has always presented itself to him as an image of decadence, and which he associates with the memory of a dynasty he held in low esteem? Will he leave the circle of mediocre advisers and ministers with which he seems satisfied? Can the sovereign invested by plebiscite with the fullness of popular rights be parliamentary? Is not the plebiscite the negation of constitutional monarchy? Has such a government ever issued from a coup d'état? Can it exist with universal suffrage? Respect for the person of the sovereign forbids us to consider these issues. The character of Napoleon III is in any case an issue on which, even when one will possess elements that nobody can have now, one will do well to speak with great caution. There will be few historical subjects where it will be more important to use corrections, and if in fifty years there is no critic as profound as Mr. Sainte-Beuve,[30] as conscientious, as attentive not to erase contradictions and to explain them, the Emperor Napoleon III will never be well judged. We will offer a single reflection. The considerations of race and blood, which were once decisive in history, have lost much of their strength. Substitutions that would have been impossible under the old order may have become possible. The character of families, which was formerly inflexible, so that a Bourbon, for example, could be of use only in a particular role, is now capable of many modifications. Historical role and race are no longer two inseparable things. There is nothing absolutely inadmissible in an heir of Napoleon I accomplishing a task in contradiction to the work of Napoleon I. Public opinion has become the sovereign master to such an extent, that every name, every man are but what it makes them. The a priori objections that some people raise against the possibility of a constitutional future with the Bonaparte family are therefore not decisive. The Capetian family, which became the veritable representation of French nationality and of the Third Estate, was originally ultra-Germanic, ultra-feudal.

As architecture creates a style from mistakes and inexperience, so a country derives what advantage it will from the actions to which fate led it. We enjoy the benefits of royalty, even though royalty was founded by a series of crimes; we profit from the consequences of the Revolution, even though the Revolution was a tissue of atrocities. A sad law of human affairs decrees that one becomes wise when one is spent. We were too difficult, we rejected the excellent; we now keep the mediocre for fear of worse. The coquette who refused the finest suitors often ends up in a marriage of convenience. Those who have dreamed of a Republic without republicans similarly indulge in the thought of a reign of the Bonaparte family without the Bonapartists: a state of affairs in which this family, freed from the compromising entourage of those who brought about its second accession, would find its best backers, its surest counselors among those who did not make it, but who accepted it because it was desired by France and it was capable of finding some kind of exit to the strange impasse in which destiny has led us. It is very true that there is no example of a constitutional dynasty issuing from a coup d'état. The Visconti, the Sforza,[31] tyrants who sprung from republican discord, are not the material from which legitimate royalties are made. Such royalties are based only on the particular hardness and loftiness of the Germanic race in barbaric and unconscious times, in which forgetting was possible and humanity lived in the mysterious darkness that establishes respect. *Fata viam invenient!* . . .[32] The strange challenge France has presented to all the laws of history imposes extreme restraint in such inductions. Let us go further back, and, neglecting what can be foiled by an accident tomorrow, let us search for the reasons for the existence of constitutional monarchy in the country, the reasons that seem to suggest its triumph, and the fears that may remain regarding its establishment.

## IV

We have seen that the specific feature of France, the feature that sets it apart significantly from England and other European countries (Italy and Spain to some extent excepted), is that the republican party is a considerable element within it. This party, which was strong enough to overthrow Louis-Philippe and impose its theory on France for a few months, was, after December 2, the target of a sort of proscription. Has it disappeared as a consequence? Certainly not. The progress it has made in the past seventeen years has been quite considerable. It has not only remained in control of the majority in Paris and the main cities, it has conquered entire regions; the entire Parisian conurbation belongs to it. The democratic spirit as we know it in Paris, with its rigidity, its absolute tone, its discouraging simplicity of ideas, its meticulous suspicion, its ingratitude, has conquered some rural districts in an astonishing manner. In certain villages, the situation of farmers and farm laborers is exactly that of workers and employers in a manufacturing city; peasants there will be arrogant, radical, and jealous in politics as confidently as workers in Belleville or the Faubourg Saint-Antoine.[33] The idea of equal rights for all, the manner of conceiving of government merely as a public service one pays for and to which one owes neither respect nor gratitude, a kind of American impertinence, the pretention to be as wise as the best statesmen and to reduce politics to a simple consultation of the will of the majority, this is the spirit that prevails more and more, even in the countryside. I have no doubt that this spirit will grow every day, and that at the next election, wherever it is the master, it will prove itself both more demanding and more intractable than it was this year.

Will the republican party, however, one day become the majority and impose American institutions in France? I do not think so. The essence of this party is to be a minority. If it led to a social revolution, it could create new classes, but these classes would become monarchical the day after their enrichment. The most pressing interests of France, its character, its qualities, and its faults make royalty indispensable for it. The day after the radical party overthrows a monarchy, journalists, literary people, artists, people of intellect, socialites, women will all conspire to establish another one, for the monarchy responds to some of France's deep needs. Our amiability suffices on its own to make bad republicans of us. The charming exaggerations of the old French politeness, the courteousness that puts us at the feet of those with whom we are in relations, are the opposite of the rigidity, the harshness, the dryness that the constant awareness of his rights gives the democrat. France excels only in the exquisite, loves only the distinguished, can produce only the aristocratic. We are a race of gentlemen; our ideal was created by gentlemen, not, like that of America, by honest bourgeois, serious businessmen. Such habits are not satisfied except with high society, a court, and princes of the blood. To hope that the great and refined French creations will continue to be produced in a bourgeois world, admitting of no other inequality than that of wealth, is an illusion. The people of intellect and feeling who expend the most enthusiasm for the republican utopia would be precisely those who would fit least in such a society. The individuals who aim so eagerly for the American ideal forget that this race does not have our brilliant past, that it has not made a single discovery of pure science nor created a masterpiece, that it has never had a nobility, that business and wealth occupy it exclusively. Our own ideal can only be achieved with a government that gives luster to what comes into contact with it and that creates social distinctions apart from wealth. A society in which a man's merit and his superiority over another can only reveal itself in the form of industry and trade does not appeal to us; not that trade and industry do not seem honest to us, but we see that the best things (for example, the office of the priest, the magistrate, the scholar, the artist, and the serious man of letters) are the opposite of the industrial and commercial spirit, the first duty of those who devote themselves to such things being not to attempt to enrich themselves, and never to consider the market value of what they do.

The republican party therefore may prevent any liberal government from establishing itself, for, by causing seditions, it will always be capable of forcing governments to arm themselves with repressive laws, to restrict freedoms, and to strengthen the military element; it is doubtful that it will be able to establish itself. The hatred between it and the peaceable part of the country will become ever more poisonous, because the country will perceive it more and more as the eternal spoilsport. It will only succeed, I fear, in causing those sorts of periodic crises, followed by violent expulsions, that the conservative party will present as purifications, but that will in fact be diminishments, and in any case will deplorably consume the temperament of France. Indeed, in these convulsive fits of retching, excellent elements, necessary to the life of a nation, will be rejected with the impure elements. As happened after 1848, liberal ideas will suffer for their inevitable solidarity with a party that, full of generous illusions, exercises a great attraction on young imaginations and, moreover, has an entire part of its program in common with the liberal school. It is to be feared that long-enduring habits of mind, a certain rigidity, the consolidated routine and habit of judging everything on the basis of Paris (a habit easy to understand in a party that was essentially Parisian in origin) will induce this party to believe that revolutions of the kind of 1830 and 1848 could be repeated. Nothing could be more disastrous. The time of Parisian revolutions has come to an end. I base this opinion much less on the material changes that have taken place in Paris than on two reasons that in my opinion will weigh heavily on future destinies.

The first is the establishment of universal suffrage. A people in possession of this suffrage will not allow its capital to make revolutions. If such a revolution took place in Paris (which fortunately is impossible), I am persuaded that the *départements* would not accept it, that barricades would arise on the railway tracks to stop the spread of the conflagration and prevent the supplying of the capital, that the Parisian insurrection, quickly starved, would only have a few days of life. The emancipation of the provinces has progressed markedly since 1848.

A second event, moreover, must be taken into great consideration. The whole philosophy of history is dominated by the question of armaments. Nothing has contributed as much to the triumph of the modern spirit as the invention of gunpowder. Artillery killed chivalry and feudalism, created the force of monarchies and states, brought barbarism definitively to heel, rendered those strange hurricanes of the Tartar world, which formed at the center of Asia and came to shake Europe and terrify the Christian world, impossible. In our own day, the subtle application of science to the art of war will cause revolutions almost as grave. War will increasingly become a scientific and industrial problem; the richest, the most scientific, the most industrious nation will hold the advantage. And if we examine the effects of this change within states, it is clear that the application of science to armaments on a large scale will only benefit governments. The effect of artillery was to demolish one after the other all the feudal castles; a salvo from some such perfected machine will stop a revolution. In times when armaments are not advanced, a citizen almost equals a soldier; but as soon as the means of aggression become technical, demanding precision instruments and requiring special training, the soldier enjoys an immense superiority over the unarmed masses. Everything thus leads us to believe that revolutions undertaken by citizens will henceforth be crushed at the outset.

This is what the Jesuits have grasped with their usual skill, when they take over the alleyways of the school of Saint-Cyr[34] and the Polytechnic. They see the future of those who know how to handle advanced weapons and disciplined forces, and recognize full well that the advantage, in this respect, belongs to the old noble classes, less concerned than the bourgeoisie with industry or lucrative civilian positions, and for this very reason more capable of abnegation. Abnegation always wins out. The Teuton conquered the world because he was capable of loyalty, that is to say abnegation. It is true that the democratic party is also capable of great sacrifices, but not of the kind that consists in dying for the sake of loyalty and suffering the disdain of the aristocrat to whom one is morally superior.

France therefore seems destined not to be a republic for a long time yet, even if the republican party were to compose the numerical majority. Every day, France sees growing within it a popular mass devoid of religious ideals and rejecting any social principle superior to the will of individuals. The other mass, which is not yet won over by this selfish notion, is reduced every day by primary education and the employment of universal suffrage; but against this rising tide of invading ideas, which, being young and inexperienced, do not take any difficulty into account, superior interests and needs are arrayed that require the organization and management of society by means of a principle of reason and science separate from the will of individuals. The democrat always imagines that the consciousness of the nation is perfectly clear, he does not accept that public opinion has anything obscure, hesitant, or contradictory about it. To count votes and do what the majority wants seem quite simple things to him; but these are illusions. Long will public opinion still have to be guessed, intuited, hypothesized, and, to a certain degree, guided. Hence the monarchical interests, which, the day after the establishment of the republic, will prove formidable, even in the minds of those who will have brought about or not prevented the republic.

The movement occurring among the popular classes that tends to lend individuals a progressively clearer consciousness of their rights is so evident a fact that the desire to oppose it would be madness. The task of politics is not to fight such a movement, but to anticipate it and adapt to it. The learned have never sought a way to stem tides; they have done better; they have understood the laws of the phenomenon so well, that the seaman knows the state of the sea at every minute, and derives great benefit from it. The key is for the rising tide not to sweep away the necessary dams, and not to produce disastrous reactions by withdrawing. Now, this is what, in all likelihood, will happen whenever French democracy will be led by acrimonious, surly, pedantic Jacobinism, which stirs up the country, sometimes even gives it an impulse, but which will never lead it to a stable constitution. This party can cause a revolution, but it will not reign longer than two months after having caused it. Even the day in which it were to reach an electoral majority (a rather unlikely occurrence), it would not have established anything, because the elements it has at its disposal, though excellent for agitation, are unstable, easy to split, and completely incapable of providing the solid elements of a construction. Its strength, though large, is in part a force of circumstance. Ten times, during an election campaign, was I given the opportunity to hear the following dialogue:

We are not happy with the government; it costs too much; it rules in the interest of ideas that are not our own; we shall vote for the candidate of the most extreme opposition.—So, are you revolutionaries?—By no means; a revolution would be the worst misfortune. It is only a question of making an impression on the government, to force it to change, to restrain it vigorously.—But if the Lower House is composed of revolutionaries, the government will be overthrown.—No; there will be twenty or thirty at most, and anyway the government is so strong! It has *chassepots*![35]

This simpleminded reasoning gives the measure of the illusion under which the radical Left labors, when it imagines that the country wants it for its own merits. A large part of the country uses it as a stick to chastise power, not as a support on which to lean. "They appoint us, therefore they love us," would be on the part of the honorable members of the so-called extreme opposition the most dangerous of conclusions. They are appointed to teach the government a lesson, and with the conviction that the government is strong enough to endure the lesson. The day it were no longer so and one found that the existence of the government had been endangered, there would be a reversal, to the extent that the radical party is subject to this strange law according to which the hour of its victory spells the beginning of its defeat. Its triumph is its termination; often those who appointed and promoted it themselves celebrate its proscription.

In effect, order has become so imperious a requirement in our modern societies of Europe that long civil wars are impossible. Sometimes the example of these illustrious Greek and Italian republics, which created an admirable civilization in the midst of a political state rather similar to our Terror, is cited; but we cannot conclude anything from this for societies like ours, whose springs are much more complicated. Spain, the Spanish republics of America, Italy itself can withstand anarchy more than France, because these are countries in which material life is easier, in which there are fewer sources of wealth, in which special interests and credit have developed less. The Terror, at the end of the past century, was the suspension of life. In our day, it would be even worse. Just as a creature with a simple structure is resistant to very different environments, while superior animals, such as humans, have very narrow limits for life, to the extent that slight changes in their habits lead them to death, so are our civilizations, which are set up like clever devices, unable to tolerate crises. They are, if I dare say so, of delicate constitution; one degree more or less can kill them. Eight days of anarchy would cause incalculable losses; after a month perhaps, the railways would stop. We have created mechanisms of an infinite precision, apparatuses that run on trust and that all presuppose deep public tranquility, a government both strongly established and seriously controlled. I know that in the United States matters do not follow this course; disorders that would draw cries of alarm from us are tolerated there. This derives from the fact that the constitutional foundations of the United States are never truly compromised. These American lands, lightly governed, resemble the European ones in which the dynasty is not in question. They have respect for law and the constitution, which represents among them what the dogma of legitimacy is in Europe. To compare countries with socialist tendencies, like our own, where so many people expect to improve their fate by a revolution, with such states, which are completely free of socialism, and where man, completely taken by his private affairs, requires very few guarantees from government, is the most profound error that can be committed in the realm of philosophical history.

The need for order experienced by our old European societies, coinciding with the perfecting of weaponry, will in sum give governments as much force as they are deprived of daily by the progress of revolutionary ideas. Like religion, order will have its fanatics. Modern societies present the feature of being extremely mild when their principle is not in danger, but becoming pitiless if doubts are inspired in them regarding the conditions of their duration. A society that has been afraid is like a man who has been afraid: it no longer possesses its moral value in its entirety. The means that Catholic society employed in the thirteenth and sixteenth century to defend its threatened existence will be employed by modern society, in ways more expeditious and less cruel, but no less terrible. If the old dynasties are powerless to do this, or if, as is likely, they refuse power in conditions unworthy of them, one will resort to the *pacieri* and *podestà* of medieval Italy,[36] who will be tasked, for a flat fee and on the basis of a bloody program agreed in advance, with reestablishing the preconditions for social life. This era of the *podestà*, quite jaded as to glory and demanding nothing but handsome profits as the price for their services, will be the era of torture. Torture always reappears in times of selfishness and treachery, which have extinguished all personal loyalty, when the hierarchy of humanity no longer rests on anything but fear, and man has no other hold on his fellow being except by torturing his flesh. We will once again see the *carême*[37] of the Viscontis, the torments of the Achaemenids[38] and of Tamerlane. Adventurer dictators similar to the generals of Spanish America will alone charge themselves with such a task. However, because our races have a core of loyalty from which they cannot be parted, and because moreover there will long be some survivors of the ancient dynasties, there will probably be some recurrence of legitimacy and even of feudalism after each cruel dictatorship. In some provinces, the people will ask old families, wealthy and accustomed to wielding weapons, to place themselves at their head in order to fight anarchy and form local centers of resistance. More than once will one beg the old traditional recipients of national roles again to resume their work and restore at all costs a little peace, good faith, and honor to the countries that long ago had made a pact with their ancestors. Perhaps they will hesitate, and make their acceptance dependent upon clauses on which one will not be disposed to haggle. Perhaps they might even be asked not to accept any conditions at all, and to keep intact, in the interests of the people, a fullness of power that will be considered the most valuable property of the nation. Confronted with certain facts such as those that occurred recently in Greece, Mexico, Spain,[39] the democratic party sometimes says with a smile, "Kings can no longer be found." Indeed, a time will come when depreciated kingship will not present a sufficient attraction to tempt capable and self-respecting princes. May God forefend that one day, for having excessively disparaged graciously granted liberties, we be obliged to pray the sovereign to reserve them all, or to untie their bundle only slowly, through personal, local, momentary concessions and charters!

A return of the barbarians, that is to say a new triumph of the less conscious and less civilized parts of humanity over the more conscious and more civilized parts, seems, at first glance, impossible. Let us be clear in this regard. A reservoir of barbarian forces still exists in the world, and is placed almost entirely in the hands of Russia. As long as civilized nations retain their strong organization, the role of this barbarism is almost reduced to naught; but undoubtedly, if (God forbid!) the plague of selfishness and anarchy were to destroy our Western states, barbarism would recover its function, which is to regenerate the virility of corrupt civilizations, to effect an invigorating reappearance of instinct when reflection has stifled subordination, to show that the willingness to be killed out of loyalty for a leader (which the democrat considers a base and senseless thing) is what grants strength and a title to possession of the land. One should not hide from oneself, in fact, that the final consequence of democratic socialist theories would be a complete enervation. A nation that gave itself over to this program, rejecting any notion of glory, social brilliance, individual superiority, reducing everything to the satisfaction of the materialistic desires of the crowd, that is to say to the obtainment of the pleasure of the greatest number, would become completely open to conquest, and its existence would run the greatest dangers.

How to prevent these sad eventualities, which we have wanted to present as possibilities rather than as specific fears? By means of the reactionary program? By compressing, smothering, constricting, governing ever more? No, a thousand times no; this policy was the root of all evil; it would be the way to ruin everything. The liberal program is at the same time the truly conservative program. Constitutional monarchy, limited and held in check; decentralization, reduced government, strong organization of the municipality, the canton, the *département*; strong impulse to individual activity in the fields of art, intellect, science, industry, colonization; unambiguously peaceful policy, abandonment of any claim to territorial aggrandizement in Europe; development of a good primary education and of a higher education capable of giving the manners of the educated class the foundation of a solid philosophy; creation of an Upper House deriving from several varied modes of election and achieving alongside the simple numerical representation of citizens the representation of diverse interests, functions, specialties, aptitudes; in social issues, governmental neutrality; full freedom of association; gradual separation of church and state, the precondition of all seriousness in religious opinions: this is what we dream of when we seek, with a cold reflection free from the blindness of an intemperate patriotism, a viable path. In some respects, this is a policy of atonement, involving the admission that, for the moment, it is less a question of continuing the Revolution than of criticizing it and of repairing its mistakes. Indeed, often I fancy that the French character is traversing a period of fasting, a sort of political diet, during which the appropriate attitude is that of the man of intellect who atones for the sins of his youth, or of the disappointed traveler who by a long detour skirts the elevation he had intended to climb at its steepest. Revolutions, like civil wars, are strengthening if one emerges from them; they are deathly if they last. We have done poorly at dazzling and bold enterprises; let us try humbler paths. The initiatives of Paris have been disastrous; let us see what provincial simplicity can accomplish. Let us beware these imperious and haughty demands, so seldom followed by action.

Show me an example, in France at least, of a freedom conquered in battle and ultimately maintained.

No one admires and loves more than I do this extraordinary center of life and thought called Paris. A disease if you will, but a disease the way a pearl is, a precious and exquisite hypertrophy, Paris is France's reason for existence. A center of light and of warmth, I accept that it may be termed a center of moral decay as well, as long as one grants that upon this heap of manure charming flowers bloom, some of which are surpassingly rare. The glory of France is that it knows how to maintain this wonderful permanent exhibition of its most excellent products; but one should not hide at what price this marvelous result is obtained. Capitals consume and do not produce. One should not, by taking the illness to extremes, risk making France alternately into a head without a body and a body without a head. The political activity of Paris should no longer be dominant. The provinces have begun to welcome with equal antipathy the two things they have so far received from Paris, revolutions and government. On its own, Parisian democracy will create nothing solid; if we do not take heed, it will bring periodic exterminations, disastrous for France, since Parisian democracy is also a necessary ferment, an excitant without which the life of France would languish. Public meetings during the latest electoral campaign in Paris displayed a complete lack of political sense. Mistress of the field, democracy has placed on the agenda a sort of competition in terms of paradoxes; the candidates allowed themselves to be led by the demands of the crowd, and were hardly appreciated except in proportion to their declamatory vigor; moderate opinion could not make itself heard, or was obliged to force its tone. Paris ignores the first two virtues of political life, patience and forgetting. The politics of the Patriarch Jacob, who wanted the pace of his entire tribe to be set by that of the newborn lambs, is not at all to its liking.

In general, the error of the French liberal party is that it does not understand that any political construction must have a conservative foundation. In England, parliamentary government was only possible after the exclusion of the radical party, an exclusion that was accomplished with a sort of legitimist frenzy. Nothing is certain in politics until one has brought around the heavy and solid parts, which are the ballast of the nation, to the service of progress. The liberal party of 1830 imagined too easily that it could attain its program by force, openly antagonizing the Legitimist party. The withdrawal or hostility of this party remains the great misfortune of France. Removed from common life, the Legitimist aristocracy refuses society what it is owed, patronage, models and lessons of noble life, fine images of seriousness. Vulgarity, France's absence of education, the ignorance of the art of living, monotony, the lack of respect, and the childish parsimony of provincial life derive from the fact that the people who owe the country the types of gentlemen who fulfill public duties with an authority recognized by all are the ones deserting general society, and retreating more and more into a solitary and closed life. The Legitimist party is in a sense the indispensable basis of any political establishment among us; in its own way, even the United States possesses this foundation, essential to any society, in the form of religious memories, heroic in their own way, and in this class of moral, proud, serious, ponderous citizens, which are the stones with which the edifice of the state is built. The rest is just sand; nothing lasting can be done with it, whatever spirit, indeed whatever passion one sets to it.

What does this provincial party, which daily becomes more conscious of its strength, think? What does it want? Never was a state of opinion more obvious. This party is liberal, not revolutionary, constitutional, not republican; it desires that power be controlled, not destroyed, the end of personal government, not the overthrow of the dynasty. I have no doubt that if, eight months ago, the government had resolutely made up its mind, refrained from official candidacies[40] and the artificial fragmentation of constituencies, and let the country handle the elections freely, the ballot would have produced a Lower House unambiguously imbued with these principles, and which, being considered by the country as a representation of its will, would have possessed the strength to surmount the most difficult circumstances. One day it will be as complicated to understand why the Emperor Napoleon III did not seize this means of obtaining a second signature of the country to his marriage contract and sharing with him the responsibility for an obscure future, as it is to understand why Louis-Philippe had not seen in the cooptation of capacities[41] a way to broaden the base of his dynasty. The provinces, in effect, take elections much more seriously than Paris. Having no political life except once every six years, they lend elections an importance that Paris, with its perpetual levity, does not afford them. Paris, concerned with its radical protests, takes elections not as a choice of serious delegates, but rather as an opportunity for ironic demonstrations. The provinces do not understand these subtleties; their representatives are truly their mandataries, and they care about them. Would a Lower House elected freely and without the intervention of the administration have been dangerous for the dynasty? Would the radical opposition have been represented therein by a larger number of representatives? I believe just the opposite. In many cases, the election of hostile or even insulting candidates was a form of protest against the official or complaisant candidate. The official candidacy completely disrupts the electoral process and alters its sincerity, not just by the direct pressure the administration exercises in its favor, but especially by the awkward position in which it places the independent voter. For him, indeed, it no longer is a question of choosing the candidate who best represents his opinion or whom he thinks most capable of rendering services to the country; it is a question of defeating the official candidate at all costs. Thence, no more nuances, no more preferences. Extreme views being assured of the favor of the crowd, on which sharp assertions and loud declamations exert a greater impact than moderate opinions, and the democratic party in any case possessing an organization that no other party has and having a real fanaticism at its disposal, liberals follow the current, and adopt the radical candidate despite their revulsion. It is a widespread error in France to believe that by asking for more one obtains less, and that the radical opposition is the instrument of progress, the government's propulsive force; this is true of the moderate opposition, but not of the radical opinion, which is an obstacle to progress, an impediment to concessions, by the terror it inspires and the repressive measures to which it leads.

More than ever, politics must strive not to resolve the issues, but to wait until they wear out. The life of nations, like that of individuals, is a compromise between contradictions. Of how many things must we admit that we can live neither with nor without, and yet we still live! The Prince Napoleon,[42] a few days ago, said wittily to those who wish to adjourn freedom until there are neither rival dynasties nor a revolutionary party any longer in France: "You will wait a long time." History will not blame the policies of those who, in such a state of affairs, will have resigned themselves to expedients. Suppose that one day a member of the eldest or youngest branch of the Bourbons reigns over France; it will not be because the majority of France has become Legitimist or

Orléanist, it is because the *wheel of fortune* will have brought back circumstances in which a given member of the House of Bourbon will be found to be expedient. France has allowed dynastic attachment to perish within it so completely, that even legitimism would only return by chance, on a transitory basis. Contemporary positivism has suppressed all metaphysics to such a degree, that a most narrow-minded idea tends to spread, namely, that a popular vote has all the more force the more recent it is, so that after fifteen years this strange argument is voiced: "The generation that voted for such a plebiscite has died in part, the vote has lost its value and needs to be renewed." This is the opposite of the idea of the Middle Ages, according to which a pact was all the more valid if it was older. This is in a sense the negation of the national principle, for the national principle, like religion, presupposes pacts independent of the will of individuals, pacts transmitted and received from father to son like an inheritance. By denying the nation the power to bind the future, everything is reduced to lifetime contracts, indeed, even passing contracts; the ranters, I believe, would even want them to be annual, as a step toward what they call direct government, a condition in which the national will would be nothing more than the whim of each hour. What becomes of the integrity of the nation with similar political conceptions? How can the right to secession be denied when everything is reduced to the material fact of the current will of the citizens? The truth is that a nation is not simply the collection of the units that compose it, that it cannot depend on a vote, that it is in its own way an idea, an abstract thing, superior to individual wills. The principle of government likewise cannot be reduced to a simple consultation of universal suffrage, that is to say, to determining and implementing what the greatest number considers its interest. This materialistic conception ultimately contains a call to arms; by proclaiming itself the ultima ratio, universal suffrage rests on the idea that the greatest number is an indicator of strength; it assumes that if the minority did not acquiesce in the opinion of the majority, it would have every chance of being defeated. But this reasoning is incorrect, since the minority can be more energetic and better versed in the handling of weapons than the majority. "We are twenty, you are one," says universal suffrage. "Yield, or we will force you!—You are twenty, but I am right, and on my own I can force you; yield," says the armed man.

*Fata viam invenient!* Lucky is he who may write his *Consolation of Philosophy* on the ruins of a world, like Boethius.[43] The future of France is a mystery that defies all sagacity. Certainly, other countries are debating serious problems; England, with a calm that one cannot admire enough, resolves bold questions that among us pass for the domain of utopians alone; but the debate is everywhere circumscribed, everywhere there is a limited arena, with rules of engagement, heralds, and judges. Among us, it is the constitution itself, the form and to some extent the existence of society that are perpetually in question. Can a country survive such a regime? This is what we ask ourselves anxiously. We are reassured by thinking that a great nation is, like the human body, an admirably weighted and balanced machine, that it creates the organs it needs, and that if it loses them, it creates new ones. It is possible that, in our revolutionary ardor, we have gone too far with the amputations, that while we believed we were only excising unhealthy superfluities we hit some vital organ, so that the obstinacy the patient displays in not being well may have to do with some large wound we caused in the patient's entrails. It is a reason to take many precautions henceforth and leave this body, robust after all, though deeply affected, to heal its own inner wounds and return to the normal conditions of life.

Let us hasten to say it, in any case: defects as dazzling as France's are, in their way, qualities. France has not lost the scepter of intellect, of taste, of subtle art, or of Atticism; long will it yet draw the attention of the civilized world, and set the stakes upon which the European public will place its bets. The affairs of France are of such a nature that they divide and fascinate foreigners as much as and often more than the affairs of their own countries. The greatest drawback of its political condition is the unexpected; but the unexpected is two-sided: beside bad eventualities, there are good ones, and we would not at all be surprised if, after some deplorable misadventures, France were to traverse years of a singular brilliance. If, having finally tired of astonishing the world, it wanted to opt for a kind of political pacification, how wide and glorious a revenge it could achieve along the path of private activity! How it could rival England in the peaceful conquest of the world and the subjection of all the inferior races! France can do anything, except be mediocre. What it suffers, in sum, it suffers for having been too daring against the gods. Whatever evils the future holds in store, and even if the fate of the

Frenchman, like that of the Greek, the Jew, the Italian, were one day to arouse the pity of the world and almost its smile, the world shall not forget that if France fell into this abyss of misery, it is because it conducted bold experiments from which everyone benefits, because it loved justice to madness, because it accepted with generous imprudence the possibility of an ideal that the miseries of humanity do not entail.

# 6

## THE WAR BETWEEN FRANCE AND GERMANY
## (*LA GUERRE ENTRE LA FRANCE ET*
## *L'ALLEMAGNE*, 1870)

As I begin to write these pages, I ignore what state the world will be in when they are completed. One would need quite a frivolous character to attempt to tease out the future when the present is so uncertain. Nonetheless, it is permissible for those whom a philosophical conception of life has raised, certainly not above patriotism, but above the mistakes an unenlightened patriotism entails, to attempt to discern something through the thick smoke that lets nothing appear on the horizon except the image of death.

I have always considered a war between France and Germany as the worst misfortune that might befall civilization. We all completely accept the duties of the fatherland, its rightful sensitivities, its hopes; we all have full confidence in the deep forces of the country, in that resilience that more than once already has caused France to rebound under the pressure of misfortune; but even supposing all permissible hopes are greatly exceeded, the war that has begun will nevertheless be an immense bane. It will have sown the seeds of a violent hatred between the two portions of the European race whose union mattered most to the progress of the human spirit. The great mistress of scholarly investigation and the ingenious, lively, and quick initiator of the world to all fine and delicate thought are set against each other for a long time to come, maybe forever; each of them will sink into its flaws, one becoming ever rougher and coarser, the other ever more superficial and backward. The intellectual, moral, and political harmony of humanity is broken; a sour dissonance will pervade the concert of European society for centuries.

In fact, setting aside the United States of America, whose future, bright no doubt, is still obscure, and which in any case occupies a secondary position in the original work of the human mind, the intellectual and moral greatness of Europe rests upon a triple alliance whose breakup is a bereavement for progress: the alliance of France, Germany, and England. United, these three great forces would lead the world and lead it well, carrying with them by necessity the other, still considerable, elements that compose the European network; they would especially trace the path in an imperious way for another force, which must be neither exaggerated nor minimized: Russia. Russia is not a danger unless the rest of Europe abandons it to the false idea of an originality that it perhaps does not possess, and allows it to gather together all the barbarian tribes of the center of Asia, completely powerless on their own, but capable of discipline and fully liable, if we are not careful, to coalesce around a Muscovite Genghis Khan. The United States is not a danger unless the division of Europe allows it to indulge the illusions of a presumptuous youth and its ancient resentment against the mother country. With the union of France, England, and Germany, the Old Continent would have preserved its equilibrium, powerfully mastered the New, and kept in tutelage that vast Oriental world, which it would be unhealthy to let form exaggerated hopes. It was but a dream. One day has sufficed to topple the edifice that sheltered our hopes, to expose the world to all dangers, all desires, and all brutalities.

In this situation, for which we are in no way responsible, the duty of all philosophical minds is to silence their emotion and to study, with cold and clear thinking, the causes of the illness, to attempt to glimpse the way in which it is possible to palliate it. Peace will be made between France and Germany. Extermination only lasts so long; it finds its end, like contagious diseases, in its very devastation, as does the flame in the destruction of the object that provided its nourishment. I have read, I forget where, the parable of the two brothers who, in the days of Cain and Abel without doubt, came to hate each other and decided to fight until they were no longer brothers. When, exhausted, they both fell to the ground, they found themselves to still be brothers, still neighbors, dependent on the same well, living along the same brook.

Who will make peace between France and Germany? In what conditions will this peace be made? There would be a great risk of erring in talking about the provisional peace, or rather armistice, that will be concluded in a few weeks or a few months. We speak here instead of the settling of scores that will take place one day for the good of the world between the two great nations of the center of Europe. To form an idea in this regard, one must first of all correctly understand in what way Germany came to conceive of the idea of its own nationality.

I

Germany's law of historical development in no way resembles France's; Germany's destiny, however, is in many ways similar to Italy's. Italy, founder of the old Roman Empire, jealous custodian of its traditions, never could become a nation like the others. Germany, succeeding the Roman Empire, founder of the new Carolingian Empire, considering itself the custodian of a universal power, of rights greater than national, had until recently not been a people. The Roman Empire and the papacy, which was its continuation, had doomed Italy. The Carolingian Empire almost doomed Germany. The Germanic emperor was no more capable of bringing about the unity of the German nation than the pope was of the Italian. One is not master in one's own home until one has no pretense to reign outside one's home. All countries that come to exert a political, intellectual, religious primacy over other peoples atone for it by the loss of their national existence for centuries.

Things did not go the same way with France. From the tenth century onward, France withdraws very distinctly from the empire. It loses the two jewels of the Western world, the imperial crown and the papal tiara, to its own advantage. Beginning with the death of Charles the Fat,[1] the empire becomes an exclusive appanage of the Germans, no king of France is ever Western emperor again. On the other hand, the papacy becomes the property of Italy. Francia, as the Treaty of Verdun[2] made it, is privileged precisely because of what it lacks: it has neither empire nor papacy, the two universals that perpetually trouble the country that possesses them in the task of its inner accretion. From the tenth century onward, Francia is completely national, and in fact in the second half of this century it substitutes the Carolingians, cumbersome Germans that defend it poorly, with a family, without doubt still Germanic, but quite truly wedded to the soil, the family of the dukes of France,[3] which has its own domain, and not, like the Carolingians, simply an abstract title. Hence begins around Paris that admirable progression of national development, which culminates in Louis XIV,[4] in the Revolution, and of which the nineteenth century will be able to witness the obverse, by consequence of the sad law that condemns human creations to enter upon the path of decadence and destruction as soon as they are completed.

Up until the French Revolution, Germany's idea was never to form a compact nationality. This great German race takes the taste of regional independence much farther than France. The possibility of wars we would call civil between parts of the same national family does not frighten it. It does not desire unity for its own sake, it desires it solely out of fear of the foreigner; it cares above all for the liberty of its interior divisions. This is what allowed it to accomplish the most beautiful act of modern times, the Lutheran Reformation, an act that was in our opinion superior to [Enlightenment] philosophy and Revolution, accomplishments of France, and second only to the Renaissance, the work of Italy; but one always has the defects of one's qualities. After the fall of the Hohenstaufen,[5] the general politics of Germany was indecisive, weak, marked with a sort of awkwardness; following the Thirty Years' War,[6] the consciousness of a German fatherland scarcely exists. French royalty exploited this pitiable political condition of a great race. It departed from its project, which was to assimilate only countries whose language was French; it seized Alsace, a German land. Time has legitimated this conquest, for Alsace subsequently took a brilliant role in the common endeavors of France. Nonetheless, in this fact, which in the seventeenth century shocked no one, lay the seed of a serious embarrassment for the age in which the idea of nationalities would become the mistress of the world and lead to assume, in questions of territorial delimitation, language and race as the criterium of legitimacy.

The French Revolution was, truth be told, the fact that generated the idea of German unity. The Revolution responded in a way to the wishes of the best minds in Germany; but they were quickly revolted by it. Germany remained legitimist and feudal; its conduct was nothing but a series of hesitations, of misunderstandings, of errors. The conduct of France was supremely inconsequent. While raising before the world the standard of national rights, it violated all nationalities in the intoxication of its victories. Germany was trampled by horses; German genius, which was then developing in such a marvelous manner, went unrecognized; its serious value was not grasped by the narrow minds that formed the intellectual elite of the Empire years; Napoleon's conduct with regard to the Germanic countries was a tissue of blunders. This great captain, this eminent organizer, was devoid of the most elementary principles in the realm of foreign policy. His idea of a universal domination of France was mad, for it is well established that any attempt at hegemony by one European nation provokes, by way of necessary reaction, a coalition of all the other states, a coalition of which England, guardian of the equilibrium, is always the originating core.*

A nation ordinarily does not attain complete consciousness of itself except under pressure from abroad. France existed before Joan of Arc and Charles VII; however, it is under the weight of English domination that the word *France* gained a particular note. An *I*, to employ the language of philosophy, is always constituted in opposition to another *I*. France thus created Germany as a nation. The wound had been too visible. A nation in the full flowering of its genius and at the highest point of its moral force had been yielded without defense to a less intelligent and less moral adversary by the wretched divisions of its petty princes, and for the lack of a central banner. Austria, a barely German aggregate, which introduced within the Germanic body a host of non-Germanic elements, constantly betrayed the German cause and sacrificed German interests to its own dynastic combinations. A point of rebirth then appeared: it was the Prussia of Frederick. A recent formation within the Germanic body, Prussia harbored all its effective strength. In terms of the background of its population it was more Slavic than Germanic; but this was not an inconvenience—on the contrary. It is almost always thus that the mixed and frontier countries effect the political unity of a race: recall the role of Macedonia in Greece and of Piedmont in Italy. The reaction of Prussia against the oppression of the French Empire was very fine. It is well known how the genius of Stein[7] derived from prostration itself the preconditions of force, and how the organization of the Prussian army, the starting point of the new Germany, was the direct consequence of the

---

* This was true only in the past. The old England, it seems, no longer exists nowadays (September 1871).

battle of Jena.[8] With his habitual presumption and lack of understanding of the Germanic race, Napoleon failed to see any of this. The battle of Leipzig[9] was the signal of a resurrection. From that day, it became clear that a new power of the first order (Prussia, holding in its hand the German banner) had made its entry into the world. Ultimately, the Revolution and the Empire had understood nothing about Germany, as Germany had understood nothing about France. The great Germanic minds had been able to salute with enthusiasm the great accomplishment of the Revolution, because the principles of this movement originally had been theirs, or rather those of the eighteenth century as a whole; but this lowly terrorist democracy,[10] transforming itself into military despotism and into the instrument of enslavement for all peoples, filled them with horror. By reaction, enlightened Germany showed itself to be in some ways hungering for the old order. The French Revolution found the obstacle that was to stop it in the organized feudality of Prussia, Pomerania, Holstein, that is to say in this stock of populations from the edges of the Baltic, antidemocratic to the highest degree, loyal to legitimacy, accepting to be led, beaten down, serving well when they are well commanded, having at their head a small village nobility, strong with all the strength that prejudice and narrow-mindedness afford. The true Continental resistance to the Revolution and the Empire came from this Vendée[11] of the north; it is there that the country gentleman, covered in ridicule among us by the high nobility, the court, the bourgeoisie, the common people themselves, took his revenge on French democracy, and prepared secretly, without noise, without plebiscites, without newspapers, the startling apparition that in the past few years has unfolded before us.

The necessity that under the Restoration obliged France to forswear any foreign ambition and the wise policy that under Louis-Philippe[12] reassured Europe held off for a time the danger that this anti-France of the Baltic, which is the complete negation of our most firm principles, harbored for the France that emerged from the Revolution. Apart from a few imprudent words by statesmen of a mediocre caliber and a few second-rate verses[13] by an empty-headed poet,* the France of this time worried little about Germany. Activity was focused inward and not toward outward aggrandizement. And this was completely appropriate. France is

---

*    It must be said that he was but responding to a provocation coming from Germany.

big enough; its mission does not consist in absorbing foreign countries, it consists in offering at home one of those dazzling developments of which it is eminently capable, to show the prosperous implementation of the democratic system it has proclaimed, and whose viability has so far not been fully proven. That a country with seventeen or eighteen million inhabitants, as was once the case with Prussia, would wager everything to exit, even at the cost of the gravest of perils, a situation that had it floating between large and small states, is only natural; but a country of thirty or forty million inhabitants has all that is necessary to be a great nation. That the borders of France may have been drawn poorly in 1815 is possible; but if one excludes a few faulty contours toward the Saarland and the Palatinate, which were traced, apparently, under the influence of puny military considerations, the rest seems all right to me. The Flemish lands are more Germanic than French; the Walloon lands have been prevented from coalescing with the French conglomerate by historical circumstances that have nothing fortuitous about them; it depended on the deep municipal spirit that rendered French royalty insufferable to these lands. The same can be said of Geneva and Swiss Romandy; one may add that the usefulness of these small French lands, politically separated from France, is considerable; they offer exile to the émigrés of our internal dissentions, and, in times of despotism, they serve as a refuge for free thought. Rhenish Prussia and the Palatinate are former Celtic lands, but profoundly Germanized over the past two thousand years. Except for a few isolated valleys separated from France in 1815 for reasons of strategy, France does not therefore have an inch of land to desire. England and Scotland have an area no greater than two-fifths of France, but does this mean England is obliged to aspire to territorial conquest in order to be great?

The fate of the year 1848, in this issue as in others, was to raise questions that it could not settle and that, after a year or two, received solutions by means diametrically opposed to those imagined by the parties then in power. The issue of German unity was loudly raised; according to the fashion of the times, it was thought that everything would be set right by means of a constituent assembly.[14] These efforts resulted in a resounding failure. Whether one calls the men of 1848 utopians or whether one blames the masses for not having been enlightened enough to follow them, it is certain that the attempts of that year were all fruitless. For ten years, the problems dozed, German patriotism appeared to be in mourning; but already a man was saying to those willing to listen: "These problems are not resolved the way you believe, by the free association of the people; they are resolved by fire and sword."[15]

The Emperor Napoleon III broke the ice with the Italian War,[16] or rather by the conclusion of that war, which was the annexation to France of Savoy and Nice. The first of these two annexations was fairly natural; of all the French-speaking lands not reunited to France, Savoy was the only one that could be ceded to us without inconvenience; since the duke of Savoy had become king of Italy, such a cession was almost in the nature of things. Nonetheless, this annexation produced many more inconveniences than advantages. It banned France from what makes its true strength, the right to invoke a disinterested policy, solely inspired by love of principles; it gave an exaggerated idea of the expansionary plans of the Emperor Napoleon III, displeased England, awakened the suspicions of Europe, provoked the daring initiatives of Mr. von Bismarck.

It is clear that, if ever there was a legitimate movement in history, it is the one that has drawn Germany to form into a single nation over the past sixty years. In any case, if someone has the right to complain about it, it is not France, since Germany only submitted to this tendency following our example, and in order to resist the oppression France subjected it to in the seventeenth century and under the Empire. France, having renounced the principle of legitimacy, which saw in this or that agglomeration of provinces into a realm or an empire only the consequence of the marriages, inheritances, or conquests of a dynasty, can understand one sole principle of delimitation in political geography, that is to say the principle of nationalities, or, what amounts to the same, the free wish of peoples to live together, demonstrated through serious and effective acts. Why refuse Germany the right to do in its own home what we have done in our own, what we have helped Italy to do in its own? Is it not evident that a hard, chaste, strong, serious race like the Germanic race, a race placed in the first rank by the gifts and the labors of thought, a race scarcely inclined to pleasure, all taken with its dreams and the satisfactions of its imagination, would wish to play in the order of political matters a role commensurate to its intellectual importance? The title of a nationality resides in its men of genius, "national treasures," who give an original shape to the sentiments of this or that people, and offer the great subject matter of the national spirit, something to love, to admire, to boast about in common.

Dante, Petrarch, the great artists of the Renaissance were the true founders of Italian unity. Goethe, Schiller, Kant, Herder created the German
fatherland. The wish to oppose a flowering announced by so many signs
would have been as absurd as the wish to oppose the rising tide. The wish
to give it advice, to trace the fashion in which we would have desired it
to be accomplished, was childish. This movement was occurring because
of distrust of us; to suggest rules for it was tantamount to furnishing a
suspicious and susceptible national consciousness with a positive criterium, and clearly inviting it to do the opposite of what we demanded.
Certainly I am the first to recognize the fact that some strange excesses
were mixed with the German nation's need for unity. The German patriot,
like the Italian patriot, is not easily separated from the old universal role
of his fatherland. Certain Italians still dream of the *primato*;[17] a great number of Germans link their aspirations to the memory of the Holy Roman
Empire, exercising over the whole European world a sort of suzerainty.
Now, the first precondition of a national spirit is to renounce any claim
of a universal role, universal roles being destructive of nationality. More
than once German patriotism has shown itself to be unjust and partial in
this guise. This theoretician of German unity who maintains that Germany must everywhere take back the fragments of its old empire refuses
to hear any argument when one talks to him of abandoning a land as
purely Slavic as the Grand Duchy of Posen.* The truth is that the principle
of nationality must be understood in a broad sense, without subtleties.
History has traced the borders of nations in a way that is not always the
most natural; each nation has too much, and too little; one must limit
oneself to what history has wrought and to the wishes of the provinces, in
order to avoid impossible analyses and inextricable difficulties.

If the idea of German unity was legitimate, it was also legitimate that
such unity be brought about by Prussia. The parliamentary attempts in
Frankfurt having failed, nothing remained except the hegemony of Austria, or of Prussia. Austria contains too many Slavs, it is too disagreeable

---

\* The possession of Posen by Prussia cannot be equated with France's possession of Alsace.
Alsace has Frenchified and no longer protests against its annexation, while Posen has
not Germanized and does protest. The parallel of Alsace is Silesia, a Slavic province by
race and language but sufficiently Germanized, whose legitimate possession by Prussia
nobody challenges any longer.

to Protestant Germany, it has failed too much, for centuries, in its duties as the leading power in Germany for it to be called upon once more to play a role of this type. On the other hand, if ever there was a well-defined historical calling, it was that of Prussia since Frederick the Great. It could not escape a discerning mind that Prussia was the center of a new ethnic vortex, that it played for the northern German nationality the role of the heart in an embryo, only to be absorbed, later, by the Germany it had created, as we see Piedmont absorbed by Italy. One man appeared to seize all these latent tendencies, to represent them and bring them to full fruition with matchless energy.

Mr. von Bismarck had two objectives that the most severe of philosophers could declare legitimate, if in practice the rather unscrupulous statesman had not demonstrated that force was for him synonymous with legitimacy: first of all, to chase Austria out of the German Confederation,[18] as Austria was a body more than half foreign that prevented it from existing; second, to gather around Prussia the members of the German fatherland that the accidents of history had dispersed. Did Mr. von Bismarck see beyond this? Did his necessarily limited point of view as a practical man allow him to suspect that one day Prussia would be absorbed by Germany and would disappear in a certain sense in its victory, just as Rome ceased to exist as a city the day it achieved its task of unification? I do not know, as Mr. von Bismarck has so far not made himself available for analysis; he will perhaps never do so. One of the questions a curious mind poses most often, when reflecting on contemporary history, is to determine whether Mr. von Bismarck is a philosopher, whether he sees the vanity of what he does, while still toiling at it eagerly, or whether he is a believer as to politics, whether he is fooled by his own work, as all absolute characters are, and does not see its deciduous nature. I lean toward the first hypothesis, as it seems difficult to me for so complete a mind not to be critical, not to determine in his most passionate action the limits and the weak side of his designs. Be that as it may, if he perceives in the future the impossibility of the solution that would consist of making Germany into an enlarged Prussia, he refrains from saying so, because the narrow fanaticism of the party of the Prussian squirearchy could not for a minute tolerate the thought that the goal of Prussia's actions is not to Prussianize all of Germany, and later the entire world, in the name of a sort of political mysticism whose secret it seems to want to keep to itself.

Mr. von Bismarck's plans were developed in the confidence and with the backing of the Emperor Napoleon III, as well as the small number of people who were privy to his designs. It is unjust to reproach the Emperor Napoleon for it. It was France that raised the banner of nationalities in the world; every nationality that is born and grows should do so with the encouragement of France, and become a friend to it. German nationality was a historical necessity; wisdom would have dictated not to stand in the way. The right policy is not to oppose what is inevitable; the right policy is to contribute to it and benefit from it. A great liberal Germany, created in full friendship with France, would have become a capital part of Europe, and would have created an invincible trinity with France and England, driving the world, and especially Russia, along the path of progress through reason. It was therefore supremely desirable that German unity come to pass not despite France, but, on the contrary, with our consent. France was not obliged to assist, but it was obliged not to oppose it; it was even natural to care about the goodwill of the future young nation, to reserve for ourselves something of that deep feeling that the United States of America will still long hold toward France in memory of La Fayette.[19] Was it appropriate to profit from the circumstances for our territorial enlargement? Not in principle, for such enlargements are more or less useless. How is France greater since the addition of Nice and Savoy? Nevertheless, since superficial public opinion set much store by these enlargements, it would have been possible, in the time of amicable negotiations, to agree upon certain transfers, relating to lands willing to be reunified with France, as long as it was well understood that these enlargements were not the goal of the negotiation—that its only goal was the friendship of France and Germany. To respond to the taunts of the statesmen of the opposition and satisfy certain military exigencies that no doubt have some grounds, one could have, for instance, agreed before the war on the transfer of Luxemburg, had it been willing, and the rectification of the Saarland, to both of which Prussia probably would have acceded at the time. I repeat, I consider that it would have been better not to demand anything: Luxemburg would not have brought us more force than Savoy or Nice did. As for the strategic contours of borders, how much better a bulwark a good policy would have been! The effect of a good policy would have been that nobody would have attacked us, or that, if somebody had taken the initiative against us, we would have been defended by the sympathy of the whole of Europe. Be that as it may, no choices were made; a lamentable indecision paralyzed the pen of the Emperor Napoleon III, and Sadowa[20] came without anything having been agreed upon for the future. This battle, which could have been a victory for France had one followed a consistent policy, thus became a defeat, and, eight days later, the French government went into mourning over the event to which it had itself contributed more than anyone.

Besides, at that moment, two elements that had played no part in the Biarritz conversations[21] entered the scene: French public opinion and Prussian public opinion, both exalted. Mr. von Bismarck is not Prussia; beside him is a fanatical, absolutist, monolithic party with which he must reckon. Mr. von Bismarck belongs to this party by birth but he does not share its prejudices. To capture the mind of the king, silence his scruples, and dominate the narrow counsels that surround him, Mr. von Bismarck is forced to make some sacrifices. After the victory of Sadowa, the fanatical party found itself more powerful than ever; any transaction became impossible. What happened to the Emperor Napoleon III will happen, I fear, to many of those who have relations with Prussia. This intractable spirit, this rigidity of character, this exaggerated pride will be the cause of many difficulties. In France, the Emperor Napoleon III similarly proved to be outflanked by a certain sector of public opinion. This time, the opposition was what it too often is, superficial and declamatory. It was easy to prove that the conduct of the government had been lacking in foresight and decisiveness. It is clear that at the time of Mr. von Bismarck's overtures, the government should either have refused to listen or have possessed a plan of action that it could support with a good army on the Rhine; but that was not a reason to keep arguing each year, as the opposition did, that France had been beaten at Sadowa, nor especially to make a doctrine of the idea that the border of France must be protected with small weak states that are enemies with one another. Could one invent more effective a means to persuade them to be united and strong? Mr. Thiers[22] contributed considerably by his avowals to excite German public opinion, which is persuaded that this honorable statesman represents the French bourgeoisie's prevailing opinion and its secret instincts.

The settlement of the Luxemburg matter placed this disastrous situation in stark relief. Nothing had been agreed upon between France and Prussia before Sadowa: Prussia therefore did not evade any engagement by refusing any concession; but, if moderation had been in the character of the Berlin court, how would it have failed to suggest that the emotion of France be taken into account, that its rights and its advantage not be pushed to the extreme? Luxemburg is an insignificant country, completely hybrid, neither German nor French, or, if one will, both. Its annexation to France, preceded by a plebiscite, had nothing in it to displease the primmest of Germans in his patriotism. Prussia's systematic rigidity demonstrated that it did not intend to preserve any grateful memory of the negotiations that had preceded Sadowa, and that France, despite the genuine support it had provided, remained its eternal enemy. On the French side, this result had been obtained by a series of errors; we had been so unadvised we did not even have the right to complain. We had tried to play subtly, but had found someone subtler still. We had acted like the man who, having an excellent hand, has not managed to resolve himself to play his cards, always keeping them for points that never come.

Is this to say, as many people believe, that since 1866 war between France and Prussia has been inevitable? Certainly not. When one can wait, few things are inevitable; now, one could have gained some time. The death of the king of Prussia and what one knows of the sensible and moderate character of the prince and princess of Prussia[23] could have changed many things. The Prussian feudal military party, which is one of the great sources of danger for the peace of Europe, seems destined in time to yield much of its ascendancy to the Berlin bourgeoisie, to the German character, so broad, so free, and which will become profoundly liberal as soon as it is delivered from the grasp of the Prussian barracks. I know that the symptoms of this hardly present themselves yet, and that Germany, always rather timid in action, has been conquered by Prussia, without any indication that Prussia is disposed to lose itself in Germany; but the time has not yet come for such an evolution. Accepted as a means of fighting France, Prussian hegemony will only weaken when such a fight no longer has reason to exist. The force with which the German movement is launched will produce very rapid developments. No analogy in history is valid any longer, if conquered Germany does not in turn conquer Prussia and absorb it. It is inconceivable that the German race, as averse to revolution as it is, will not overcome the Prussian core, as resistant as it may be. The Prussian principle, according to which the basis of a nation is an army, and the basis of an army a petty aristocracy, could not be applied to Germany. Germany, indeed even Berlin, has a bourgeoisie. The basis of the true German nation, as of all modern nations, will be a rich bourgeoisie. The Prussian principle has accomplished something very powerful, but which cannot last beyond the day Prussia completes its task. Sparta would have ceased to be Sparta, if it had brought about the unity of Greece. The Roman constitutions and mores disappeared once Rome became mistress of the world; beginning that day, Rome found itself governed by the world, and that was only fair.

Each year would thus have brought about the greatest transformations to the state of affairs that issued from Sadowa. The aberration of an hour dashed all the hopes of the best minds. Without considering that a young nation, in all the blaze of its development, has an immense advantage over an aged nation that has already fulfilled its project and achieved equality, we cheerfully plunged into the abyss. The arrogance and ignorance of military men, the thoughtlessness of our diplomats, their vanity, their foolish faith in Austria (an out-of-joint machine that should hardly be taken into consideration), the absence of serious equilibrium within the government, the outlandish outbursts of a will as intermittent as the awakenings of Epimenides,[24] have brought upon the human race the greatest woes it has known for the past fifty-five years. An incident[25] that a shrewd diplomat would have smoothed over in a few hours was sufficient to unleash hell. . . Let us withhold our curses; there are moments in which horrible reality is the cruelest of profanities.

II

Who made war? I believe we have answered that question. One must refrain, in these sorts of matters, from only seeing the immediate and proximate causes. If one were to limit oneself to the narrow consider-ations of an inattentive observer, France would be fully in the wrong. If one places oneself on a higher plane, responsibility for the horrible mis-fortune that has befallen humanity in this disastrous year must be shared. In Prussia's way of acting there easily is something hard, self-interested, and ungenerous. Feeling its own force, it made no concessions. From the moment Mr. von Bismarck decided to carry out his great undertakings in concert with France, he was obliged to accept the consequences of the policy he had chosen. Mr. von Bismarck was not required to take the Emperor Napoleon III into his confidence, but, having done so, he was required to have some consideration for the emperor and for the French statesmen, as well as for a sector of public opinion that had to be humored. Prussia's great ill is pride. As a powerful center of the old order, it is irritated by our bourgeois prosperity; its gentlemen are wounded to see commoners, I will not say richer than them, but exercising as they do the profession that elsewhere is the privilege of the nobility. Jealousy among them joins pride. "We are poor youths," they say, "younger branches seeking to make a position for ourselves in the world." One of the causes that produced Mr. von Bismarck was the wounded vanity of the diplomat steeped in insults by his Austrian colleagues who treated Prussia as an upstart. The sentiment that created Prussia was something analogous: the serious, poor, intelligent, charmless man suffers with difficulty the worldly successes of a rival who, while clearly inferior in solid qualities, shines in polite society, dictates fashion, and manages through aristocratic disdain to prevent him from being accepted.

France was no less guilty. The newspapers were superficial, the military party showed itself to be presumptuous and stubborn, the opposition seemed to care for nothing but the search for a false popularity, blaming the government if it prepared for war, insulting it if it did not wage it, speaking ceaselessly of the disgrace of Sadowa and the necessity of revenge; but the great ill was the excess of personal power. The conversion to parliamentary monarchy was lacking in seriousness to such an extent that an entire government, the Lower Chamber, the Senate all deferred almost without resistance to a personal notion of the sovereign that did not correspond in any way to their ideas or their desires.

Who now will make peace? The worst consequence of the war is to render those who did not want it powerless, and to open a fateful spiral in which common sense is termed cowardice, and at times treason. We will speak frankly. Only one force in the world will be capable of repairing the harm done to civilization in this circumstance by feudal pride, exaggerated patriotism, the excess of personal power, and the lack of development of parliamentary government on the continent.

This force is Europe. Europe has a major interest in preventing both nations from being either too victorious or too vanquished. The disappearance of France from the ranks of the great powers would be the end of the European equilibrium. I dare say that England in particular would feel its conditions of existence fully changed the day such an event came to pass. France is one of the preconditions of England's prosperity. England, following the great law that states that the primitive race of a country in the long run gains the upper hand against all invasions, becomes with each passing day more Celtic and less Germanic; in the great struggle of races, it is on our side; the alliance of France and England is established for centuries to come. Let England focus its thoughts on the United States, Constantinople, India; it will see it needs France, and a strong France.

Indeed, make no mistake: a weak and humiliated France cannot exist. Once France loses Alsace and Lorraine, France is no longer. The edifice is so compact, that the removal of one or two large stones would cause it to collapse. Natural history teaches us that an animal whose organization is strongly centralized cannot bear the amputation of a large member; we often see a man whose leg is cut off die of consumption; similarly, France, affected in its main limbs, would see general life extinguished and its central organs insufficient to circulate life to its extremities.

Thus, one should not hope to reconcile two contradictory things, preserving France and diminishing it. There are some absolute enemies of France who believe that the supreme goal of contemporary politics should be to suppress a power that, according to them, represents evil. That these fanatics advise finishing off the enemy they have temporarily beaten, is to be expected; but those who believe the world would be mutilated if France disappeared should take heed. A diminished France would lose all its parts in succession; the whole would dislocate, the south would separate; the centuries-long work of the kings of France would be demolished and, I swear to you, the day it occurred nobody would have grounds to rejoice. Later, when one will want to form the great coalition that all overweening ambition rouses, in Europe one will regret not having been more farsighted. Two great races face one another; both have accomplished great things, both have a great task to fulfill in common; one of them must not be placed in a state that is tantamount to its destruction. The world without France would be as mutilated as without Germany; these great organs of humanity each have their purpose: it is important to preserve them for the accomplishment of their various missions. Without attributing to the French spirit the leading role in the history of the human spirit, one must recognize that it plays an essential role: the concert would be affected if this note were lacking. Now, if you want the bird to sing, do not disturb its grove. If France were humiliated, you would no longer have the French spirit.

An intervention of Europe guaranteeing Germany complete freedom in its interior movements, maintaining the boundaries set in 1815, and barring France from dreaming of other ones, leaving France beaten, but proud in its integrity, consigning it to the memory of its errors and allowing it to disengage freely and as it pleases from the strange internal situation that it has created for itself: such is the solution that, according to us, the friends of humanity and civilization must desire. Not only would this solution put a stop to the horrible dispute that is now disrupting the European family, it would in addition contain the seed of a power destined to wield the most beneficent action for the future.

Indeed, how was a frightful event such as the one that will cast a memory of terror upon the year 1870 possible? Because the various European nations are too independent one from the other and have nobody above them, because there is no congress, no diet, and no amphictyonic court[26] superior to national sovereignties. Such an establishment exists in a virtual state, because Europe, especially after 1814, has frequently acted as a collective body, pressing forward its resolutions by dint of the threat of a coalition; but this central power has not been strong enough to prevent terrible wars. It must become so. The dream of the peace utopians, a court without an army to support its decisions, is a chimera; nobody will obey it. On the other hand, the opinion according to which peace will be secured only on the day in which one nation has an uncontested superiority over the others is the opposite of truth; any nation exercising hegemony prepares its own ruin by that alone, evoking the coalition of all against it. Peace cannot be established and maintained except by the common interest of Europe, or, if you prefer, by the league of neutrals shifting to a minatory attitude. Justice between two contending parties has no chance of prevailing; but among ten contending parties justice carries the day, for it is the only possibility for a common basis of understanding, a common ground. The force capable of maintaining against the most powerful of states a decision deemed useful to the preservation of the European family therefore only resides in the power of intervention, mediation, and coalition of the several states. Let us hope that this power, assuming ever more concrete and regular forms, will lead in the future to a true congress, periodical, if not permanent, and will be the heart of the United States of Europe, bound to each other by a federal pact. No nation then will have the right to call itself "the great nation," but each will be permitted to be a great nation, provided that it expect this title from the others and not claim to bestow it on itself. It will belong to history, later, to specify what each people has done for humanity and to designate the country that, at a certain time, managed to have over others some form of superiority.

In this fashion, we can hope that the frightful crisis in which humanity is entangled will experience a pause. The day after the scythe of death has been stopped, what should we do? Vigorously attack the cause of the illness. The cause of the illness was a lamentable political regime that made the existence of a nation dependent on the presumptuous boastfulness of obtuse military men, on the spite and wounded vanity of inconsistent diplomats. Let us oppose to this a parliamentary regime, a true government of the serious and moderate parts of the country, not the democratic chimera of the reign of popular will and all its vagaries but the reign of the national will, the result of the good instincts of the people skillfully interpreted by thoughtful reflection. The country did not want war; it never will; it wants its internal development, in the form of both wealth and public freedoms. Let us offer the foreigner the spectacle of prosperity, of liberty, of calm, of equality correctly understood, and France will regain the ascendancy it lost through the reckless acts of its military men and its diplomats. France has principles that, though debatable and dangerous in some respects, are made to seduce the world, when France is the first to give the example of the respect of these principles; let it display at home the model of a truly liberal state in which the rights of all are guaranteed, of a state that is benevolent toward other states and that definitively forswears the idea of enlargement, and everyone, far from attacking it, will strive to imitate it.

There exist in the world, I am aware of it, centers of fanaticism where temper still reigns sovereign; in certain countries there exists a military nobility, the natural-born enemy of these reasonable ideas, that dreams of exterminating what does not resemble it. The feudal element of Prussia on one side, Russia on the other, is of the age in which one possesses the sharpness of barbarian blood, without regress or disillusionment. France and, to a certain extent, England have achieved their goal. Prussia and Russia have not yet reached that moment when one has what one wanted, when one considers coolly what one has troubled the world for, and realizes that it is naught, that everything on earth is but an episode of an eternal dream, a wrinkle on the surface of infinity that in turn produces and absorbs us. These new and violent races of the north are much more naive; they are fooled by their desires; driven by the goal they set themselves, they resemble the young man who imagines that, once he obtains the object of his passion, he will be fully happy. Joined with this is a character trait, a sentiment that the sandy plains of the north of Germany always seem to have inspired, the sentiment of the uncorrupted Vandals faced with the customs and luxury of the Roman Empire, a sort of puritan fury, the jealousy and rage against the easy life of those who enjoy themselves. This somber and fanatical temper still exists in our day. Such "melancholy characters," as one used to say, believe they are charged with avenging virtue, redressing corrupted nations. For these ranters, the idea of the German empire is not that of a limited nationality, free in its own home, not busying itself with the rest of the world; what they want is a universal action of the Germanic race, renewing and dominating Europe. It is a completely chimerical frenzy; for let us suppose, to humor these sad characters, that France were annihilated, Belgium, Holland, Switzerland crushed, England passive and silent; what of the great specter of the Germanic future, the Slavs, who will aspire all the more to separation from the Germanic body the further the latter individualizes? Slavic consciousness mounts in proportion to Germanic consciousness, and contrasts it like an opposite pole; the one creates the other. The German has the right to a fatherland like everyone else; he has no more right to domination than anyone else. In any case, it must be noted that such fanatical aims are nowise the product of enlightened Germany. The most complete embodiment of Germany is Goethe. What is less Prussian than Goethe? Imagine this great man in Berlin, and the overflow of Olympian sarcasms that this rigidity devoid of gracefulness or spirit, this heavy mysticism of pious warriors and god-fearing generals would have inspired in him! Once delivered from the fear of France, these keen populations of Saxony, of Swabia will evade Prussian regimentation; the south in particular will resume its gay, serene, harmonious, and free life.

The way to bring this to pass is for us not to meddle with it. The great factor for Prussia is France, or, better said, the apprehension of interference by France in German affairs. The less France busies itself with Germany, the more German unity will be compromised, because Germany only wants unity as a precautionary measure. In this sense, France is Prussia's entire force. Prussia (I mean military and feudal Prussia) will have been a crisis, not a permanent condition; what will truly last is Germany. Prussia will have been the energetic means employed by Germany to rid itself of the menace of Bonapartist France. The reunion of German forces in the hands of Prussia is but a fact brought about by a passing necessity. Once the danger vanishes, the union will vanish, and Germany will soon return to its natural instincts. The day after its victory, Prussia will thus find itself faced with a hostile Europe and a Germany recovering its taste for individual autonomy. This is what makes me say with assurance: Prussia will pass, Germany will remain. Now, Germany, left to its own spirit, will be a liberal nation, peaceful, democratic even, in the legitimate sense; I believe that the social sciences will owe it some remarkable advances, and that many ideas that among us have donned the frightful mask of socialist democracy will appear there in beneficent and workable form.

The greatest error the liberal school could commit amid the horrors that besiege us would be to despair. The future is ours. This war, the subject matter of future curses, has happened because of a deviation from liberal maxims, maxims that are at one and the same time those of peace and of the union of peoples. The disastrous desire for revenge, a desire that would prolong extermination indefinitely, will be set aside by a wise development of liberal politics. It is a wrong idea to think that France can imitate Prussian military institutions. The social conditions of France do not permit all citizens to become soldiers, or those who are soldiers to remain so forever. To maintain an army organized in the Prussian fashion, a petty aristocracy is necessary; now, we do not have an aristocracy, and, if we did, the French spirit would dictate that we had a grand rather than a petty one. Prussia bases its strength on the development of primary education and on the identification of the army with the nation. The conservative party in France hardly accepts these two principles, and, as a matter of fact, it is not certain that the country would be capable of them. Prussia having, as Plutarch would put it, a more virtuous disposition than France, it can bear institutions that, applied without precautions, would perhaps produce among us some completely different results, and would be a source of revolutions. Prussia in this reaps the benefit of the great political and social abnegation of its populations. By obliging its rivals to tend to their primary education and imitate its *Landwehr*[27] (innovations that in Catholic and revolutionary countries will probably be anarchical), it forces them into a regime healthy for it, but unhealthy for them, like the drinker who obliges his partner to drink a wine that will inebriate her, while he keeps his reason.

In sum, the immense majority of the human race hates war. The truly Christian ideas of gentleness, justice, goodness increasingly conquer the world. The warlike spirit only survives among professional soldiers, in the noble classes of the north of Germany and in Russia. Democracy does not desire, does not understand war. The progress of democracy will be the end of these men of iron, survivors of another age, whom our century has witnessed with terror arising from the entrails of the old Germanic world. Whatever the outcome of the present war, this party will be beaten in Germany. Democracy has numbered its days. I have some qualms about certain tendencies of democracy, and I voiced them with sincerity a year ago;* but certainly, if democracy limits itself to ridding the human race of those who, for the satisfaction of their vanity and their grudges, would have millions of men slain, it will have my full approval and my grateful sympathy.

The principle of independent nationalities is not liable, as many think, to deliver the human race from the scourge of war; on the contrary, I have always feared that the principle of nationalities, substituting the gentle and patronizing doctrine of legitimism, would cause the struggles of peoples to degenerate into exterminations of races, and would expel from the code of the law of peoples those temperaments, those civilities that the erstwhile small political and dynastic conflicts allowed. One will see the end of war when one appends to the principle of nationalities the principle that is its corrective, that of a European federation, superior to all nationalities; let us add: when democratic issues, the counterpart of issues of pure politics and diplomacy, regain their importance. Recall 1848: the French movement was reproduced in simultaneous shocks throughout Germany. Everywhere the military leaders managed to smother the naive

---

\* The article on constitutional monarchy, reprinted at the end of this volume (text 5 in the present edition).

aspirations of the time; but who knows whether the poor folk these same military leaders are driving to slaughter today will not end up enlightening their consciousness? Certain German naturalists, who have the pretention to apply their science to politics, maintain, with a coldness that would pass for depth, that the law of the destruction of races and the fight for life can be discovered in history, that the stronger race necessarily drives out the weaker, and that the Germanic race, being stronger than the Latin race or the Slavic race, is called upon to overcome and subordinate them. We shall let this last pretention go, despite the fact that it may elicit quite a few qualifications. Similarly, let us not object to such eminent materialists that rights, justice, morality, things that have no meaning in the animal kingdom, are laws of humanity; minds so emancipated from the old ways of thinking would probably answer us with a smile. Let us limit ourselves to an observation; animal species do not enter into alliances with one another. Never has one seen two or three species in danger of being destroyed forming a coalition against their common enemy; the animals of one same country do not have alliances or congress with each other. The federative principle, guardian of justice, is the basis of humanity. Here is the guarantee of the rights of all; no European people can avoid bowing to such a tribunal. This great Germanic race, truly much greater than its clumsy apologists make it, will certainly have one loftier title in the future, if it can be said that its powerful action will have definitively introduced so essential a principle into European law. All the great military hegemonies, that of Spain in the sixteenth century, that of France under Louis XIV, that of France under Napoleon, promptly exhausted themselves. Let Prussia be warned, its radical policy may lead it into a series of complications that it will not be in a position to evade; a discerning eye could perhaps see even now the knot of the future coalition already formed. The wise friends of Prussia say softly, not as a threat, but as a warning: *Vae victoribus!*[28]

# 7

## TWO LETTERS TO MR. STRAUSS
### (*LETTRE & NOUVELLE LETTRE À M. STRAUSS,* 1870-1871)

### LETTER TO MR. STRAUSS

On August 18, 1870, a letter that Mr. Strauss paid me the honor of addressing to me on the events of the time appeared in the *Gazette d'Augsbourg*. It ended thus:

> Perhaps you will also find it strange that these lines only reach you through the intermediary of a newspaper. Without a doubt, in less turbulent times I would have obtained your prior agreement; but in the present circumstances before my request had reached your hands, and your answer mine, the appropriate moment would have passed. And besides, I think there may be some utility in having, in this crisis, two men belonging to the two rival nations, independent one from the other and alien to any partisan spirit, exchange their views without passion, but quite frankly, on the causes and the scope of the present struggle; for the pages I have written here will not have achieved their aim completely unless they provoke you to a similar exposition of your feelings on the matter, from your own point of view.

I allowed myself to be persuaded by this invitation; on September 16, 1870, the reply I reproduce hereafter appeared in the *Journal des débats*.

The previous day, the translation of Mr. Strauss's letter had appeared in the same newspaper.

*Dear sir and learned scholar,*

Your high and philosophical words reached us like a message of peace through this hell unleashed; they offered solace to us, and especially to me, who owe to Germany what I hold most dear, my philosophy—I would almost say, my religion. I was in the seminary of Saint-Sulpice around 1843 when I began to learn about Germany through Goethe and Herder. I felt as if I were entering a temple, and from that time on, everything I had held as pomp worthy of divinity produced upon me the effect of yellowed and withered paper flowers. Hence, as I wrote you the moment hostilities began, this war filled me with suffering, firstly, because of the frightful calamities it could not avoid bringing, secondly, because of the hatreds, the erroneous judgments it will spread and the wrongs it will cause to the progress of truth. The great misfortune of the world is that France does not understand Germany, and that Germany does not understand France: this misunderstanding can only get worse. Fanaticism can only be fought with an opposite fanaticism; after the war, we will confront characters narrowed by passion who will accept our free and broad equanimity with difficulty.

Your ideas on the history of the development of German unity are perfectly accurate. At the time I received the issue of the *Gazette d'Augsbourg* containing your fine letter, I was precisely busy writing an article[1] for the *Revue des deux Mondes*, to appear shortly, in which I exposed views identical to your own. It is clear that, once one has rejected the principle of dynastic legitimacy, all that is left as a basis for the territorial delimitation of states are the rights of nationalities, that is to say, of the natural groups determined by race, history, and the will of the populations. Now, if there is a nationality that has an obvious right to existence in all its independence, it is assuredly the German nationality. Germany has the best national title,

by which I mean a historical role of the first order, a soul, a
literature, men of genius, a particular conception of things
human and divine. Germany undertook the most important
revolution of modern times, the Reformation. Furthermore,
in the past century Germany has produced one of the finest
intellectual developments that ever was, a development that
has, if I dare say so, added one more degree to the human spirit
in depth and breadth—so much so that those who have not
assimilated this new culture are to those who have penetrated
it what those who only know arithmetic are to those who know
calculus.

That so great an intellectual force in connection with so
much morality and seriousness was destined to produce a
corresponding political movement, that the German nation
would be called to assume in the external, material, and
practical world an importance proportional to what it wielded
in the world of the mind, was evident to any educated person
not blinded by routine or superficial bias. What added to the
legitimacy of Germany's aspirations was that the need for unity
was, for it, a precautionary measure justified by the deplorable
lunacies of the First Empire,[2] lunacies that enlightened
Frenchmen condemn as much as the Germans do, but against
whose return it was reasonable to guard, as certain persons still
raise such memories with much thoughtlessness.

This is to say that in 1866 we (I speak here for a small
group of true liberals) greeted with great joy the omen of the
constitution of Germany into a great power. We found it no
more agreeable than you did to see this great and happy event
brought about by the Prussian army. You have demonstrated
better than anyone how far from the truth it is that Prussia is
the same thing as Germany. But no matter; we had on this an
opinion that I believe you share: German unity, having been
accomplished by Prussia, would absorb Prussia, in line with
the general law by which leaven disappears in the dough it
caused to rise. Thus, we saw the arrogant and jealous pedantry
that at times displeases us in Prussia gradually substituted and
finally supplanted by the German character, with its marvelous

broadness, its poetical and philosophic aspirations. We forgot, as you yourselves forgot, what was unappealing to our liberal instincts in a feudal country, very poorly parliamentarized, dominated by a small nobility besotted with a narrow orthodoxy and full of prejudices, so as to see in a coming future only Germany, that is to say, a great liberal nation, destined to bring about a decisive step forward in political, religious, and social matters and perhaps to accomplish what we have attempted in France, so far without success: a scientific and rational organization of the state.

How have these dreams been frustrated? How have they given way to the bitterest of realities? I explained my ideas on this point in the *Revue*; here they are in brief: one may magnify at will the proportion of mistakes of the French government, but it would be unfair to forget what was in many ways reprehensible in the conduct of the Prussian government. You know that the plans of Mr. von Bismarck were communicated in 1865 to the Emperor Napoleon III, who, in essence, acceded to them. If such assent derived from the conviction that the unification of Germany was a historical necessity and that it was desirable that such unification take place with the full friendship of France, the Emperor Napoleon III was completely right. I know by personal experience that, approximately a month before the beginning of hostilities in 1866, the Emperor Napoleon III believed in the success of Prussia and even hoped for it. Sadly, hesitation and the taste for successively contradictory actions dishonored the emperor in this occasion, as in many others. The victory of Sadowa[3] erupted before anything had been agreed upon. Inconceivable fickleness! Misled by the boasts of the military party, disconcerted by the rebukes of the opposition, the emperor let himself be convinced to view as a defeat what for him should have been a victory, which, in any case, he had desired and facilitated.

If success justifies everything, the Prussian government is entirely absolved; but we are philosophers, sir; we have the gullibility to believe that even the successful may have in part been wrong. The Prussian government had solicited and accepted a secret alliance with the Emperor Napoleon III and with France. Even though nothing had been stipulated, it owed the emperor and France some token of gratitude and sympathy. One of your compatriots, who presently exhibits against France more passion than I appreciate seeing in a gentleman, told me, at the time we are discussing, that Germany owed France much gratitude for the very real, though negative, role the latter had assumed at its founding. Led by a feeling of pride that will have unhappy consequences in the future, the cabinet in Berlin did not see things thus. Certainly, territorial enlargement in the case of a nation that already has thirty or forty million inhabitants bears little importance; the acquisition of Savoy and Nice[4] was more trouble than gain for France. Nonetheless, it is regrettable that the Prussian government did not moderate the severity of its claims in the Luxemburg affair. Had Luxemburg been ceded to France, France would not have been larger, nor Germany smaller; yet, this insignificant concession would have sufficed to satisfy superficial public opinion, which, in a country with universal suffrage, must be humored, and would have permitted the French government to conceal its retreat. In the greatest of the Crusader castles still extant in Syria, the Qal'at al-Hosn,[5] one can see the following inscription in beautiful twelfth-century characters on a stone amidst the ruins, an inscription the House of Hohenzollern should have carved on the escutcheon of all its castles:

*Sit tibi copia,*
*Sit sapientia,*
*Formaque detur;*
*Inquinat omnia*
*Sola superbia*
*Si comitetur.*[6]

Concerning the remote causes of the war, an impartial character can thus consider that the French government on one side and the Prussian on the other deserve almost equal parts of blame. As for the precipitating cause, this pitiful diplomatic incident[7]—or, rather, this cruel game of wounded vanity that, to avenge some diplomats' puny quarrel, unleashed all the scourges on the human race—you know what I think of it. I was in Tromsoë, where the most splendid snowy landscape of the polar seas reminded me of the isles of the dead of our Celtic and Germanic ancestors, when I learned the horrible news; I have never cursed the way I did that day the baneful fate that seems to condemn our unfortunate country to be led by nothing but ignorance, overconfidence, and ineptitude.

This war, whatever one may say, was in no way inevitable. France did not want war at all. One should not judge such things by newspaper declamations or street outcries. France is deeply peaceful; its attention is focused on the exploitation of the immense sources of wealth it possesses and on democratic and social questions. King Louis-Philippe[8] had seen the truth on this matter with much common sense. He perceived that France, with its eternal wound always ready to reopen (its lack of a universally accepted dynasty or constitution), could not wage a major war. A nation that has fulfilled its plan and attained equality cannot fight against young peoples, full of illusions and in the blaze of their development. Believe me, the sole causes of the war were the weakness of our constitutional institutions and the baleful advice presumptuous and narrow-minded generals and conceited and ignorant diplomats gave the emperor. The plebiscite played no role; on the contrary, this strange display, which demonstrated that the Napoleonic dynasty had put roots into the very innards of the country, should have led to the belief that the emperor would subsequently distance himself more and more from the behavior of a desperate gambler. A man who owns great land wealth would seem to us necessarily less inclined to take his chances on the roll of a die than the man whose wealth is doubtful. In reality, to avoid the dangers of a conflagration, it would have been sufficient to wait. How many issues, in the affairs of this unfortunate human race, must be resolved by not resolving them! After a few years, one notices with surprise that the issue no longer exists. Was there ever a national hatred comparable to the one that for six centuries divided France and England? Twenty-five years ago, under Louis-Philippe, this hatred was still fairly strong; almost everyone maintained that it could not end except in war; it has disappeared as if by a spell.

Naturally, dear sir, the enlightened liberals here have had but one wish since the fateful hour, to see the end of what never should have begun. France was completely in the wrong to appear desirous of opposing the interior developments of Germany; but Germany would commit no lesser a fault by wishing to prejudice the integrity of France. If one's goal were to destroy France, no plan is better conceived; mutilated, France would enter into convulsions, and perish. Those who, like some of your compatriots, believe that France must be eliminated from the circle of nations are consistent in demanding its diminution; they see clearly that this diminution would be its end; but those who, like you, believe that France is necessary to the harmony of the world must weigh the consequences that would follow from a partition. I may speak here with a sort of impartiality. I endeavored all my life to be a good patriot, as a gentleman should, but at the same time to avoid exaggerated patriotism as a source of error. My philosophy, after all, is idealism; where I see goodness, beauty, truth, there lies my fatherland. It is in the name of the true eternal interests of the ideal that I would be disconsolate if France ceased to exist. France is necessary as a remonstrance against pedantry, dogmatism, and narrow rigor. You who have understood Voltaire so well[9] must understand that. This levity for which we are reproached is ultimately serious and honest. Beware that, if our cast of mind, with its qualities and its shortcomings, were to disappear, human consciousness would certainly be diminished. Variety is necessary, and the first duty of the man who attempts with a truly pious heart to further the designs of the deity is to support and respect even the providential organs of the spiritual life of humanity that he finds least congenial and pleasing. Your famous Mommsen,[10] in a letter that left us rather sad, a few days ago compared our literature to the boggy waters of the Seine and attempted to preserve the world from it as from a poison. Well! This austere

scholar is therefore acquainted with our satirical papers and our
zany little farcical theater! Rest assured that, behind the wretched
charlatan literature that holds, as everywhere, the favors of the
crowd, there is still a highly distinguished France, different from
the France of the seventeenth and eighteenth century, yet of the
same lineage: first of all, a group of men of the highest worth and
the utmost seriousness, then an exquisite high society, charming
and serious at the same time, elegant, tolerant, amiable, knowing
everything without having learned anything, inferring by
instinct the latest results of any philosophy. Beware of upsetting
it. France, a very mixed country, presents the feature that certain
Germanic plants grow better here than on their native soil;
one could prove this point through examples from our literary
history of the twelfth century, the chansons de geste, Scholastic
philosophy, Gothic architecture. You seem to believe that the
diffusion of wholesome Germanic ideas would be facilitated by
certain radical measures. Think again. Such propaganda would
then be stopped short; the country would plunge wrathfully into
its national routines and its specific flaws. "So much the worse
for it!" your ranters will say. "So much the worse for humanity!"
I will add. The removal or the atrophy of a member causes the
entire body to suffer.

This is a solemn hour. There are two currents of opinion
in France. The first reasons thus: "Let us conclude this odious
game as quickly as possible; let us surrender everything,
Alsace, Lorraine; let us sign the peace treaty; then, hatred unto
death, ceaseless preparations, alliances with anyone, limitless
indulgence for all Russian ambitions; one single goal, one single
reason for life, a war of extermination against the Germanic
race." The second says: "Let us save the integrity of France,
develop the constitutional institutions, mend our flaws, not with
the dream of taking our revenge for a war in which we were
unjust aggressors, but rather by contracting an alliance with
Germany and England whose effect will be to lead the world
down the path of liberal civilization." Germany will decide
which of these two policies France will follow, and at the same
time it will decide the future of civilization.

Your hotheaded Germanists allege that Alsace is a Germanic land, unjustly separated from the German Empire. Observe that all nationalities are "rough estimates;" if one begins to discuss the ethnography of each canton, the door is open to wars without end. Some beautiful Francophone provinces do not belong to France, and this is very advantageous, even for France. Some Slavic lands belong to Prussia. These anomalies are of great use to civilization. The union of Alsace with France, for instance, is one of the events that contributed most to the propagation of Germanism; it is through Alsace that Germany's ideas, methods, books ordinarily make their way to us. It is indisputable that, if one were to put it to the Alsatian people, an immense majority would pronounce itself in favor of retaining unity with France. Is it worthy of Germany to absorb by force a rebel, resentful province that has become irreconcilable, especially since the destruction of Strasbourg? One's sensibility is truly shocked at times by the temerity of your statesmen. The king of Prussia appears to be in the process of taking upon himself the cumbersome task of solving the French question by giving, and consequently guaranteeing, a government to France.[11] Can one lightheartedly seek a similar burden? How can one fail to see that the consequence of such a policy will be to occupy France indefinitely with three or four hundred thousand men? So, does Germany wish to rival sixteenth-century Spain? What would become of its great and lofty intellectual culture then? Beware that one day, when one will want to identify the most glorious years of the Germanic race, one might prefer to the period of its military domination, branded perhaps by an intellectual and moral decline, the first years of this century, when, beaten, externally humiliated, it created for the world the highest revelation of reason humanity had ever known!

It is astonishing that some of your best minds fail to see this, and especially that they appear unwilling to contemplate the involvement of Europe in these matters. Peace, it seems, cannot be signed directly between France and Germany; it cannot but be the work of Europe, which censured the war and must desire that no members of the European family be excessively

weakened. You speak with just cause of guarantees against
the return of dangerous dreams; but what guarantee would
be worth that of Europe consecrating once again the current
borders and forbidding anyone from dreaming of changing the
boundaries set by the ancient treaties? Any other solution will
leave the door open to endless retaliations. If Europe does this,
it will have sowed the seed for the future of the most productive
institution—I mean a central authority, a sort of congress of the
United States of Europe, which would judge nations, prevail
over them, and correct the principle of nationality with the
principle of federation. Up to now, this central force of the
European community barely showed itself in action except in
the transitory coalitions against the people aspiring to universal
domination; it would be good if a sort of permanent and
preventive coalition were to form for the protection of great
common interests, which, after all, are those of reason and
civilization.

The principle of European federation can thus offer a basis
for mediation similar to what the church offered in the Middle
Ages. One is at times tempted to assign an analogous role to
democratic tendencies and to the importance social problems
have acquired in our day. The movement of contemporary
history is a sort of oscillation between patriotic questions, on
one hand, and democratic and social questions, on the other.
These latter problems have an aspect of legitimacy to them,
and they will perhaps, in a sense, be the great pacification
of the future. It is certain that the democratic party, despite
its aberrations, raises issues superior to the fatherland; the
supporters of this party join hands above any national divisions
and affect the greatest indifference for points of honor, which
especially concern the nobility and the military. The thousands
of poor folk who presently are killing one another for a cause
they only half understand do not hate each other; they have
needs, and interests, in common. That one day they manage to
reach an agreement and join hands despite their leaders, is no
doubt a dream; one may nonetheless glimpse that more than
one angle of Prussia's excessive policy favors the rise of ideas it

does not suspect. It seems difficult that this fury of a handful
of men, the remnant of old aristocracies, will lead for much
longer to the slaughtering of masses of meek populations, who
have reached a fairly advanced democratic consciousness and
are more or less infatuated with economic ideas (which are
sacred to them) the specificity of which is precisely to disregard
national rivalries.

Ah, my dear sir! Jesus did well to establish the kingdom of
God, a world superior to hatred, jealousy, and pride, in which
the worthiest of esteem are not, like in the sad times we are
traversing, those who cause the greatest harm, who hit, kill,
insult, who are the greatest liars, the least loyal, the rudest,
the most mistrustful, the most treacherous, the most prolific
in evil methods, in diabolical ideas, the most impervious to
pity, to forgiveness, those who have no civility, who surprise
their adversary, who play the most wicked tricks; but rather,
the meekest, the most modest, the farthest removed from all
assertiveness, boastfulness, callousness, those who defer to
everyone, those who consider themselves the last! War is a web
of sins, an unnatural condition in which it is recommended to
commit as a noble act what at all other times is forbidden as a
sin or a fault, in which it is a duty to rejoice in the misfortunes
of others, in which he who would render blessing for evil,
who would practice the evangelical injunction to pardon
insults, to accept humiliation, would be preposterous and even
reprehensible. What allows entry into Valhalla excludes from
the kingdom of God. Have you noticed that neither in the eight
Beatitudes nor in the Sermon on the Mount nor in the gospel
nor in the whole of primitive Christian literature is there a
single word that places the military virtues among those that
gain entry into the kingdom of Heaven?

Let us insist on these great teachings of peace, which elude
men who are duped by their pride, driven by their eternal and
so very unphilosophical neglect of death. Nobody has the right
to ignore the disasters of his own country; but the philosopher,
like the Christian, always has reasons to live. The kingdom of
God knows neither vanquisher nor vanquished; it consists in

the joys of the heart, the spirit, and the imagination, which
the vanquished savors more than the vanquisher, if he is more
advanced morally and has more character. Have your great
Goethe, your admirable Fichte not taught us how one can lead
a noble and consequently happy life surrounded by the external
abasement of one's country? One reason, after all, grants me
great peace of mind; last year, during the elections for the
renewal of the Corps législatif,[12] I offered myself to the suffrage
of the electors; I was not chosen; my posters can still be seen on
the walls of the villages of the Seine-et-Marne; they read: "No
revolution, no war. A war would be as disastrous as a revolution."
To have a clear conscience in times such as ours one must be able
to tell oneself that one has not systematically escaped public life,
any more than one has sought it out.

Please retain your friendship for me always, and accept my
highest regards.

Paris, September 13, 1870


## NEW LETTER TO MR. STRAUSS

*Paris, September 15, 1871*

*Dear sir and learned scholar,*

At the end of the letter you addressed to me through the *Gazette
d'Augsbourg* on August 18, 1870, you invited me to set forth my
views on the terrible situation created by the latest developments.
I did so; my reply to your letter appeared in the *Journal des
débats* on September 16; the previous day, the translation of your
letter, as your excellent French translator, Mr. Charles Ritter, had
sent it to us, had been placed in the same newspaper. If you will
consider the conditions prevailing in Paris at that time, you will
perhaps recognize that this newspaper demonstrated a certain
amount of courage thereby. The siege began the following day,

and all communication between Paris and the rest of the world
was severed for five months.

Several days after the signing of the armistice in February
1871, I learned some surprising information, namely that on
October 2, 1870, you had responded in the *Gazette d'Augsbourg*
to my letter of September 16. Assuredly, you must not have
believed the Prussian blockade would be as thorough as it was;
for, if you had, it is unlikely that you would have addressed
an open letter to me that I could neither read nor respond
to. Misunderstanding in these delicate matters is easy; it is
imperative that the person who has been addressed have the
opportunity to give explanations and rectify, if needs be, the
opinions attributed to him. In the case in question, the fear of
a misunderstanding was not chimerical. Indeed, among several
rectifications I would make to your response of October 2, there
is one that has some importance. Misled by the expression "the
treaties of 1814" that we often employ in France to refer to the
body of agreements that set the borders of France at the fall
of the First Empire, you believed that I demanded after Sedan
that the transfers of 1815 be revisited, that Saarlouis and Landau
be returned to us.[13] I am vexed that you presented me to the
German public as capable of such an absurdity. It seems to me
that, if there is one idea that appears clearly from what I have
written on this catastrophic war, it is that national borders
should have been kept such as history had fashioned them, that
any annexation of land without the consent of the populations
was a mistake and even a crime.

A circumstance further enhanced my distress. A few days
after I learned of the existence of your letter of October 2,
I discovered that the *Gazette d'Augsbourg* had not run the
translation of my September 16 letter, so that this newspaper,
after having invited me, by your intercession, to enter the
debate and after having seen the *Journal des débats* (whose
situation was so much more awkward than its own) insert
your haughty pages under the threat of popular riots, refused
to bring to the victorious German public the humble pages in
which I called for a bit of generosity and pity for my defeated

fatherland. I know you rued this way of proceeding; but this is
where I am astonished by what your impassioned patriotism
is capable of; for, rather than withdraw from a discussion
in which your adversary is denied a chance to speak, a few
days later you placed in that very same *Gazette d'Augsbourg* a
rejoinder to the letter you had me write and did not have the
merit to have published. Here, sir, is where I clearly perceive
the difference in our ways of understanding life. The passion
that fills you and appears sacred to you is capable of eliciting
from you a distressing act. One of our weaknesses, on the
contrary, one of the weaknesses of us Frenchmen of the old
school is to believe that the sensitivities of a gentleman come
before any duty, any passion, any belief, before the fatherland,
before religion. This is a disadvantage, because we are not
always returned the favor, and, like all sensitive people, we play
the role of fools in a world that fails to understand us.

It is true that you have subsequently done me an honor,
which I appreciate, as I should. You have translated my reply
yourself and have published it in a pamphlet, together with
your two letters.* You have decided that the proceeds from this
pamphlet should finance an institution for German invalids.
God forbid I quibble with you over intellectual property! The
work to which you had me contribute is, after all, humanitarian
work, and if my spindly prose managed to fetch a few cigars
for those who ransacked my house in Sèvres, I thank you for
having offered me the opportunity to fit my conduct to some of
the precepts of Jesus I believe are the most authentic. But again,
notice the slight nuances. Most certainly, if you had allowed me
to publish a work of yours, never, never would I have conceived
the idea of turning it into an edition whose proceeds would flow
to our Hôtel des Invalides. The goal sweeps you away; passion
prevents you from noticing these affectations of jaded people
that we call taste and tact.

In the past year, I have experienced what those who counsel
moderation in times of crisis always experience. The events,

---

* Leipzig, Hirzel, 1870.

as well as the immense majority of public opinion, disagreed.
I cannot say, however, that I have changed my mind. Let us wait
ten or fifteen years; my conviction is that the enlightened part
of Germany will then acknowledge that, by suggesting it make
light use of its victory, I was its best friend. I do not believe in
the staying power of things taken to extremes, and I would be
quite surprised if so absolute a faith in the virtue of a race as
what Mr. von Bismarck and Mr. von Moltke[14] profess did not
lead to a severe disappointment. Germany, by turning itself over
to the statesmen and warriors of Prussia, has climbed atop a
fiery steed that will lead it where it knows not. You wager too
heavily. What does your conduct resemble? Precisely France's
at the time for which it is most blamed. In 1792,[15] the European
powers provoked France. France defeated the powers, as it had
a right to do; then it pushed its victories to excess, in which it
was wrong. Excess is bad; pride is the only vice that is punished
in this world. To triumph is always a demerit and, in any case, is
very unphilosophical. *Debemur morti nos nostraque.*[16]

Do not imagine you are more shielded from error than
others. For the past year, your newspapers have shown
themselves to be no doubt less ignorant than ours, but quite as
vehement, quite as immoral, quite as blind. They do not see a
mountain that stands in front of their eyes, the ever-growing
opposition of Slavic consciousness to Germanic consciousness,
opposition that will lead to a frightful conflict. They do not see
that by destroying the northern pole of a battery one destroys
the southern one also, that French solidarity caused German
solidarity, that, by its death, France will have its revenge and
serve Germany ill. In other terms, Germany made the mistake
of crushing its adversary. Those who lack an antithesis lack
a purpose. If there no longer were any orthodox persons,
neither you nor I would exist; we would be facing a stupid
vulgar materialism, which would kill us much better than
the theologians. Germany behaved with France as if it would
never have another enemy. Now the precept of the old sage
*ama tanquam osurus*[17] must today be reversed; one should hate
as if one were to become someday the ally of the hated one;

we ignore whose friendship we will be compelled to seek in the future.

It serves no purpose to state that sixty or seventy years ago we acted exactly in the same fashion, that we then conducted the war of pillage, massacre, and conquest in Europe for which we now blame the Germans of 1870. We have always condemned these wrongdoings of the First Empire; they are the work of a generation with which we have little in common and whose glory is not our own. Wrongly, it seems, we had accustomed ourselves to believing that the nineteenth century had ushered in an era of civilization, peace, industry, and sovereignty of populations. "How, one says, can you call the surrender of souls to which, in the past, other races fully as noble as yours consented, and from which you yourselves benefited, crimes and disgraces?" Let us distinguish the dates. The rights of the past are not the rights of today. The sentiment of nationality is not a hundred years old. Frederick II[18] was no more of a bad German in his disdain for the German language and literature than Voltaire was a bad Frenchman to rejoice for the outcome of the battle of Rossbach.[19] The surrender of a province was, at the time, nothing more than a transfer of real estate from prince to prince; the people remained most often indifferent. We brought this self-consciousness of peoples into the world by our Revolution; we have brought it to those we fought, and often fought unjustly; it is our dogma. This is why we French liberals were for the Venetians, for the Milanese against Austria; for Bohemia, for Hungary against Viennese centralism; for Poland against Russia; for the Greeks and the Slavs of Turkey against the Turks. There was an outcry on the part of Milan, Venice, Bohemia, Hungary, Poland, the Greeks and Slavs of Turkey: that sufficed for us. We were similarly for the Romagnols against the pope, or rather against the foreign coercion that kept them subject to the pope against their wishes; for we could not accept that a population be sequestered against its will for the benefit of a religious idea that claims it needs a territory in order to survive. In the American War of Secession, many good minds, while feeling little sympathy for

the Southern states, could not bring themselves to deny them
the right to recede from an association to which they no longer
wished to belong, since they had proven by harsh sacrifices that
their will in this matter was serious.

This rule of politics has nothing deep or transcendent to it;
but one must guard against losing one's justice and humanity
by dint of erudition and metaphysics. War will be endless if one
does not accept a statute of limitations for the violence of the
past. Lorraine was part of the German Empire, without the least
doubt; but Holland, Switzerland, Italy itself, down to Benevento,
and reaching back before the Treaty of Verdun,[20] the whole of
France, comprising even Catalonia, have also been a part of it.
Alsace is a Germanic land now by language and race; but before
being invaded by the Germanic race Alsace was a Celtic land,
as was a part of southern Germany. We do not conclude from
it that southern Germany must be French; but one should no
more claim that by ancient right Metz and Luxemburg must be
German. Nobody can say where this archaeology would stop.
Almost anywhere the fiery patriots of Germany claim Germanic
rights we could claim prior Celtic rights, and before the Celtic
period there were, they say, the foreign tribes, the Finns, the
Laplanders; and before the Laplanders, there were the cavemen;
and before the cavemen, there were the orangutans. With this
philosophy of history, the only legitimate rights in the world
will be the rights of the orangutans, unjustly dispossessed by the
perfidy of the civilized.

Let us be less absolute; next to the rights of the dead, let us
grant a small part to the rights of the living. The treaty of 843,
an agreement reached among three barbarian headmen who
most definitely only heeded their own personal convenience
in the division, cannot be an eternal basis for national rights.
The marriage of Mary of Burgundy with Maximilian[21] cannot
impose itself forever on the people's will. It is impossible to
accept that humanity be bound for an indefinite number of
centuries by the marriages, the battles, the treaties of obtuse,
ignorant, selfish creatures who, in the Middle Ages, headed
the affairs of this fallen world. Those of your historians, such

as Ranke, Sybel, who see in history nothing but the canvas of princely ambition and diplomatic intrigue, for whom a province is summed up by the dynasty, often of foreigners, who owned it, are as unphilosophical as the naive school that considers the French Revolution to have marked an absolutely new era in history. Only a middle ground between these extremes seems practical to us. Sure, we reject the equality of human individuals and the equality of races as a fundamental factual error; the high parts of humanity must dominate the low parts; human society is a building with several stories, where mildness, kindness must reign (man is held to it, even toward animals), not equality. But the European nations, as history has made them, are the peers of a great senate in which each member is inviolable. Europe is a confederation of states united by the common idea of civilization. The character of each nation is no doubt formed by race, language, history, religion, but also by something much more tangible—by present consent, by the will the various provinces of a state have to live together. Before the unfortunate annexation of Nice, not one canton of France wished to separate itself from France; that sufficed for it to be a European crime to dismember France, though France is not of one language or race. On the contrary, parts of Belgium and Switzerland and, up to a point, the Channel Islands, though French speaking, in no way wish to belong to France; this suffices for it to be criminal to attempt to annex them by force. Alsace is German by language and race; but it does not desire to be part of the German state; that settles the matter. One speaks of the rights of France, the rights of Germany. These abstractions affect us much less than the right of the Alsatians, living beings of flesh and bones, to obey only the power to which they have consented.

Thus, do not criticize our French liberal school for considering as a sort of divine right the right of populations not to be transferred without their consent. For those who, like us, no longer accept the dynastic principle that equates the unity of the state with the personal rights of the sovereign, there is no longer any other law of peoples than that. As a legitimist nation lets itself be hacked to pieces for its dynasty, so are we obliged to

make the most extreme sacrifices in order that those who were
bound to us by a life-and-death pact may not suffer violence.
We do not accept the surrender of souls; if the territories to be
surrendered were deserted, nothing better; but the men who
inhabit them are free beings, and our duty is to have them
respected.

Our policy is the policy of the law of nations; yours is the
policy of races: we believe ours has greater worth. The excessively
accentuated division of humanity into races, in addition to
resting on a scientific error—since very few countries possess a
truly pure race—can only lead to wars of extermination. These
"zoological" wars, allow me to say so, are analogous to those the
different species of rodents or carnivores wage for life. It would
be the end of this fertile intermixture, composed of numerous
and equally necessary elements, that is called humanity. You
have raised in the world the standard of ethnographic and
archaeological politics instead of liberal politics; this politics
will be fatal to you. Comparative philology, which you have
created and wrongly transported to the field of politics, will
play evil tricks on you. The Slavs are becoming passionate for
it; each Slavic schoolteacher is an enemy for you, a termite
who wrecks your house. How can you believe the Slavs will not
do to you what you do to others, they who march behind you
in all things, follow your trail step after step? Every assertion
of Germanism is an assertion of Slavism; each movement of
concentration on your part is a movement that "precipitates" the
Slav, extricates him, makes him exist separately. A glance at the
affairs of Austria shows this clearly. The Slav, in fifty years, will
know that it is you who have made his name into a synonym of
"slave"; he will see this long historical exploitation of his race
by yours, and the number of Slavs is two times your own, and
the Slav, like the dragon of the Apocalypse, whose tail sweeps
away a third of the stars,[22] will drag behind him one day the
herd of Central Asia, the old clientele of Genghis Khan and
Tamerlane. How much better it would have been to preserve for
yourselves against that day the appeal to reason, to morality, to
friendships of principles! Imagine what a weight will bear upon

the balance of the world the day Bohemia, Moravia, Croatia, Serbia, all the Slavic populations of the Ottoman Empire, surely destined to emancipation, races who are still heroic, completely military, and needful of nothing but leadership, group around the great Muscovite conglomeration, which already encompasses within a Slavic gangue so many different elements, and which indeed appears the chosen core of the future Slavic unity, just as Macedonia, barely Greek, Piedmont, barely Italian, Prussia, barely German, were the center of the formation of Greek, Italian, German unity. And you are too wise to count on the gratitude Russia owes you. One of the secret causes of the bad feelings of Prussia against us is that it owes us a part of its culture. One of the wounds of the Russians will one day be to have been civilized by the Germans. They will deny it, but they will admit it to themselves as they deny it, and the memory will exasperate them. The academy of Saint Petersburg will one day resent the Berlin one, for having been entirely German, the way the Berlin one blames us for having, in the past, been half French. Our century is the century of the triumph of the serf over his master; the Slav was, and in some respects still is, your serf.

Now, on the day of the Slavic conquest, we will be worth more than you, just as Athens under the Roman Empire kept a clear role, while Sparta had none.

Hence, beware of ethnography, or, rather, do not apply it overmuch to politics. With the pretext of a Germanic etymology, you seize for Prussia a given village of Lorraine. The names of Vienna (Vindobona), Worms (Borbetomagus), Mainz (Mogontiacum) are Gallic; we will never demand these cities; but if one day the Slavs come to demand Prussia proper, Pomerania, Silesia, Berlin, for the reason that all these names are Slavic, if they do on the Elbe and the Oder what you have done on the Moselle, if they map the villages of the Obotrites and the Veleti,[23] what will you have to say? Nation is not synonymous with race. Tiny Switzerland, so solidly built, contains three languages, three or four races, two religions. A nation is a great, centuries-long (but not eternal) association among provinces, part of which are of the same kind and form the core

around which other provinces gather, bound to one another
by common interests or by ancient events that have been
accepted and have become interests. England, which is the most
perfect of nations, is the most mixed from the point of view
of ethnography and history. Pure Britons, Romanized Britons,
Irishmen, Caledonians, Anglo-Saxons, Danes, pure Normans,
Frenchified Normans, everything is merged therein.

And I dare say that no nation will stand to suffer as much by
this spurious way of reasoning than Germany itself. You know
better than I do that what set apart the great ascendancy of
the Germanic race in the world, from the fifth to the eleventh
century, was not so much that it occupied vast contiguous lands
as a compact population but that it swarmed over Europe and
introduced a new principle of authority. While Germanism
lorded over the entire West, Germania proper had a meager
extension. The Slavs came up to the Elbe, the old Gallic base
endured; so much so that the Germanic empire was not much
more than a Germanic feudal class ruling over a Slav and
Gallic base. Beware: in this century of resurrections of the
dead, strange things may come to pass. If Germany gives in
to a sentiment that is too exclusively national, it will see its
area of moral influence shrink in proportion. Bohemia, which
was half-digested by Germanism, slips from you, like the prey
already swallowed by a boa snake who revived in the esophagus
of the monster and made desperate efforts to break out. I am
ready to believe Slav consciousness is dead in Silesia, but you
will not assimilate Posen.[24] These operations need to be brought
off straightaway, while the patients sleep; if they happen to
awake, they can no longer be resumed. A universal suspicion
of your power of assimilation, of your schools, will spread. A
vast effort to exclude your nationals, who will be considered
the forerunners of your armies, will long be the order of the
day. The silent infiltration of your emigrants into the large
cities, which had become one of the most important and most
beneficial social facts of our century, will be much attenuated.
The German, having revealed his zest for conquest, will only
advance as a conqueror. Under the most peaceful exterior, one

will see an enemy attempting to become the boss in someone else's home. Believe me, what you have lost is not nearly compensated by the five billion[25] you have gained.

Everyone must mistrust whatever absolute and exclusivist traits are in his character. Let us never imagine that we are so far in the right that our adversaries are completely wrong. The heavenly Father arranges His sun to rise with equal benevolence on the most diverse spectacles. What we find evil is often useful and necessary. As for myself, I would be irritated with a world where everyone led the same type of life as me. Being a former cleric, I have compelled myself, as you have, to follow the rule of manners strictly; but I would be saddened if there existed no fashionable people to represent a freer way of life. I am not rich; but I could hardly live in a society where there were no affluent people. I am not Catholic; but I am pleased that there are Catholics, Sisters of Charity, country priests, Carmelites, and if I had the power to suppress them all I would not. Similarly, Germans, tolerate what does not resemble you! If everyone were made in your image, the world would perhaps be a bit dreary and boring; your wives themselves have trouble tolerating this excessively virile austerity. This universe is a spectacle a god offers himself. Let us serve the intent of the great choragus by contributing to make the spectacle as brilliant and varied as possible.

Your Germanic race still seems like it believes in Valhalla; but Valhalla will never be the kingdom of God. With this military splendor, Germany is at risk of missing its true vocation. Let us all resume work together on the great and true problems, social problems, which may be summarized thus: to find a rational organization of humanity that is as just as possible. These problems were stated by France in 1789 and 1848; but generally the one stating the problems is not the one that resolves them. France tackled them in too simple a manner; it thought it had found a solution by pure democracy, universal suffrage, and dreams of the communist organization of labor. The two attempts have failed, and this double setback was the cause of disagreeable reactions, toward which it is good to be indulgent, if one considers that initiative in these matters has at least some

merit. Tackle these problems yourselves. Create for people
an association outside of the state and beyond the family that
raises them, supports them, corrects them, helps them, makes
them happy—what the church was and is no longer. Reform
the church, or put something else in its place. The excess of
patriotism harms such universal projects whose basis is Saint
Paul's expression: *Non est Judaeus neque Graecus.*[26] It is precisely
because your great men of eighty years ago were not too patriotic
that they opened this broad road, on which we are their disciples.
I fear that your ultrapatriotic generation, by rebuffing anything
that isn't purely Germanic, is fashioning itself a much narrower
audience. Jesus and the founders of Christianity were not
German. Saint Boniface[27] and the Irishmen who taught you to
write in the time of the Carolingians, the Italians, who have been
the teachers of all of us twice or three times, were not German.
Your Goethe recognized he owed something to that "debauched"
France of Voltaire and Diderot. Let us relinquish this petty
fanaticism to the inferior regions of public opinion. Allow me
to say so: you have diminished yourselves. You have been more
pettily patriotic than us. Among us, some superior men have
found calm and impartiality in their philosophy; among you,
I know of no one, outside the democratic party, who has not
been shaken in the coolness of his judgment, who has never been
unjust, who did not recommend doing in the sphere of national
relations what would have been a disgrace according to the
principles of private morality.

But I shall stop here; it is too naive nowadays to speak of
moderation, of justice, of fraternity, of the gratitude and respect
peoples owe one another. The conduct you will be obliged
to assume in the provinces annexed against their will shall
consummate your loss of morality. You will be obliged to disown
all your principles, to treat as criminals men you should respect,
men who will not have done anything but what you yourselves
did so nobly after Jena;[28] all moral ideas will be corrupted.
Our system of European equilibrium and amphictyony[29] will
be dismissed to dreamland; our liberal theses will become
an outmoded jargon. Thanks to Prussian statesmen, France
will long have but one goal: to reconquer the lost provinces.

Fomenting the Slavs' ever-growing hatred of the Germans, furthering Pan-Slavism, seconding all Russian ambitions unconditionally, dangling the reestablishment of the pope in Rome[30] in front of the Catholic party that is present everywhere; at home, surrendering to the legitimist and clerical party of the west,[31] that alone possesses intense fanaticism: this is the policy such a situation demands. It is precisely the opposite of what we had dreamed of. One cannot serve two rival causes in turn. We will not be the ones who advocate the destruction of what we have loved, provide a plan cleverly to profit from the Roman question, become Russians and papists, recommend mistrust and malevolence toward foreigners; but we would be guilty in another respect if we attempted, by advocating once again for a generous and disinterested course, to prevent the country from hearing the voices of two million Frenchmen who demand the help of their former fatherland.

France is saying, like your Herwegh,[32] "enough of this kind of love, let us try hate now."[33] I will not follow it in this new experiment, in which, anyway, one may doubt it will succeed; the resolution France keeps least is that of hating. In any case, life is too brief for it to be wise to waste one's time and consume one's forces in so wretched a game. I have worked in my humble sphere for the friendship of France and Germany; if now is "the time to refrain from embracing," as the Ecclesiastes says,[34] I step back. I will not recommend hatred, having recommended love. I will be silent. Harsh and proud is this Germanic virtue, which punishes us, like Prometheus, for our rash attempts, for our crazy "philanthropy." But we can say along with the great vanquished: "Jupiter, despite all his pride, would do well to be humble. Now, for he is the winner, for he sits in state at ease, trusting the sound of his thunder and shaking his flame-tongued spear in his hand. All this will not protect him from falling ignominiously one day with a horrible plunge. I see him fashioning his own enemy, a very difficult monster to fight, who will discover a flame superior to lightning, a sound superior to thunder. Beaten then, he will discover how different it is to reign and to serve."[35]

Please accept, learned sir, my highest regards.

# 8

## INTELLECTUAL AND MORAL REFORM OF FRANCE (*LA RÉFORME INTELLECTUELLE ET MORALE DE LA FRANCE*, 1871)

### PREFACE[1]

The lengthiest of the pieces contained in the present volume encompasses the reflections that occurred to me during those painful weeks in which a good Frenchman should have had no thought but for the sufferings of his fatherland. I harbor no illusions as to the influence these pages may exert. The role of writers whose lot is to voice unseasonable truths does not differ much from the fate of that madman of Jerusalem who ceaselessly walked the walls of the city destined to extermination, exclaiming: "A voice from the East! A voice from the West! A voice from the four winds! Woe to Jerusalem and to the temple!" Nobody took heed, up to the day when, hit by the stone of a catapult, he fell, saying: "Woe to me!"[2] The small number of people who have followed in politics the line I have felt it my duty to adopt, not for the sake of interest or ambition, but out of a simple desire for the public good, are the most comprehensively vanquished in the baneful crisis unrolling before our eyes; however, I fundamentally wish to avoid the reproach of having denied to the affairs of my time and my country the attention that every citizen owes them. Considering what has become of human societies, one should have little esteem for those who ardently seek a part of the responsibility in running the affairs of their time and their country. The careerist of the old school, who drew his enjoyment, his honor, and his hope of advancement from participation in government, would in our day be practically non-sensical, and if at the present stage we saw a young man approach public life with the somewhat vain eagerness, the intensity of feeling and naive optimism that characterized, for instance, the age of the Restoration,[3] we could not hold back a smile nor refrain from foretelling cruel disappointments. One of the most pernicious results of democracy is to make the commonwealth the prey of a class of mediocre and jealous *politicians*, naturally ill-respected by the crowd, which saw its current representative humiliate himself before it yesterday, and knows by what charlatanism its suffrage was captured. However, before proclaiming that the wise man should confine himself to pure thought, one must be quite certain that one has exhausted all means of making the voice of reason heard. When we have been ten times beaten, when the crowd has ten times preferred the declamations of the complaisant or the hothead to our counsel, when it is well proven that, having been legally offered, we have been shunned and rejected, only then will we have the right to withdraw proudly, calmly, and to take credit for our defeat. We are not required to succeed, we are not required to compete with the means a vulgar ambition grants itself; we are required to be sincere. Had Turgot[4] lived to see the Revolution, he would have been almost the only one with a right to remain calm, for he had been alone in pointing out what needed to be done to prevent it.

I have added to this essay on the reforms that seem most urgent one or two pieces that appeared in 1869,[5] which serve as its commentary and explanation.* It will be felt, perhaps, that these are the wrecks of quite a backward politics; the solutions of moderate liberalism always tend to be shelved in the case of extreme situations, but they should not be abandoned for this reason, since public opinion reverts to them sooner or later. Despite the ostensible rebuttal the facts have afforded me, I have reread these pieces with no bitterness and felt they still held some value.

It is, on the contrary, with deep suffering that I reprint the two or three pieces regarding the war that appear in this volume.[6] I had made it the dream of a lifetime to strive, to the feeble extent of my abilities, toward the intellectual, moral, and political alliance of Germany and France, an alliance entailing one with England as well, and constituting a force capable

---

\*   Certain points that may appear obscure in these various studies are developed more thoroughly in my *Questions contemporaines* (Paris, 1868).

of governing the world, of guiding it, that is, on the road to liberal civilization, equally far from the naively blind enthusiasms of democracy and the puerile aspirations for a return to a past that will not live again. My chimera, I freely admit it, is destroyed forever. A gulf has come between France and Germany; centuries will not suffice to fill it. The violence done to Alsace and Lorraine will long remain an open wound; the supposed peace guarantee that German journalists and statesmen dream of will in fact guarantee wars without end.

Germany had been my mistress; I was conscious of owing to it all that was best in me. One may conceive how I suffered, when I saw the nation that had taught me idealism mock all ideals, when the fatherland of Kant, Fichte, Herder, and Goethe took to pursuing the aims of an exclusive patriotism and nothing else, when the people I had always described to my compatriots as the most moral and cultivated manifested themselves to us in the form of soldiers who differed in nothing from the troopers of all ages, wicked, thieving, drunk, devoid of morals, looting as in the time of Waldstein;[7] when, finally, the noble rebel of 1813, the nation that roused Europe in the name of "generosity," proudly excluded from politics any consideration of generosity, stated as a matter of principle that the duty of a people is to be firm and selfish, and treated as a crime the touching folly of a poor nation, betrayed by fate and by its sovereigns, a superficial nation, free of political discernment, I admit it, but guilty only of thoughtlessly attempting an experiment (universal suffrage) with which no other people will have any better results. Germany characterizing for the whole world duty as ridiculous, the struggle for the fatherland as criminal: what a sad disappointment for those who thought they had seen in German culture a future for general civilization! What we loved in Germany, its broad-mindedness, its high conception of reason and humanity, is no more. Germany is no longer anything but a nation; at present, it is the strongest of nations; but it is well known how little these hegemonies last, and what they leave in their wake. A nation that confines itself to the pure consideration of its own self-interest no longer has a general role. A country only exerts its mastery through the universal aspects of its genius; patriotism is the opposite of moral and philosophical influence. How are we, who have spent our lives abstaining from the errors of French chauvinism, supposed to espouse the narrow thinking of a foreign chauvinism, fully as unjust, fully as intolerant as French chauvinism? Man may rise above the prejudices of his nation; however, among errors, he will always prefer patriotic prejudices to those that present themselves as menacing insults or unjust disparagements.

No one more than I has always recognized the great qualities of the German race, the seriousness, the knowledge, the conscientiousness that almost compensate for genius and are worth a thousand times more than talent, the sense of duty, which I much prefer to the motivation of vanity and honor that is our strength and our weakness. But Germany cannot assume mankind's entire work. Germany does not act disinterestedly for the rest of the world. German liberalism is very noble, taking as its goal less the equality of classes than culture and the elevation of human nature in general; but the rights of man count for something too, and it is our philosophers of the eighteenth century, it is our Revolution that founded them. The Lutheran Reformation was carried out only for the Germanic countries; Germany never experienced something analogous to our chivalrous attachment to Poland, to Italy. German character, in any case, appears to contain two opposite poles: the gentle, obedient, respectful, resigned German; and the German knowing nothing but force, the leader wielding inflexible and harsh authority, in short the old man of iron; *jura negat sibi nata*.[8] One may say that there is nothing better in the world than the moral German and nothing more evil than the German devoid of morals. If the masses are less susceptible to discipline here than in Germany, the middle classes are less capable of vileness. Let it be said to France's honor that, throughout the last war, it was almost impossible to find a Frenchman capable of playing the role of the spy passably; we loathe lies and low cunning too much.

Germany's great superiority lies in the intellectual sphere; but even in this it should not fancy it has everything. It lacks tact and charm. Germany has far to go to have a society like the French society of the seventeenth and eighteenth centuries, gentlemen like La Rochefoucauld,[9] Saint-Simon,[10] Saint-Évremond,[11] ladies such as Mrs. de Sévigné,[12] Miss de la Vallière,[13] Ninon de Lenclos.[14] Even today, does Germany have a poet like Mr. Victor Hugo, a prose writer like Ms. Sand,[15] a critic like Mr. Sainte-Beuve,[16] an imagination like that of Mr. Michelet,[17] a philosophic character like that of Mr. Littré?[18] It is for the experts of other nations to say. We limit ourselves to refusing the unjust judgment of those who would know contemporary France only through its low press, through its petty literature, through those small mediocre theaters whose foolish character, as alien to the French character as can be, is the work of foreigners and in part of Germans. If one judged Germany by its popular newspapers, one would judge it just as poorly. What pleasure can one derive in nourishing oneself thus of false ideas, hateful opinions, and partiality? Whatever one says, a world without France would be as deficient as one in which France was the entire world; a dishful of salt is nothing, but a dish without salt is tasteless. The goal of humanity is superior to the triumph of this or that race; all races are useful; all in their own way have a mission to accomplish.

May a league of men of goodwill from all tribes, all languages, and all peoples at last be formed that will be able to create and maintain above these fiery struggles an empyrean of pure ideas, a heaven where there will be neither Greek nor barbarian, neither Teuton nor Latin! When he was urged to write verses against France, Goethe responded: "How shall I preach hatred, when I do not feel it in my own heart?" Such must be our response when we will be urged to slander Germany. Let us be inexorably just and cool. France did not heed us when we begged it not to fight the inevitable; Germany mocked us when we incited it to moderation in victory. Let us know how to wait. The laws of history are the justice of God. In the Book of Job, God, to show He is strong, delights in crushing the triumphant and exalting the humble. The philosophy of history is in agreement with the old poem on this point. All human creations have their worm consuming them; a defeat is atonement for past glory and often the guarantor of future victory. Greece and Judaea paid with their national existence for their exceptional fate and the incomparable honor of establishing teachings for the whole of mankind. Italy atoned with two hundred years as a nonentity for the glory of having ushered in civil life during the Middle Ages and for having created the Renaissance; in the nineteenth century, this double glory was its main title to a new life. Germany atoned with a lengthy political eclipse for the glory of having created the Reformation; now, it reaps the profit of the Reformation. France today atones for the Revolution; it will perhaps one day benefit from it in the thankful memories of emancipated peoples.

Consolations of the defeated, some will say, cheap fodder you afford yourselves to sweeten present ills with dreams of the future! Be it so; nonetheless, one is also forced to admit that never were consolations more solid. Hopes based on the fickleness of fortune have never once failed to be realized since humanity has existed. *Nil permanet sub sole,*[19] said that amiable skeptic, so marvelously acute, the Ecclesiastes, the most inspired of the sacred authors. History will follow its course, the victors of today will be the vanquished tomorrow. Whether this be a happy or sad truth matters little; it is a truth that will stay true for all time. This is why the philosopher must wish that there be as few victors and vanquished as possible.

"O, world, how evil and perverse in nature you are!" cries the greatest of Persian poets. "What you have raised up, you yourself destroy. Look what became of Féridoun, the hero who snatched the empire from the old Zohak. He reigned for five centuries; in the end, he died. He died as we all will, whether we have been the shepherd, or the flock."

## PART I: THE ILLNESS

Those who at all costs wish to discover in history the application of a rigorous distributive justice submit themselves to a forceful challenge. If in many cases we see national crimes followed by prompt punishment, in several instances we also witness a world governed by less severe judgments; many countries were able to be weak and corrupt with impunity. It is certainly one of the signs of the greatness of France that it was not allowed to do so. Enervated by democracy, demoralized by its very prosperity, France atoned in the cruelest fashion for its years of sin. The reason for this fact lies with the importance itself of France, and the nobility of its past. There is justice for France: it is not allowed to abandon itself, to neglect its vocation; it is evident that Providence loves it, for Providence punishes it. A country that has played a leading role does not have the right to reduce itself to a bourgeois materialism that does not ask for anything but to enjoy its acquired wealth in peace and quiet. Mediocrity is not available to everyone. The man who drags a great name in the mud, who does not live up to a mission inscribed in his nature, cannot allow himself, without consequence, a series of things that one would pardon in an ordinary man, who has neither a past to continue, nor a great obligation to fulfill.

To notice in these past few years that the moral fiber of France was severely compromised, it was necessary to possess some acuity of spirit, a certain familiarity with political and historical reasoning. To see the sickness today, alas!, one needs but eyes. The edifice of our illusions has crumbled like the fairy castles one builds in dreams. Presumption, puerile vanity, indiscipline, lack of seriousness, perseverance, honesty, weakness of judgment, inability to consider many ideas together, absence of scientific spirit, naive and vulgar ignorance: this is the summary of our history in the past year. The army, so proud and pretentious, has not had one favorable break. The statesmen, so sure of themselves, have turned out to be children. The self-important public administration has been proven incompetent. The public education system, impermeable to progress, has been shown to have allowed the spirit of France to decay into absolute mediocrity. The Catholic clergy, which vigorously preached the inferiority of Protestant nations, has remained the terrified spectator of a disaster it had contributed to cause. The dynasty, whose roots in the country appeared so deep, did not have a single defender on September 4.[20] The opposition, which claimed to have solutions to all ills in its revolutionary doctrines, has found itself, in a few days, as unpopular as the deposed dynasty. The republican party, which, full of the tragic errors spread in the past half-century on the history of the Revolution, thought itself capable of repeating a struggle that was won eighty years ago only as a result of circumstances completely different from those of today, has discovered that it was but the victim of a hallucination, mistaking its dreams for reality. Everything has crumbled, as in an apocalyptic vision. Even the legends were mortally wounded. The legend of the Empire was destroyed by Napoleon III; the legend of 1792[21] was finished off by Mr. Gambetta; the legend of the Terror (for even terror has its own legend among us) had its hideous parody in the Commune; that of Louis XIV[22] will not be the same since the day in which the descendant of the Elector of Brandenburg reestablished the empire of Charlemagne in the ballroom of Versailles. Bossuet alone appears to have been prophetic, when he said, *et nunc, reges, intelligite!*[23]

In our day (and this is what makes the reformers' task difficult), it is the people who must understand. Let us attempt, by an analysis as exact as possible, to take cognizance of the illness of France, so as to try to discover the remedy that should be applied. The strength of the patient is very great; his resources are nearly infinite; his good intentions are real. It is up to the doctor to avoid mistakes, for a narrowly conceived diet or an inopportunely applied medication would cause revulsion in the patient, kill him or worsen his illness.

I

The history of France is a whole composed of parts so intimately interconnected that it is impossible to understand a single one of our contemporary afflictions without searching for its cause in the past. Two years ago, we set out* what we believe to be the standard path of states originating from the feudalism of the Middle Ages, of which path England is the most perfect example, because England, without breaking with its royal house, its nobility, its counties, its communes, its church, its universities, found the way to become the freest, most prosperous, and most patriotic state of all. The path of French society since the twelfth century has been entirely different. The Capetian royalty,[24] as generally happens to great forces, pushed its principle to extremes. It destroyed the possibility of any provincial life, of any representation of the nation. Already, under Philip the Fair,[25] the illness is evident. The element that elsewhere created parliamentary life, the small rural nobility, has lost importance. The king gathered the Estates General only to be begged to do what he had already decided. As instruments of government he only wished to employ his rather self-serving relatives, powerful aristocracy of princes of the blood, and ennobled lawmen and administrators (*milites regis*), obliging servants of absolute power. This state of affairs is pardonable in the seventeenth century, given the incomparable splendor it affords France; soon thereafter, however, the contrast becomes blatant. The most spiritual nation of Europe had nothing but a shapeless political machine to put its ideas into practice. Turgot considered the *parlements*[26] as the principal obstacles to all achievement; he held no hope for assemblies. Was this admirable man, so free of any self-love, mistaken? No. He saw things right, and what he saw amounted to saying that the illness had no cure. Add to this a profound moral debasement of the people; Protestantism, which would have uplifted them, had been banished; Catholicism had failed to educate them. The ignorance of the low

---

\*    In the work on constitutional monarchy, reprinted at the end of this volume (text 5 in the present edition).

classes was frightful. Richelieu,[27] the Abbé Fleury[28] clearly state as a principle that the people should know neither how to read nor how to write. Side by side with this barbarism, a charming society, full of wit, enlightenment, and gracefulness. One never saw more clearly the inner tendencies of France, what it can and cannot do. France is admirable at lacework; it is incapable of producing household linen. The humble tasks, like that of the schoolteacher, will always be carried out poorly among us. France excels at the exquisite; it is mediocre at the commonplace. By what whim is it at the same time democratic? By the same whim that makes Paris, which lives off the court and off luxury, a socialist city, that makes Paris, which spends all its time jeering at any belief or virtue, intractable, fanatical, credulous in all matters concerning its chimera of a republic.

The beginnings of the Revolution were assuredly admirable, and if one had limited oneself to summoning the Estates General, regularizing them, making them annual, one would have been completely in the right. But the false politics of Rousseau prevailed. It was decided to create an a priori constitution. One failed to note that England, the most constitutional of countries, had never had a written constitution, strictly defined. One let oneself be outflanked by the people; in a childish fashion the disorder of the taking of the Bastille was cheered, without considering that such disorder would sweep everything away later on. Mirabeau,[29] the greatest, the only great politician of the time, began his career with some indiscretions that would probably have ruined him, had he lived; for it is much more advantageous for a statesman to begin with reaction rather than with an indulgence for anarchy. The thoughtlessness of the Bordeaux lawyers,[30] their empty declamations, their moral levity completed the ruin. One imagined that the state, which had been embodied by the king, could do without a king, and that the abstract idea of the commonwealth would suffice to sustain a country where the public virtues are too often lacking.

The day France cut off its king's head it committed suicide. France cannot be compared to those small ancient fatherlands, composed most often of a city with its suburbs, where everyone was related. France was a great shareholding company formed by a first-class speculator, the House of Capet. The shareholders thought they could do without the boss, and carry on business on their own. This will work as long as business is good; but when business slumps, there will be calls for liquidation. France had been created by the Capetian dynasty. Even supposing that old Gaul had

had a sentiment of national unity, Roman domination and Germanic conquest would have destroyed it. The Frankish Empire, whether under the
Merovingians[31] or the Carolingians,[32] was an artificial construction whose
unity resided only in the force of the conquerors. The Treaty of Verdun,[33]
which destroyed this unity, divided the Frankish Empire into three bands
from north to south: Charles's part, or Carolingia, was so dissimilar from
what we call France that all of Flanders and Catalonia were part of it, while
toward the east it only reached the Saône and the Cévennes. Capetian
politics rounded out this faulty shred, and in eight hundred years made
France as we intend it, the France that has created all we live of, all that
binds us together, all our reason for existence. France thus is the result of
Capetian politics, pursued with admirable consistency. Why is Languedoc
united with the north of France, a union that neither language, nor race,
nor history, nor the character of the populations demanded? Because
the kings of Paris, throughout the thirteenth century, exercised a persistent and victorious pressure on these lands. Why is Lyon part of France?
Because Philip the Fair, by means of the subtleties of his jurists, managed
to trap it in his net. Why are the Dauphinois our compatriots? Because,
the Dauphin Humbert[34] having fallen into a sort of lunacy, the king of
France happened to be present to purchase his lands, with cash. Why was
Provence absorbed by the whirlwind of Carolingia, into which nothing at
first glance seemed to suggest it should be brought? Thanks to the cunning of Louis XI[35] and his accomplice Palamède de Forbin.[36] Why are the
Franche-Comté, Alsace, Lorraine united to Carolingia, despite the merid-
ian line traced by the Treaty of Verdun? Because the House of Bourbon
rediscovered the secret so admirably practiced by the first Capetians to
enlarge the royal demesne. Why, lastly, is Paris, so peripheral a city, the
capital of France? Because Paris was the city of the Capetians, because the
abbot of Saint-Denis became the king of France.* Unsurpassed naivety!

---

\*  *"Challes, li rois de Saint Denis"* ["Charles, the king of Saint Denis"] (*Roman de Roncevaux*,
   stanza 40).
   Hugh the White owed his fortune to the possession of the great abbeys of Saint-Denis, Saint-Germain-des-Prés, Saint-Martin de Tours, which made him into the tutor
   of rich and prosperous lands. The standard of the Capetian king was the standard of
   Saint-Denis. His rallying cry was *Montjoie Saint-Denis*. The first Capetians sang in the
   chorus in Saint-Denis.

This city that claims an aristocratic privilege of superiority over the rest of France and owes this privilege to royalty is at the same time the center of the republican utopia. How can Paris not see that it is what it is thanks to royalty, that it will not regain all its importance as a capital except through royalty, and that a republic, according to the rule established by the illustrious founder of the United States of America, would necessarily create for its central government a small Washington in Amboise or Blois?

This is what the ignorant and obtuse men who took hold of the destinies of France at the end of the past century did not understand. They imagined one could do without the king; they did not understand that, once the king was eliminated, the edifice of which the king was the keystone would collapse. The republican theories of the eighteenth century managed to work in America, because America was a colony formed by the voluntary participation of emigrants seeking liberty; they could not work in France, because France had been built on the basis of a completely different principle. A new dynasty almost emerged from the terrible convulsion that shook France; but we learned in that circumstance how difficult it is for modern nations to create for themselves reigning houses different from those issued from the Germanic conquest. The extraordinary genius that had raised Napoleon to power toppled him from it, and the old dynasty returned, apparently determined to attempt the experiment of a constitutional monarchy that had so sadly failed in the hands of poor Louis XVI.

It was destined that, in this great and tragic history of France, the king and the nation would rival in recklessness. This time, the royalty's mistakes were the gravest. The decrees of July 1830[37] may truly be described as a political crime; their grounding in Article 14 of the Charter was an obvious sophism. In the intentions of Louis XVIII, this Article 14 in no way had the meaning attributed to it by the ministers of Charles X. It cannot be admitted that the author of the Charter would have placed in the Charter an article that overturned its whole balance. This was a case for the axiom: *Contra eum qui dicere potuit clarius praesumptio est facienda.*[38] If before Mr. de Polignac[39] someone had imagined that this article gave the king the right to abolish the Charter, it would have been the matter of constant protests; but no one protested, because no one ever thought this insignificant article contained the implicit right to coups d'état. The inclusion of this article did not come from royalty, which would have left itself a way to evade its commitments; it was part of the constitutional project devised by the parliament of 1814, which was quite careful not to overstate the rights of the king; it did not give cause for any observation; "one saw in it only a sort of commonplace, borrowed from previous constitutions, and nobody suspected the formidable and mysterious meaning it was later lent."[*]

The representatives of 1830 were therefore right to resist the decrees, and the citizens who were in the position to heed their appeal were right to take arms. The situation resembled that of the king of England, who more than once entered into conflict with his parliament. But once the beaten king had revoked the decrees, one should have stopped and kept the king in his palace. It suited him to abdicate: the one in whose favor he abdicated should have been chosen. A different choice was made. Let us hasten to state that eighteen years of a reign full of wisdom justified, in many respects, the choice of August 10, 1830, and that this choice could be justified by some of the precedents of the Revolution of 1688 in England; but for so bold a substitution to become legitimate, it needed to last. Through a series of unpardonable lapses of judgment on the part of the nation and following a regrettable weakness of the new dynasty, this consecration did not occur. The king and his sons, rather than defending their rights with the force of arms, drew back and let the Parisian riot outrageously violate the will of the nation. Disastrous rending of a title somewhat fragile to begin with and that could only have acquired force by persisting. A dynasty owes it to a nation, which is always supposed to support it, to resist a turbulent minority. Humanity is satisfied, as long as after the battle the victorious power proves generous and treats the rebels not as if they were guilty, but defeated.

Most of us were entering public life when the fateful events of February 24 occurred. With a perfectly sound instinct, we sensed that what happened that day was a great misfortune. Being liberals by philosophical principle, we understood that the liberty trees that were being planted with such naive joy would never flourish; we comprehended that the social problems that were stated in such a bold manner were destined to play a leading role in the future of the world. The baptism of blood of the June days, the reactions that followed anguished us; it was

---

[*]    Mr. de Viel-Castel, *Histoire de la Restauration*, vol. I, p. 429.

clear that the soul and the character of France were truly in danger. The levity of the men of 1848 was truly unexampled. They gave France, which had not demanded it, universal suffrage. They did not consider that this suffrage would only benefit five million peasants, foreign to any liberal idea. At that time I frequently saw Mr. Cousin.[40] During the long walks this profound expert of all French glories took me on through the streets of Paris on the Left Bank, explaining the history of each house and its inhabitants in the seventeenth century, he often said these words: "My friend, it is still not understood what a crime the February Revolution was; the ultimate consequence of this Revolution will perhaps be the dismemberment of France."

The coup d'état[41] of December 2 distressed us deeply. For ten years, we mourned the rule of law; we protested according to our forces against the system of intellectual debasement cunningly directed by Mr. Fortoul,[42] and barely mitigated by his successors. Nonetheless, the same occurred as always does. A power that was ushered in by violence became better as it aged; it began to see that the liberal development of man is a major interest of any government. The country, on the other hand, was enchanted with this mediocre government. It had what it wanted; it would have been senseless to attempt to topple such a government despite the evident support of the majority. The wisest course was to make the best of a bad situation, to act like the bishops of the fifth century and the sixth, who attempted to enlighten the barbarians, not being able to fend them off. Therefore, we consented to serve the government of the Emperor Napoleon III for what was good in it, that is to say inasmuch as it touched on the eternal interests of knowledge, of public education, of the progress of enlightenment, in short those social duties that never rest.

It is undeniable, anyway, that the reign of the Emperor Napoleon III, despite its immense shortcomings, had resolved a part of the problem. The majority of France was perfectly content. It had what it wanted, order and peace. It lacked liberty, it is true; political life was extremely feeble; but this only aggrieved a minority comprised of a fifth or a sixth of the nation, and even within this minority one must distinguish a small number of educated, intelligent, truly liberal men from a scarcely reflective crowd, animated by that seditious spirit whose only program is always to oppose the government and attempt to topple it. Public administration was very bad; but whoever did not deny the principle of the rights of the dynasty suffered little. The men of the opposition themselves were hampered in their activities rather than persecuted. The wealth of the country grew in unheard-of proportions. On May 8, 1870, after some very serious mistakes had been committed, seven and a half million electors still declared themselves satisfied. It did not come into almost anyone's mind that such a state might be exposed to the most fearsome of catastrophes. This catastrophe, in fact, did not derive from a general necessity of the situation; it came from a particular trait of the character of the Emperor Napoleon III.

II

The Emperor Napoleon III had established his fortune by responding to the need for reaction, order, and rest that was the consequence of the Revolution of 1848. If the Emperor Napoleon III had limited himself to this program, if he had contented himself with repressing domestically all ideas, all political liberties, with developing material interests, with the support of a moderate clericalism lacking all conviction, his and his dynasty's reign would have long been secured. The country was sinking further and further into vulgarity, forgetting its old history; the new dynasty had been founded. France such as universal suffrage has fashioned it has become deeply materialist; the noble preoccupations of the past, patriotism, enthusiasm for beauty, love of glory, have disappeared along with the noble classes that represented the soul of France. The judgment and the government of things have been conveyed to the masses; and now the masses are dull, coarse, dominated by the most superficial notion of self-interest. Its two poles are the worker and the peasant. The worker is not enlightened; the peasant wants first and foremost to buy land, to round off his field. If you speak of France, of its past, of its national genius to the peasant, to the socialist of the International, he will not understand such a language. Military honor, from this limited point of view, seems a folly; the taste for great things, the glory of the spirit are chimeras; money spent for art and science is money lost, spent madly, taken from the pocket of people who care as little as possible for art and science. This is the provincial spirit that the emperor marvelously served in the first years of his reign. If he had remained the docile and blind servant of this small-minded reaction, no opposition would have managed to undermine him. All the oppositions united would have found their limit in two million votes at the most. The score of the opponents grew each year, by which some concluded that it would continue to grow until it would become a majority. Mistake: this score would have found a resting point that it would not have surpassed. Let us say it, for we are certain these lines will not be read except by intelligent people: a government wishing only to establish itself in France and to last indefinitely now has, I fear, quite a simple route to take: imitate the program of Napoleon III, minus the war. By so doing, it will lead France to the level of debasement any society attains that abandons lofty goals; but it will only perish with the country, of the slow death of those who abandon themselves to the current of destiny without ever fighting it.

The Emperor Napoleon III was not like this. He was superior in a sense to the majority of the country; he loved goodness; he had a taste, doubtless an unenlightened taste, but a real taste nonetheless, for the noble culture of humanity. In many respects he was in total dissonance with those who had appointed him. He dreamed of military glory; the ghost of Napoleon I haunted him. This is all the stranger since the Emperor Napoleon III saw full well that he possessed neither aptitude nor preparation for war, and he knew that France had lost all its qualities in this respect. But the innate idea won over. The emperor felt so clearly that his personal views on the matter were a sort of *naevus*[43] in need of being hidden, that we always see him, at the time of the foundation of his power, declaring that he wants peace. He recognized it was the means of making himself popular. The Crimean War[44] was accepted in public opinion only because it was thought to be without consequence for the general peace. The Italian War[45] was not forgiven until it was seen to be cut short and remain unfinished.

The simplest common sense enjoined Napoleon III never to make war. France, he knew it, did not desire it in any way.\* Furthermore, a country tormented by revolutions, with dynastic divisions, is not capable of a great military effort. King John,[46] Charles VII,[47] Francis I,[48] and even Louis XIV passed through situations as critical as that of Napoleon III after the capitulation of Sedan; they were not toppled for it, or even momentarily

---

\*    Prefects' inquest, *Journal des débats*, October 3 and 4, 1870.

undermined. The king of Prussia Frederick William III, after the battle of Jena,[49] remained as solidly as ever on his throne; but Napoleon III could not sustain a defeat. He was like a gambler who gambled on the condition that he would be shot if he lost a game. A country divided by dynastic questions must give up war; for, at the first setback, this cause of weakness appears, and turns any accident into a fatal case. The man who has a poorly healed wound can engage in the actions of ordinary life without people noticing his infirmity; but any vigorous exercise is forbidden for him; at the first strain his wound reopens, and he collapses. It is inconceivable that Napoleon III would have been so completely deluded as to the solidity of the edifice he himself had built out of clay. How could he not have seen that such an edifice would not resist a jolt, and that the clash of a powerful enemy would necessarily make it collapse?

The war declared in the month of July 1870 was thus a personal aberration, the explosion or rather the aggressive return of an idea long latent in the mind of Napoleon III, an idea that the peaceful tastes of the country obliged him to conceal, and which it seems he himself had almost given up. There is no example of more complete a betrayal of a state by its sovereign, taking the word betrayal to designate the act of the agent who substitutes his will to that of the principal. Is this to say that the country was not responsible for what happened? Alas! We cannot claim that. The country was guilty of having given itself an unenlightened government and especially a wretched parliament, which, with a thoughtlessness surpassing all imagination, voted for the most catastrophic of wars taking a minister at his word. France's misdeed was that of a rich man who chooses a bad manager for his estate, and gives him unlimited power of attorney; this man deserves to be ruined; but it is not fair to allege that he himself accomplished the acts his proxy did without him and against his will.

Whoever knows France, in fact, both as a whole and in its provincial varieties, will not hesitate to admit that the movement that has swept this country for the past half-century is essentially peaceful. The military generation, crushed by the defeats of 1814 and 1815, had essentially disappeared under the Restoration and the reign of Louis-Philippe.[50] A profoundly honest, but often superficial patriot recounted our old victories in a triumphal tone that often might have offended abroad; but this dissonance weakened by the day. One may say it had ceased since 1848. Two movements then began that were destined to spell the end not only of the martial spirit, but of patriotism more generally: I speak of the extra-ordinary awakening of material desires among the workers and peasants. It is clear that the socialism of the workers is the antithesis of the military spirit; it is practically the negation of the fatherland; the doctrines of the International are there to prove it. The peasant, on the other hand, once the road to wealth has been opened to him and he has been shown that his line of business is the most securely lucrative, the peasant has felt his horror for conscription redouble. I speak from experience. I ran in the electoral campaign of May 1869 in an entirely rural constituency of the Seine-et-Marne; I can assure you I did not find on my path one single ele-ment of the old military life of the country. An inexpensive government, unimposing, untroubling, an honest desire for liberty, a great thirst for equality, a complete indifference to the glory of the country, the deter-mined will not to make any sacrifices for nonpalpable interests, this is what the peasant character appeared to me to be in the part of France where the peasant is, as they say, the most advanced.

I do not mean to say that no traces remained of the old character that feeds on the memories of the First Empire. The not particularly numer-ous party that one may call Bonapartist in the proper sense of the term surrounded the emperor with deplorable agitations. The Catholic party, with its erroneous commonplaces on the alleged decadence of Protestant countries, also attempted to rekindle a fire that was almost extinguished. But this had no effect on the country. The experience of 1870 proved it; the news of the war was received with consternation; the foolish bragging of newspapers, the cries of the hawkers on the boulevards are facts history will have to consider only to show to what extent a band of lunatics can deceive the true sentiments of a country. The war demonstrated to the point of obviousness that we no longer possessed our old military facul-ties. This is not something that should startle those who have conceived an accurate idea of the philosophy of our history. The France of the Middle Ages was a Germanic construction, built by a Germanic military aristoc-racy out of Gallo-Roman materials. The centuries-long task of France has consisted in expelling from its bosom all the elements introduced by the Germanic invasion, up to the Revolution, which was the last convulsion in this effort. The military character of France came from its Germanic side; by violently ousting the Germanic elements and replacing them with a philosophical and egalitarian conception of society, France by the same stroke rejected all that was military within it. It has remained a rich country, which considers war a foolish career, and rather unprofitable. France has thus become the most peaceful country on earth; all its activity has turned toward social problems, toward the acquisition of wealth and the progress of industry. The enlightened classes have not allowed the taste for art, for science, for literature, for elegant luxury to wither; but the military career has been abandoned. Few families of the well-to-do bourgeoisie, having to choose an occupation for their son, preferred a profession whose social importance they do not understand to the substantial prospects of commerce and industry. The Academy of Saint-Cyr[51] received hardly more than the dregs of youth, until the ancient nobility and the Catholic party began to populate it, a change whose consequences have not yet had time to develop. This nation was once dazzling and warlike; but it was so by selection, if I dare say it. It maintained and produced an admirable nobility, full of valor and luster. Once this nobility collapsed, what remained was an indistinct background of mediocrity, without originality or daring, a commonfolk that included neither the privilege of the intellect nor that of the sword. A nation thus fashioned may reach the peak of material prosperity; it no longer has a role in the world, or action abroad. On the other hand, it is impossible to exit such a condition with universal suffrage. For one does not tame universal suffrage by means of itself; one can deceive it, benumb it; but as long as it reigns it obliges those who are dependent on it to compromise with it and undergo its law. It is a vicious circle to dream of reforming the errors of an unconvertible public opinion by relying on public opinion alone.

France, in any case, has done nothing but follow in this the general movement of all the nations of Europe, Prussia and Russia excepted. Mr. Cobden,[52] whom I saw around 1857, was delighted with us. England had outpaced us on this path of industrial and commercial materialism; however, the English, much wiser than us, managed to make their government proceed in accordance with the nation, while our clumsiness was such that the government of our choice managed to commit us against our will to the war. I do not know if I am deceived, but there is a concept of historical ethnography that imposes itself more and more in my mind. The similarity of England and northern France appears to me more every day. Our thoughtlessness comes from the Midi, and if France had not dragged Languedoc and Provence into its area of activity we would be serious, active, protestant, parliamentary. Our racial background is the same as that of the British Isles; the Germanic influence, while it was strong enough in these isles to make a Germanic idiom prevail, was not more considerable on the whole of the three kingdoms than on the whole of France. Like France, England appears to me to be expelling its Germanic element, the obstinate, proud, intractable nobility that governed it in the age of Pitt,[53] Castlereagh,[54] Wellington.[55] How far this peaceable and wholly Christian school of economists is from the passion of the men of iron who imposed upon their country such great things! The public opinion of England, as it has manifested itself for the past thirty years, is in no way Germanic; one perceives in it the Celtic character, gentler, more congenial, more human. These sorts of sketches must be taken very broadly; one may state nonetheless that what is still left of the military spirit in this world is Germanic. It is probably by the Germanic race, being feudal and military, that socialism and egalitarian democracy, which among us Celts would not easily find a limit, will ultimately be tamed, and this will be congruent with historical precedent; for one of the traits of the Germanic race has always been to equate the idea of conquest with the idea of guarantee; in other words, to let the material and brutal fact of property derived from conquest prevail over all considerations of the rights of man and the abstract theories of the social contract. The response to each advance of socialism accordingly may be an advance of Germanism, and one can foresee the day when all the countries of socialism will be governed by Germans. The invasion of the fourth and fifth centuries occurred for analogous reasons, the Roman countries having become incapable of producing good constables, good maintainers of property.

In effect, our country, and especially the provinces, was moving toward a social form that, despite the difference in appearances, bore more than passing similarity to America, a social form in which many of the things formerly considered to pertain to the state would be left to private initiative. Of course, one could fail to be a supporter of such a future; it was clear that France by developing in this guise would remain much inferior to America. America compensates for its lack of education, of distinction, for that vacuum that the absence of a court, of high society, of ancient institutions always leaves in a country, by the blaze of its young development, by its patriotism, by the perhaps exaggerated faith it has in its own force, by the conviction that it is working at the great task of humanity, by the effectiveness of its Protestant convictions, by its daring and its spirit of enterprise, by the almost total absence of the germs of socialism, by the ease with which the difference between the rich and the poor is accepted there, and especially by the privilege it has of developing in the open air, in infinite space and without neighbors. Deprived of these advantages, experimenting, so to speak, in isolation, both too heavy and too light, too credulous and too mocking, France would never have been anything but a second-rate America: paltry, mediocre, perhaps more similar to Mexico or to South America than to the United States. In our old societies royalty preserves a host of things worth keeping. Given the idea I have of the old France and its spirit, I would call this farewell to glory and great things: *Finis Franciae*.[56] But in politics one must be cautious of taking one's inclinations as what should be; what is successful in this world is ordinarily the opposite of the instincts of us idealists, and we are almost always authorized to conclude from the fact that we dislike something that it will come to pass. This desire for a political condition involving the least possible central government is the universal wish of the provinces. The antipathy they demonstrate for Paris is not only the rightful indignation against the attacks of a factious minority; it is not only revolutionary Paris, it is governing Paris that France does not like. Paris for France is the synonym of troublesome requirements. It is Paris that enrolls men, absorbs money, employs it in a host of pursuits that the provinces do not understand. The most capable of the administrators of the past reign told me with regard to the elections of 1869 that what appeared to him most compromised in France was the system of taxation, since the provinces at each election forced their representatives to make commitments that it would be necessary to honor sooner or later in some measure and whose fulfillment would cause the destruction of the finances of the state. The first time I met Prévost-Paradol[57] upon his return from his electoral campaign in the Loire-Inférieure, I asked him what his prevailing impression was: "We will soon see the end of the State," he told me. It is exactly what I would have answered, if he had asked me my impressions of Seine-et-Marne. Let the prefect[58] meddle with as few things as possible, reduce taxes and military service as much as possible, and the provinces will be satisfied. Most people hardly have more than a single demand, to be left in peace to enrich themselves. Only the poor parts of the country still display some eagerness for posts; in the rich *départements* public office is

not considered highly and is held to be one of the less advantageous uses
to be made of one's activity.

Such is the character of what one may call provincial democracy. This
character, as one can see, differs considerably from the republican character; it can adapt to empire and constitutional monarchy just as well as
to the republic, and even better in some respects. As indifferent to any
single dynasty as it is to anything that can be called glory or splendor, it
ultimately prefers to have a dynasty as a guarantee of order; but it does
not want to make any sacrifices for the establishment of this dynasty. It is
pure political materialism, the antithesis of the measure of idealism that is
the soul of the Legitimist and republican theories. Such a party, which is
that of the immense majority of the French, is too superficial, too narrow-
minded to lead the destinies of a country. Twenty times over will it repeat
the immense folly it committed from its own point of view when in 1848
it took the Prince Louis-Napoléon as the manager of its affairs. Its destiny
is to be endlessly fooled, for the basely self-interested man is precluded
from being clever; simple bourgeois dullness cannot produce the amount
of devotion necessary to create an order of affairs and maintain it.

Indeed, there is truth in the Germanic principle that a society only
has a full right to its patrimony as long as it can guarantee it. In a general
sense, it is not advantageous that owners be incapable of defending what
they own. The duel of the knights of the Middle Ages, the threat of the
armed man coming to offer battle to the owner who has relaxed into luxury, was in some respects legitimate. The rights of the courageous established property; the man of the sword is indeed the creator of all wealth,
for by defending what he has conquered he ensures the good of the people
who are gathered under his protection. Let us at least say that a status like
the one the French bourgeoisie had dreamed of, a status in which those
who owned and enjoyed did not really wield the sword to defend their
property (as a consequence of the law on replacements[59]), represented a
genuine cantilever of social architecture. A propertied class living in relative idleness, providing few public services, and nevertheless appearing
arrogant, as if it had a birthright to property and others had a duty by
birth to defend it, such a class, I claim, will not hold property for long.
Our society is becoming too exclusively an association of the weak; such
a society defends itself poorly; it is difficult for it to produce that great
legal and voluntarist *criterium* that a gathering of men has in order to

live together and protect each other, I mean a powerful armed force. The author of wealth is as much he who secures it by his weapons as he who creates it by his labor. Political economy, exclusively preoccupied with the creation of wealth through labor, has never understood feudalism, which basically was just as legitimate as the constitution of the modern army. The dukes, the marquesses, the counts were basically the generals, the colonels, the captains of a *Landwehr*[60] whose compensation consisted of lands and seigneurial rights.

III

Thus the tradition of a national politics was being lost, day after day. Since the taste that the majority of the French have for monarchy is essentially materialist in origin and as far removed as possible from what may be called fidelity, loyalism, and love of one's princes, France, while wanting a dynasty, proves very lax in the choice of the dynasty itself. The ephemeral but brilliant reign of Napoleon I had sufficed to create a title for this people, alien to any idea of centuries-long legitimacy. As the Prince Louis-Napoléon presented himself in 1848 as the heir to this title, and as he appeared to be made on purpose to extricate France from a condition it dislikes and whose dangers it exaggerated, France clung to him like a life buoy, aided him in his most reckless enterprises, became an accomplice in his coups d'état. For almost twenty years, the perpetrators of December 10[61] were allowed to believe they had been in the right. France developed its domestic resources prodigiously. It was truly a revelation. Thanks to order, peace, and treaties of commerce, Napoleon III taught France of its own wealth. The domestic political degradation displeased an intelligent fraction; the rest had found what they wanted, and there is no doubt that for certain classes of the nation the reign of Napoleon III will remain a veritable ideal. I repeat, had Napoleon III chosen not to make war, the dynasty of the Bonapartes would have been established for centuries to come. But such is the weakness of a condition devoid of a moral foundation: a day of folly suffices to lose everything. How could the emperor not have seen that the war with Germany was too hard a test for a country as weakened as France? An ignorant inner circle lacking seriousness, a consequence of the original sin of the new monarchy, a court where there was but one intelligent man (this prince,[62] full of intelligence and marvelously knowledgeable about his times, whom the vagaries of destiny left almost without authority) rendered all surprises, all misfortunes possible.

In fact, while public wealth experienced unprecedented growth, while the peasant acquired by his thrift an affluence that in no way uplifted his intellectual condition, his civility, his culture, the debasement of all aristocracy took place at a frightening rate; the intellectual average of the public declined strangely. The number and worth of the distinguished men who emerged from the nation remained constant, perhaps increased; in more than one scale of value, the newcomers were not inferior to any of the illustrious names of generations that had flowered in better times; but the atmosphere was becoming impoverished; one died of cold. The universities, already weak, scarcely enlightened, were systematically weakened; the only two strong subjects it possessed, history and philosophy, were practically suppressed. The École polytechnique, the École normale[63] were uncrowned. Some efforts at improvement that were attempted from 1860 onward remained inconsistent and desultory. The men of goodwill who staked their reputation on them were not supported. The clergy's demands, to which one submitted, only permitted a harmless mediocrity; anything even slightly original saw itself condemned to a sort of banishment within its own country. Catholicism remained the only organized force outside of the state, and hijacked for its own benefit the external affairs of France. Paris was invaded by the foreign viveur, by the provincials, who only encouraged a ridiculous petty press and foolish literature, as un-Parisian as possible, in the new farce genre. The country, meanwhile, was sinking into a hideous materialism. Having no nobility to provide an example, the enriched peasant, content in his cumbersome and vulgar affluence, did not know how to live, remained graceless, without ideas. *Oves non habentes pastorem*,[64] such was France: a fire without flame or light, a heart without warmth; a people without prophets capable of telling it what it feels; a dead planet, traveling on its orbit by mechanical movement.

Administrative corruption was not organized robbery, as seen in Naples, or Spain; it was carelessness, idleness, a universal permissiveness, a complete indifference for the commonwealth. Every public office had become a sinecure, the right to an annuity in exchange for doing nothing. Everyone was thereby unassailable. Thanks to a law on defamation that gives the impression of having been passed to protect the least honorable of citizens, and especially thanks to the universal discredit in which the press had fallen due to its venality, an enormous premium was guaranteed to mediocrity and dishonesty. He who ventured any criticism was quickly singled out, and soon became a dangerous man. He was not persecuted; that was quite useless. Everything got lost in a general sluggishness, in a complete lack of attention, of precision. Some men of intellect and of feeling, who gave useful advice, were powerless. The conceited impertinence of the official administration, convinced that Europe admired and envied it, made any observation useless and any reform impossible.

Was the opposition more enlightened than the government? Barely. The orators of the opposition proved themselves to be, with regard to German affairs, even more thoughtless than Mr. Rouher.[65] In sum, the opposition in no way represented a superior principle of morality. Alien to any idea of skillful politics, it did not break from the mold of superficial French radicalism. Apart from a few worthy men one was surprised to see issue from so turbid a source as the Parisian polls, the rest were nothing but declamation, democratic bias. The provinces, in certain respects, fared better. The needs of a regular local life, of a serious decentralization in favor of the city administration, the canton, the *département*, the imperious desire for free elections, the firm will to reduce the government to what was strictly necessary, shrink the armed forces considerably, suppress the sinecures, abolish the aristocracy of public servants, all constituted a program liberal enough, albeit miserly, as the substance of this program was to pay as little as possible, and forswear anything that may be termed glory, strength, or splendor. From the achievement of these wishes, in time a small provincial life would have resulted, materially quite prosperous, indifferent to education and intellectual culture, passably free; a life of the wealthy bourgeois, independent from one another, with no care for knowledge, for art, for glory, for genius; a life, I repeat, similar enough to American life, excluding the differences in manners and temperament.

Such would have been the future of France, if Napoleon III had not run voluntarily to his own ruin. We were speeding with full sails toward mediocrity. On the one hand, the advances in material prosperity absorbed the bourgeoisie; on the other, social issues completely muffled national and patriotic issues. These two sorts of issues in a certain sense balance each other; the advent of the former signals the eclipse of the latter. The great improvement that had been made in the conditions of the worker was far from being favorable to his moral improvement. The people are much less capable than the higher or enlightened classes of resisting the attraction of easy pleasures, which are without inconvenience only when one is jaded about them. For well-being not to sap morality, you must be accustomed to it; the man who lacks education spoils himself rapidly through pleasure, he takes it seriously in a clumsy fashion, he is not revolted by it. The superior morality of the German people comes from the fact that up to our time they have been much mistreated. The political thinkers who maintain that the people must suffer in order to be good are unfortunately not altogether mistaken.

Shall I say it? Our political philosophy contributed to the same result. The first principle of our morals is to suppress temperament, to allow reason to control animal nature as much as possible; now this is the opposite of the martial spirit. What could the rule of conduct be, for us liberals, who cannot accept divine right in politics, since we do not accept the supernatural in religion? A simple human law, a compromise between absolute rationalism after the fashion of Condorcet[66] and the eighteenth century (which only recognized the right of reason to rule humanity) and the rights deriving from history. The failed experiment of the Revolution cured us of the cult of reason; but, even with all possible goodwill, we have proven incapable of shifting to the cult of force, or of right based on force, which is the summation of German politics. Such were our principles, and they had two essential flaws: the first was that there happened to be people in the world who had entirely different principles, who lived by the harsh doctrines of the old order, which made the unity of the nation consist of the rights of the sovereign, while we believed that the nineteenth century had ushered in a new right, the right of populations; the second flaw was that we were not always able to make these principles prevail in our own home. The principles I mentioned just now are indeed French principles, in the sense that they logically follow from our [Enlightenment] philosophy, from our Revolution, from our national character with its virtues and its shortcomings. Unfortunately, the party that professes them is, like all intelligent parties, only a minority, and this minority has too often been defeated among us. The Rome expedition was the most evident departure from the only policy that could suit us. Our attempt to meddle in German affairs was a glaring inconsistency, and it must not be attributed exclusively to the deposed government; the opposition had not stopped advocating it since Sadowa.[67] Those who have always repudiated the policy of conquest have the right to say, "To seize Alsace against its will is a crime; to surrender it save in the face of absolute necessity would also be a crime." But those who preached the doctrine of natural borders and national expediency do not have the right to consider it evil that they be treated the way they wanted to treat others. The doctrines of natural borders and of the right of populations cannot be invoked by the same mouth, under penalty of an evident contradiction.

Thus, we found ourselves to be weak, disavowed by our own country. France could ignore all foreign action, as Louis-Philippe wisely did. As soon as it acted abroad, it could only serve its own principle, the principle of free nations, composed of free provinces, mistresses of their destiny. It was from this viewpoint that we were sympathetic with the Emperor Napoleon III's Italian War, even in some regards with the Crimean War, and especially with the assistance he provided for the creation of a northern Germany[68] around Prussia. For a fleeting moment, we believed that our dream, that is to say, a political and intellectual union of Germany, France, and England, forming among the three of them a driving force of humanity and civilization, containing Russia, or rather steering it on its path and uplifting it, was going to come true. Alas! What to do with a strange and inconsistent mind? The Italian War had as its obverse the prolonged occupation of Rome,[69] a complete denial of all French principles; the Crimean War, which would not have been legitimate unless it had led to the emancipation of the good peoples held in subjection by Turkey, had as its only result the strengthening of the Ottoman principle; the Mexico expedition[70] was a challenge to all liberal ideas. The real titles that had been garnered to the gratitude of Germany were lost after Sadowa by adopting an attitude of petulance and provocation.

It is unjust, let us say it once more, to dismiss all these mistakes as the responsibility of the past regime, and one of the most dangerous turns national self-love could take would be to believe that our woes have no other cause than the mistakes of Napoleon III, so that, Napoleon III once discarded, victory and happiness would return to us. The truth is that all our weaknesses had a deeper root, a root that has in no way disappeared: democracy incorrectly understood. A democratic country cannot be well governed, well administered, well led. The reason is simple. Government,

208 INTELLECTUAL AND MORAL REFORM OF FRANCE

administration, leadership are in society the result of a selection that draws from the mass a certain number of individuals who govern, administer, lead. This selection can occur in four ways, which have been applied, at times individually, at times concurrently in different societies: first, by birth; second, by the drawing of lots; third, by popular election; fourth, by competitive examinations.

The drawing of lots has hardly ever been practiced, except in Athens and in Florence, that is to say in the only two cities where there has been an aristocratic people, a people offering by its history, in the midst of the strangest deviations, the most elegant and delightful spectacle. It is clear that in our societies, which resemble vast Scythias,[71] within which the courts, the great cities, the universities represent something akin to Greek colonies, such a mode of selection would lead to absurd results; there is no need to linger on it.

The system of competitive examinations has not been adopted on a large scale anywhere but in China. There it produced a general and incurable senility. We ourselves have traveled far enough down this road, and it is not the least of causes of our decadence.

The system of election cannot be taken as the sole basis of government. Applied to military leadership, in particular, election is a sort of contradiction, leadership's negation itself, since, in military affairs, leadership is absolute; now, the elected never command their electors absolutely. Applied to the choice of the person of the sovereign, election encourages charlatanism, preemptively destroys the prestige of the elected, obliges him to humiliate himself before those who must obey him. All the more do these objections apply if suffrage is universal. Applied to the choice of members of parliament, universal suffrage, as long as it is direct, will always lead to mediocre choices. It is impossible to draw from it a higher chamber, a judiciary, or even a good departmental or municipal council. Essentially narrow-minded, universal suffrage does not understand the necessity of knowledge, the superiority of the noble and the learned. Its only use is to create a body of notables, and even then only on condition that the election be conducted in the fashion we will specify presently.

It is indisputable that, if we had to limit ourselves to a single means of selection, birth would be better than election. The role of chance in birth is lesser than the role of chance in balloting. Birth ordinarily entails advantages in education and at times a certain superiority of race. With respect to the designation of the sovereign and of military leaders, the *criterium* of birth prevails almost by necessity. This *criterium*, after all, only offends the French prejudice, which sees in public office much more an annuity to assign to a public official than a public duty. This prejudice is the opposite of the true principle of government, which enjoins to consider in the choice of public officials nothing but the good of the state, or, in other terms, the proper discharge of the office. Nobody has the right to a position; everyone has the right to have the positions appropriately filled. If the hereditary transmission of certain offices were a guarantee of good management, I would not hesitate to propose hereditary transmissions for these offices.

One can understand now how the selection of leadership, which had been performed so admirably in France until the end of the seventeenth century, is now so degraded, and how it could have produced the body of rulers, ministers, deputies, senators, field marshals, generals, and administrators we had in the month of July of last year, which one can consider as among the weakest staffs of statesmen a country has ever seen in office. All this issued from universal suffrage, because the emperor, the source of all initiative, and the Corps législatif,[72] the only counterweight to the emperor's initiatives, both issued from it. This wretched government was indeed the result of democracy; France had wanted it, had drawn it from its entrails. The France of universal suffrage will never have a much better one. It would be contrary to nature for an intellectual average that barely reaches that of an ignorant and narrow-minded man to be represented by an enlightened, brilliant, and strong governmental corps. From such a selection procedure, from such a misconceived democracy, only the complete obfuscation of a country's consciousness can result. An electoral college composed of everyone is inferior to the most mediocre sovereign of old; the court of Versailles was more apt at choosing public servants than universal suffrage today; such a suffrage will produce a government inferior to the worst of the eighteenth century.

A country is not the simple sum of the individuals who comprise it; it is a soul, a consciousness, a person, a living result. This soul may reside in a very small number of men; it would be best if all could participate in it; but what is indispensable is that, through governmental selection, a head is created that stands vigil and thinks while the rest of the country does not think and is hardly conscious. Now, the French selection is the weakest of all. With its unorganized universal suffrage, which is left to chance, France can only have a social head lacking intelligence and knowledge, prestige and authority. France wished for peace, and chose its representatives so foolishly that it was plunged into war. The assembly of a super-pacific country enthusiastically voted for the most disastrous war. A few roadside bawlers, a few imprudent journalists managed to pass for the expression of the public opinion of the nation. There are in France as many men of feeling and men of intellect as in any other country; but all this is not exploited. A country that has no other organ save direct universal suffrage is as a whole, whatever the value of the men it possesses, an ignorant, foolish being, unable to decide wisely on any issue whatsoever. The democrats judge the old order very harshly for bringing to power sovereigns who were often incompetent or wicked. Certainly, the states that let national consciousness reside in a royal family and its entourage have highs and lows; but let us consider the Capetian dynasty, which reigned for almost nine hundred years, as a whole; for a few lows in the fourteenth, sixteenth, and eighteenth centuries, what admirable runs in the twelfth, thirteenth, and seventeenth centuries, from Louis the Young to Philip the Fair, from Henry IV to the second half of the reign of Louis XIV! No electoral system can give a representation such as that. The most mediocre man is superior to the collective result issuing from thirty-six million individuals, each counting for one unit. May the future prove me wrong! But one may fear that with infinite resources of courage, of goodwill, and even of intelligence, France will nonetheless be choked off like an ill-built fire. Selfishness, the source of socialism, and jealousy, the source of democracy, will never produce anything but a weak society, incapable of resisting powerful neighbors. A society is only strong as a consequence of recognizing the existence of natural superiorities, which essentially can be reduced to a single one, that of birth, since intellectual and moral superiority itself is nothing but the superiority of a seed of life that burgeoned in particularly favored conditions.

IV

If we had been alone in the world or without neighbors, we could have continued our decadence indefinitely and even reveled in it; but we were not alone in the world. Our past glory and empire came like a specter to trouble our celebrations. He whose ancestors have participated in great struggles is not free to lead a quiet and vulgar life; the descendants of those who were killed by his forefathers always come to wake him from his bourgeois happiness and point a sword at his brow.

Always improvident and inconsiderate, France had literally forgotten that half a century ago it had insulted most of the nations of Europe, and in particular the race that presents in all respects the contrary of our qualities and defects. French consciousness is short and lively; German consciousness is long, persistent, and deep. The Frenchman is good, but heedless: he quickly forgets the evil he does and the evil he is done; the German is rancorous, scarcely charitable; he understands glory and points of honor poorly; he does not know forgiveness. The revenges of 1814 and 1815 had not satisfied the enormous hatred that the disastrous wars of the Empire had set ablaze in the heart of Germany. Slowly, skillfully it prepared its vengeance for injuries that for us were events of a different time, with which we felt no tie and for which we in no way believed we bore responsibility.

While we carelessly slid down the slope of an unintelligent materialism or an overgenerous philosophy, allowing practically all memory of a national character to dissipate (without realizing that our social condition was so lacking in solidity that the whim of a few reckless men would suffice to lose everything), a completely different character, the ancient character of what we call the old order, was alive in Prussia, and in many respects in Russia. England and the rest of Europe, excluding these two countries, had taken the same path as us, a path of peace, industry, and commerce, presented by the school of the economists and by most statesmen as the path of civilization itself. But there were two countries where ambition in the sense of yore, the desire to expand, national faith, the pride of race still endured. Russia, by its deep instincts, by its fanaticism both religious and political, preserved the sacred fire of ancient times, which one finds quite little in a people consumed like ours with selfishness, that is to say the ready disposition to be killed for a cause to which no personal benefit is attached. In Prussia, a privileged nobility, peasants submitted to a nearly feudal regime, a military and national character driven almost to coarseness, a harsh life, a certain general poverty, with a tinge of envy for peoples that lead a gentler life, all maintained the conditions that up to now have made the strength of nations. There, the military condition, which among us is belittled or considered a synonym of idleness and an aimless life, is the main title of honor, a sort of learned career. The German mind had applied to the art of killing the power of its methods. While on this side of the Rhine all our efforts strove to root out the memories of the First Empire, which we thought noxious, the old spirit of Blücher,[73] of Scharnhorst[74] was still alive there. Among us, patriotism related to military memories was ridiculed with the term *chauvinism*; there, they all are what we call *chauvins*, and they pride themselves on it. The tendency of French liberalism was to diminish the state for the benefit of individual liberty; the state in Prussia was much more tyrannical than it ever was among us; the Prussian, raised, trained, moralized, educated, regimented, constantly monitored by the state, was much more governed (also no doubt much better governed) than we ever were, and did not complain. This people is essentially monarchical; they have no need for equality; they have virtues, but virtues of classes. While among us one same type of honor is everyone's ideal, in Germany, the nobleman, the bourgeois, the professor, the peasant, the worker each has its particular formula of duty; the duties of man, the rights of man are poorly understood; and this is a great strength, for equality is the greatest cause of political and military weakening there is. Add knowledge, the critical faculty, the scope and precision of the mind, all qualities that Prussian education develops in the highest degree and our French education obliterates or does not develop; add especially the moral qualities and in particular the quality that always grants victory to a race over the peoples that have it in a lesser degree, chastity,* and you will understand that, for whomever possesses a bit of philosophy of history and has understood what the virtue of nations is, for whomever has read the two fine treatises by Plutarch, "On the Virtue and Fortune of Alexander" and "On the Virtue and Fortune of the Romans,"[75] there could remain no doubt regarding what was in store. It was easy to see that the French Revolution, only slightly and momentarily checked by the events of 1814 and 1815, would once again see rise against it its eternal enemy, the Germanic or rather Slavic-Germanic race of the north, in other terms, Prussia, which had remained a country of the old

---

*   Women in France account for an enormous part of social and political life; in Prussia, they account for infinitely less.

order, and hence had preserved itself from the industrial, economic, socialist, revolutionary materialism that had tamed the manliness of all the other peoples. Hence, the fixed resolve of the Prussian aristocracy to vanquish the French Revolution had two distinct phases, one from 1792 to 1815, the other from 1848 to 1871, both victorious, and it will probably again be so in the future, unless revolution takes over its own enemy itself, for which the annexation of Germany to Prussia will provide great advantages, though not for the immediate future.

War is essentially a thing of the old order. It presupposes a great absence of selfish reflection, for, after victory, those who contributed most to secure it, I mean the dead, do not benefit from it; it is the contrary of this lack of abnegation, this acrimony in the claiming of individual rights that is the character of our modern democracy. With this type of character, no war is possible. Democracy is the strongest solvent of military organization. Military organization is based upon discipline; democracy is the negation of discipline. Germany has its democratic movement, too; but this movement is subordinated to the national patriotic movement. Germany's victory, therefore, could not have failed to be complete, because an organized force always beats a force that is not organized, even if it is numerically superior. Germany's victory was the victory of the disciplined man over the man who is not, of the dutiful, careful, vigilant, methodical man over the man who is not; it was the victory of knowledge and reason; but it was also the victory of the old order, of the principle that repudiates the sovereignty of the people and the right of populations to determine their destiny. These latter ideas, far from strengthening a race, disarm it, make it unfit for any military action, and, as a crowning blow, do not protect it from placing itself in the hands of a government that will allow it to commit the gravest mistakes. The inconceivable act of the month of July 1870 hurled us into a chasm. All the putrid germs that, without it, would have induced a slow consumption developed into a poisonous outburst; all the veils were torn asunder; barely suspected character flaws appeared in a sinister manner.

An illness never comes alone, for a weakened body no longer has the force to repress the causes of destruction that are always latent in the organism and that good health prevents from erupting. The horrible episode of the Commune came to display an ulcer under the ulcer, an abyss below the abyss. March 18, 1871,[76] is, in the past thousand years, the day

French consciousness was at its lowest ebb. For an instant we feared that it might not re-form, that the vital force of this great body, hit in the part of the brain that houses the *sensorium commune* itself, might not suffice to prevail over the rottenness that tended to flood it. The work of the Capetians appeared compromised, and it was conceivable that the future philosophical formulation of our history would close in 1871 the great development begun by the dukes of France in the ninth century. Matters turned out differently. French consciousness, though smitten by a terrible blow, has found itself once again; it recovered from its faint in three or four days. France has regained life, the corpse that worms were already fighting over has recovered its warmth and its movement. In which conditions will this existence of the afterlife take place? Will it be the short radiance of the life of the resuscitated? Will France resume an interrupted chapter of its history? Or rather will it enter an entirely new phase of its long and mysterious destinies? What hopes can a good Frenchman harbor in such circumstances? What suggestions can he give his country? We will attempt to answer, not with the assurance that at such an hour would be the sign of a very superficial mind indeed, but with the reserve that allows generously for the contingencies of every day and the uncertainty of the future.

## PART II: THE REMEDIES

One thing known to all is the ease with which our country reorganizes itself. Some recent facts have demonstrated how little France was affected in its wealth.[77] As for the human losses, if it were permissible to speak of a similar subject with a coldness that has a cruel air to it, I would say that they are barely perceptible. Thus, a question arises for every thoughtful mind. What shall France do? Will it return to the downward path of national weakening and political materialism it was following before the War of 1870, or will it react energetically against foreign conquest, respond to the sting that touched a raw nerve, and, like Germany in 1807, take its defeat as the point of departure for an age of renewal? France is very forgetful. If Prussia had not demanded territorial concessions, I would not have hesitated to answer that the industrial, economic, social-ist movement would have continued to follow its course; the financial losses would have been recovered within a few years; the sense of military glory and national vanity would have disappeared further and further. Yes, Germany after Sedan had the finest role in the history of the world in its hands. By remaining content with its victory, by not doing violence to any part of the French population, it could have buried war for eternity, insomuch as it is permissible to speak of eternity with regard to human affairs. It did not accept this role; it violently took two million Frenchmen, of which only a tiny fraction may be presumed favorable to such a separa-tion. It is clear that all that remains of French patriotism will long have one sole aim, to recover the lost provinces. Even those who are philosophers before they are patriots will not be able to remain unmoved by the cries of two million people, whom we were obliged to cast into the sea to save the rest of the shipwrecked, but who were bound to us for life and death. Thus, France has a steel spike sunk in its flesh that will not let it sleep. But which path shall it follow in the task of its reform? In what way will its rebirth resemble so many other attempts at national resurrection? What role will French originality play? This is what needs discovering, while considering it probable a priori that a consciousness as impressionable as French consciousness will lead, in the grip of unique circumstances, to the least expected manifestations.

I

There is an excellent model for the manner in which a nation can recover from the worst disasters. Prussia itself provided it to us, and cannot reproach us for following its example. What did Prussia do after the peace of Tilsit?[78] It resigned itself, and collected itself. Its remaining territory was at most a fifth of what we have left; this territory was the poorest in Europe, and the military stipulations that had been imposed on it seemed liable to condemn it forever to powerlessness. The situation would have discouraged less caustic a patriotism. Prussia organized silently; far from banishing its dynasty, it closed ranks around it, worshiped its mediocre king, its Queen Louise, even though she had been one of the proximate causes of the war. All the competences of the nation were called upon; Stein[79] supervised everything with his concentrated vehemence. The reform of the army was a masterpiece of study and reflection; the University of Berlin was the center of Germany's regeneration; a cordial collaboration was demanded of the scholars and philosophers, who set only one condition for their participation, the one they always set and must set: their freedom. From this serious effort, pursued over fifty years, Prussia emerged the leading nation of Europe. Its regeneration had a solidity that simple patriotic vanity could not have provided, it had a moral basis; it was founded on the idea of duty, on the pride that adversity nobly borne confers.

It is clear that, if France wished to imitate Prussia's example, it would be ready more quickly. If France's difficulties derived from a profound exhaustion, there would be nothing left to do; but such is not the case; the resources are immense; it is a question of organizing them. It is indisputable that the circumstances would come to our aid. "The fashion of this world passeth away," says the scripture.[80] Certain individuals will die; the domestic difficulties of Germany will return; the Catholic party and the democratic party of the two Internationals, as they say in Prussia, will cause Mr. von Bismarck and his successors perpetual difficulties; one must consider that the unity of Germany is in no way yet the unity of France; there are parliaments in Dresden, Munich, Stuttgart; imagine Louis XIV in such conditions. In Prussia, the rivalry of the feudal party and the liberal party, skillfully staved off by Mr. von Bismarck, will erupt; the fruitful and peaceful diffusion of Germanism will cease. The maker of Slavic consciousness is German consciousness; the consciousness of the Slavs will grow and will resist that of the Germans more and more; the disadvantage for a state in detaining countries against their wishes will become more and more apparent; Austria's endless crisis will bring the most dangerous adventures; Vienna in any case will become an entanglement for Berlin; whatever one does, this empire was born bicephalous; it will live with difficulty. The wheel of fortune turns and always will turn. Having risen, one descends; and that is why pride is so unreasonable a thing. Military organizations are like industrial plants; industrial plants age quickly, and it is rare that an industrialist will refurbish the plant that is in his possession of his own free will; these plants, in fact, represent an immense fixed investment; one wishes to preserve them; one only substitutes them if forced to by the competition. In this case, it so happens that the competitor almost always holds the advantage, for he builds from scratch, and needs to make no compromises with previous establishments. Without the needle gun, France would never have replaced its flintlock guns; the needle gun having spurred it to action, it made the *chassepot*.[81] Military organizations succeed each other in this fashion like machines in industry. The military machine of Frederick the Great was in its own time the best; in 1792, it was completely outdated and powerless. Thereafter, Napoleon's machine had strength; in our day, the machine of Mr. von Moltke[82] has demonstrated its immense superiority. Either human affairs change their course, or what today is the best will no longer be so tomorrow. Military capabilities change from one generation to the next. The armies of the Republic and the Empire succeeded those that were beaten at Rossbach.[83] Once France is roused, once its bourgeois portliness and its habits of domesticity are shaken, it is impossible to say what will happen.

Therefore it is certain that if France wishes to submit to the conditions of a serious reform it can very quickly recover its place in the European concert. I cannot believe that any serious statesman in Germany has thought what the German newspapers ceaselessly repeated: "Let us seize Alsace and Lorraine to make France incapable of resuming." If we only consider territorial size and number of souls, France is barely damaged. The question is whether it will wish to enter upon the path of a serious reform, in other words, imitate the conduct of Prussia after Jena.

This path would be austere: it would be the path of penance. In what does true penance consist? All the fathers of the spiritual life agree on this point: penance does not consist in leading a harsh life, in fasting, in self-mortification. It consists in ridding oneself of one's flaws, and among one's flaws of ridding oneself precisely of those one loves, of the favorite flaw that is almost always the substance itself of our nature, the secret origin of our actions. Which is this favorite flaw for France, of which it is supremely important it rid itself? It is the taste for superficial democracy. Democracy causes our military and political weakness; it causes our ignorance, our foolish conceit; it causes, together with hidebound Catholicism, the inadequacy of our national education. Thus, I would think that a good character and a good patriot, more desirous of being useful to his fellow citizens than liked by them, would express himself more or less in these terms:

"Let us rid ourselves of democracy. Let us reestablish kingship, let us to a certain extent reestablish nobility; let us create a solid national primary and higher education; let us make education tougher, and military service compulsory for all; let us become serious, conscientious, obedient to public powers, friendly to rules and discipline. Let us above all be humble. Let us be suspicious of presumptuousness. Prussia took sixty-three years to avenge Jena; let us employ at least twenty to avenge Sedan; for ten or fifteen years, let us abstain completely from world affairs; let us limit ourselves completely to the obscure toil of our domestic reform. Let us not have a revolution, whatever the cost, let us cease believing that we have the privilege of the initiative in Europe; let us give up the attitude that makes us into the perpetual exception to the general order. In this way, it is indubitable that, with the help of the ordinary transformations of the world, we will have recovered our rank in fifteen or twenty years.

"We shall not recover it otherwise. Prussia's victory has been the victory of quasi-divine-right kingship (of historical-right kingship); a nation cannot reform itself on the Prussian model without a historic kingship and without the nobility. Democracy does not bring discipline or morality. One cannot discipline oneself; children gathered together without a schoolmaster do not learn; they play and waste time. From the masses there cannot emerge enough reason to govern and reform a people. Reform and education must come from without, from a force that has no other interest except that of the nation, yet distinct from the nation and independent from it. There is something democracy will never do, and that is war, I mean studied war as Prussia has inaugurated it. The age of the undisciplined volunteers and of the militias has passed. The age of the dazzling, ignorant, brave, shallow officers has also passed. War henceforth is a scientific and administrative problem, a complicated task that superficial democracy is as incapable of seeing through to a successful outcome as sailboat builders are of producing an armored frigate. French-style democracy will never endow the knowledgeable with enough authority for them to be able to make a rational course prevail. How could democracy choose a rational course, besieged as it is by charlatans and lacking the competence to choose among them? Besides, democracy will not be sufficiently steadfast to sustain for long the enormous effort necessary for a great war. Nothing can be done in these gigantic common enterprises, if everyone may, as the vulgar expression has it, "pick and choose;" now, democracy cannot abandon its fecklessness without entering into terror. Ultimately, the republic must always be suspicious of the hypothesis of a victorious general. Monarchy is so natural to France that any general who had given his country a spectacular victory would be able to topple the republican institutions. The republic cannot exist except in a vanquished country or in a completely pacified one. In all countries exposed to war, the cry of the people will always be the cry of the Hebrews to Samuel: 'A king to march at our head and wage war with us.'

"France has been mistaken about the form the people's consciousness can take. Its universal suffrage is like a pile of sand, without cohesion or fixed relationship between the atoms. You cannot build a house with it. A nation's consciousness resides in the enlightened part of the nation, which leads and commands the rest. Civilization originally was an aristocratic accomplishment, the accomplishment of a very small number (nobles and priests), who imposed it by what democrats call force and fraud; the preservation of civilization is an aristocratic accomplishment, too. Fatherland, honor, and duty are things created and maintained by a very small number in the midst of a crowd that, left to its own devices, would discard them. What would Athens have become, if suffrage had been granted to its two hundred thousand slaves and if the small aristocracy of free men that had made it what it was had been drowned by numbers? Similarly, France has been created by the king, the nobility, the clergy, the Third Estate. The people in the proper sense of the term and the peasants, who today are the absolute masters of the house, in reality are intruders here, hornets turned into bosses in a hive they did not build. The soul of a nation will not be preserved without an order officially charged with maintaining it. A dynasty is the best institution for this, because, by associating the fortunes of a nation with those of a family, such an institution creates the most favorable conditions for a good continuity. A senate like that of Rome or of Venice fulfills the same role quite well; the religious, social, pedagogical, gymnastic institutions of the Greeks were perfectly sufficient for it; a prince elected for life has also supported relatively strong social states; but what is unexampled is the dream of our democrats, a house made out of sand, a nation without traditional institutions, without a body charged with guaranteeing the continuity of national consciousness, a nation based on the deplorable principle that a generation does not bind the following one, so that there is no chain from the dead to the living, no assurance for the future. Recall what caused the demise of all workers' cooperative associations: the inability to set up a serious management in such associations, the jealousy against those the association had invested with any authority whatsoever, the pretension always to subordinate them to their constituents, the obstinate refusal to offer them a dignified position. French democracy will make the same mistake in politics; an enlightened direction will never issue from what is the denial itself of the value of intellectual work and the necessity of such work.

"And do not claim that an assembly will be able to fill the role of the old dynasties and the old aristocracies. The word 'republic' itself is an encouragement to a certain unhealthy democratic development; we will see it well in the progressive exaltation that will manifest itself in the elections, as happened in 1850 and 1851. To stem this movement, an assembly will be ruthless; but then another tendency will be uncovered, the one that leads to prefer a liberal monarchy to a reactionary republic. The fate of the republic is both to provoke anarchy and to repress it very severely. An assembly is never a great man. An assembly has the defects that in a sovereign are the most crippling: narrow-minded, passionate, easily carried away, quick to decide—without responsibility—on the spur of a moment's whim. It is a chimera to hope that an assembly composed of departmental notables, of honest provincials, can take up and maintain the dazzling heritage of French royalty and nobility. A permanent aristocratic center is necessary to preserve art, science, taste against democratic and provincial dulling. Paris clearly realizes it; no aristocracy ever cared for its ancient privileges as much as Paris does for the privilege it claims, to be an institution of France, to act on certain days as its head and sovereign, and to demand the obedience of the rest of the country; but it is one of the strongest inconsistencies of which the history of centuries has retained the memory that Paris, while demanding its privilege as a capital, still considers itself republican and has established the suffrage of all.

"The synagogue in Prague has among its traditions an old legend that has always seemed to me a striking symbol. A cabbalist of the sixteenth century had made a statue so perfectly congruent with the proportions of the divine archetype that it lived and acted. By placing under its tongue the ineffable name of God (the mystical tetragrammaton), the cabbalist even bestowed reason on the man of plaster, though an obscure, imperfect reason always in need of being guided; he made use of it as a domestic servant for various menial tasks; on Saturdays, he took the marvelous talisman from its mouth, so it could observe the holy rest. Now, one time he forgot this very necessary precaution. While he was attending the divine service, a terrible noise was heard in the ghetto; it was the man of plaster breaking, smashing everything. People ran up and grabbed it. From then on, the tetragrammaton was removed from it forever, and it was placed under lock and key in the garret of the synagogue, where it can still be seen. Alas! We believed that, by having the formless being that does not shine with an interior light utter a few words of reason, we had made a man of it. The day we left it to itself, the brutal machine broke down; I fear it should be stored for centuries.

"Thus, the task we should set ourselves is to reestablish a historical right, in place of that ill-fated formula of 'divine' right the publicists of fifty years ago made fashionable. Monarchy, by tying the interests of a nation to those of a rich and powerful family, constitutes the system of greatest fixity for national consciousness. Even the mediocrity of the sovereign is only a feeble inconvenience in such a system. The degree of national reason emanating from a people that has not contracted a centuries-long marriage with a family is, on the contrary, so weak, so discontinuous, so intermittent that it can only be compared to the reason of a completely inferior man, or even to the instinct of an animal. The first step therefore is evidently for France to take back its dynasty. A country only has one dynasty, the one that created its unity at the end of a state of crisis or dissolution. The family that created France over nine hundred years still exists; luckier than Poland, we possess our old banner of unity; however, a terrible rent defiles it. The countries whose existence is based on kingship always suffer the greatest ills when there are disputes on the legitimate inheritance. On the other hand, what is impossible is impossible. Doubtless, one cannot claim that the Orléans branch, after its retreat from combat in February[84] (an act appropriate perhaps for good citizens, but not for princes), has any firm royal rights; but it has an excellent title, the memory of the reign of Louis-Philippe, the esteem and the affection of the enlightened part of the nation.

"One should not deny, however, that the Revolution and the years that followed were in many respects one of those constitutive crises in which all political casuists recognize that the rights of dynasties are established. The house of Bonaparte emerged from the revolutionary chaos that accompanied and followed the death of Louis XVI, just as the Capetian house issued from the anarchy that accompanied, in France, the decadence of the Carolingian house. Without the events of 1814 and 1815, it is likely that the house of Bonaparte would have inherited the title of the Capetians. The recovery of the Bonapartist title following the Revolution of 1848 gave it actual strength. If the revolution of the end of the past century one day comes to be considered the starting point of a new France, it is possible that the house of Bonaparte will become the dynasty of this new France; for Napoleon I saved the Revolution from an unavoidable shipwreck, and embodied the new needs quite fittingly. France is undoubtedly monarchical; but heredity rests on political reasons too deep for it to comprehend. What it desires is a monarchy without a well-set rule, analogous to that of the Roman Caesars. The House of Bourbon must not lend itself to this wish of the nation; it would fail all of its duties if it ever accepted to play the role of the *podestàs*, of the *stadtholders*, of the interim presidents of aborted republics. One cannot cut a jerkin out of the mantle of Louis XIV. The house of Bonaparte, on the other hand, does not betray its role by accepting these indecisive positions, which are not in contradiction with its origins and are justified by the full acceptance it has always professed for the dogma of popular sovereignty.

"France is in the position of the Hercules of the sophist Prodicus, *Hercules in Bivio*.[85] In the next few months it must decide on its future. It can keep the republic; but one cannot desire contradictory things. Some imagine a powerful, influential, glorious republic. Let them disabuse themselves and choose. Yes, the republic is possible in France, but a republic barely superior in importance to the Helvetic Confederation, and less taken into consideration. The republic can have neither armed forces nor diplomacy; the republic would be a military condition of rare inanity; discipline would be very imperfect; for, as Mr. Stoffel proved quite well, there is no discipline in the armed forces if there is none in the nation. The principle of the republic is election: a republican society is as weak as an army corps that appointed its own officers; the fear of not being reelected paralyzes all energies. Mr. von Savigny[86] has shown that a society needs a government coming from outside, from beyond, from before it, that social power does not emanate entirely from society, that there is a philosophical and historical right (divine, if you prefer) that imposes itself on the nation. Kingship is in no way a hereditary presidency, as our superficial constitutional school pretends to believe. The president of the United States did not create the nation, whereas the king did create the nation. The king is not an emanation of the nation; the king and the nation are two separate things; the king stands outside the nation. Kingship therefore is a divine fact for those who believe in the supernatural, a historical occurrence for those who do not. The current will of the nation, the plebiscite, even if seriously implemented, is not sufficient. The essential point is not that such-and-such a particular will of the majority be done; the essential point is that the general reason of the nation triumph. The numerical majority can will injustice, immorality; it can will the destruction of its history, and then the sovereignty of the numerical majority is nothing more than the worst of mistakes.

"It is, in any case, the mistake that weakens a nation the most. An elected assembly does not reform. Give France a young, serious king, austere in his habits; let him reign for fifty years, let him gather around him men hardened for work, fanatical about their task, and France will have one more century of glory and prosperity. With the republic, it will have indiscipline, disorder, irregular troops, volunteers who try to convince the country they are ready to die for it, while not even having enough abnegation to accept the common conditions of military life. These conditions, obedience, hierarchy, and so forth, are the contrary of all the recommendations of the democratic catechism, and that is why a democracy would not be capable of surviving with a considerable military state. This military state cannot develop under such a regime, or, if it does, it would absorb the democracy. America will be raised as an objection; but apart from the fact that the future of this country is quite unclear, one must say that America, by its geographical position, is placed, with regards to the armed forces, in a very particular situation, which could not be compared to our own.

"I can conceive of only one exit from the hesitations that are killing the country; it is a great act of national authority. One can be a royalist without accepting divine right, just as one can be a Catholic without believing in the infallibility of the pope, or a Christian without believing in the supernatural and the divinity of Jesus Christ. The dynasty is, in a sense, anterior and superior to the nation, because it is the dynasty that created the nation; but it can do nothing against the nation or without it. Dynasties have rights over the countries they have historically represented; but the country also has rights on them, because dynasties only exist for the benefit of the country. A summons addressed to the country in extraordinary circumstances might constitute an action analogous to the great national occurrence that created the Capetian dynasty, or the decision of the university of Paris at the time of the accession of the Valois.[87] Our ancient theorists of monarchy agree on the fact that the legitimacy of dynasties is established in certain solemn moments, in which it is a question foremost of retrieving the nation from anarchy and of replacing an outdated dynastic title.

"Similarly, it is by the historical process, I mean by skillfully benefiting from the sections of walls left over from a more ancient building, and by developing what exists, that one could create something to replace the ancient family traditions. No royalty without nobility; the two ultimately rest on the same principle, a selection artificially creating a sort of separate race for the good of society. Nobility among us no longer holds any connotation of race. It issues from an almost fortuitous co-optation, in which the usurpation of titles, the misunderstandings, the small frauds, and especially the childish notion that consists in believing that the preposition *de* is a mark of nobility, have almost as much weight as birth and legal ennoblement. A two-tier suffrage would introduce a much superior aristocratic principle. The armed forces would be another means of ennobling. The officer of our future *Landwehr*, a constantly trained local militia, would soon become a village squire, and this office would often have a tendency to become hereditary; the captain of the canton, toward the age of fifty, would want to transmit his position to his son, whom he would have groomed and whom everyone would know. The same occurred in the Middle Ages for the necessities of self-defense. The *Ritter*,[88] who had a horse, a sort of brigadier of the constabulary, became a small lord.

"The foundation of provincial life should thus be an honest, quite loyal village gentleman, and a good country priest completely devoted to the moral education of the people. Duty is aristocratic: it should have its special representation. The master, Aristotle says, has more duties than the slave; the higher classes have more duties than the lower classes. This provincial *gentry*[89] must not be everything, but it is a necessary foundation. The universities, centers of high intellectual culture, the court, school of elegant manners, Paris, residence of the sovereign and city of high society, will correct the slightly dull tendency of the provincial *gentry*, and prevent the bourgeoisie, too proud of its morality, from degenerating into pharisaism. One of the advantages of dynasties is precisely that they attribute to exquisite and serious things a value the public cannot confer on them, they perceive certain particularly aristocratic products that the masses do not understand. It was much easier for Turgot to be minister in 1774 than it would be nowadays. These days, his modesty, his clumsiness, his lack of talent as an orator and a writer would have thwarted him from the very beginning. One hundred years ago, to be successful, he only needed to be understood and appreciated by the Abbé de Very, a philosophical priest, very influential with Madame de Maurepas.

"Everybody is more or less in agreement on this point, that we need military legislation patterned in its general lines upon the Prussian system. In the first moment of emotion, there will be the votes in parliament to pass it. But, once this moment passes, if we remain a republic, there will not be votes in parliament to support it or to have it implemented. At each election, members of parliament will be obliged to undertake engagements in this respect that will paralyze their future activity. If Prussia had universal suffrage, it would have neither universal military service nor compulsory education. The pressure of the electorate would have long since lightened these two burdens. The Prussian system is possible only with country noblemen, born leaders of their village, always in contact with their men, whom they have long had in training and can call together in the wink of an eye. A people without noblemen is in time of danger a panicked herd, beaten in advance by an organized enemy. Indeed, what is nobility if not the military function, considered as hereditary and placed at the forefront of social functions? When war disappears from the world, so will nobility: no sooner. One does not staff an army the way one staffs an administration of the public domain or of the tobacco monopoly, by the free choice of families and of young men. The military career thus conceived is too puny to attract good subjects. The military selection of democracy is wretched; a Saint-Cyr established under such a regime will always be excessively weak. If on the contrary there is a class that is destined to war by birth, this will provide the armed forces an average of good characters, who would otherwise follow other avocations.

"Are these dreams? Perhaps; but if so I assure you that France is lost. It would not be, if it were believable that Germany would itself be led into the circle of the democratic sabbath, where we have lost all our virtue; but this is unlikely. That people is obedient, and resigned beyond all belief. Its national pride is so strongly exalted by its victories that, for the next generation or two at least, social problems will occupy only a limited part of its activity. A people, like a man, always prefers to concentrate on what it excels in; now, the Germanic race senses its military superiority. As long as it does, it will have neither a revolution nor socialism. This race is destined for a long period of war and patriotism; this will distract it from domestic politics, from anything that weakens the principle of hierarchy and discipline. If it is true, as it seems, that kingship and the aristocratic organization of the armed forces are lost to the Latin peoples, one must state that the Latin peoples are calling for a new Germanic invasion, and they will suffer it."

II

Fortunate are those who find in family traditions or in the fanaticism of a narrow mind the assurance that alone resolves all these doubts! As for us, too accustomed to seeing the different sides of matters to believe in absolute solutions, we would also conceive that a very honest citizen might speak as follows:

"Politics does not discuss imaginary solutions. The character of a nation cannot be changed. It is sufficient that the plan of reform you sketched was Prussia's plan for me to make bold to predict that it will not be France's. Reforms that require France to recant its democratic prejudices are chimerical reforms. Rest assured that France will remain a land of amiable, gentle, honest, just, merry, superficial people, full of good heart, of weak political intelligence; it will keep its mediocre administration, its stubborn committees, its habit-bound bodies, convinced they are the best in the world; it will forge ahead evermore on this path of materialism, of vulgar republicanism toward which all the modern world, except for Prussia and Russia, seems headed. Does this mean it will never have its revenge? It is perhaps precisely by these means that it will attain it. Its revenge, then, will be that one day it will have preceded the world on the road that leads to the end of all nobility, of all virtue. As long as the Germanic and Slavic peoples maintain their illusions of young races, we will remain inferior to them; but these races will age in their turn; they will follow the path of all flesh. This will not occur as quickly as the socialist school believes, convinced as it is that the issues that hold its attention absorb the world in the same degree. The issues of rivalry between races and nations seem destined for a long time yet to trump issues of salaries and welfare in the parts of Europe one can ascribe to the old world; but the example of France is contagious. There has never been a French revolution without repercussions abroad. The cruelest revenge that France can obtain over the prideful nobility that was the main tool of its defeat would be to live in a democracy, to prove by example the possibility of a republic. We would perhaps not have to wait long to say to our victors like the dead of Isaiah: *Et tu vulneratus sicut et nos; nostri similis effectus es!*[90]

"Therefore, let France remain what it is; let it maintain without wavering the banner of liberalism that has given it a role for the past hundred years. This liberalism is often a cause of weakness: it is a reason for the world to come around to it; for the world is slackening and losing its old rigor. In any case, France is more assured of its revenge, if it owes it to its flaws, than if it is reduced to awaiting it from the qualities it never had. Our enemies can rest assured, if Frenchmen, in order to recover their rank, must begin by becoming Pomeranian or Dithmarsian. What conquered France was a residue of moral strength, of roughness, of gravity and sense of abnegation that, in a lost corner of the world, happened to have survived the deleterious effects of selfish reflection. If French democracy manages to constitute a viable state, this old leaven will soon disappear under the effect of the most powerful solvent of any virtue the world has yet known."

Perhaps, in fact, the decision France has made, on the advice of some statesmen who know it well, to table the constitutional and dynastic questions, is the wisest one. We will comply with it. Without forsaking this commitment, we might point out some reforms that, under any scenario, must be considered.

III

The same people who do not accept that France was mistaken in proclaiming the sovereignty of the people without reservation cannot deny at least, if they have a modicum of philosophical character, that it has chosen a very imperfect mode of national representation.* The appointment of the social powers by direct universal suffrage is the crudest political machine that has ever been employed. A country is composed of two essential elements: (1) citizens considered in isolation as simple units and (2) social functions, groups, special interests, property holders. Two chambers are thus necessary, and no regular government of any type shall ever survive without two chambers. A single chamber appointed by the suffrage of citizens considered as simple units might not contain a single magistrate, a single general, a single professor, a single administrator. Such a chamber might poorly represent property holders, special interests, what one may call the moral constituencies of the nation. It is therefore absolutely necessary that side by side with an assembly elected by citizens without distinction of professions, titles, social classes there be an assembly constituted with a different procedure, and representing the competences, the specializations, the various special interests without which there is no organized state.

Is it indispensable that the first of these two chambers be appointed by the universality of citizens, in order to be a true representation of citizens? Certainly not, and the sudden establishment of universal suffrage in 1848 was, as all political thinkers admit, a great mistake. But dwelling on this is no longer a question. All the measures, like the law of May 31, 1851,[91] whose goal is to deprive citizens of a right they have exercised for

---

\*    I was pleased to concur, in the following views, with some good minds who are presently searching for the remedy to our ever-so-defective institutions: J. Foulon-Ménard, *Fonctions de l'État* (Nantes, 1871); J. Guadet, *Du suffrage universel et de son application d'après un mode nouveau* (Bordeaux, 1871).

the past twenty-three years, would be blameworthy. What is legitimate, possible, and just is to ensure that suffrage, while remaining completely universal, is no longer direct, to introduce different levels in the suffrage. All the constitutions of the First Republic, except the one of 1793, which was never put into practice, accepted this elementary principle. The two levels would correct what is necessarily superficial in universal suffrage; the assembly of grand electors at the second level would constitute a political public worthy of serious candidates. One may grant that all citizens possess a certain right to the management of the commonwealth; but this right must be regulated, its employment must be enlightened. Let a hundred citizens of the same canton, by entrusting their mandate to one of their fellow citizens who lives in the same canton, make him a grand elector; this will produce approximately eighty thousand grand electors for the whole of France. These eighty thousand grand electors would form departmental constituencies, each cantonal subdivision of which would meet in the canton's seat, would hold its free sessions, and would vote for the whole *département*. List voting, so absurd with direct universal suffrage, would then be fully appropriate, especially if the number of members of the first chamber were reduced, as it should be, to four or five hundred. In this system, the procedures for the selection of the grand electors at the second level would be public, it is true; but that would be a guarantee of morality. The electoral mandate should be conferred for fifteen or twenty years; if the electoral college is created anew for each individual election, almost all the advantages of the reform in question are lost.

I admit that I would prefer an even more representative system, and one in which women and children were counted. I would have it that, in first-level elections, a married man voted for his wife (in other words, that his voice counted for two), and a father voted for his underage children; I would even conceive of the mother or the sister entrusting their power to a son or a brother of legal age. It is certainly impossible for women to participate directly in political life; but it is fair that they be counted. There would be too many inconveniencies if they could choose the individuals to whom they would give their political mandate; but the woman who has a husband, a father, or a brother, a son of legal age has natural mandataries, of which she must be in a position to double the voting power, if I dare say so, on election day. In this way, society becomes an interlinked, cemented unity, where all is mutual duty, responsibility, solidarity. The grand electors at the second level would be local aristocrats, authorities, notables appointed almost for life. These grand electors could be gathered by canton in times of crisis; they would be the guardians of the mores, the stewards of public monies; they would teach gravitas and seriousness. The general councils of the *départements* would issue from analogous electoral procedures, slightly modified.

The means of composing the second chamber would be completely different and infinitely more varied. Let us assume that the number of members were three hundred and sixty. First of all, there should be about thirty hereditary seats, reserved for the survivors of ancient families, whose titles would resist a historical and critical analysis. Life members would be appointed by various procedures. One could have the general council of each *département* appoint one member. The head of state would appoint fifty members; the higher chamber itself would co-opt up to thirty members; the first chamber would appoint thirty more. The hundred and twenty or hundred and thirty left would represent the national bodies, the social functions. The army and the navy would be present through their marshals and admirals; the judiciary, the teaching corps, the clergies would have their leaders sit there; each class of the Institut[92] would appoint a member; the same would be the case for the industrial corporations, the chambers of commerce, and so on. Finally, the great cities are moral persons, with an individual character. I would like every large city of more than one hundred thousand souls to have a representative in the higher chamber; Paris would have four or five. This chamber thus would represent everything that is an individuality within the state; it would truly be a conservative body of all rights and all freedoms.

We are permitted to hope that two chambers thus created would contribute to liberal progress and not to revolution. In view of certain particularities of the French character, it would be good to forbid the publicity of the sessions, which too often causes the debates to degenerate into a display. One would thus establish a simple and true type of eloquence, much preferable to the tone of our lengthy and declamatory harangues in bad taste. The parliamentary record has the inconvenience of redirecting the aim of the orator, of leading him to target the public rather than the chamber, and of having the government of the country used for the agitation of the country. If France desires a future of reform and revenge, it must avoid wearing out its forces in parliamentary battles. Parliamentary government is excellent for times of prosperity; it serves to avoid very serious mistakes and excesses, which is certainly of capital importance; however, it does not rouse great moral efforts. Prussia would not have accomplished its rebirth following Jena, if it had practiced parliamentary life. It lived through forty years of silence, which served admirably to forge the nation's character.

It is incontestable that Paris is the only possible capital of France; but this privilege must be offset by obligations. Not only must Paris forswear its aggressions against the representation of France; Paris being granted the status of a special city due to the residence of the central authorities, it cannot have the rights of an ordinary city. Paris can have neither a mayor, nor a council elected in the ordinary fashion, nor a civic guard. The sovereign power must not encounter in the city where it resides another sovereignty apart from its own. The usurpations of which the city government of Paris has rendered itself guilty so often in the past more than justify any fears on this count.

With solid institutions, the freedom of the press might be left intact. In a truly stable social condition, the working of the press is very useful as a control; without the press, extremely serious abuses are inevitable. It is up to the honest classes to discourage the scandalous press by their disdain. As for the freedom of association, experience shows that such freedom has no serious advantage, and that it is not worthwhile making sacrifices for it.

The cause of administrative decentralization is too completely proven for us to insist on it. But if we want to speak of a deeper decentralization, which would turn France into a federation of states analogous to the United States of America, we must understand each other. There are no examples in history of a unitary and centralized state decreeing its partition. Such a partition was at risk of occurring last March; it would occur the day France falls even lower than it did with the War of 1870 and the Commune; it will never occur by legal means. An organized power only cedes what is wrenched from it. When great governmental machines, such as the Roman Empire or the Frankish Empire, begin to weaken, the dislocated parts of these aggregates impose their conditions on the central power, draw up charters, force the central power to sign them. In other words, the formation of a confederation (except in the case of colonies) is the symptom of an empire collapsing. Let us therefore table such proposals, the more so since, if the iron hooks were loosened that hold the stones of the old building together, it is not certain that these stones would remain in their place and not come apart altogether.

Colonization on a large scale is an absolutely first-order political necessity. A nation that does not colonize is irrevocably destined to socialism, to the war of the rich against the poor. The conquest of a country of an inferior race by a superior race, which settles there to govern it, has nothing shocking to it. England practices this type of colonialism in India, to the great benefit of India, humanity in general, and its own people. The Germanic conquest of the fifth and sixth centuries has become the basis of all conservation and legitimacy in Europe. In the same way that conquests between equal races are reprehensible, the regeneration of inferior or mongrel races by superior races fits within the providential order of humanity. The man of the people is, among us, almost always a declassed nobleman; his heavy hand is much better suited to wielding the sword than the slavish tool. Rather than work, he chooses to fight, that is to say he returns to his original condition. *Regere imperio populos*,[93] this is our avocation. Direct this devouring activity toward countries that, like China, call for foreign conquest. Make a *ver sacrum*[94] out of the adventurers that trouble European society, a swarm like those of the Franks, the Lombards, the Normans; all will fit their role. Nature has made a race of workers: it is the Chinese race, with its marvelous manual dexterity and hardly any feeling of honor; govern it with justice, drawing from it an ample endowment for the benefit of the conquering race in exchange for the advantage of such a government, and it will be satisfied. The Negro is a race of field laborers; be good and humane toward it, and everything will be in order. The European race is a race of lords and soldiers. Reduce this noble race to toiling in prison like Negroes and Chinamen, and it rebels. Each rebel among us is, to some extent, a soldier who missed his calling, a creature made for the heroic life, which you assign to a task contrary to his race: a mediocre worker, too good a soldier. Now, this life that disgusts our workers would make the happiness of a Chinaman, a *fellah*, creatures who are in no way military. Let all do what they are made for, and everything will go well. The economists are mistaken in considering labor to be the origin of property. The origin of property is conquest and the guarantee given by the conqueror to the fruits of labor around him.

The Normans were the creators of property in Europe because, the day after these bandits gained some land, they established for themselves and for all the people of their domain a social order and a security no one had seen until then.

IV

In the struggle that just came to a close, France's inferiority was above all intellectual; what we lacked was not in the heart but in the head. Public education is an issue of capital importance; French intellect has weakened; it must be strengthened. Our greatest mistake is to believe that man is born completely reared; the German, it is true, believes too much in education; he becomes pedantic; but we believe in it too little. The loss of faith in science is France's deep flaw; our military and political inferiority has no other cause; we are too skeptical of what can be achieved through reflection, skillful combination. Our educational system needs radical reforms; almost everything the First Empire accomplished in this respect is bad. Public education cannot be imparted directly by the central authority; a ministry of public education will always be a very mediocre educational machine.

Primary education is the hardest to organize. We envy Germany its superiority in this respect; but it is not philosophical to desire the fruits without the trunk and the roots. In Germany, popular education came from Protestantism. Lutheranism, having made religion consist in reading a book, and later having reduced Christian dogmatics to an impalpable quintessence, gave an outsized importance to the schoolhouse; the illiterate were almost expelled from Christianity; occasionally communion is refused them. Catholicism, on the contrary, making salvation consist in sacraments and supernatural beliefs, considers schools a secondary matter. To excommunicate those who cannot read or write seems impious to us. Schools, not being the extension of the churches, are the rivals of the churches. The curate does not trust them, wants them to be as weak as possible, even prohibits them if they are not completely clerical. Now, without the collaboration and goodwill of the curate, the village school will never prosper. How we hope Catholicism will reform itself, free itself from outdated rules! What services a curate, a Catholic pastor, would render, offering in each village a model of a well-regulated family, overseeing the school, almost a schoolmaster himself, dedicating to the education of the peasant the time he [now] devotes to the annoying repetition of the breviary! In truth, the church and the school are equally necessary; a nation can do without neither the one nor the other; when the church and the school gainsay each other, all goes awry.

We have reached the issue that is at the center of all others. France decided to remain Catholic; it bears the consequences. Catholicism is too hieratical to give intellectual and moral nourishment to a population; it causes transcendent mysticism to bloom beside ignorance; it has no moral efficacy; it produces terrible effects on the development of the brain. A pupil of the Jesuits will never be an officer liable to be pitted against a Prussian officer; a pupil of Catholic elementary schools will never be able to wage specialized war with advanced weapons. Catholic nations that do not reform will always invariably be beaten by Protestant nations. Supernatural beliefs are like a poison that is fatal if ingested in too high a dosage. Protestantism does mix some quantity of them into its brew, but the proportion is feeble and then becomes beneficial. The Middle Ages had created two proficiencies of the life of the mind, the church and the university; Protestant countries have kept these two structures; they have introduced freedom into the church, freedom in the university, to such a degree that these countries can have established churches, official education, and a full freedom of conscience and education at the same time. As for us, in order to have liberty we have been obliged to separate ourselves from the church; the Jesuits had long reduced our universities to a secondary role. Consequently, our efforts have been weak, not being connected to any tradition or institution of the past.

Liberals such as ourselves are quite perplexed by this, for our first principle is that the state must never meddle in matters concerning freedom of conscience. Faith, like all exquisite things, is vulnerable; at the slightest contact it cries violence. What is to be desired is a liberal reform of Catholicism without the intervention of the state. May the church recognize two categories of believers, those who are for the letter and those who keep to the spirit. At a certain degree of rational culture, belief in the supernatural becomes an impossibility for many; do not oblige them to wear a lead weight. Do not meddle in what we teach or what we write, and we will not fight you for the people; do not object to our place in the universities or the academies, and we will give the rural schools over to you entirely. The human spirit is a ladder in which each step is necessary; what is good at a given level is not good at another; what is disastrous for one is not so for the other. Let us preserve religious education for the people, but allow us to be free. There is no strong development of the head without freedom; moral energy is not the result of a particular doctrine, but rather of race and the vigor of education. We have heard enough of the decadence of Germany, which was presented as a dispensary of paralyzing errors, of dangerous subtleties! It was being killed, we were told, by sophism, Protestantism, materialism, pantheism, fatalism. Indeed, I cannot swear that Mr. von Moltke does not profess one of these errors; but one will admit that this does not prevent him from being a good general-staff officer. Let us give up these dull declamations. The freedom of thought, together with high culture, far from weakening a country is a precondition of the great development of intellect. What strengthens the mind is not a given solution; what strengthens it is debate, and freedom. One may say that for the cultivated man there is no evil doctrine, because for him all doctrines are an effort toward truth, a useful exercise for the health of the mind. You wish to keep your young men in a sort of intellectual gynaeceum; you will make narrow-minded men of them. To produce good scientific heads, serious and meticulous officers, it is necessary to have an education open to anything, without constricting dogmas. Intellectual and military superiority will belong henceforth to the nation that will think freely. Anything that exercises the brain is healthy. What is more, freedom of thought within the universities has the advantage that the freethinker, satisfied with reasoning at his leisure from his chair among people who share his point of view, no longer dreams of spreading propaganda among the elites and the people. The German universities offer the most curious spectacle in this regard.

Our secondary education, while deserving of blame, is the best part of our teaching system. The good pupils of a Paris lycée are superior to young Germans in their talent for writing and the art of composition; they are better prepared to become lawyers or journalists; but they do not know enough things. We must persuade ourselves that science is progressively gaining the upper hand on what we in France call letters. Teaching must above all be scientific; the result of education must be that the young man know as much as possible of what the human mind has discovered on the reality of the universe. When I say scientific, I do not mean practical, professional; the state need not concern itself with craft applications;

but it must ensure that the education it imparts does not limit itself to an empty rhetoric, which does not strengthen the intellect. With us, the brilliant gifts, talent, wit, and genius are alone held in esteem; in Germany, these gifts are rare, perhaps because they are not much prized; good writers are not very numerous there; journalism, the political rostrum do not have the glamor they have among us; but force of mind, education, and the solidity of judgment are much more widespread, and form an average of intellectual culture superior to anything one has been able to obtain from a nation so far.

It is especially in higher education that reforms are urgent. The special schools, devised by the Revolution, the stunted colleges created by the Empire in no way replace the great and fine system of autonomous and rival universities, a system that Paris created in the Middle Ages and that all of Europe has preserved, except precisely for France, which pioneered it around 1200. By returning to it, we will be imitating nobody, we will only be resuming our tradition. We must create five or six universities in France, independent of one another, independent from the cities in which they will be located, independent from the clergy. Concurrently, we must abolish the special schools, the École polytechnique, the École normale, and so on, useless institutions when one possesses a good university system, as they prevent the universities from developing. These schools, in fact, are simply a baneful skimming of the universities' audience.* The university teaches everything, prepares for everything, and in its bosom all the branches of the human spirit are in contact and embrace one another. Next to the universities, there can, there must be professional schools; there cannot be closed-number state schools that compete against the universities. There are complaints that the colleges of letters, of sciences do not have assiduous students. What is surprising about it? Their natural audience is at the École normale, at the École polytechnique, where they receive the same instruction, but without experiencing any of the healthy movement, of the community of spirit the university creates.

---

*. We do not wish to deny the usefulness of such institutions as residential colleges or seminaries; but instruction for interns should not go beyond conferences among students, following the ancient customs.

These universities, established in the provincial cities,* naturally without prejudice for the University of Paris and the great individual institutions, such as the Collège de France, which are peculiar to Paris, seem to me the best means of awakening the French mind. They would be schools of seriousness, gentlemanliness, and patriotism. The true freedom of thought, which cannot do without solid study, would be created there. There a salutary change in the character of the youth would be effected, as well. It would be educated to respect; it would assume the sense of the value of knowledge. Here is a fact that gives us much to reflect on. It is recognized that our schools are hotbeds of scarcely reflective democratic spirit and of unbelief disposed toward an inconsiderate popular propaganda. It is the exact opposite in Germany, where the universities are dens of aristocratic spirit, reactionary (as we say) and almost feudal, dens of free thought, but not of indiscrete proselytism. Whence this difference? From the fact that freedom of discussion, in German universities, is absolute. Rationalism is far from leading to democracy. Reflection teaches that reason is not the simple expression of the ideas and desires of the multitude, that it is the result of the apperceptions of a small number of privileged individuals. Far from being inclined to deliver the commonwealth to the whims of the crowd, a generation thus raised will jealously maintain the privilege of reason; it will be painstaking, studious, and not at all revolutionary. Knowledge will be its title of nobility, as it were, which it will not forsake easily, and will defend even somewhat harshly. Young people brought up with the feeling of their own superiority will balk at only counting for one, like the man in the street. Filled with rightful pride afforded by the consciousness of knowing the truth that the rabble ignores, they will not wish to be the interpreters of the superficial thoughts of the crowd. Thus the universities will be nurseries of aristocrats. Then, the sort of antipathy the French conservative party encourages against the high culture of the mind will seem the most inconceivable nonsense, the most annoying mistake.

---

* A circumstance of a different order will render the implementation of this system almost indispensable: the establishment of mandatory military service for all. Such a military organization is only possible if young men can pursue their university studies (law, medicine, etc.) while performing their military service, as is done in Germany. This combination presupposes regional college towns that are, at the same time, serious centers of military instruction.

It goes without saying that next to these universities financed by the state, and in which all opinions presented in a scholarly fashion would have access, a full latitude would be left for the establishment of free universities. I believe these free universities would produce very mediocre results; any time freedom truly exists within the university, freedom outside the university is of little consequence; but, by allowing them to be established, one would have a clean conscience and would silence the naive people who are led to believe they would work wonders without the tyranny of the state. It is quite probable that the most fervent Catholics, such as an Ozanam,[95] for example, would prefer the open ring of the state universities, where everything would take place in full view, to those small universities behind closed doors, founded by their sect. In any case, they would have the choice. With a similar regime, what might the Catholics most prone to inveigh against the state monopoly complain about? Nobody would be excluded from university appointments because of his beliefs; the Catholics would obtain them like everyone. The Privatdozent system, furthermore, would allow all doctrines to develop outside the endowed chairs. Finally, the free universities would remove up to the last pretext for recriminations. It would be the opposite of our French system, which proceeds by exclusion of the brilliant subjects. It is believed that enough has been done for impartiality if, after dismissing or refusing to appoint a freethinker, a Catholic is dismissed or refused appointment. In Germany, they are placed face to face; rather than only serving mediocrity, such a system encourages emulation and the awakening of the mind. By distinguishing scrupulously between educational degrees and the right to exercise a profession, as one does in Germany, by determining that the university does not make physicians or lawyers, but makes people capable of becoming physicians or lawyers, one would eliminate the difficulties certain people have with the state's conferral of educational degrees. The state, in such a system, does not salary specific scientific or literary opinions; it opens, in the high interest of society and for the benefit of all opinions, large enclosed fields, vast arenas, where the various sensibilities can develop, struggle with each other, and fight for the favor of the youth, already ripe for reflection, which attend these debates.

This would be the ideal: to train through the universities a rationalist head of society, reigning through knowledge, proud of this knowledge and hardly disposed to let its privilege perish for the benefit of an ignorant crowd; to honor pedantry (if I may be allowed this paradoxical form of expressing my thought), thus to contrast the excessive influence of women, high society, and journals [*revues*], which absorb so many live forces or only offer them a superficial employment; to care more for specialization, for knowledge, for what the Germans call *Fach*, less for literature, for talent in writing or speaking; to complete this solid summit of the social edifice with a brilliant court and capital, from which the splendor of an aristocratic character does not exclude solidity and the strong culture of reason; at the same time, to raise the people, to revive its somewhat weakened faculties, to inspire in it, with the aid of a good clergy devoted to the fatherland, the acceptance of a superior society, the respect of knowledge and of virtue, the spirit of sacrifice and of devotion. It would be lovely to at least try to come close.

I have said at several points that these reforms cannot be carried out properly without the cooperation of the clergy. It is clear that our theoretical principle can no longer be other than the separation of the church and the state; but practice cannot be theory. Up to now, France has only experienced the two extremes, Catholicism and democracy; swaying constantly from one to the other, it never rests between the two. To atone for its demagogical excesses, France plunges into narrow Catholicism; to react against narrow Catholicism, it plunges into false democracy. It should atone for both at the same time, since false democracy and narrow Catholicism are equally opposed to a reform of France on the Prussian model, that is to say to a strong and healthy rational education. We are with respect to Catholicism in the strange position of not being able to live with it or without it. The church is too important a part of education to do without, if on its side it makes the necessary concessions and does not become more harmful than useful by exaggerating its doctrines. If a Gallican reform movement were possible, such as the one Father Hyacinthe[96] dreams of with so much candor, sincerity, and warmness of feeling, a reform, I say, entailing the marriage of country priests and the replacement of the breviary with an almost daily teaching, it should be welcomed solicitously; but I fear that the Catholic Church will harden and prefer to fall rather than change. A schism within it seems to me more likely than ever; or rather, the schism has already occurred; from latent, it will become actual. The hatred of the Germans and the French, the occupation of Rome by the king of Italy have added a new explosive element to those accumulated by the council.[97] If the pope remains in Rome, capital of Italy, the non-Italians will grieve to see their spiritual leader thus subordinated to an individual nation. If the pope leaves Rome, the Italians will say, as in 1378:[98] "The Pope is the Bishop of Rome; let him return, or we will choose a Bishop of Rome, who, by that fact itself, will be the Pope." Truth be told, a pope such as the council made him cannot reside anywhere; he would need a craggy island with no shores; he has no place in the world; now, if the papacy ceases to have a small politically neutralized territory for its use, it will see its unity shattered. It seems to me almost inevitable that soon we will have two popes or even three, because it will be quite difficult for Frenchmen, Italians, and Germans to be of the same religion. The principle of nationalities was bound in the long run to produce the ruin of the papacy. It is often said: "Religious issues in our day are of too little moment to produce schisms." This is a mistake; there will be no more heresies, no more divisions on abstract dogmas,* because dogmas are hardly taken seriously anymore; but it is absolutely possible, indeed there will be schisms such as the Avignon one, rifts over individuals, contested elections whose uncertainty will long keep parts of the Catholic world in conflict with one another. Once the schism has arisen over individuals, once two popes are established, one in Rome, the other outside Italy, the decomposition of the Catholic world will come about through the choice of allegiances, like water under the action of an electrical battery; each of the two popes will become a pole that will attract all the elements homogeneous to it; one will be the pope of retrograde Catholicism, the other, the pope of progressive Catholicism, because both will wish for partisans, and in order to have partisans one must represent something. We will see Pedro de Luna once more claiming to contain the universal church within his rock of Peñíscola;[99] the line of separation of allegiances may even already have been traced. A host of reforms now impracticable will become practicable then, and the horizon of Catholicism, now so closed, may suddenly open and reveal unexpected depths.

---

\* The dogma of infallibility is an exception, for this dogma is "practical" in the highest degree and affects the entire organization of the Catholic Church in its relationship with the civil order.

## V

With serious efforts a rebirth would thus be possible, and I am persuaded that, if France proceeded for ten years along the path we have attempted to point out, the esteem and goodwill of the world would render any revenge unnecessary. Yes, it is possible that one day we will have to bless this terrible war and consider it the beginning of a regeneration. It would not be the only time war has proved more beneficial for the vanquished than for the victor. If the foolishness, negligence, sloth, and thoughtlessness of states did not have the consequence of leading them to defeat, it is hard to say to what level of debasement humankind might fall. In this way, war is one of the preconditions of progress, the crack of the whip that prevents a country from falling asleep by forcing self-satisfied mediocrity to emerge from its apathy. Man is sustained only by exertion and struggle. Struggle against nature is insufficient; man would reduce it through industry to inconsequential proportions. The struggle of races thus arises. When a population has had its essence produce all it could, it would become lax if the terror of its neighbors did not awaken it; for the goal of humanity is not enjoyment; acquisition and creation are the affair of strength and of youth: enjoyment is the affair of decrepitude. Fear of conquest is therefore, in human affairs, a necessary spur. The day in which humanity became a great, pacified Roman Empire with no more foreign enemies would be the day in which morality and intellect would face the greatest dangers.

But will these reforms be accomplished? Will France strive to correct its flaws, recognize its errors? The issue is complex, and, to resolve it, one must have gained a precise notion of the movement that seems to be leading the entire European world toward an unknown goal.

The nineteenth century has two types of societies that have proven themselves and that, despite the uncertainties that may weigh on their future, will have a great role in the history of civilization. One is the American type, essentially based on freedom and property, without class privileges, without ancient institutions, without history, without aristocratic society, without a court, without a glamorous power, without serious universities or strong scientific institutions, without mandatory military service for citizens. In this system, the individual is protected very little by the state, and also inconvenienced very little by the state. Thrown into life's battle without a master, he does as best he can, he grows rich, he grows poor, without once thinking of complaining about the government, of toppling it, of asking something of it, or of holding forth against freedom and property. The pleasure of deploying his activity at full speed is sufficient for him, even when the vagaries of the lottery have not been favorable to him. These societies lack distinction and nobility; they hardly produce original works in terms of art and science; but they can come to be very powerful, and excellent things can develop in their midst. The key question is to know how long they will last, which specific illnesses will affect them, how they will behave with regard to socialism, which up to now has affected them little.

The second type of society that our century sees flourish is what I will call the old order, revised and corrected. Prussia offers the best example of it. Here the individual is taken, raised, shaped, trained, disciplined, and continually sequestered by a society that derives from the past, is cast into old institutions, and proclaims its mastery of morality and reason. The individual, in this system, gives very heavily to the state; in exchange, he receives a strong intellectual and moral culture from the state, together with the joy of participating in a great undertaking. These societies are particularly noble; they create knowledge; they lead the human spirit; they make history; but with every passing day they are weakened by the demands of individual egoism, which finds the burden the state imposes on it too cumbersome to bear. These societies, in fact, imply the sacrifice of entire categories, people who must resign themselves to a sad life without hope of betterment. The awakening of popular consciousness and, up to a point, the education of the people sap these great feudal edifices and threaten them with ruin. France, which once was a society of this type, has fallen. England draws ever farther from the type we have just described and nearer to the American type. Germany maintains this great structure, not without some signs of revolt already being visible. To what degree will this spirit of revolt, which is none other than socialist democracy, invade the Germanic countries in turn? This is the issue that must preoccupy thoughtful minds the most. We lack the elements to respond with precision.

If the nations of the old order, when their ancient edifice is toppled, simply moved to the American system, the situation would be simple;

one could then rest on this philosophy of history of the republican school, according to which the American social type is the type of the future, to which all countries will sooner or later come. But this is not the case. The active part of the democratic party that currently troubles more or less all European states in no way has the American republic as its ideal. Apart from a few theorists, the democratic party has socialist tendencies that are the opposite of American ideas on freedom and property. The freedom to work, free competition, the free employment of property, the ability all are afforded to enrich themselves according to their powers are exactly what European democracy does not want. Will a third social type result from these tendencies, in which the state will intervene in contracts, in industrial and commercial relations, in issues of property? It can hardly be conceived, for no socialist system so far has managed to present itself with the appearance of viability. Hence, a strange doubt, which in France attains the proportions of the highest tragedy and troubles our lives: on the one hand, it seems exceedingly hard to keep the institutions of the old order in place in any form whatsoever; on the other, the aspirations of the people in Europe are in no way directed toward the American system. A series of unstable dictatorships, a caesarism of the age of decadence, this alone appears likely for the future.

France's materialist direction can in any case act to counterbalance all the manly grounds for reform that issue from the situation. This materialist direction has lasted since the years following 1830. Under the Restoration, public spirit was still very much alive; noble society had cares other than enjoyment and enrichment. Decadence became fully palpable around 1840. The shock of 1848 arrested nothing; the movement of material interests was toward 1853 what it would have been if the February Revolution had not taken place. Certainly, the crisis of 1870–1871 is much deeper than the one of 1848; but it may be feared that the temperament of the country will once more prevail, that the mass of the nation, recovering its indifference, will think only of making money and enjoying itself. Personal interest never suggests military courage, for none of the inconveniences one incurs through cowardliness outweighs what one risks through courage. To expose one's life to danger, faith in something immaterial is necessary; now, this faith is disappearing with every passing day. Having destroyed the principle of dynastic legitimacy, which founds the reason for the existence of the union of provinces on the rights of the sovereign, all we had left was a single dogma, namely that a nation consists in the free consent of all its parts. The latest peace has caused this principle the most grievous of wounds. Finally, far from reviving, intellectual culture received significant blows from the events of the year; the influence of narrow Catholicism, which will be the great obstacle to rebirth, seems in no way to be decreasing; the presumptuousness of a part of the people who preside over public administration at times seems to have doubled with the defeats and the outrages.

One cannot deny, besides, that many of the reforms Prussia imposes on us must encounter serious difficulties among us. The core of the conservative program in France has always been to set the slumbering parts of popular consciousness against the parts that were too alert, by which I mean the army against the people. It is clear that this program will have no core the day the democratic spirit penetrates within the army itself. To cultivate an army that represents a separate body within the nation and to prevent the development of primary education have thus become articles of political faith within a certain party; but France has Prussia as a neighbor, which will indirectly force even a conservative France to retreat from these two principles. The French conservative party was not mistaken in taking to mourning the day of the battle of Sadowa. This party had as its maxim to copy Metternich's Austria, that is to say to fight the democratic spirit by means of an independently disciplined army, a people of peasants rigorously kept in ignorance, a clergy armed with powerful concordats. This regime excessively weakens a nation that must fight against rivals. Austria itself was obliged to abandon it. Thus it is that, according to Plutarch's thesis, the more virtuous always wins over the less virtuous, and the emulation of nations is the precondition of general progress. If Prussia manages to avoid socialist democracy, it may provide a protection for liberty and property for a generation or two. Without the least doubt, the classes threatened by socialism would silence their patriotic antipathies the day they could no longer stem the rising tide, and some strong state would assume the mission of maintaining the European social order. On the other hand, Germany would find in the accomplishment of such a task (relatively analogous to the one it performed in the fifth century) so advantageous an employment of its activity that socialism would long be rejected there. Rich, slack, not particularly industrious, France for years had resorted to having its tiresome chores, requiring effort, performed by foreigners whom it paid well for their pains; government, inasmuch as it shades into the policeman's trade, is in certain respects one of these tiresome chores for which the Frenchman, good and weak, has little aptitude; the day can be glimpsed when he will pay arrogant, serious, hard people to do it, the way the Athenians had the Scythians fill the roles of cops and jailors.

The seriousness of the crisis will perhaps uncover unknown strengths. Much is unpredicted in human affairs, and France often enjoys proving the most reasoned of calculations wrong. Strange, at times deplorable, the destiny of our country is never vulgar. If it is true that French patriotism, at the end of the past century, awakened German patriotism, it will also perhaps be true to say that German patriotism will have awakened French patriotism on the point of being extinguished. This return to national issues would for a few years bring about a pause in social issues. What has happened in the past three months, the vitality that France demonstrated after the fearsome moral collapse of March 18 are very reassuring occurrences. We often take to fearing that France and even England, ultimately troubled by our same illness (the weakening of the military character, the prevalence of industrial and commercial considerations) will soon be reduced to a secondary role and that the stage of the European world will be occupied solely by two giants, the Germanic race and the Slavic race, which have preserved the vigor of the military and monarchical principle and whose struggle will fill the future. But one can also declare that, in a superior sense, France will have its revenge. It will be recognized one day that it was the salt of the earth, and that without it the banquet of this world will be next to tasteless. One will miss that old liberal France, which was powerless, imprudent, I admit it, but which was also generous, and of which it will one day be said, as it was of Ariosto's knights: "Oh gran bontà dei cavalieri antiqui!"[100]

When the victors of the day will have successfully rendered the world positive, selfish, alien to any other motive but self-interest, as unsentimental as possible, one will find, nonetheless, that it had been fortunate for America that the Marquis de la Fayette thought otherwise; that it had been fortunate for Italy that, even in our saddest age, we were capable of a generous folly; that it had been fortunate for Prussia that in 1865 a notion of high political philosophy had mingled with the confused plans that filled the emperor's head.

"Never hope too much and never despair," this must be our motto. Let us be reminded that only sadness bears great things, and that the true way of raising up our poor country is to show it the chasm it is in. Let us recall especially that the rights of the fatherland are imprescriptible, and that the meager attention it pays to our advice does not excuse us from offering it. Foreign or domestic emigration is the worst action one can commit. The Roman emperor[101] who, on his deathbed, condensed his opinion of life in the words *nil expedit*,[102] nonetheless gave his officers the watchword: *Laboremus*.[103]

# 9

## WHAT IS A NATION?

## (QU'EST-CE QU'UNE NATION?, 1882)

I propose to analyze with you an idea that seems clear, but lends itself to the most dangerous misunderstandings. The forms of human society are exceedingly varied. The vast agglomerations of men in China, Egypt, or the most ancient Babylonia; the tribes of the Hebrews, the Arabs; the city-states of Athens or Sparta, the assemblies of disparate lands after the fashion of the Achaemenid Empire,[1] the Roman Empire, the Carolingian Empire; the communities without a fatherland, preserved by a religious bond, such as those of the Israelites and the Parsees; nations, such as France, England, and most modern European independent entities; confederations after the fashion of Switzerland and America; kinships, such as those that race, or rather language, establishes between the different branches of the Teutons or the different branches of the Slavs—here are types of groupings, each of which exists, or has existed, and cannot be confused with another except with the direst of consequences. At the time of the French Revolution, it was believed that the institutions of small independent cities, such as Sparta and Rome, could be applied to our large nations of thirty to forty million souls. Nowadays, a far graver mistake is made: race is confused with nation, and a sovereignty analogous to that of truly existing peoples is attributed to ethnographic, or rather, linguistic groups. Let us attempt to reach some precision on these difficult questions, in which the slightest confusion regarding the meaning of words at the beginning of the argument may lead in the end to the most disastrous mistakes. It is a delicate thing that we propose to do; it is almost a vivisection; we will be treating the living as one ordinarily treats the dead. We shall employ the most absolute detachment and impartiality.

I

Since the end of the Roman Empire, or rather since the dismemberment of Charlemagne's empire, Western Europe appears to be divided into nations, some of which, in certain epochs, have attempted to exercise a hegemony over the others, without ever succeeding in a lasting fashion. It is unlikely that anyone will achieve in the future what Charles V, Louis XIV, and Napoleon I failed to do. The founding of a new Roman Empire or of a new Carolingian Empire has become an impossibility. The division of Europe is too great for any attempt at universal domination not to be met very quickly with a coalition that would force the ambitious nation back to its natural limits. A kind of equilibrium is established for the long run. Centuries from now, France, England, Germany, and Russia, despite the vicissitudes they will have encountered, will still be individual his-torical units, the essential pieces of a checkerboard, whose squares con-stantly vary in importance and size but are never wholly confused with each other.

Nations, understood in this fashion, are something fairly new in his-tory. Antiquity was not acquainted with them; Egypt, China, or ancient Chaldea were in no way nations. They were herds led by a Son of the Sun or by a Son of Heaven. There were no Egyptian citizens, any more than there were Chinese citizens. Classical antiquity had republics, municipal king-doms, confederations of local republics, empires; it hardly had nations in the sense in which we understand them. Athens, Sparta, Sidon, Tyre were small centers of admirable patriotism; but they were cities with a relatively limited territory. Gaul, Spain, and Italy, prior to their absorption within the Roman Empire, were collections of tribes, often allied with each other but possessing no central institutions or dynasties. The Assyrian Empire, the Persian Empire, and the Empire of Alexander were not fatherlands, either. There never were any Assyrian patriots; the Persian Empire was a vast feudalism. No nation traces its origins back to Alexander's colossal adventure, fruitful though its consequences were for the general history of civilization.

The Roman Empire was much closer to a fatherland. Roman domination, at first so harsh, was soon loved for the immense benefit of putting an end to war. It was a great association, a synonym for order, peace, and civilization. In the last days of the empire, there was among the lofty souls, the enlightened bishops, and the educated a real sense of the "Roman peace," as opposed to the threatening chaos of barbarism. But an empire twelve times larger than present-day France cannot form a state in the modern sense. The split of east and west was inevitable. The attempts at an empire in Gaul in the third century[2] did not succeed. It was the Germanic invasion that introduced into the world the principle that later served as a basis for the existence of nationalities.

What in fact did the German peoples accomplish, from their great invasions in the fifth century to the last Norman conquests in the tenth? They had scarce impact on the racial stock; but they imposed dynasties and a military aristocracy upon more or less extensive parts of the old Western Empire, which took the names of their invaders. Hence, France, Burgundy, Lombardy; subsequently, Normandy. The dominance rapidly assumed by the Frankish Empire reestablished the unity of the west for a period; but this empire was irreparably shattered around the middle of the ninth century; the Treaty of Verdun[3] traced divisions that were immutable in principle and, from then on, France, Germany, England, Italy, and Spain set off on paths, often circuitous and through a thousand vicissitudes, to their full national existence, such as we see it blossoming today.

What, in fact, characterizes these different states? It is the fusion of the populations that compose them. In the countries we have listed, there is nothing analogous to what you will find in Turkey, where the Turk, Slav, Greek, Armenian, Arab, Syrian, and Kurd are as distinct today as they were on the day of the conquest. Two crucial circumstances contributed to this result. First, the fact that the Germanic peoples adopted Christianity as soon as they underwent any prolonged contact with the Greek or Latin peoples. When the conqueror and the conquered have the same religion or, rather, when the conqueror adopts the religion of the conquered, the Turkish system, the absolute distinction between men according to their religion, can no longer occur. The second circumstance was the forgetting, by the conquerors, of their own language. The grandsons of Clovis, Alaric, Gundobad, Alboin, and Roland were already speaking a Romance language. This fact was itself the consequence of another important feature: the Franks, Burgundians, Goths, Lombards, and Normans had very few women of their own race with them. For several generations, the chiefs only married Germanic women; but their concubines were Latin, as were the wet-nurses of their children; the entire tribe married Latin women. This meant that once the Franks and the Goths established themselves on Roman territory the *lingua francica* and the *lingua gothica* had very short lives. Things went otherwise in England, for the Anglo-Saxon invasion undoubtedly brought women in its train; the Briton population fled, and, besides, Latin was no longer, or rather had never been, dominant in Britain. If the Gaulish language had been generally spoken in Gaul in the fifth century, Clovis and his followers would not have abandoned Old German for Gaulish.

Thence this fundamental result, that despite the extreme violence of the customs of the Germanic invaders, the mold they imposed became, with the passing centuries, the mold itself of the nation. *France* became quite legitimately the name of a country in which only an imperceptible minority of Franks had entered. In the tenth century, in the first *chansons de geste*, which are such a perfect mirror of the spirit of the times, all the inhabitants of France are French. The idea of a difference between races in the population of France, so obvious to Gregory of Tours,[4] does not occur at all to French writers and poets after Hugh Capet.[5] The difference between noble and villein was as sharply drawn as possible, but the difference between the two was in no way an ethnic difference; it was a difference in courage, habit, and education, transmitted by birth; it did not occur to anyone that the origin of all this was a conquest. The spurious system according to which the nobility owed its origin to a privilege conferred by the king for great services rendered to the nation, so that every nobleman was an ennobled person, was established as a dogma in the thirteenth century. The same thing took place after almost all the Norman conquests. After one or two generations, the Norman invaders were no longer distinguishable from the rest of the population; their influence had nonetheless been profound; they had given the conquered country a nobility, military customs, and a patriotism it had lacked previously.

The act of forgetting, I would even say, historical error, is an essential factor in the creation of a nation, which is why progress in historical studies often constitutes a danger for nationality. Indeed, historical enquiry brings back to light the deeds of violence that took place at the origin of all political formations, even of those whose consequences have been the most beneficial. Unity is always achieved brutally; the unification of northern France with southern France was the result of massacres and terror lasting almost a century. The king of France, who is, if I dare say so, the ideal type of a secular crystallizer; the king of France, who founded the most perfect national unity there ever was; the king of France, observed too closely, has lost his prestige. The nation he formed has cursed him, and, nowadays, only cultivated minds know his value and his achievements.

It is through contrast that these great laws of the history of Western Europe become discernible. Many countries failed to achieve what the king of France, partly through his tyranny, partly through his justice, so admirably brought to conclusion. Under the Crown of Saint Stephen,[6] the Magyars and the Slavs have remained as distinct as they were eight hundred years ago. Far from fusing the diverse elements of its domains, the House of Habsburg has kept them distinct and often opposed them to one another. In Bohemia, the Czech and German elements are superimposed like oil and water in a glass. The Turkish policy of the separation of nationalities according to their religion has had much graver consequences: it brought about the ruin of the east. Take a city such as Salonika or Smyrna, and you will find five or six communities, each of which has its own memories and almost nothing in common with the others. Now, the essence of a nation is that all individuals have many things in common, and also that they have forgotten many things. No French citizen knows whether he is a Burgundian, an Alan, a Taifal, or a Visigoth; every French citizen must have forgotten the Saint Bartholomew's Day massacre,[7] the massacres in the Midi in the thirteenth century.[8] There are not even ten families in France that can supply the proof of their Frankish origin, and furthermore any such proof would be essentially defective, as a consequence of the thousand unknown crossings that can disrupt all the systems of the genealogists.

The modern nation is therefore a historical result brought about by a series of convergent facts. Sometimes unity has been effected by a dynasty, as was the case for France; sometimes by the direct will of the provinces, as was the case with Holland, Switzerland, Belgium; sometimes it has been the work of a general consciousness, belatedly victorious over the caprices of feudalism, as was the case in Italy and Germany. A deep reason for existence always presided over these formations. Principles, in such cases, always emerge through the most unexpected surprises. In our time, we have seen Italy unified by its defeats, and Turkey demolished by its victories. Each defeat advanced the cause of Italy; each victory ruined Turkey; for Italy is a nation, and Turkey, outside of Asia Minor, is not. It is France's glory to have proclaimed, through the French Revolution, that a nation exists of itself. We should not be displeased that others imitate us. The principle of nationality is our own. But what, then, is a nation? Why is Holland a nation, when Hanover or the Grand Duchy of Parma are not? How can France continue to be a nation, when the principle that created it has disappeared? How is it that Switzerland, which has three languages, two religions, and three or four races, is a nation, while Tuscany, for instance, which is so homogeneous, is not? Why is Austria a state and not a nation? In what ways does the principle of nationality differ from that of races? These are points that a thoughtful mind would wish to have settled, to be at peace with itself. The affairs of this world are hardly decided by this sort of reasoning, yet diligent men wish to bring some reason into these issues and resolve the confusions in which superficial minds are entangled.

II

According to some political theorists, a nation is above all a dynasty, representing an ancient conquest, which was first accepted and then forgotten by the mass of the people. Following the theorists I speak of, the grouping of provinces produced by a dynasty, by its wars, its marriages, its treaties, ends with the dynasty that had established it. It is quite true that the majority of modern nations were made by a family of feudal origin, which had contracted a marriage with the soil and was in some sense a nucleus of centralization. France's borders in 1789 had nothing natural or necessary to them. The wide zone that the Capetian House had added to the narrow strip of the Treaty of Verdun was indeed the personal acquisition of this house. During the epoch in which these annexations were carried out, there was no idea of natural frontiers, or of the rights of nations, or of the will of provinces. The union of England, Ireland, and Scotland was likewise a dynastic fact. Italy only tarried so long before becoming a nation because, among its numerous reigning houses, none, prior to our century, turned itself into the center of unity. Strangely, it was from the obscure island of Sardinia, scarcely an Italian land, that it assumed a royal title.* Holland, which created itself by an act of heroic resolution, has nonetheless contracted an intimate marriage with the House of Orange, and would run real dangers the day in which this union is compromised.

Is such a law, however, absolute? Undoubtedly not. Switzerland and the United States, which have formed themselves as conglomerates of successive additions, have no dynastic basis. I shall not discuss the question as regards France. It would be necessary to read the secrets of the future. Let us simply say that this great French royalty had been so highly national that, on the morrow of its fall, the nation was able to endure without it. Anyway, the eighteenth century had changed everything. Man had returned, after centuries of abasement, to the ancient spirit, to self-respect, to the conception of his rights. The words 'fatherland' and 'citizen' had recovered their meaning. Thus, the boldest operation to have been conceived in history could be brought to completion, an operation one might compare with the attempt, in physiology, to make a body from which one had removed the brain and the heart live in its original identity.

It must therefore be admitted that a nation can exist without a dynastic principle and even that nations that have been formed by dynasties can separate from such dynasties without ceasing to exist because of it. The old principle, which only takes the rights of princes into account, can no longer hold; apart from dynastic rights, there are also national rights. Upon what criterion, however, should one base this national right? By what sign should one recognize it? From what tangible fact can it be made to derive?

I.—from race, many say with self-assurance. The artificial divisions, resulting from feudalism, from princely marriages, from diplomatic congresses, are passing. What remains firm and fixed is a population's race. This is what constitutes a right, a legitimacy. The Germanic family, for

---

* The House of Savoy owes its royal title only to the acquisition of Sardinia (1720).

instance, according to the theory I am expounding, has the right to take back the scattered limbs of Germanism, even when these limbs are not asking to be joined together again. The right of Germanism over such-and-such a province is stronger than the right of the inhabitants of that province over themselves. A sort of primordial right, analogous to the divine right of kings, is thus created; an ethnographic principle is substituted for a national one. This is a very great error, which, if it were to become dominant, would doom European civilization. The national principle is as just and legitimate as that of the primordial right of races is narrow and full of danger for true progress.

In the ancient tribe and city-state, race was, we admit it, of first-rate importance. The ancient tribe and city-state were but an extension of the family. In Sparta, in Athens all citizens were relatives to a greater or lesser degree. The same was true among the Bene Israel; it is still the case with the Arab tribes. Let us move from Athens, Sparta, and the Israelite tribe to the Roman Empire. The situation is completely different. First established through violence, then preserved by interest, this great agglomeration of entirely different cities and provinces deals the gravest of blows to the idea of race. Christianity, with its universal and absolute character, works even more effectively in the same direction. It formed an intimate alliance with the Roman Empire, and, through the effects of these two incomparable agents of unification, ethnographic reason was excluded from the government of human affairs for centuries.

Despite appearances, the barbarian invasion was a further step along this path. The partition of the barbarian kingdoms had nothing ethnographic about it; it was settled by the strength or the whim of the invaders. The race of the populations they subdued was the most indifferent of matters to them. Charlemagne refashioned in his own way what Rome had already fashioned: a single empire composed of the most diverse races; the authors of the Treaty of Verdun, in drawing imperturbably their two long lines from north to south, were not in the slightest concerned with the race of the peoples that fell to the right or left of these lines. The changes in borders that were effected in the rest of the Middle Ages similarly occurred outside any ethnographic tendency. If the constant policy of the Capetian House has managed more or less to group together, under the name of France, the territories of ancient Gaul, this was not an effect of the tendency these lands would have had to join together with their fellows. The Dauphiné, Bresse, Provence, and the Franche-Comté no longer recalled any common origin. All Gallic consciousness had perished by the second century of our era, and it is only by way of erudition that, in our own days, the individuality of the Gallic character has been retrospectively rediscovered.

Ethnographic considerations have therefore had no weight in the constitution of modern nations. France is Celtic, Iberian, Germanic. Germany is Germanic, Celtic, and Slav. Italy is the country where ethnography is most bewildered. Gauls, Etruscans, Pelasgians, and Greeks, not to mention many other elements, are crossed therein in an indecipherable mixture. The British Isles, as a whole, present a mixture of Celtic and Germanic blood whose proportions are singularly difficult to define.

The truth is that there is no pure race and that to base politics upon ethnographic analysis is to base it on a chimera. The noblest countries, England, France, and Italy, are those where the blood is the most mixed. Is Germany an exception in this respect? Is it a pure Germanic country? What an illusion! The entire south was once Gallic. All the east, from the Elbe, is Slav. And are the parts that are claimed to be truly pure in fact so? Here we confront problems on which it is of the utmost importance that we gain clear ideas and prevent misunderstandings.

Discussions on race are interminable, because the term 'race' is used by philological historians and physiological anthropologists in two completely different senses.* For the anthropologists, race has the same meaning as in zoology; it indicates an actual descent, a blood relation. Now, the study of languages and of history does not lead to the same divisions as physiology. Words such as brachycephalic or dolichocephalic have no place in either history or philology. Within the human group that created the Aryan languages and discipline, there already were brachycephalics and dolichocephalics. The same must be said of the primitive group that created the languages and institution known as Semitic. In other words, the zoological origins of humanity are vastly prior to the origins of culture, civilization, and language. The primitive Aryan group, the primitive Semitic group, the primitive Turanian group had no physiological unity. These groupings are historical facts that took place in a particular

---

\*    This point has been developed in a lecture, whose analysis can be read in the bulletin of the Association scientifique de France, March 10, 1878.

epoch, let us say fifteen or twenty thousand years ago, while the zoological origin of humanity is lost in incalculable darkness. What is known philologically and historically as the Germanic race is no doubt a full distinct family within the human species. But is it a family in the anthropological sense of the term? Certainly not. The emergence of a Germanic individuality occurred only a few centuries before Jesus Christ. Ostensibly, the Teutons did not emerge out of the earth at this epoch. Prior to this, mingled with the Slavs in the great indistinct mass of the Scythians, they did not have their separate individuality. An Englishman is definitely a type within the whole of humanity. Now, the type of what is quite improperly called the Anglo-Saxon race* is neither the Briton of Julius Caesar's time, nor the Anglo-Saxon of Hengist's time, nor the Dane of Canute's time, nor the Norman of William the Conqueror's time; it is the result of it all. A Frenchman is neither a Gaul, nor a Frank, nor a Burgundian. He is what emerged from the cauldron in which, under the direction of the king of France, the most diverse elements have fermented together. An inhabitant of Jersey or Guernsey differs in no way, with regard to origins, from the Norman population of the nearby coast. In the eleventh century, even the sharpest eye would not have seen the slightest difference on the two sides of the Channel. Trifling circumstances made it so that Philip Augustus[9] did not seize these islands together with the rest of Normandy. Separated from one another for almost seven hundred years, the two populations have become not only strangers to one another but wholly dissimilar. Race, as we historians understand it, is therefore something that is made and unmade. The study of race is crucial for the scholar concerned with the history of humanity. In politics, it has no applications. The instinctive consciousness that presided over the tailoring of the map of Europe took no account of race, and the leading nations of Europe are nations of essentially mixed blood.

The fact of race, originally crucial, thus becomes increasingly less important. Human history differs essentially from zoology. In it, race is not everything, as it is among the rodents or the felines, and one does

---

* The Germanic elements in the United Kingdom are not much more considerable than they were in France when it had possession of Alsace and Metz. The Germanic language has dominated in the British Isles simply because Latin had not wholly replaced the Celtic idioms, as had occurred in Gaul.

not have the right to go through the world sizing up people's skulls, then taking them by the throat and saying: "You are of our blood; you belong to us!" Beyond anthropological characteristics, there is reason, justice, the true, and the beautiful, which are the same for all. Beware, this ethnographic politics is not certain. Today you use it against others, later you will see it turn against you. Is it certain that the Germans, who have raised the banner of ethnography so high, will not see the Slavs in their turn come to analyze the names of villages in Saxony and Lusatia, search for any traces of the Veleti or of the Obotrites,[10] and demand recompense for the massacres and the mass enslavements that the Ottos[11] inflicted upon their ancestors? It is good for everyone to know how to forget.

I am very fond of ethnography; it is a science of rare interest; but, as I would wish it to be free, I wish it to be without political application. In ethnography, as in all forms of study, systems change; it is the precondition of progress. Would states then change as well along with systems? States' frontiers would follow the fluctuations of science. Patriotism would depend upon a more or less paradoxical dissertation. One would come say to a patriot: "You were mistaken; you shed your blood for such-and-such a cause; you thought you were a Celt; not at all, you are a Teuton." Then, ten years later, you will be told that you are a Slav. So as not to distort science, we should exempt it from giving an opinion on these problems, in which so many interests are involved. Rest assured that, if one tasks it with providing elements for diplomacy, one will catch it many times in the act of being complaisant. It has better things to do; let us simply ask it to tell the truth.

II.—What we have just said of race must also be said of language. Language invites unity; it does not impose it. The United States and England, Spanish America and Spain speak the same language and do not form a single nation. Conversely, Switzerland, so well made, since it was made with the consent of its different parts, has three or four languages. There is something in man that is superior to language: the will. The will of Switzerland to be united, despite the diversity of its idioms, is a fact of far greater importance than a similarity of language often obtained by vexatious methods.

An honorable fact about France is that it has never sought to obtain the unity of language by coercive measures. Can one not have the same sentiments and the same thoughts, and love the same things in different languages? We were speaking just now of the inconvenience of making international politics depend upon ethnography. There would be no less inconvenience if one were to make it depend upon comparative philology. Let us allow these interesting fields of study full freedom of discussion; let us not involve them in matters that would corrupt their serenity. The political importance lent to languages derives from their being regarded as signs of race. Nothing could be more false. Prussia, where only German is now spoken, spoke Slav a few centuries ago; Wales speaks English; Gaul and Spain speak the primitive dialect of Alba Longa;[12] Egypt speaks Arabic; the examples are innumerable. Even at the origins, similarity of language did not entail similarity of race. Let us consider, for example, the proto-Aryan or proto-Semitic tribe; there one found slaves who spoke the same language as their masters; now, the slave at the time was often enough of a different race than his master. Let us repeat it: these divisions of Indo-European, Semitic, and other languages, created with such admirable sagacity by comparative philology, do not coincide with the divisions established by anthropology. Languages are historical formations, which tell us little about the blood of those who speak them, and which, in any case, could not shackle human liberty, when it is a matter of determining the family with which one unites oneself for life and for death.

This exclusive regard for language, like the excessive attention given to race, has its dangers, its drawbacks. When we exaggerate, we enclose ourselves within a specific culture, considered as national; we limit ourselves, we sequester ourselves. We leave the heady air that one breathes in the vast field of humanity in order to enclose ourselves in the conventicles of compatriots. Nothing could be worse for the intellect; nothing could be more deplorable for civilization. Let us not abandon the fundamental principle that man is a reasonable and moral being, before he is corralled in such and such a language, before he is a member of such and such a race, an adherent of such and such a culture. Before French, German, or Italian culture there is human culture. Consider the great men of the Renaissance; they were neither French, nor Italian, nor German. They had rediscovered, through their dealings with antiquity, the secret of the veritable education of the human spirit, and they devoted themselves to it body and soul. And how well they did!

III—Religion cannot offer an adequate basis for the establishment of a modern nationality either. Originally, religion had to do with the very existence of the social group. The social group was an extension of the family. Religion and the rites were family rites. The religion of Athens was the cult of Athens itself, of its mythical founders, of its laws, of its customs; it implied no dogmatic theology. This religion was, in the strongest sense of the term, a state religion. One was not Athenian if one refused to practice it. It was, fundamentally, the cult of the Acropolis personified. To swear on the altar of Aglauros* was to swear that one would die for the fatherland. This religion was the equivalent of what the act of drawing lots[13] or the cult of the flag are for us. Refusing to participate in such a worship was what refusing military service would be in our modern societies. It was to declare that one was not Athenian. From another angle, it is clear that such a religion had no meaning for someone who was not from Athens; also, there was no attempt made to proselytize foreigners to force them to accept it; the slaves of Athens did not practice it. Things were much the same in some small republics of the Middle Ages. One was not considered a good Venetian if one did not swear by Saint Mark; one was not a good Amalfitan if one did not set Saint Andrew higher than all the other saints of paradise. In these small societies, what subsequently would be persecution or tyranny was legitimate and of no more consequence than our custom of wishing the father of a family happy birthday or a happy New Year.

What was true in Sparta, in Athens, was already no longer the case in the kingdoms that issued from Alexander's conquest, and especially not in the Roman Empire. The persecutions of Antiochus Epiphanes,[14] to compel the east to worship Olympian Jupiter, and those of the Roman Empire, designed to maintain a supposed state religion, were a mistake, a crime, a veritable absurdity. In our time, the situation is perfectly clear. There no longer are masses that believe in a perfectly uniform manner. Each person believes and practices in his own fashion, what he can, as he wishes. There no longer is a state religion; one can be French, English, or German, while being Catholic, Protestant, Jewish, or practicing no religion. Religion has become an individual matter; it concerns the conscience of each person. The division of nations into Catholic and Protestant no longer exists. Religion, which, fifty-two years ago, played so substantial a part in the formation of Belgium, [15] preserves all its importance in the

---

* Aglauros, who gave her life to save her fatherland, represents the Acropolis itself.

heart of each person; but it has ceased almost entirely to be one of the grounds that define the frontiers of peoples.

IV—The community of interests is assuredly a powerful bond between men. Do interests, however, suffice to make a nation? I do not think so. Community of interests brings about trade agreements. Nationality has a sentimental side to it; it is both soul and body at once; a *Zollverein*[16] is not a fatherland.

V—Geography, or what are called natural frontiers, certainly plays a considerable part in the division of nations. Geography is one of the essential factors in history. Rivers have led races; mountains have brought them to a halt. The former have favored historical movements, the latter have restricted them. Can one say, however, as some parties believe, that a nation's frontiers are written on the map and that a given nation has the right to assign itself what is necessary to round off certain contours, in order to reach such a mountain and such a river, to which one accords a sort of limiting faculty a priori? I know of no doctrine that is more arbitrary or more fatal. With it, one can justify any violence. And first of all, is it the mountains or the rivers that form these supposedly natural frontiers? It is indisputable that mountains separate, but rivers tend rather to unify. Moreover, not all mountains can divide states. Which are the ones that separate, and which are not? From Biarritz to Tornea,[17] there is no one estuary more suited than another to serving as a boundary. Had history so decreed, the Loire, the Seine, the Meuse, the Elbe, or the Oder could just as easily as the Rhine have had this quality of being a natural frontier, which has incited so many infractions of the fundamental right, the will of men. One speaks of strategic grounds. Nothing is absolute; it is quite clear that many concessions must be made to necessity. But these concessions should not go too far. Otherwise, everybody will claim military expediency, and there will be war without end. No, it is no more soil than race that makes a nation. The soil provides the substratum, the field of battle and of labor; man provides the soul. Man is everything in the formation of this sacred thing that is called a people. Nothing material suffices for it. A nation is a spiritual principle, the outcome of the profound complications of history, a spiritual family, not a group determined by the configuration of the earth.

We have now seen what elements are not sufficient to create such a spiritual principle: race, language, interests, religious affinity, geography, military necessities. What more then is required? Following what has been said previously, I will not have to retain your attention much longer.

### III

A nation is a soul, a spiritual principle. Two things that, in truth, are but one constitute this soul, this spiritual principle. One is in the past, the other in the present. One is the possession in common of a rich legacy of memories; the other is present consent, the desire to live together, the will to perpetuate the value of the heritage that one has received in an undivided form. Gentlemen, man cannot be improvised. The nation, like the individual, is the culmination of a long past of efforts, sacrifices, and devotion. The cult of ancestors is the most legitimate of all; our ancestors have made us who we are. A heroic past, great men, glory (I mean the genuine kind), this is the capital stock upon which one bases a national idea. To have common glories in the past, a common will in the present; to have performed great deeds together, to wish to perform still more, these are the essential preconditions for being a people. One loves in proportion to the sacrifices to which one has consented, and to the ills that one has suffered. One loves the house that one has built and passes down. The song of the Spartiates—"We are what you were; we will be what you are"—is in its simplicity the abridged hymn of every fatherland.

In the past, a heritage of glory and regrets to share, in the future, a similar program to put into effect; to have suffered, rejoiced, and hoped together: here is something more valuable than common customs houses and frontiers conforming to strategic ideas; here is something that can be understood in spite of differences of race and language. I spoke just now of "having suffered together;" indeed, suffering in common unites more than joy does. Where national memories are concerned, grief is of more value than triumphs, for it imposes duties, it requires a common effort.

A nation is therefore a vast solidarity, constituted by the sentiment of the sacrifices one has made and of those one is yet prepared to make. It presupposes a past; it is, however, summarized in the present by a tangible fact: consent, the clearly expressed desire to continue a common life. A nation's existence is (if you will pardon the metaphor) an everyday plebiscite, just as an individual's existence is a perpetual affirmation of life. Oh! I know, this is less metaphysical than divine right, less brutal than alleged historical right. In the frame of ideas I put to you, a nation has no more right than a king does to say to a province: "You belong to me, I am seizing you." A province, for us, is its inhabitants; if anyone has the right to be consulted in such an affair, it is the inhabitant. A nation never has any real interest in annexing or holding on to a country against its will. What the nation wants is, ultimately, the only legitimate criterion, the one to which one must always return.

We have driven metaphysical and theological abstractions out of politics. What remains after that? Man, his desires, his needs. Secession, you will say to me, and, in the long run, the disintegration of nations will be the consequence of a system that places these old organisms at the mercy of oft scarcely enlightened wills. It is clear that, in such a field, no principle must be taken to extremes. Truths of this order are only applicable as a whole and in a very general fashion. Human wills change; but what does not, here below? Nations are not something eternal. They had their beginnings, they will end. A European confederation will probably replace them. But such is not the law of the century in which we are living. At the present time, the existence of nations is a good thing, a necessity, even. Their existence is the guarantee of liberty, which would be lost if the world had only one law and one master.

Through their various and often opposed faculties, nations contribute to the common task of civilization; each sounds a note in this great concert of humanity, which, in sum, is the highest ideal reality we are capable of attaining. In isolation, each has its weak point. I often tell myself that an individual who had the faults that in nations are considered good qualities, who fed off vainglory, who was to such extent jealous, selfish, and quarrelsome, who could suffer no affront without unsheathing his sword, would be the most intolerable of men. But all these discordant details disappear in the aggregate. Poor humanity! How you have suffered! How many trials still await you! May the spirit of wisdom guide you, to shield you from the countless dangers with which your path is strewn!

Let me summarize, Gentlemen. Man is a slave neither to his race, nor to his language, nor to his religion, nor to the course of rivers, nor to the direction of mountain chains. A large aggregate of men, healthy in mind and warm of heart, creates a moral consciousness that is called a nation.

So long as this moral consciousness demonstrates its strength by the sacrifices that the abdication of the individual for the benefit of the community demands, it is legitimate, it has the right to exist. If doubts arise regarding its frontiers, consult the disputed populations. They certainly have the right to have a say in the matter. This will bring a smile to the lips of the high priests of politics, these infallible individuals who spend their lives deceiving themselves and, from the height of their superior principles, take pity upon our lack of pretention: "Consult the populations, indeed! What simplemindedness! A fine example of those puny French ideas that claim to replace diplomacy and war with methods of a childish simplicity." Let us wait a while, Gentlemen; let the reign of the high priests pass; let us bear the scorn of the powerful. Perhaps, after much fruitless groping, one will revert to our modest empirical solutions. The way to be right in the future is, in certain periods, to know how to resign oneself to being unfashionable.

# 10

## ISLAM AND SCIENCE
## (*L'ISLAMISME ET LA SCIENCE*, 1883)

L adies and Gentlemen,

Having already experienced many times the benevolent attention of this audience, I ventured to select for discussion before you today a most subtle topic, full of those delicate distinctions in which it is necessary to enter resolutely if history is to be rescued from the domain of vague approximation. What causes almost all misunderstandings in history is the lack of precision in the employment of words designating nations and races. One speaks of the Greeks, the Romans, the Arabs as if these words designated human groups that are always identical to themselves, without considering the changes occasioned by military, religious, linguistic conquest, by fashion and the great currents of all sorts that traverse the history of humanity. Reality is not governed by categories of such simplicity. We the French, for instance, are Roman by language, Greek by civilization, Jewish by religion. The race factor, fundamental at the outset, increasingly loses its importance as the great universal factors called Greek civilization, Roman conquest, Germanic conquest, Christianity, Islam, the Renaissance, [Enlightenment] philosophy, Revolution roll like millstones over the primitive varieties of the human family and oblige them to mix in more or less homogeneous masses. I would like to try to sort out with you one of the greatest confusions of ideas committed in this guise, I mean to say the equivocation contained in these words: Arab science, Arab philosophy, Arab art,

Muslim science, Muslim civilization. Many mistaken judgments, and even some practical errors that at times can be rather serious, flow from the vague ideas held on this point.

Any person with a modicum of instruction in the affairs of our time clearly sees the current inferiority of Muslim countries, the decadence of the states governed by Islam, the intellectual nonentity of the races that derive their culture and education solely from this religion. Anyone who has been to the Orient or Africa is struck by the fatefully narrow-minded character of the true believer, by this sort of iron band that encircles his head, rendering it completely impervious to science, incapable of learning anything or opening itself up to any new idea. Beginning with his religious initiation, toward the age of ten or twelve, the Muslim child, up to that point sometimes fairly bright, suddenly becomes fanatical, full of a foolish pride in possessing what he believes to be absolute truth, pleased with what causes his inferiority as if it were a privilege. This senseless pride is the radical flaw of the Muslim. The apparent simplicity of his worship inspires in him an ill-founded disdain for other religions. Convinced that God grants riches and power to whomever He chooses, without considering education or personal merit, the Muslim has the greatest disdain for education, for science, for all that makes up the European spirit. This turn of thought instilled by the Muslim faith is so strong that all the differences of race and nationality disappear as a consequence of the conversion to Islam. The Berber, the Sudanese, the Circassian, the Malay, the Egyptian, the Nubian, having become Muslims, are no longer Berber, Sudanese, Egyptian, and so forth; they are Muslim. Only Persia is an exception to this rule; it managed to retain its own ethos; for Persia managed to assume a separate position within Islam; it is ultimately much more Shiite than Muslim.

To attenuate the disagreeable generalizations against Islam that one is led to draw from this very basic fact, many point out that such a decadence, after all, may simply be a transitory phenomenon. To gain confidence in the future they appeal to the past. Muslim civilization, currently so humbled, was once very dynamic. It boasted scholars, philosophers. It was for centuries the teacher of the Christian West. Why should what has been not be once again? This is precisely the point on which I would like to focus the debate. Was there really such a thing as a Muslim science, or at least a science accepted by Islam, tolerated by Islam?

There is in the facts one invokes a very real degree of truth. Yes, from approximately the year 775 to the middle of the thirteenth century, that is, for about five hundred years, there were some very distinguished scholars and thinkers in Muslim countries. One may even claim that, during this time, the Muslim world was superior to the Christian world in intellectual culture. But this fact must be analyzed correctly in order not to draw erroneous consequences from it. One must follow the history of civilization in the Orient century by century in order to distinguish the different elements that brought about this momentary superiority, which soon changed into an altogether typical inferiority.

No time was more alien to anything one might call philosophy or science than the first century of Islam. The result of a centuries-long religious struggle that held the consciousness of Arabia suspended between the different forms of Semitic monotheism, Islam is a thousand miles from anything one might call rationalism or science. The Arab horsemen who joined it as a pretext for conquest and pillage were, in their time, the foremost warriors of the world; but they were assuredly the least philosophical of men. An Oriental writer of the thirteenth century, Abu'l Faraj,[1] tracing the character of the Arab people, expresses himself thus: "The science of this people, the science in which they gloried, was the science of language, the knowledge of its idiomatic forms, the structure of its verses, the skillful composition of prose. . . . As for philosophy, God had taught them nothing of it, and had not predisposed them for it." Nothing is truer. The nomadic Arab, the most literary of men, is the least mystical of men, the least inclined to reflection. The religious Arab contents himself, in order to explain things, with a creator God, who governs the world directly and reveals Himself to man through successive prophets. Thus, as long as Islam remained in the hands of the Arab race, that is to say under the first four caliphs[2] and the Omayyads,[3] no intellectual movement of a secular character developed within it. Omar did not, as is often alleged, burn the library of Alexandria; the library, at that time, had essentially vanished; but the principle he imposed on the world was in fact truly destructive of learned research and the varied endeavors of the mind.

Everything changed when, around the year 750, Persia took over and imposed the dynasty of the children of Abbas[4] in place of the Banu Umayya. The center of Islam found itself transported to the region of the Tigris and Euphrates. Now, this country was still replete with traces of one of the most dynamic civilizations the Orient has known, that of the Sassanid Persians,[5] which had reached its zenith under the reign of Chosroes Anushiruwan.[6] The arts and industry had been flourishing in this country for centuries. Chosroes added intellectual activity. Philosophy, chased from Constantinople,[7] sought refuge in Persia; Chosroes had books from India translated. The Nestorian Christians, who made up the most considerable segment of the population, were well versed in Greek science and philosophy; medicine was entirely in their hands; their bishops were logicians, geometers. In the Persian epics, whose local color is borrowed from Sassanid times, when Rostam[8] wants to build a bridge, he has a *djathalik* (*catholicos*, the term for Nestorian patriarchs or bishops) come to act as an engineer.

The tremendous gale of Islam stopped all this fine Persian development in its tracks for about a century. But the advent of the Abbasids seemed like a resurrection of the splendor of the Chosroes. The revolution that brought this dynasty to the throne was carried out by Persian troops, with Persian leaders. Its founders, Abu al-'Abbas[9] and especially Al-Mansur,[10] are always surrounded by Persians. They are, in a sense, resurrected Sassanids; the personal advisers, the tutors of the princes, the prime ministers are Barmakids, an extremely enlightened ancient Persian family that remained loyal to the national religion, Parsism, and only converted to Islam late and without conviction. The Nestorians soon surrounded these caliphs of moderate faith and became, by a sort of exclusive privilege, their first physicians. A city that has fulfilled a very exclusive role in the history of the human mind, the city of Harran, had remained pagan and had preserved the entire scientific tradition of Greek antiquity; it furnished a considerable contingent of scholars foreign to any revealed religion to the new school, especially some skillful astronomers.

Baghdad arose as the capital of this renascent Persia. The language of the conquest, Arabic, could not be supplanted any more than the religion could be entirely disowned; the character of this new civilization, however, was essentially mixed. The Parsis, the Christians carried the day. The administration, especially the police, was in the hands of the Christians. All those splendid caliphs, the contemporaries of our Carolingians,[11] Al-Mansur, Harun al-Rashid,[12] Al-Ma'mun,[13] are barely Muslim. They practice outwardly the religion of which they are the leaders, its popes, if one may express oneself thus; but their mind is elsewhere. They are curious of all things, and principally of exotic and pagan things; they examine India, ancient Persia, and above all Greece. At times, it is true, Muslim pietists bring about strange reactions at court; the caliph, at certain moments, turns devout and sacrifices his infidel or freethinking friends; then the spirit of independence regains the advantage; then the caliph recalls his scholars and his fellow revelers, and the free life resumes, to the dismay of puritan Muslims.

This is the account of this curious and appealing Baghdad civilization, of which the fables of the *Arabian Nights* have set the features in all imaginations, a strange mix of official rigor and secret laxity, age of youth and inconsequence, in which the serious arts and the arts of the merry life flourished thanks to the protection of the nonconformist leaders of a fanatical religion; where the libertine, though he is always menaced by the most cruel punishments, is blandished, sought after at court. Under the reign of these caliphs, at times tolerant, at times reluctantly persecutory, free thought developed; the *mutakallimūn*, or "disputants," held sessions in which all religions were examined on the basis of reason. We have, in a sense, the proceedings of one of these sessions, composed by a zealot. Allow me to read it to you, in Mr. Dozy's[14] translation:

A doctor of Kairouan[15] asks a pious Spanish theologian, who had been to Baghdad, if, during his sojourn in that city, he had ever attended the sessions of the *mutakallimūn*. "I attended them twice," answers the Spaniard, "but I made a point of not returning. "Why is that?" asked his interlocutor. "You will be the judge of it," answered the traveler. "In the first session I attended, there were not only Muslims of all sorts, orthodox and heterodox, but also misbelievers, Zoroastrians, materialists, atheists, Jews, Christians; in short, unbelievers of all stripes. Each sect had its leader, charged with defending the opinions it professed, and each time one of these leaders entered the hall, all rose as a sign of respect, and nobody took his place again before the leader was seated. The hall was soon full, and once the gathering realized everyone had arrived, one of the unbelievers spoke: 'We are assembled to ratiocinate,' he said. 'You all know the rules. You Muslims will not invoke justifications derived from your book or based on the authority of your prophet; for we believe in neither one nor the other. Everyone must limit himself to arguments derived from reason.' All applauded these words. As you can understand," adds the

Spaniard, "after hearing such things I never returned to such an assembly. I was persuaded to visit a different one, but it was the same scandal."

A veritable philosophical and scientific movement was the consequence of this transitory slackening of orthodox rigor. The Christian Syrian physicians, successors of the last Greek schools, were very well versed in peripatetic philosophy, in mathematics, in medicine, in astronomy. The caliphs employed them to translate into Arabic the encyclopedia of Aristotle, Euclid, Galen, Ptolemy—in a word, the whole of Greek science as it was then known. Some active minds, such as Al-Kindi,[16] began to speculate on the eternal problems man poses but cannot resolve. They were called *failasūf* (*philosophos*), and from then on, this exotic word was taken amiss as designating something alien to Islam. *Failasūf* became for Muslims a dreaded label, often entailing death or persecution, like *zindīq* and later *firmasōn* (Freemason). It must be admitted that within Islam the most complete form of rationalism was engendered. A sort of philosophic society, which was named the Ikhwan as-Safa', "the Brethren of Sincerity," began to publish a philosophical encyclopedia, remarkable for the wisdom and elevation of its ideas. Two very great men, Al-Farabi[17] and Avicenna,[18] soon range themselves with the most complete thinkers who ever lived. Astronomy and algebra, especially in Persia, see some remarkable developments. Chemistry follows its long subterranean work, which reveals itself externally by some astonishing results, such as distillation, and perhaps gunpowder. Muslim Spain tackles these studies following the Orient; Jews actively collaborate. In the twelfth century, Ibn-Bajja,[19] Ibn Tufail,[20] Averroes[21] raise philosophical thought to heights one had not seen since antiquity.

This is the great philosophical aggregate, customarily called Arab, because it is written in Arabic, but in fact Greek-Sassanid. It would be more exact to say Greek, because the truly fruitful element in it all came from Greece. One's value, in those fallen times, was proportional to what one knew of old Greece. Greece was the sole source of knowledge and correct thought. The superiority of Syria and Baghdad over the Latin West derived solely from the fact that they were much closer to the Greek tradition. It was easier to procure a Euclid, a Ptolemy, an Aristotle in Harran or in Baghdad than in Paris. If only the Byzantines had deigned to be less jealous custodians of the treasures that at the time they hardly read! If only from the eighth or ninth century there had been some Bessarions[22] or Lascarises![23] There would have been no need for the strange detour following which we received Greek science in the twelfth century through Syria, Baghdad, Córdoba, Toledo. But the form of secret Providence that decrees that, when the beacon of the human spirit dies out in the hands of one people, another people will be there to take it up and set it ablaze again, placed a very high value on the endeavors, otherwise obscure, of these poor Syrians, these persecuted *falāsifa*, these Harranians, whose unbelief placed them outside the bounds of humanity of that time. It was through these Arabic translations of the works of Greek science and philosophy that Europe received the leaven of ancient tradition necessary for the blooming of its spirit.

In fact, while Averroes, the last Arab philosopher, was dying in Morocco in dejection and abandonment, our Western world was experiencing a full awakening. Abelard[24] has already uttered the rallying cry of renascent rationalism. Europe has found its essence and begins its extraordinary evolution, whose last word will be the complete emancipation of the human spirit. Here, on the montagne Sainte-Geneviève,[25] a new *sensorium* was created for the work of the mind. What was missing were the books, the pure sources of antiquity. It would seem at first glance that it would have been easier to seek them in the libraries of Constantinople, where the originals were to be found, than in oft-mediocre translations in a language that hardly lent itself to express Greek thought. Religious debates, however, had caused a regrettable hostility between the Latin and Greek worlds. The baneful crusade of 1204[26] merely exasperated it. Moreover, we had no Hellenists; three hundred more years needed to pass for us to have a Lefèvre d'Étaples,[27] a Budé.[28]

Lacking true authentic Greek philosophy, which was to be found in the Byzantine libraries, badly translated and adulterated Greek science in Spain was sought out. I will not speak of Gerbert,[29] whose voyages among the Muslims are very doubtful; but from the eleventh century onward, Constantine the African[30] is superior in knowledge to his time and his country because he has received a Muslim education. From 1130 to 1150, an active group of translators, gathered in Toledo under the patronage of the archbishop Raymond,[31] renders into Latin the most important work of Arab science. From the first years of the thirteenth century, the Arabic Aristotle makes its triumphant entry into the University of Paris. The West has shaken away its four- or five-hundred-year-long inferiority. Up to this point, Europe has been a scientific tributary to the Muslims. Toward the middle of the thirteenth century, the comparison is still uncertain. Beginning approximately around 1275, two movements clearly appear: on one hand, the Muslim countries sink into the most dismal intellectual decadence; on the other, Western Europe resolutely enters on its own behalf into the great path of the scientific search for truth, an immense trajectory whose span cannot yet be measured.

Woe to those who become useless to human progress! They are almost immediately suppressed. Once so-called Arab science has transmitted its seed of life to the Latin West, it disappears. While Averroes's fame becomes almost equal to Aristotle's in the Latin schools, he is forgotten by his coreligionists. After about the year 1200, there is no longer a single Arab philosopher of consequence. Philosophy had always been persecuted within Islam, but in a manner that had failed to suppress it. Beginning in 1200, theological reaction wins out completely. Philosophy is eradicated in Muslim countries. The historians and polygraphs speak of it only as a memory, and a bad memory. The philosophical manuscripts are destroyed, and become rare. Astronomy is tolerated only for the part that serves to determine the direction of prayer. Soon enough the Turkish race becomes hegemonic within Islam and imposes its complete lack of philosophical and scientific spirit everywhere. From this moment on, with some rare exceptions such as Ibn Khaldun,[32] Islam will no longer witness any broad-mindedness; it has killed science and philosophy within itself.

I have not attempted, Gentlemen, to belittle the role of this great allegedly Arab science, which represents such an important milestone in the history of the human spirit. Its originality has been exaggerated in some respects, especially with regards to astronomy; one should not fall into the opposite excess by demeaning it beyond measure. Between the disappearance of ancient civilization, in the sixth century, and the rise of European culture in the twelfth and thirteenth, there was what may be termed an Arab period, during which the tradition of the human spirit was led by the regions won over to Islam. But what is Arab in this allegedly Arab science? The language, nothing but the language. The Muslim conquest had brought the language of the Hejaz[33] to the ends of the world. The same fate befell Arabic as did Latin, which, in the West, came to express feelings and thoughts that had nothing in common with the old Latium.

Averroes, Avicenna, Al-Battani[34] are Arabs the way Albert the Great,[35] Roger Bacon,[36] Spinoza are Latin. It is as great a mistake to attribute Arab science and philosophy to Arabia as it would be to attribute the entirety of Christian Latin literature, all the Scholastics, all the Renaissance, all the science of the sixteenth and part of the seventeenth centuries to the city of Rome simply because it is written in Latin. What is quite remarkable, in fact, is that of all the allegedly Arab philosophers and scholars, there was in practice only one, Al-Kindi, who had Arab origins; all the others are Persians, inhabitants of Transoxiana, Spaniards, people of Bukhara, Samarkand, Córdoba, Seville. Not only are they not Arabs by blood; their character has nothing Arab about it. They employ Arabic; but they are hampered by it, the way the thinkers of the Middle Ages are hampered by Latin and break its rules for their purposes. Arabic, which is so well suited to poetry and a certain kind of eloquence, is a very impractical instrument for metaphysics. The Arab philosophers and scholars are, generally speaking, rather bad writers.

This science is not Arab. Is it at least Muslim? Did Islam offer this rational research any protective support? Hardly! This fine movement of studies is wholly the work of Parsis, of Christians, of Jews, of Harranians, of Ismailis, of Muslims who were intimately in revolt against their own religion. It received nothing but curses from orthodox Muslims. Al Ma'mun, the caliph who exhibited the greatest zeal in introducing Greek philosophy, was damned mercilessly by the theologians; the troubles that beset his reign were presented as punishments for his tolerance of doctrines alien to Islam. It was not a rare occurrence to see books of astronomy, of philosophy burned on the public square, thrown in wells and cisterns, to appease a crowd roused by the imams. Those who cultivated such studies were termed *zindīqs* (misbelievers): they were beaten in the middle of the street, their houses burned to the ground, and often the powerful, when they wished to enhance their own popularity, would have them put to death.

Islam, in fact, has always persecuted science and philosophy thus. It has ended up smothering them. One must simply distinguish in this respect two periods in the history of Islam: one, from its origins to the twelfth century, the other, from the thirteenth century to our times. In the first period, Islam, undermined by the sects and tempered by a type of protestantism (what is called Mu'tazila), is much less organized and less fanatical than it became in the second age, when it fell into the hands of the Tartar and Berber races, dull and brutal races devoid of culture. Islam presents the peculiarity of having obtained from its devotees an ever-increasing faith. The first Arabs that committed themselves to the movement barely believed in the Prophet's mission. For two or three centuries, unbelief is barely veiled. Then comes the absolute reign of dogma, with no possible separation of the spiritual from the temporal, with coercion and bodily punishment for those who do not practice; a system, in short, that has only really been surpassed in terms of oppressiveness by the Spanish Inquisition. Freedom is never more deeply wounded than by a social organization in which religion completely dominates civil life. In modern times, we have seen but two examples of such a regime: on one hand, the Muslim states; on the other, the former papal states in the age of temporal power. And one is obliged to note that the temporal papacy only bore down on quite a small country, while Islam oppresses vast portions of our globe, imposing on them the most antithetical idea to progress: a state founded on a supposed revelation, theology governing society.

The liberals who defend Islam are not acquainted with it. Islam is the indiscernible union of the spiritual and the temporal, it is the reign of a dogma, it is the heaviest chain humanity has ever carried. In the first part of the Middle Ages, I repeat, Islam tolerated philosophy, because it was not able to forbid it; it was not able to forbid it, because it was lacking cohesion, unequipped for terror. The police, as I said, were in the hands of the Christians and principally occupied with responding to the attempts of the Alids.[37] A host of things passed through the rather loose holes of this net. But, when Islam came to have masses of fervent believers at its disposal, it destroyed everything. Religious terror and hypocrisy were the order of the day. Islam has been liberal when weak, violent when strong. Let us not honor it for what it was not able to suppress. To honor Islam for the philosophy and science it did not immediately wipe out would be akin to honoring theologians for the discoveries of modern science. These discoveries were made despite the theologians. Western theology was no less persecuting than Islamic theology. Simply, it failed, it did not crush the modern spirit the way Islam crushed the spirit of the countries it conquered. In our Western world, theological persecution only succeeded in one country: Spain. There, a terrible system of oppression smothered the scientific spirit. Let us hasten to add, this noble country will have its revenge. In the Muslim countries, things went the way they would have in Europe if the Inquisition, Philip II,[38] and Pius V[39] had succeeded in their plan to halt the human spirit. Frankly, I have a great deal of difficulty in being grateful to people for the evil they were unable to commit. No; religions have their great and beautiful moments, when they comfort and uplift the weak parts of our poor human race; but they should not be complimented for what was born despite them, for what they tried to suffocate in the cradle. One does not inherit from those one assassinates; one should not allow the persecutors to benefit from the things they persecuted.

Yet this is the mistake one makes, through excessive generosity, when one attributes to the influence of Islam a movement that developed despite Islam, against Islam, and that luckily Islam failed to prevent. To honor Islam for Avicenna, Avenzoar,[40] Averroes is tantamount to honoring Catholicism for Galileo. Theology hampered Galileo; it was not strong enough to block him altogether; that is not a sufficient reason to be particularly thankful toward it. Far be it from me to utter bitter words against any of the symbols in which human consciousness has sought repose amid the insoluble problems with which the universe and its own destiny presented it! Islam has some beautiful aspects as a religion; I have never entered a mosque without strong emotion, without—shall I say it?—a certain regret for not being a Muslim. For human reason, however, Islam has only been detrimental. The minds it closed off to enlightenment were already doubtlessly closed to it by their own internal limits; however, it persecuted free thought, I would not say more violently than other religious systems did, but more effectively. It rendered the countries it conquered a domain closed to the rational culture of the mind.

Indeed, the distinguishing trait of the Muslim is his hatred of science, his persuasion that research is useless, frivolous, almost ungodly: in natural science, because it enters into competition with God; in historical science, because, by focusing on the ages before Islam, it might revive ancient errors. One of the most curious pieces of evidence in this respect is that of sheikh Rifa'a,[41] who had resided for several years in Paris as the chaplain of the Egyptian School and who, upon his return to Egypt, produced a work full of the most curious of observations on French society. His obsession is that European science, especially as a consequence of its principle of the permanence of nature's laws, is a heresy from beginning to end; and, it must be said, from the point of view of Islam he is not entirely mistaken. A revealed dogma always opposes free research, which may contradict it. The result of science is not to expel the holy, but always to distance it, to distance it, I say, from the world of particular facts in which one thought one saw it. Experimentation obliges the supernatural to retreat and shrinks its domain. Now, the supernatural is the basis of all theology. Islam, by treating science as its enemy, is only being consistent; but it is dangerous to be too consistent. Islam has succeeded to its own detriment. By killing science, it has killed itself, and condemned itself to complete inferiority in the world.

When one begins with the idea that research threatens the rights of God, one ends up inevitably with laziness of the mind, lack of precision, incapacity to be exact. *Allah aalam*, "God knows best," is the last word in every Muslim conversation. It is a good thing to believe in God, but not that much. In the early days of his sojourn in Mosul, Mr. Layard,[42] as the clear mind he was, wished to obtain some facts on the population of the town, its commerce, its historical traditions. He approached the *qadi*,[43] who answered him with the following reply, whose translation I owe to an affectionate communication:

My illustrious friend, joy of the living!

What you seek from me is both useless and harmful. Despite the fact that I have spent all my days in this country, it never occurred to me to count its houses, or to inform myself of the number of their inhabitants. And, as for what kind of merchandise this man puts on his mule, or that man in the hold of his boat, it is none of my business at all. Regarding the earlier history of this town, only God knows, and only He could say how many errors its inhabitants imbibed before the Islamic conquest. It would be dangerous for us to want to discover it.

My dear friend, my lamb, do not attempt to learn what does not concern you. You have come among us and we have given you the greeting of welcome; go in peace! In truth, all the words you have said to me did not hurt me in any way; for he who speaks is one, he who listens is another. Following the customs of the men of your nation, you have traveled through many lands, until you were no longer able to find happiness anywhere. We (may God be blessed!) were born here, and we do not wish to leave.

Harken, my son, there is no wisdom equal to that of believing in God. He created the world; should we attempt to equal Him by trying to penetrate the mysteries of His creation? See that star that revolves up there around that other star; watch that other star with a tail that takes so many years to come and so many to return; let it go, my son; He whose hands made it will know how to lead and direct it.

Perhaps, you will say: "Man! Withdraw, for I am more learned than you, and have seen things you ignore!" If you think such things have made you better than me, you are twice as welcome; but I bless the Lord that I do not search for what I do not need. You are well educated in things in which I have no interest, and whatever you have seen I scorn it. Will greater knowledge make you a second stomach, and will those eyes, which go ferreting everywhere, find you a paradise?

My friend, if you wish to be happy, cry out: "Only God is God!" Do not do evil, and so you will fear neither men nor death, for your hour will come.

This *qadi* is very philosophical, after his own fashion; but here is the difference. We find the *qadi*'s letter charming, while he would find what we are saying here abominable. It is for society, anyway, that the repercussions of such a mentality are disastrous. Of the two consequences entailed by the lack of a scientific spirit, superstition or dogmatism, the second is perhaps worse than the first. The Orient is not superstitious; its great illness is its narrow dogmatism, which imposes itself through the force of society as a whole. The goal of mankind is not to rest in a resigned ignorance; the goal is relentless war on falsity, the struggle against wrongfulness.

Science is the soul of a society, because science is reason. It creates military superiority and industrial superiority. One day it will create social superiority, by which I mean a state of society where the amount of justice compatible with the essence of the universe will be obtained. Science places force in the service of reason. There are, in Asia, elements of barbarism analogous to those that formed the first Muslim armies and the great whirlwinds of Attila and Genghis Khan. But science stands in their way. If Omar or Genghis Khan had come up against some good artillery, they would not have crossed the borders of their desert. One should not dwell on momentary aberrations. What was not said, originally, against firearms? They nevertheless contributed substantially to the victory of civilization. For my part, I am convinced that science is a good thing, that only science furnishes weapons against the evil that can be done with it, that ultimately it will only serve progress, I mean true progress, the kind that is inseparable from respect for man and for liberty.

## APPENDIX TO THE FOREGOING LECTURE

A remarkably intelligent Afghan sheikh, who was passing through Paris, presented some observations on the foregoing conference in the May 18, 1883, issue of the *Journal des débats*.[44] I responded the following day, in the same newspaper, as follows:

> Yesterday I read with the attention they deserve the very judicious re-flections that my latest conference at the Sorbonne suggested to sheikh Jamal ad-Din. Nothing is more informative than to study the conscious-ness of the enlightened Oriental thus, in its original and sincere manifes-tations. It is by listening to the most diverse voices from the four corners of the horizon in favor of rationalism that one reaches the conviction that, if religions divide human beings, reason brings them closer, and that there is ultimately but one form of reason. The unity of the human spirit is the great and reassuring outcome of the peaceful clash of ideas, when one sets aside the opposed pretenses of alleged supernatural revelations. The alliance of the upright intellects of the entire world against fanati-cism and superstition is ostensibly the undertaking of a vanishingly small minority; but in the end it is the only lasting alliance, because it rests upon truth, and it will win out in the end, when the rival fables will have exhausted themselves in centuries-long series of impotent convulsions.
>
> Approximately two months ago, I made the acquaintance of sheikh Jamal ad-Din through our dear assistant Mr. Ganem. Few people have made a livelier impression on me. It was due in large part to the con-versation I had with him that I decided to choose the relationship of the scientific spirit with Islam as the topic of my conference at the Sorbonne. Sheikh Jamal ad-Din is an Afghan who is completely free of the preju-dices of Islam; he belongs to those energetic races of upper Iran, neigh-boring India, where the Aryan spirit still resides so energetically beneath

the superficial layer of official Islam. He is the best proof of the axiom we have often asserted, namely that religions are worth only as much as the races that profess them. The freedom of his thought, his noble and loyal character led me to believe, while we were conversing, that I had before me, in a resuscitated state, one of my ancient acquaintances, Avicenna, Averroes, or another one of those great infidels who for five centuries represented the tradition of the human spirit. The contrast was especially marked for me when I compared this striking apparition with the sight the Muslim countries on this side of Persia offer, countries in which scientific and philosophical curiosity is so rare. Sheikh Jamal ad-Din is the most splendid example one may quote of ethnic remonstrance against religious conquest. It confirms what the more intelligent European orientalists have often maintained: that Afghanistan is, with the exception of Japan, the country in the whole of Asia that presents the most numerous constitutive elements of what we call a nation.

I only see one point in the learned article of the sheikh on which we truly differ. The sheikh does not accept the distinctions that historical criticism has led us to make in these great complex entities called empires and conquests. The Roman Empire, with which the Arab conquest has so much in common, caused Latin to become the organ of the human spirit throughout the West up to the sixteenth century. Albert the Great, Roger Bacon, Spinoza wrote in Latin. Nonetheless they are not Latins for us. In a history of English literature, a place is made for Bede[45] and Alcuin;[46] in a history of French literature, we place Gregory of Tours[47] and Abelard; we most certainly do not disregard the role of Rome in the history of civilization, no more than we disregard the Arab role. But these great human currents call for analysis. Not all that is written in Latin is the glory of Rome; not all that is written in Greek is a Hellenic work; not all that is written in Arabic is an Arab product; not all things made in a Christian country are the effect of Christianity; not all things made in a Muslim country are the fruit of Islam. This is the principle Mr. Reinhart Dozy, the profound historian of Muslim Spain whose passing scholarly Europe is presently mourning, applied with rare sagacity. These sorts of distinctions are necessary, if we do not want history to be a web of vague approximations and misunderstandings.

A facet for which the sheikh may have thought me unjust was that I did not sufficiently develop the concept that *any* revealed religion is led to show hostility toward positive science, and that Christianity in this respect has nothing to envy Islam. This is not in question. Galileo was no better treated by Catholicism than Averroes by Islam. Galileo found truth in a Catholic land, despite Catholicism, the way Averroes philosophized nobly in a Muslim land, despite Islam. If I did not insist further on this point, it is only because, in all truth, my opinions on the matter are familiar enough for me not to restate them in front of an audience conversant with my works. I have stated often enough for me not to have to repeat it on every occasion that the human mind must be freed of all supernatural belief, if it wishes to strive for its essential mission, the building of positive science. This does not imply violent destruction, or an abrupt break. It is not a question of the Christian abandoning Christianity, or the Muslim abandoning Islam. It is a question, for the enlightened section of Islam and Christianity, to attain the state of benevolent indifference in which religious beliefs become innocuous. This has been accomplished in about half of Christian countries; let us hope it will be accomplished for Islam. Naturally, that day the sheikh and I will be united in our vigorous applause of such a development.

I have not said that all Muslims, with no distinction of race, are and always will be ignorant; I have said that Islam causes great difficulties to science, and that unfortunately it has almost managed to suppress it in the countries it controlled in the past five or six hundred years, which for these countries is a source of extreme weakness. Indeed, I believe that the regeneration of the Muslim countries will not be brought about by Islam: it will be brought about through the weakening of Islam, in the same way the great momentum of the so-called Christian countries began, after all, with the destruction of the tyrannical church of the Middle Ages. Some have seen in my talk a malevolent attitude toward the individuals who profess the Islamic religion. It is not so: Muslims are the first victims of Islam. Many times during my travels in the Orient I have had the opportunity to observe that fanaticism originates with a small number of dangerous men who keep the others in religious worship through terror. The best favor one can bestow upon a Muslim is to emancipate him from his religion. By expressing the wish that these populations, among which there are so many good characters, be freed from the yoke that weighs upon them, I do not believe I am wishing them ill. And since the sheikh Jamal ad-Din wishes me to keep an equal balance between religions, no more would I think I am wishing certain European countries ill if I desired Christianity to assume among them a less dominant character.

Disagreement between liberals on these different points is not deep, since, whether they be favorable to Islam or not, they all reach the same practical conclusion: spread education among the Muslims. This is excellent, provided we are talking about serious education, of the kind that cultivates reason. If the religious leaders of Islam contribute to this superb endeavor, I would be delighted. To speak frankly, I am rather doubtful they will. Some distinguished personalities will spring up (few will be as distinguished as sheikh Jamal ad-Din) who will separate themselves from Islam, as we separate ourselves from Catholicism. Certain countries, in time, will break almost completely with the religion of the Koran; but I doubt that the movement of rebirth will take place with the support of official Islam. The scientific rebirth of Europe did not take place with Catholicism either, and even now, without it needing to cause much surprise, Catholicism still fights to prevent the full achievement of what epitomizes the rational code of humanity, the neutral state, extraneous to allegedly revealed dogmas.

Above all, as a supreme rule, we place liberty and respect for human beings. The duty of civil society is not to destroy religions, and even to treat them benevolently, as free manifestations of human nature, but not to guarantee them either, and especially not to defend them against their believers who attempt to separate themselves from them. Reduced thus to the status of a free and individual matter, such as literature or taste, religions will be entirely transformed. Divested of the bonds deriving from their established or concordat status, they will become separate, and lose the greater part of their drawbacks. All this is utopian at present; it will all be reality in the future. How will each religion respond to a regime of freedom, which will prevail in human societies after much action and reaction? Such an issue cannot be examined in a few lines. In my talk, I simply wanted to discuss a historical question. Sheikh Jamal ad-Din has, I believe, contributed some considerable grounds to my two main theses: during the first half of its existence, Islam did not prevent a scientific movement from manifesting itself in Muslim countries; during the second half of its existence, it smothered the scientific movement in its midst, to its own detriment.

# 11

## ORIGINAL UNITY AND GRADUAL SEPARATION OF JUDAISM AND CHRISTIANITY (*IDENTITÉ ORIGINELLE ET SÉPARATION GRADUELLE DU JUDAÏSME ET DU CHRISTIANISME*, 1883)

I am infinitely thankful, Baron,* for the words with which you had the kindness to introduce me to this assembly. I have, indeed, been among those who from the very start applauded the creation of this Society of Jewish Studies, which I believe is destined to a great future. I applauded in particular the article of your statutes that allows individuals foreign to the Israelite community to become members of your society.

You were perfectly right, Gentlemen, to introduce this clause in your regulations. Without a doubt, Jewish studies rightfully belong to you; but, allow me to say this to your lasting credit, they also belong to humanity. Research relating to the Israelite past is of interest to everyone. All beliefs find the secret of their formation in your books. All who wish to search for their religious origins necessarily come to Hebrew. These studies, while they are your particular domain, are thus at the same time the common domain of everyone who believes or searches. (*Applause.*)

What marvelous destiny, indeed, your sacred book has had, this Bible that has become the intellectual and moral nourishment of civilized humanity! If there is a part of the world that scarcely resembles Judaea, it is our lost islands of the west and the north. Nonetheless! With what does one concern oneself in these faraway countries, inhabited by races

---

\* The Baron Alphonse de Rothschild had opened the proceedings with an address.

so different from those of the Orient? With what? With the Bible, Gentlemen, with the Bible first and foremost.

In the north of Scotland, thirty leagues from the coast, surrounded by
a wild sea, there is an isolated rock that during half the year is practically
plunged in darkness. This small island is called Saint Kilda. Lately I read
some very curious information on this isle, which could furnish us with
some interesting facts on the Celtic race in its pure state. For months at
a time, all relations with the rest of the world are interrupted. One must
suffer boredom quite severely in Saint Kilda, and society must be hardly
varied there. (*Laughter.*) Nonetheless! What do people do in this small
forgotten land? They read the Bible from dawn to dusk; they attempt to
understand it.

I have traveled somewhat in the north of Scandinavia; I have glimpsed
some encampments of Laplanders. These Laplanders are half-civilized.
They now know how to read. Well, what do they read? The Bible, once again
the Bible. They understand it after their own fashion, interpreting it in the
most original way, with a sort of somber passion and profound intelligence.

You thus have the incomparable privilege that your book has become
the book of the entire world; consequently, blame no one but yourselves if
everyone wishes to meddle in your studies. You share this privilege of universality with another race that also imposed its literature on all centuries
and all countries: Greece. Assuredly, we would complain if modern Greeks
were to tell us: "We alone have the right to concern ourselves with Greek."
"Excuse us," we would reply, "but everyone admires your ancient literature, and everyone has the right to study it." Similarly, the Bible, being the
common possession of humanity, belongs to the human race as a whole;
we have the right to collaborate with you. Hence, we thank you, Gentlemen, for having decided to allow us, as good Samaritans, to toil side by
side with you at the task that interests us all equally. (*Very well! Very well!
And lively applause.*)

To such a degree are Hebrew studies the common foundation of our
world's religious studies that all who try to account for their faith are
led to concern themselves with your religious past. When one wishes
to deepen one's knowledge of Christianity, it is Judaism that one must
study. Bound by one of those habits of youth, which are the most dear
and long-lasting—bound, I was saying, to Christianity by one of these
habits, I believed I could prove my respect for Christian doctrine best

by examining it closely. I think that a serious, conscientious examination is the greatest sign of respect one can give to religious beliefs. (*Signs of approbation.*)

Where did I find myself led by this analysis of Christianity? To the study of Judaism; for, I repeat, the Christian who wishes to account for his faith is necessarily driven to Hebrew. And, without a doubt, such a study produced in my intellect the most profound revolution. From the day I began to be acquainted with your past my ideas have, I may well say, fixated on the religious history of humanity.

The study of Christianity inspired in me the resolution to write the history of Christian origins. But what is the history of Christian origins, Gentlemen? It is essentially your history. I recognize that, to be completely logical, I should have begun my history of the *Origins of Christianity* with a history of the Jewish people. If I jumped, as one says, into the middle of the subject, it was because we do not know the length of our lives and we focus first on the matters of greatest urgency. For this reason, now that I have recounted as best I could the first one hundred and fifty years of Christianity I would like to consecrate what I have left of life and energy to the previous history, wherein resides, I realize it, the veritable explanation of Christianity.

The origins of Christianity must be placed, indeed, at least seven hundred and fifty years before Jesus Christ, in the age in which the great prophets appear, the creators of an entirely new idea of religion.

This is your glory, Gentlemen, the glory of Israel; this is the great secret of which you are the custodians: it is within your race, around seven or eight centuries before Jesus Christ (those years can hardly be gauged in a rigorous fashion), it is within Israel that the passage from a primitive religion, full of unwholesome superstitions, to the pure and, one may well say, definitive religion of humanity was definitively accomplished. Primitive religion, insofar as one is permitted to discern, must have shared in the coarseness inherent in the origins of humanity. It was a wholly selfish religion. God or the gods were envisaged in a form more or less analogous to man, and one attempted to relate to the deity or deities as one does with men, that is, through interest, donations, gifts. One attempted to ingratiate oneself with the gods by offering them something attractive, especially sacrifices, which one thought must be well received by them. It was an essentially self-interested worship. Man was surrounded by terrors, by unknown causes, and imagined reaching his goals by winning the favor of these unknown causes, by yoking them to his ambition and his passion.

Read the inestimable inscription of Mesha[1] that we have at the Louvre, which illustrates so well the state of conscience of a king of Moab nearly nine hundred years before Jesus Christ. Mesha offers sacrifices; he tries to be pleasing in every way to the god Camos, who rewards his piety by granting him victories and protecting him on all occasions. Mesha, in a word, is Camos's favorite. And why is that? Because Mesha is a man of great moral stature? That is very unlikely. We do not have much knowledge of this distant age; but I think we would not go too far by saying that Camos was attached to Mesha by reasons wholly other than because the latter was very much a gentleman. The god Camos appears not to have been sensitive to such considerations. (*Laughing.*)

How striking the contrast, if we move from the religion of Moab to the religion of Israel. Let us read, for instance, Psalm 15, which, like most psalms, is not dated, but in which we find the expression of a quite ancient sentiment. What do we read in it?

The psalmist asks himself what one must do to be the protégé of Jehovah, to be his *ger*, "his neighbor." This condition of *ger* with respect to the god he served has become quite clear through Phoenician inscriptions, bearing a likeness to certain Arabic expressions. The *ger*, the neighbor of a god, was the individual who lived next door to the temple of such a god; he was his parasite, his table companion, participating in the blowouts resulting from the sacrifices offered to the god. (*Laughing.*) The neighbor of the god was thus covered by the protection of the god, which extended like two great wings around the temple. Now, among the Phoenicians, for example, did the *ger* attempt to make himself worthy of this protection, of these advantages, of this favor by behaving honestly, by perfecting his moral being? Certainly not; the information we have on these *gerim* would lead us to believe quite the opposite. Let us now read our Psalm 15. We will see what the qualities must be of the protégé, of the neighbor of Jehovah, of the individual the God of Israel covers with his wings.

> Lord, who shall abide in[2] thy tabernacle?
> Who shall dwell in thy holy hill?

Witness the reply:

> He that walketh uprightly, and worketh righteousness,
> and speaketh the truth in his heart.
> He that backbiteth not with his tongue,
> nor doeth evil to his neighbour,
> nor taketh up a reproach against his neighbour. . . .
> He that taketh not reward against the innocent.

Here, Gentlemen, are the qualities of the *ger*, of the neighbor, of the protégé of Jehovah. One becomes the protégé of Jehovah by behaving honestly.*

I am not claiming that Psalm 15 was the first to express it; but it was definitely Israel that said it first. If the psalm is not dated, here is a text that, beyond a doubt, is; it is the first chapter of Isaiah:

> Hear the word of the Lord, ye rulers of Sodom; give ear unto the law of our God, ye people of Gomorrah: to what purpose is the multitude of your sacrifices unto me? saith the Lord: I am full of the burnt offerings of rams, and the fat of fed beasts; and I delight not in the blood of bullocks, or of lambs, or of he goats. . . . Bring no more vain oblations; incense is an abomination unto me. . . . Your new moons and your appointed feasts my soul hateth: they are a trouble unto me; I am weary to bear them. . . . Yea, when ye make many prayers, I will not hear: your hands are full of blood. Wash you, make you clean; put away the evil of your doings from before mine eyes; cease to do evil; learn to do well; seek judgment, relieve the oppressed, judge the fatherless, plead for the widow.

Gentlemen, here is a completely new god, profoundly different from the Camos of King Mesha and all the gods of antiquity. Morality has entered religion; religion has become moral. The essential is no longer the material sacrifice. The disposition of the heart, the integrity of the soul is the true worship. (*Prolonged applause.*)

These words have a date; they are authentic, they are from around seven hundred and twenty-five years before Jesus Christ. They signal

---

\* Also recall the beautiful formulation: *Lo iegurka ra*, "neither shall evil dwell with thee" (literally, "an evildoer cannot be your *ger*"), Psalm 5:5.

the beginning of pure religion for humanity. Logically speaking, such a movement should have led to the suppression of sacrifices; but one rarely attains the absolute ideal; it is difficult to eliminate customs that are dear to a people and have become national. The spirit at least remained. The spirit of the prophets is the spirit of Israel itself. After the captivity, we encounter it again in those admirable writers of the sixth century BCE, whose dream is a religion that may befit all humanity.

As long as worship consists in material practices, one cannot ask all peoples to accept it; each nation has its own practices; why change them? But a worship that consists in the pure ideal of morality and goodness, such a worship, I say, is good for everyone.

And this is an idea that recurs endlessly with the ancient prophets: this purified worship of Israel will become the religion of mankind. It is no longer an individual worship; it is a universal worship, the reign of justice. (*Applause.*)

The reign of justice! Indeed, such is the faith of the ancient prophets; it is the ideal that appears in their works. This ideal is not realized completely—never is the ideal realized in its entirety—but the stubborn belief that, thanks to Israel, justice will reign on earth becomes, in the thought of the pious Jew, a sort of obsession.

This is where the marvelous originality of the prophets resides; this is the idea at the core of pure religion, which was necessarily adopted by all of humanity. This idea, proclaimed with such a popular and touching tone by the founders of Christianity, is expressed with admirable grandeur by the prophets of the seventh century BCE.

It is in this sense that I have claimed that the origins of Christianity lie in Judaism. The true founders of Christianity were the prophets who announced the pure religion, detached from coarse practices and dwelling in the dispositions of the spirit and the heart, a religion that consequently can and must be common to all, an ideal religion, consisting in the proclamation of the kingdom of God on earth and the hope for an era of justice for suffering humanity.

The Sibylline poems of the school of Alexandria, as apocryphal a work as you please, but so touching, revolve around the same dream, which, through mysterious echoes, made its way to Virgil: a bright future, a future of peace, happiness and fraternity destined for the world made anew. This paradise on earth will result from humanity joining the worship of Israel.

It is very difficult for us to speak in a precise way of these first founders of Christianity, whose physiognomy is hidden from our view by a triple veil; what is certain is that the entire first Christian generation is essentially Jewish. Had one asked these great founders if they thought they were placing themselves outside the bounds of the Jewish family, they would have replied: "No, we are continuing the lineage of the seers of Israel; we are the true successors of the ancient prophets." They believed, in short, that they were fulfilling the law, not abolishing it.

To encounter some factual evidence, one must come to Saint Paul, whose most ancient epistles to reach us date approximately from the year 54 AD. Here, the break is ostensibly glaring. Nonetheless, Paul protests ceaselessly that he is not abandoning his faith in the promises. He wants to enlarge Judaism, to aid the entry of the populations that wish to join it. He sometimes has some harsh words for his former people; but he also has tender words, full of gentleness, and Saint Paul never thought he was separating himself from the Jewish church. In the primitive church, anyway, Paul is considered almost a heretic, an audacious character, a sort of contrarian. In any case, he was an exception, and the small epistles, such as those that appear in the Christian canon under the name of Saint James or Saint Jude, are much more representative of the spirit of the early church. Now, such writings are completely Jewish; they could have been read in the synagogue had they been written in Hebrew.

The same is true of the so-called Apocalypse of Saint John, the one that is in the Christian canon. This book, which dates to the end of the year 68 or the beginning of the year 69, is a Jewish book in the highest degree. The author is passionate for the Jewish nation. The Jewish War[3] has begun, Jerusalem is about to be besieged; one senses in the seer the most profound sympathy for the insurgents in Judaea. Jerusalem for him is "the cherished city"; his ideal of humanity is a Jerusalem made of gold, pearls, and jewels. One cannot be more Jewish than the author of the Apocalypse.

Directly following the fall of Jerusalem, the composition of the so-called synoptic Gospels[4] occurs. Here there is a split. The character of these Gospels is in some sense double. In the old Christian books, there is a word that gives a fairly correct idea of the moral state of the Evangelists; it is the word δίψυχος, "two-souled," meaning "floating between two states of mind." In the Synoptics one reads very stern, occasionally unjust words against the Pharisees; what proves that the break had not yet taken place, however, is that the least Jewish of all the Synoptics, Luke, makes a point of noting that Jesus practiced all the rites of the law, and in particular that he had been circumcised. A rather curious fact, in any case, is the following:

Toward 75 or 80 and in the following years, many books inspired by Jewish patriotism emerge, such as the Book of Judith, the Apocalypse of Esdras, the Apocalypse of Baruch, and even the Book of Tobias, which only appears at a late date. Nothing is more Jewish than the Book of Judith, for example. Yet these books are lost among the Jews and are only preserved by the Christians; so true was it that the bond between the church and the synagogue had not yet been broken when they appeared.

The Epistle of Clement of Rome, whoever its author may be, expresses quite well the sentiments of the Roman Church toward the year 98 AD. This pamphlet is quite orthodox in its Judaism; Judith is quoted therein as a heroine for the first time, demonstrating that the schism, toward the year 100, had in no way been consummated.

If we move now to the epistles and the Gospel attributed to John, the situation is quite different. We may place the composition of these writings toward the year 125 AD, that is to say around a hundred years after the death of Jesus. Judaism here is treated as an enemy. One senses the arrival of the systems that, under the name of Gnosticism, will lead the Christians to disown their Jewish origins. Gnosticism is completely opposed to Judaism. According to the Gnostics, Christianity was born spontaneously and without antecedent; or rather, it is a reaction against the previous law. It is inconceivable that so erroneous a historical conception could have developed in so little time (one hundred or one hundred and twenty years after Jesus!). The new doctors declare that Christianity has nothing to do with Judaism. Marcion,[5] even more extreme, claims that the Jewish religion is an evil religion, which Jesus Christ came to abolish. It is, I repeat, quite singular that in the space of a century, a similar error could develop; but note that Gnosticism is to the Christian Church what a side channel is to a river. The orthodox church in the second century always considered itself tied to the synagogue by the most intimate of bonds.

Papias[6] is definitely a Jewish Christian, confined within the ideas of the synoptic Gospels and the Apocalypse. The Testaments of the Twelve Patriarchs, which appears toward the same time, is a wholly Jewish work. *The Shepherd* of Hermas remains an edifying book in the Jewish sense, a veritable *agada*.[7] I wish someone would translate it; I am certain it would charm readers, both among the faithful and among those who are simply interested in religious history. Finally, there is this bishop of Sardis, Melito,[8] who toward the year 160 spends his life searching for the sacred books among the Jews. The list of the sacred books, in remote Asia Minor, was known in a very incomplete form. Melito leads an investigation, travels to Syria, manages to gain exact knowledge of the canon of the Jews; for him, that *is* the canon of the sacred books.

We reach the time of Marcus Aurelius. The break, now, is more and more pronounced. Polycarp[9] and his entourage are enemies of the Jews. The Apologists also are, in general, great adversaries of Judaism. They are lawyers: they set up the cause they defend with sheer surfaces, like a fortress. The anonymous writing known by the name of *Epistle to Diognetus* is especially striking in this regard. It permits one to grasp quite well the strange error into which, at the end of the second century, entire branches of the Christian family had fallen: one would have thought that Christianity had sprouted from the ground on its own, independently of Judaism. The author of the *Epistle to Diognetus* treats the Jewish rituals, from which Christianity had originated, as "superstitions." Never had one seen a contradiction more extraordinary.

The separation, I repeat, was caused especially by the influence of Gnostic doctrines. Under Marcus Aurelius the divorce was still far from being absolute. Witness the rise of Montanism toward 170; Montanism was a recurrence of the old millenarian, prophetic, apocalyptic spirit among the fervent and credulous populations of Phrygia.[10] What is the fixed idea of Montanism? That Jerusalem will come establish itself in Pepuza, Phrygia. Its devotees spent their days with their eyes raised to the sky, to see this new Jerusalem burst forth in the clouds, then descend and come establish itself in the burnt lands of Catacecaumene Phrygia. For them, the tie with the ancient hopes of Israel was in no way broken.

There is one book especially that is a historical treasure: it is the romance of which Clement of Rome is the hero and that is known by the name of *Recognitions*. If one wants to understand correctly the relations between Christianity and Judaism under Marcus Aurelius, this is the book one must read. The problem is addressed in a certain sense *ex professo* in a sermon that Saint Peter is supposed to have pronounced in Tripoli, on the coast of Syria. The bases of the system of conciliation described by

Saint Peter are as follows: Judaism and Christianity do not differ from one another; Moses is Jesus; Jesus is Moses. Since the beginning there has been, strictly speaking, only one prophet, constantly reborn; the same prophetic spirit has inspired all the prophets. Judaism is sufficient for those who do not know Christianity. One may be saved both in one and the other.

The expressions employed by this very interesting author are worth pondering. According to the plot of the romance, the family of Clement of Rome converts to the truth. They are very virtuous pagans who, as a prize for their virtue, accede to the true faith: "They turn into Jews," Ἰουδαίους γεγενημένους. Turning into a Jew, for the author, means adopting religious truth, which is not split in two. For him, there is only one revelation, of which Judaism and Christianity are the two equivalent and parallel forms. This is how, under Marcus Aurelius, one understood the relationships between Judaism and Christianity.

Later, in the third century, the split becomes more marked, under the influence of the school of Alexandria, heiress of a mitigated Gnosticism. Clement of Alexandria[11] and Origen[12] do not love Judaism and speak of it with much injustice. One can feel that the separation is taking place; nonetheless, it only occurs in a complete fashion when Christianity affects the gait of a state religion, under Constantine.[13] At that point, Christianity becomes official, while Judaism maintains its free character. Is the separation wholly completed then? Well, no, not yet.

I mentioned lately the sermons of Saint John Chrysostom[14] against the Jews.[15] There is hardly a more interesting historical document. The orator shows himself to be naturally harsh, dogmatic; he makes all sorts of arguments, some of which are not very strong. (*Laughter.*) But one can see that his believers were still in a most intimate community with the synagogue. He tells them more than twenty times (for Saint John Chrysostom repeats himself a lot; he is a bit long-winded): (*Laughing.*) "Why do you go to the synagogue? Do you want to celebrate Easter? Well, we celebrate Easter, too; come with us!" (*General hilarity and applause.*)

The Christians of Antioch, in 380, therefore still went to the synagogue in many circumstances. To give an oath more force, one went to the synagogue because the sacred books were there. This, as a matter of fact, is the cause of the custom John Chrysostom combats as an abuse of the gravest sort. "I know full well," says Chrysostom, "what you will reply. You will tell me that is where the Law and the prophets are." The Christians did not frequent the Hebrew Bible enough, and had the sense that the Jews were its true custodians.

But these are nothing more than the traces of the primitive community, for the separation grows deeper and deeper. We enter the Middle Ages, the barbarians arrive, and there begins the deplorable ingratitude of humanity, which has become Christian, against Judaism. This is always how things happen: when one works for humanity, one is guaranteed to be robbed first, and, in addition, to be beaten for it. (*Laughing.—Applause.*)

The world had taken religious truth from Judaism, and treats Judaism in the cruelest manner. It is not in the first half of the Middle Ages, however, that the most deplorable incidents occur. At that time, there is hostility; it is undeniable; but there are no organized persecutions yet, or at least there are few. The Crusades give the signal for the massacres of the Jews. Scholasticism would also contribute significantly to making things worse.

Christian theology had organized itself into a sort of science, wherein revelation was framed, after a fashion, by the syllogisms of Aristotle's dialectics. One of the most pernicious aspects of this Scholasticism was the tendency to search for and find errors everywhere. We have enumerations of such errors that fill volumes, and often, among these supposed errors thus condemned, there are some very good things. In this fury of theological condemnation, it occurred to someone that the Talmud must harbor the gravest errors. Renegades got involved, and became informers. Then, the Trial of the Talmud[16] was conducted (1248); it was burned, and as my learned master, Mr. Victor le Clerc, says in his *Discours sur l'histoire littéraire de la France au XIVe siècle*: "One burned the Talmud, and sometimes the Jew with the Talmud." (*Laughter and applause.*) This was the time of the abominable persecutions, of the autos-da-fé like the one in Troyes in 1288.

At the end of the thirteenth century, the fiscal policies of Philip the Fair[17] came to wreck everything. Grand designs began to be made, but money was necessary, and, at that time, money was obtained by unpleasant means indeed. The despoilment of the Jews offered itself from the very outset. It is one of the most deplorable acts in the history of France. Up to then, France had been a relatively tolerant land for Israel; and, if any conclusion can be drawn from the work we have inserted in the *Histoire littéraire de la France* on the conditions of the Jews in France during the

Middle Ages, work whose merit I am happy to attribute entirely to Mr. Neubauer,[18] it is that up to the end of the thirteenth century the Jews practiced exactly the same professions as other Frenchmen. It is as a consequence of the sad events we have just mentioned that the distinction of professions between Israelites and non-Israelites is enacted. The Israelites were forced to lead a different kind of life than other people. The life of the Israelite becomes a life of isolation, of banishment. Now, it is a historical law that the society that condemns a part of its members to a separate life is the first victim of such unwieldy measures; for one of the consequences of banishment is, up to a point, to create a privilege for the banished. They are relieved of responsibilities; they are condemned to professions that are merely lucrative. Thus were Israelites almost forced to be rich. In this medieval society, at least from the end of the thirteenth century, the Israelite has but one free profession, which consists in enriching himself, to such an extent that a most remarkable vicious circle develops. The Middle Ages reproach the Israelite for the profession to which they have condemned him. They have denied him the tilling of land, they have forbidden him from practicing any onerous profession, yet they find it wicked that the Israelite should profit from the lucrative side of this situation. It is a most deplorable sophism.

The fact that monetary and financial matters were devolved to the Jews in the Middle Ages depended, in any case, on their position outside canon law. The church, at least in France, professed at that time the most exaggerated and false ideas on usury. The doctrines of the casuists on the topic of interest on money rendered almost all business impossible for Christian society.* To conduct the simplest of financial operations, one was obliged to have recourse to persons who were not subject to canon law. Usury (and one was a usurer if one made the slightest profit from an investment), usury, I was saying, was an ecclesiastical crime; the usurer was not allowed to make a will, he was not buried in consecrated land, his family was marked with infamy, to such an extent that Christians were completely excluded from banking and even from insurance and

---

* See the communication by Mr. Jourdain on the beginnings of political economy in the schools of the Middle Ages, in the *Mém. de l'Acad. des inscr. et belles lettres*, t. XXVIII, part 2.

commerce. Therefore, it is the Middle Ages that are guilty of what they reproached the Israelites for.

Let us not dwell on this sad spectacle. Let us reach a more encouraging age, the eighteenth century that finally proclaimed the rights of reason, the rights of man, the true theory of human society, by which I mean the state lacking an official dogma, neutral between metaphysical and theological opinions: that is the day in which equality of rights began for the Jews. It was the Revolution that proclaimed the equality of the Jews with all other citizens within the state. (*Lively and unanimous applause.*)

The Revolution found in this matter the true solution, with a sentiment of the most absolute accuracy, and everyone will come round to it. (*General assent.*)

And who better than the Jewish people, Gentlemen, could accept such a solution? It was the Jewish people themselves who had prepared it; they had prepared it by their entire history, by their prophets, the great religious creators of Israel, who had called for the future unity of mankind in faith and in law.

The promoters of such a movement are: first of all, the ancient and authentic Isaiah; then, the author who continued his book in the time of the captivity, this unparalleled religious genius; then, the Essenes,[19] these poetic ascetics who dreamed of an ideal that we have yet to reach. Christianity also has contributed powerfully to the progress of civilization; now, Christianity, so admirable in its fight against the barbarians, when it attempts to maintain some trace of reason and law in the midst of the excesses of brutality, Christianity, I say, was but the continuation of your prophets. The glory of Christianity is the glory of Judaism. Indeed, the world has become Jewish by converting to the laws of meekness and humanity preached by the disciples of Jesus. (*Applause.*)

And now that these great processes have occurred, let us state with conviction that Judaism, which served so much in the past, will also serve in the future. It will serve the true cause, the cause of liberalism, of the modern spirit. Every Jew is a liberal.* (*General assent and applause.*)

---

\*     This naturally goes for French Jews, as they were shaped by the Revolution. We are convinced, however, that any country that replicates the experiment, relinquishing state religion, secularizing civil life, and practicing the equality of all citizens before the law, will come to the same result and find excellent patriots in the Israelite religion like in the others.

He is so by his essence. The enemies of Judaism, on the contrary—observe them closely, you will see that they are in general the enemies of the modern spirit. (*New signs of approbation.*)

The creators of the liberal dogma in religion are, I repeat, your ancient prophets, Isaiah, the Sibyllines, the Jewish school of Alexandria, the early Christians, continuators of the prophets. These are the veritable founders of the spirit of justice in the world. By serving the modern spirit, the Jew, in fact, does nothing but serve the work to which he has contributed more than anyone in the past and, let us add, for which he has suffered greatly. (*Stir.*)

The pure religion, in short, which we discern will manage to gather to it all of humanity, will be the realization of the religion of Isaiah, the ideal Jewish religion, unencumbered by the impurities that may have been mixed with it.

Therefore, you have done well, Gentlemen, to establish the Society for Jewish Studies, which will cast a very specific light on these truths. Let us all work together, for the endeavor is a common one. I have, at times, enjoyed dreaming of the day when humanity, in thanks to Greece, would bring back to the Acropolis of Athens the pieces that everyone has stolen from it. (*Laughter.*) Such a dream shall never come to pass. Well, I would dream at least something analogous for your own Parthenon. Your Parthenon, Gentlemen, is, I admit, Jerusalem, this unique and eminently respectable city; but you are idealists foremost, and your true Parthenon is the Bible. (*Unanimous applause.*)

The study, the clarification, the explanation of the Bible: this is your work—to which we are all grateful to have been invited. And what better homage offered to the spirit of Israel than this prodigious work of modern exegesis, than these innumerable critical studies, to elucidate I would not even say each sentence, but rather each word, each letter of your ancient texts?

Your book is a thing so unique within humanity that each of the syllables you have written has become the subject of an unending battle. (*Laughter and bravos.*)

The Hebrew dictionary dictates the destiny of humanity. There are certain dogmas that rest upon an error of interpretation of a certain passage of your Bible, on a mistake of your copyists. Certain ancient scribes of yours have determined, by one of these distractions, the theology of the future.

When I had the honor of being associated with the manuscript department of the Imperial Library—the National Library, today—I received the visit of the famous Doctor Pusey, a respectable man if ever there was one, and, as is well known, very orthodox. Once I had handed him the Arabic manuscripts he wished to consult, he noticed Gesenius's *Thesaurus*[20] on my table. Immediately his countenance turned somber, became severe, and he told me: "That is a very dangerous book, full of rationalism and errors." (*Laughing.*) The following day, I received from him a letter more than ten pages long—which I jealously treasure—to demonstrate to me that one only needed eyes to see the clearest of predictions of the Messiah in the fifty-third chapter of Isaiah.

Well, this is your glory, Gentlemen; how many volumes has this fifty-third chapter already produced? What has one not written on a certain pronoun contained in this fifty-third chapter? How much research, how much effort to determine if this pronoun *lamo* should be taken as a singular or a plural! The faith of a mass of people has rested on the syntax of this pronoun *lamo*.

These are subtleties; but, at the same time, they are as many homages rendered to the greatness of your past.

Hence, labor on, Gentlemen, as you have up to now, and please accept our collaboration. (*Very well! Very well!—Assent.*)

Your Bible, Gentlemen, is the book of humankind as a whole, it is the fundamental document of the history of the development of the religious idea in humanity. (*Lively accord and prolonged applause.*)

# NOTES

## SERIES EDITOR'S FOREWORD

1. This volume was planned before the U.S. election of 2016 brought the wholly unexpected and yet-to-be-studied election of Donald Trump to the presidency. The meaning of the "nationalism" that captured the imagination of so many remains to be "studied" —to use Renan's phrasing. Certainly, the idea of a continued progress of popular enlightenment and political rationality has been challenged, as a dark side of progress, a reaction, has become evident. That the legitimately elected U.S. president sees fit to continue to hold mass political rallies as if he were still campaigning makes one wonder about Renan's appeal to an "everyday plebiscite."

## INTRODUCTION

1. "Although knowledge of the present is less instructive than knowledge of the past, the present is a face of reality also; it deserves to be studied."
2. Among notable contributions to the vast biographical literature on Renan, see Mary James Darmesteter, *La vie de Ernest Renan* (Paris: Calmann-Lévy, 1898); Jean Pommier, *Renan d'après des documents inédits* (Paris: Perrin, 1923); Harold Wardman, *Ernest Renan: A Critical Biography* (London: Athlone, 1964); Richard Chadbourne, *Ernest Renan* (New York: Twayne, 1968); Francis Mercury, *Vie de Renan* (Paris: Olivier Orban, 1990); Charles Chauvin, *Renan* (Paris: Desclée de Brouwer, 2000); Jean-Pierre van Deth, *Ernest Renan: simple chercheur de vérité* (Paris: Fayard, 2012); and Jean Balcou, *Ernest Renan: une biographie* (Paris: Honoré Champion, 2015).
3. As described by Renan himself in his memoirs, *Souvenirs d'enfance et de jeunesse* (1883).
4. See Erving Goffman, *The Presentation of Self in Everyday Life* (New York: Random House, 1959).

5. This aspect of Renan's approach was clearly recognized by his lifelong friend Marcellin Berthelot:

> Si nous étions tous deux également dévoués à la science et à la libre pensée, Renan, en raison de ses origines bretonnes et de son éducation ecclésiastique et contemplative, tournée vers le passé, avait moins de goût pour la démocratie, pour la Révolution française, et surtout pour cette transformation à la fois rationnelle, industrielle et socialiste, dans laquelle est engagée la civilisation moderne. Les anciennes manières d'envisager la protection des sciences, des lettres et des arts, par un pouvoir supérieur et autocratique, l'attiraient davantage: il n'en a jamais fait mystère.
>
> (*Correspondance, 1847–1892*, Paris: Calmann Lévy, 1898, 2)

6. It is worth recalling, however, that for Renan and his generation, the term *orientalism* held no negative connotation (see, for example, Renan's *La chaire d'hébreu au Collège de France: explications à mes collègues*, [Paris: Michel Lévy, 1862], 6).

7. There is hardly a doubt that misunderstanding or miscalculation played no role in the controversy: the first part of Renan's inaugural lecture, "De la part des peuples sémitiques dans l'histoire de la civilisation" (speedily issued in pamphlet form), reads as a preemptive, comprehensive liberal defense of the right to free expression against either crowd or government interference.

8. See Robert D. Priest, *The Gospel According to Renan: Reading, Writing, and Religion in Nineteenth-Century France* (Oxford: Oxford University Press, 2015).

9. Later reprinted in Renan's collection of plays, *Drames philosophiques* (1888).

10. As mentioned by Pierre Rosanvallon in Henry Laurens (ed.), *Ernest Renan: la science, la religion, la République* (Paris: Jacob, 2013).

11. On this topic, see Sudhir Hazareesingh, *Intellectual Founders of the Republic: Five Studies in Nineteenth-Century French Republican Political Thought* (New York: Oxford University Press, 2001).

12. *Examen de conscience philosophique* (1889); *Feuilles détachées* (1892).

13. See Larry Siedentop, "Two Liberal Traditions," in Raf Geenens and Helena Rosenblatt (eds.), *French Liberalism from Montesquieu to the Present Day* (Cambridge: Cambridge University Press, 2012).

14. See, for example, Pierre Rosanvallon, *Le moment Guizot* (Paris: Gallimard, 1985); Lucien Jaume, *L'individu effacé, ou: Le paradoxe du libéralisme français* (Paris: Fayard, 1997); Annelien De Dijn, *French Political Thought from Montesquieu to Tocqueville: Liberty in a Levelled Society?* (Cambridge: Cambridge University Press, 2008).

15. Benjamin Constant, *De l'esprit de conquête et de l'usurpation dans leurs rapports avec la civilisation européenne* (1814).

16. Alexis de Tocqueville, *L'ancien régime et la révolution* (1856).

17. On the wider intellectual context of protectionism, see David Todd, *Free Trade and Its Enemies in France, 1814–1851* (Cambridge: Cambridge University Press, 2015).

18. Benjamin Constant, "De la liberté des Anciens comparée à celle des Modernes" (1819).

19. See, for example, François Furet, *Penser la révolution française* (Paris: Gallimard, 1972).

20. See Helena Rosenblatt, "On the Need for a Protestant Reformation: Constant, Sismondi, Guizot and Laboulaye," in Raf Geenens and Helena Rosenblatt (eds.), *French Liberalism from Montesquieu to the Present Day* (Cambridge: Cambridge University Press, 2012).

21. See Jennifer Pitts, *A Turn to Empire: The Rise of Imperial Liberalism in Britain and France* (Princeton, NJ, and Oxford: Princeton University Press, 2005); Uday Singh Mehta, *Liberalism and Empire: A Study in Nineteenth-Century British Liberal Thought* (Chicago: University of Chicago Press, 1999); and Bart Schultz and Georgios Varouxakis (eds.), *Utilitarianism and Empire* (Lanham, MD: Lexington Books, 2005).

22. Jennifer Pitts, "Republicanism, Liberalism, and Empire in Post-revolutionary France," in Sankar Muthu (ed.), *Empire and Modern Political Thought* (Cambridge: Cambridge University Press, 2012).

23. On this, see Owen White and J. P. Daughton (eds.), *In God's Empire: French Missionaries and the Modern World* (Oxford: Oxford University Press, 2012).

24. See Aurelian Craiutu, *Liberalism Under Siege: The Political Thought of the French Doctrinaires* (Lanham, MD: Lexington Books, 2003).

25. Pierre Rosanvallon, *Le sacre du citoyen: Histoire du suffrage universel en France* (Paris: Gallimard, 1992).

26. See Aurelian Craiutu, *A Virtue for Courageous Minds: Moderation in French Political Thought, 1748–1830* (Princeton, NJ: Princeton University Press, 2012).

27. On this topic, see Keith Gore, *L'idée de progrès dans la pensée de Renan* (Paris: A.G. Nizet, 1970).

28. Hayden White, *Metahistory: The Historical Imagination in Nineteenth-Century Europe*, (Baltimore, MD: Johns Hopkins University Press, 1973), chap. 10.

29. See Peter Bergmann, *Nietzsche: The Last Antipolitical German* (Bloomington, IN: Indiana University Press, 1987). For further detail on Renan's influence on Nietzsche, especially with relation to the social role of intellectuals, see Sandro Barbera and Giuliano Campioni, *Il genio tiranno. Ragione e dominio nell'ideologia dell'Ottocento: Wagner, Nietzsche, Renan* (Milano: Angeli, 1983).

30. Shared by thinkers as diverse as Benedetto Croce, Henry James, Émile Durkheim, Georges Sorel, and Max Weber.

31. M. F. N. Giglioli, *Legitimacy and Revolution in a Society of Masses: Max Weber, Antonio Gramsci, and the Fin-de-Siècle Debate on Social Order* (New Brunswick, NJ: Transaction Publishers, 2013), chap. 1.

32. See Robert D. Priest, "The 'Great Doctrine of Transcendent Disdain': History, Politics and the Self in Renan's Life of Jesus," *History of European Ideas* (2014): 761–776.

33. See, e.g., Michel Winock, *Le siècle des intellectuels* (Paris: Seuil, 1997).

34. This shift away from racialism as a relevant explanatory factor in politics was mirrored in the subsequent generation by Max Weber, who used a very similar term of condemnation, *zoological nationalism*, to refer to his early position (see his "Freiburger Kollegen," letter of November 15, 1911, in M. Weber, *Gesamtausgabe. Abteilung II: Briefe (1911) 1911–1912*, Tübingen: J.C.B. Mohr, 1998, 352–357).

35. One of the polemical targets of Renan's argument in the "Nation" lecture—that the freedom of science requires that it not be used for political ends—appears to be the philological nationalists behind the "national awakenings" of the second half of the nineteenth century in Mitteleuropa. See István Bibó, *Miseria dei piccoli Stati dell'Europa orientale* [*A kelet-európai kisállamok nyomorúsága*], It. transl. A. Nuzzo (Bologna: Il Mulino, 1994).

36. For an overview of the history of the intellectual and political debate on this point, see Robert D. Priest, "Ernest Renan's Race Problem," *The Historical Journal* 58, 1 (2015): 309–330.

37. See Claude Digeon, *La crise allemande de la pensée française, 1870–1914* (Paris: PUF, 1959).

38. See, for example, Friedrich Nietzsche, *Die fröhliche Wissenschaft*, §377 in Giorgio Colli and Mazzino Montinari (eds.), *Nietzsche Werke: kritische Gesamtausgabe* 5.2 (Berlin: Walter de Gruyter, 1973).

39. See chapter 2 in this anthology.

40. See Richard Chadbourne, "Renan, or the Contemptuous Approach to Literature," *Yale French Studies* 3 (1949): 96–104.

41. On which L. Rétat has written most notably, for instance in the general introduction to Renan's *Histoire et parole: oeuvres diverses* (Paris: R. Laffont, 1984).

42. Pierre Rosanvallon, "Renan, père fondateur de la République?" in Henry Laurens (ed.), *Ernest Renan: La science, la religion, la République* (Paris: Jacob, 2013).

43. See Yves-Marie Hilaire (ed.), *De Renan à Marrou: L'histoire du christianisme et la mé-thode historique (1863–1968)* (Lille: Presses universitaires du Septentrion, 1999).

44. Already in his lifetime, Renan's fame as a cultural icon of secularism had spread internationally. See his *Vingt jours en Sicile* for the description of his triumphal 1875 trip to the island, in the context of the new Kingdom of Italy's anticlerical nation-building campaigns.

45. Zeev Sternhell, *La droite révolutionnaire: 1885–1914 (les origines françaises du fascisme)* (Paris: Seuil, 1978).

46. See Maurice Barrès, *Huit jours chez M. Renan* (Utrecht: J.J. Pauvert, 1965).

47. See Georges Sorel, *Le système historique de Renan* (Geneva: Slatkine Reprints, 1971).

48. See Richard Gowan, "Raymond Aron: The History of Ideas and the Idea of France," *European Journal of Political Theory* 2, 4 (October 2003): 383–399.

49. Edgar Quinet, *Les révolutions d'Italie* (Paris: Chamerot, 1848–1851).

50. Antonio Gramsci, *Quaderni del carcere*, ed. Valentino Gerratana (Torino: Einaudi, 1975). See, for instance, Quaderno 3 §40, Q. 4 §75, Q. 10 §41, Q. 11 §16, Q. 13 §1, Q. 16 §9, Q. 21 §1, and so forth.

51. The French term *réforme* also translates to "reformation."

52. See, e.g., Alasdair MacIntyre, *After Virtue* (Notre Dame, IN: University of Notre Dame Press, 1981).

53. An echo of which can be found in Pierre Bourdieu and Jean-Claude Passeron, *Les héritiers: Les étudiants et la culture* (Paris: Minuit, 1964).

54.  On this, see François Hartog's thought-provoking new book, *La nation, la religion, l'avenir: Sur les traces d'Ernest Renan* (Paris: Gallimard, 2017).

55.  Edward W. Said, *Orientalism* (Harmondsworth, UK: Penguin, 1978).

56.  See Henry Laurens, "Présentation générale de l'oeuvre de Renan," in Henry Laurens (ed.), *Ernest Renan: la science, la religion, la République* (Paris: Jacob, 2013), 11.

57.  See Benedict R. Anderson, *Imagined Communities: Reflections on the Origin and Spread of Nationalism*, rev. ed. (London: Verso, 2006); Ernest Gellner, *Nations and Nationalism* (Oxford: Blackwell, 1983); and Eric J. Hobsbawm, *Nations and Nationalism since 1780: Programme, Myth, Reality* (Cambridge: Cambridge University Press, 1990).

58.  The Israeli historian Shlomo Sand has recently taken Renan's arguments about nationalism, filtered through Anderson's interpretation, as corroboration for his own broader argument on the socially constructed nature of Jewish identity. See Sand, *De la nation et du peuple juif chez Renan* (Brignon: Les Liens qui Libèrent, 2009) and Sand, *Comment le peuple juif fut inventé: De la Bible au sionisme* (Paris: Fayard, 2008).

59.  See Michel Foucault, *Il faut défendre la société: Cours au Collège de France, 1975–1976* (Paris: Gallimard/Seuil, 1997); Pierre-André Taguieff, *La couleur et le sang: Doctrines racistes à la française* (Paris: Éd. Mille et une nuits, 1998); and Eugen Weber, *My France: Politics, Culture, Myth* (Cambridge, MA: Belknap Press, 1991).

60.  See Maurice Olender, *Les langues du paradis: Aryens et Sémites, un couple providentiel* (Paris: Seuil, 1989), especially chap. 4; and Gil Anidjar, *Semites: Race, Religion, Literature* (Redwood City, CA: Stanford University Press, 2008), 6.

61.  Renan, *The Future of Science* (Boston: Roberts Brothers, 1891); Renan, *Caliban: A Philosophical Drama Continuing "The Tempest" of William Shakespeare* (New York: Shakespeare Press, 1896).

62.  The latter was translated as "Islamism and Science" in William G. Hutchison (ed.), *The Poetry of the Celtic Races, and Other Studies* (London: Scott, 1896), 84–108.

## 1. ON CLERICAL LIBERALISM
### (DU LIBÉRALISME CLÉRICAL, 1848)

1.  Renan appears to be speaking of the trees of liberty, the planting of which was a traditional republican ritual in France since the Revolution of 1789.

2.  The reference is to the previous regime change in France, the Revolution of July 1830.

3.  "Son of the Church" was one of the titles of the king of France; hence, in this context, it designates Charles X, of the eldest branch of the royal family, as opposed to the newcomer, Louis-Philippe of Orléans.

4.  The Revolution of 1848 in Paris erupted in late February.

5.  The Bourbon dynasty, like many others in Europe, traditionally employed Swiss mercenary troops as their palace guards.

6.  Louis-Philippe of Orléans became "king of the French" on August 9, 1830.

7. "Let them be as they are, or not be at all" is a phrase attributed to Pope Clement XIII on changing the statutes of the Jesuits in order to avoid their expulsion from France in 1767.

8. In Latin in the original: "Per me reges regnant.—Subjecti . . . estote omni humanae creaturae propter Deum, sive regi quasi praecellenti, sive ducibus tanquam ab eo missis, . . . quia sic est voluntas Dei.—Omnis anima potestatibus sublimioribus subdita sit; non est enim potestas nisi a Deo; quae autem sunt, a Deo ordinatae sunt. Itaque qui resistit potestati, Dei ordinationi resistit. Qui autem resistunt, ipsi sibi damnationem acquirunt. . . . Dei enim minister est . . . Ideo necessitate subditi estote, non solum propter iram, sed etiam propter conscientiam . . . Ministri enim Dei sunt, in hoc ipsum servientes."

9. In Latin in the original: "Non tribuamus dandi regni atque imperii potestatem nisi Deo vero."

10. Constantine the Great (272–337) was emperor of Rome from 306 to his death.

11. Lucius Caecilius Firmianus Lactantius (ca. 250–c. 325) was an early Christian author and adviser to Constantine the Great.

12. In Latin in the original: "Reddite ergo quae sunt Caesaris Caesari et quae sunt Dei Deo."

13. Jacques-Bénigne Bossuet (1627–1704), bishop of Meaux, was a Catholic theologian, orator, and controversialist. His *Politics Drawn from the Very Words of Holy Scripture* was written for the Dauphin while Bossuet was his tutor (1670–1681) and published posthumously in 1709.

14. Bossuet sees the ideal of royalty in the passage he cites from Ecclesiastes in the footnote: "Omne quod voluerit faciet: et sermo illius potestate plenus est, nec dicere ei quisquam potest: Quare ita facis?" (Ecclesiastes 8:3, 4).

15. Joseph-Marie, comte de Maistre (1753–1821), was a Savoyard lawyer, diplomat, and counter-Enlightenment political thinker of the Napoleonic and Restoration eras, known inter alia for his arguments in favor of capital punishment.

16. Pierre Jurieu (1637–1713) was a French Calvinist pastor, theologian, and pamphleteer.

17. Throughout the nineteenth century in France (as in most of the rest of Europe), suffrage was exclusively male.

18. Renan's note is in Latin in the original: "Idem est presbyter qui episcopus, et antequam diaboli instinctu studia in religione fierent, . . . communi presbyterorum consilio Ecclesiae gubernabantur."

19. Council of Florence (1439–1445).

20. In Latin in the original: "Definimus romano pontifici . . . in beato Petro pascendi, regendi universalem Ecclesiam a Christo plenam potestatem traditam esse."

21. Second Council of Lyon (1272–1274).

22. In Latin in the original: "Ecclesia romana summum et plenum primatum super universalem Ecclesiam catholicam obtinet."

23. Council of Trent (1545–1563).

24. In Latin in the original: "Pontifices maximi, pro suprema potestate sibi in Ecclesia universa tradita."

25. Council of Constance (1414–1418); Council of Basel (1431–1437).

26. The Jansenists represented a rigorist, mainly French Catholic theological movement of the late seventeenth century, opposed to Jesuit casuistry and ultimately condemned by the papacy with the bull *Unigenitus* (1713).

27. Here, Renan appears to be referring to the Civil Constitution of the Clergy, the Revolution's attempt to reorganize the French Catholic Church; it was adopted in the summer of 1790.

28. In Latin in the original: "Si quis in me non manserit, mittetur foras sicut palmes, et arescet, et colligent eum, et in ignem mittent, ET ARDET" (John 15:6)

29. "Compel them to come in" (Luke 14:23) is the scriptural basis for the coercion of heretics, according to Saint Augustine.

30. In Latin in the original: "Infans non debet apud eas remanere personas de quibus potest esse suspicio quod saluti vel vitae insidiantur illius."

31. In Latin in the original: "Judaeorum filios baptizatos, ne parentum involvantur erroribus, ab eorum consortio separari decernimus, deputandos autem monasteriis aut christianis viris, ut in moribus et fide proficiant."

32. Louis XIV (1638–1715) was king of France from 1643 to his death.

33. The Edict of Nantes, granting religious toleration to Huguenots in France, was issued by King Henry IV in 1598 and revoked by King Louis XIV in 1685.

34. Henri-Dominique Lacordaire (1802–1861) was an ecclesiastic, preacher, journalist, and political activist.

35. Saint Ambrose (ca. 340–397) was bishop of Milan and doctor of the Catholic Church.

36. Dioscorus (d. 454), patriarch of Alexandria in 444, was deposed by the Council of Chalcedon but venerated as a saint by the Coptic Church.

37. In Latin in the original: "Tantorum scelerum confessionem . . . virgarum verberibus eruisti. Qui modus correctionis a magistris artium liberalium, et ab ipsis parentibus, et saepe etiam in judiciis solet ab episcopis adhiberi" (S. Aug., Epist. 159 [aliis 133]).

38. Hilary of Poitiers (ca. 310–367) was bishop of Poitiers and doctor of the Catholic Church.

39. Saint Gregory the Great (ca. 540–604) was pope from 590 until his death.

40. Saint Leo the Great (ca. 400–461) was pope from 440 until his death.

41. Jan Hus (1369–1415), a Bohemian religious reformer, was burned at the stake for heresy.

42. "Due to hatred for the author."

43. Nicolas Malebranche (1638–1715) was a rationalist philosopher.

44. This literary masterpiece was written in 1656–1657 by Blaise Pascal in defense of the Jansenist Antoine Arnauld.

## 2. MR. DE SACY AND THE LIBERAL TRADITION
### (M. DE SACY ET L'ÉCOLE LIBÉRALE, 1858)

1. *Journal des débats*, one of the newspapers with the highest circulation in France under the July monarchy, followed a liberal line in politics.

2. Namely, before and after the fall of the liberal Orléanist regime.

3. François Guizot (1787–1874) was a historian and statesman. Active in politics under the July monarchy, he was foreign minister from 1840 to 1848 and prime minister in the six months before the outbreak of the 1848 Revolution.

4. Académie française, founded in 1635, is the preeminent authority of the French literary world. It is composed of forty life members, who are replaced by co-optation.

304 2. MR. DE SACY AND THE LIBERAL TRADITION

5. Antoine-Isaac, baron Silvestre de Sacy (1758–1838), was a linguist and orientalist and perpetual secretary of the Académie des inscriptions from 1832.

6. See note 26 in chapter 1.

7. The Académie des inscriptions et belles-lettres, founded in 1663, is one of the five sections of the Institut de France (along with the Académie française).

8. Jean Duvergier de Hauranne, abbot of Saint-Cyran (1581–1643), introduced Jansenism into France.

9. Pasquier Quesnel (1634–1719) was a French Jansenist theologian.

10. Charles Le Beau (1701–1778) was a historian of late antiquity and a member of the Académie des inscriptions.

11. Charles Rollin (1661–1741) was a historian of antiquity and a pedagogue.

12. A 1514 allegorical engraving by German Renaissance artist Albrecht Dürer (1471–1528).

13. Johannes Tauler (1300–1361) was a German mystic, disciple of Meister Eckhart, and member of the Dominican order.

14. Henry Suso (d. 1366), a German Dominican friar, was beatified by the Catholic Church in 1831.

15. Niels Henrik Abel (1802–1829) was a Norwegian mathematician.

16. "Food and clothing."

17. A desert in upper Egypt in which Anthony the Great, the first Christian hermit, lived in the late third and early fourth centuries.

18. Hindu religious texts from the second millennium BCE, forming the oldest stratum of Sanskrit literature.

19. A medieval Latin hymn, generally dated to the thirteenth century.

20. Jean-Baptiste de Santeul (1630–1697) was a French poet in Latin and author of hymns.

21. Nicolas Boileau-Despréaux (1636–1711) was a French poet and critic, as well as the chief theorist of poetics of the French classical age.

22. Port-Royal-des-Champs, an abbey on the outskirts of Paris, was the center of diffusion of Jansenism.

23. "This once helped me as a child" (Boileau, *Satira I*, 3).

24. Francus, a legendary eponymous king of the Franks, was an invention of the High Middle Ages, with a distinguished literary tradition from the seventh-century *Chronicle of Fredegar* to Pierre de Ronsard's *Franciade* (1572).

25. Henri de Boulainvilliers (1658–1722), a French historian, interpreted the division between aristocrats and commoners as the result of a difference of race between the invading Franks and the conquered Gallo-Roman population in the High Middle Ages.

26. An oxen-drawn cart employed by the city-republics of Italy during the Middle Ages to carry their standard into battle.

27. Philip IV (1268–1314) was king of France from 1285 to his death.

28. Louis XI (1423–1483) was king of France from 1461 to his death.

29. Cardinal Armand Jean du Plessis, Duke of Richelieu and Fronsac (1585–1642), was chief minister of King Louis XIII from 1624 to his death.

30. See note 32 in chapter 1.

31. A classic of Chinese political and organizational thought, now generally dated to the third century BCE.

32. One of the five sections of the Institut de France, founded in 1795.

33. Qianlong was the sixth emperor of the Qing dynasty (reigned 1735–1796).

34. Diocletian (244–311), emperor of Rome from 284 to 305, ended the crisis of the third century by reforming the administration and taxation of the Empire in an absolutist direction.

35. The Convention nationale (September 1792–October 1795) was the legislative body that governed France at the height of the Revolution and proclaimed the First Republic.

36. Since 1829, the French Ministry of Education has been located in the Hôtel de Rochechouart at 110 rue de Grenelle.

37. A series of emperors in the mid-second century CE whose peaceful and benevolent reign marked the apogee of the empire.

38. "Roman world."

39. Stoicism was a school of philosophy of antiquity, stressing duty, fortitude, and the immanent order of the cosmos, largely adopted as the ethos of the senatorial class under the Roman Empire.

40. Quintus Aurelius Symmachus (ca. 345–402), a Roman statesman and orator, was a defender of paganism.

41. Severinus Boethius (480–524) was a Roman statesman and philosopher. He entered public service under the Ostrogothic king Theodoric the Great but was later imprisoned and executed on charges of conspiracy. His great philosophical treatise, the *Consolation of Philosophy*, was composed in jail.


## 3. THE PHILOSOPHY OF CONTEMPORARY HISTORY
### (*PHILOSOPHIE DE L'HISTOIRE CONTEMPORAINE*, 1859)

1. See note 3 in chapter 2.

2. John 8:7.

3. Charles Augustin Sainte-Beuve (1804–1869) was the most influential literary critic in nineteenth-century France.

4. Jules Michelet (1798–1874) was a French historian and author of *History of the French Revolution*.

5. Victor Cousin (1792–1867) was a French philosopher.

6. See chapter 2.

7. François-René, vicomte de Chateaubriand (1768–1848), French writer and politician, was considered the founder of Romanticism in French letters.

8. See note 15 in chapter 1.

9. Hugues-Félicité Robert de Lamennais (1782–1854) was a Catholic priest and political theorist.

10. Jacques Nicolas Augustin Thierry (1795–1856) was a French historian.

11.  Jean de Joinville (1224–1317) was a biographer of Louis IX of France.

12.  Louis IX (1214–1270), king of France from 1226 to his death, was canonized in 1297.

13.  See note 10 in chapter 1.

14.  Theodosius I (347–395) was emperor of Rome from 379 to his death.

15.  Gregory VII (ca. 1015–1085), pope from 1073, canonized in 1728, was a key figure in the investiture controversy.

16.  Charles V of Valois (1338–1380) was king of France from 1364, during the Hundred Years' War.

17.  Georg Gottfried Gervinus (1805–1871) was a German historian.

18.  See note 27 in chapter 2.

19.  See note 32 in chapter 1.

20.  These were associations with political and religious functions between city-states in ancient Greece. Amphictyon, son of Deucalion, mythical ancestor of Hellenic people, was said to have founded them.

21.  The *Charte*, granted by Louis XVIII in June 1814, was the linchpin of the legal system of the Bourbon Restoration.

22.  Louis XVIII (1755–1824) was king of France from 1814.

23.  See note 28 in chapter 2.

24.  Judicial courts of the ancien régime; though the offices were venal, the institution was often perceived as a counterweight to the absolute power of the French monarchy.

25.  Charles X (1757–1836), the last Bourbon king of France, reigned from the death of his brother Louis XVIII to the July 1830 Revolution.

26.  Jules, third duke of Polignac (1780–1847), was prime minister of France from August 1829 until the July 1830 Revolution.

27.  Also known as the Ordinances of Saint-Cloud, after the royal residence where they were signed; they were the attempt by Charles X to overcome liberal parliamentary opposition to the Polignac government by restricting constitutionally guaranteed freedoms.

28.  Louis-Philippe of Orléans (1773–1850) was king of the French from 1830 to 1848.

29.  The city hall building in Paris was the epicenter of revolutionary activity in 1830.

30.  Gilbert du Motier, marquis de Lafayette (1757–1834), was a military commander during the American Revolutionary War and a key figure in the French Revolutions of 1789 and 1830.

31.  See note 33 in chapter 1.

32.  This form of religious persecution, adopted in 1681, consisted in billeting troops in Protestant households with the implicit permission to wreak havoc.

33.  Chief magistrates in medieval Italian city-states, who were typically not natives in order to guarantee impartiality.

34.  Joseph Fouché (1759–1820) was head of police under Napoleon.

35.  Matthew 16:25.

36.  Three great philosophical schools of ancient Greece (the Platonic, Aristotelian, and Stoic, respectively).

37.  In English in the original.

38.  The 1848 Revolution began with a "banquet campaign," a form of struggle adopted to circumvent legal restrictions on the freedom of assembly.

39.  Presumably a reference to Tocqueville's *L'ancien régime et le Révolution*.

40.  See note 29 in chapter 2.

## 4. THE ROLE OF THE FAMILY AND THE STATE IN EDUCATION (*LA PART DE LA FAMILLE ET DE L'ÉTAT DANS L'ÉDUCATION*, 1869)

1.   In a central passage of the speech, Renan distinguishes *instruction*, the transfer of factual knowledge to the pupil, from *éducation*, the formation of the pupil's moral personality. In this case, the former is translated as "schooling" and the latter as "education." However, Renan also uses the term *instruction* more loosely elsewhere, in locutions such as *instruction publique*, which have been rendered with the usual English expression of "public education."

2.   See note 13 in chapter 1.

3.   Lazare Hippolyte Carnot (1801–1888) was a Republican politician and minister of public education under the Second Republic (1848).

4.   Johann Gottfried von Herder (1744–1803) was a poet, theologian, and philosopher.

5.   Charles Ernest Beulé (1826–1874) was a renowned archaeologist and future minister of the interior (1873).

6.   Marcus Cocceius Nerva (30–98 CE) was emperor of Rome from 96 to 98.

7.   Marcus Aurelius Antoninus (121–180 CE) was a stoic philosopher and emperor of Rome from 161 to 180.

8.   Philip II Augustus (1165–1223) was king of France from 1180 to 1223.

9.   Louis VII the Younger (1120–1180) was king of the Franks from 1137 to 1180.

10.  Suger of Saint-Denis (ca. 1080–1151), abbot and statesman, was regent of France from 1147 to 1149.

11.  Pierre Abelard (1079–1142) was a theologian and nominalist philosopher.

12.  Charles-Maurice de Talleyrand-Périgord (1754–1838) was a statesman and diplomat.

13.  Nicolas de Caritat, marquis de Condorcet (1743–1794), was a mathematician, Enlightenment philosopher, and politician.

14.  Alphonse de Lamartine (1790–1869) was a Romantic writer and politician, who served as minister of foreign affairs under the Second Republic (1848).

15.  Adolphe Thiers (1797–1877) was a lawyer, journalist, historian, and statesman, who went on to serve as president of the Third Republic from 1871 to 1873.

16.  John Chrysostom (ca. 344–407) was an archbishop of Constantinople and father of the Church.

17.  Libanius (314–393) was a Greek-language rhetorician and sophist.

18.  The Lycée Louis-le-Grand, one of the most prestigious secondary schools in Paris, was founded by the Jesuit Order in 1563 as the Collège de Clermont and was nationalized in the late eighteenth century.

## 5. CONSTITUTIONAL MONARCHY IN FRANCE
## (*LA MONARCHIE CONSTITUTIONNELLE EN FRANCE*, 1869)

1.   This anecdote is famously discussed in Pascal's *Pensées*.
2.   See note 35 in chapter 2.
3.   The Consulate was the regime that ruled France, under the authoritarian constitution of the year VIII, from Napoleon's coup of 1799 against the Directory to the proclamation of the Empire in 1804.
4.   The collegial regime that ruled France after the Terror, 1795–1799.
5.   Anne Robert Jacques Turgot, baron de l'Aulne (1727–1781), was an economist and statesman. In his role as controller-general of finances (1774–1776) and in his *Réflexions sur la formation et la distribution des richesses* (1776), he advocated for economic liberalization in response to the financial crisis of the kingdom of France.
6.   The descendants of Hugh Capet, the dynasty ruling France from 987 to 1328.
7.   See note 12 in chapter 3.
8.   Refers to the day in 1793 when Louis XVI was guillotined.
9.   See note 13 in chapter 1.
10.   See note 32 in chapter 1.
11.   See note 29 in chapter 2.
12.   The *Great Eastern* steamboat, launched in 1838, was, in its time, the biggest vessel afloat; it was plagued by a series of malfunctions and misadventures.
13.   See note 28 in chapter 3.
14.   William III of Orange (1650–1702) became king of England as a consequence of the Glorious Revolution of 1688.
15.   The restoration of the English monarchy in 1660 following the Cromwellian Commonwealth.
16.   Alludes to the revolt in the Vendée region in 1796, led by François de Charette and Jean-Nicolas Stofflet with English assistance, and the renewed strength of the Royalists in the Council of 500, which led to the Fructidor coup by the Directory against the Council in 1797.
17.   Louis-Philippe's father, Louis-Philippe Joseph, duc d'Orléans (1747–1793), had renounced his title and assumed the name Philippe Égalité. He voted for death at the trial of Louis XVI.
18.   Penal colonies in French Guiana and Algeria, respectively, where political prisoners were deported.
19.   See note 38 in chapter 3.
20.   Refers to the day in 1848 when Louis-Napoléon Bonaparte was elected president of the Republic.
21.   In Latin in the text: "Quis tulerit Gracchos de seditione querentes?"
22.   Matthew 26:52.
23.   Paul Jean Pierre Sauzet (1800–1876) was president of the lower chamber of Parliament from 1839 to the fall of the July Monarchy.
24.   Refers to the day of Louis-Napoléon's coup against the Second Republic.

25. In Latin in the original: "Excidat illa dies aevo, nec postera credant / Saecula; nos etiam taceamus, et oblita multa / Nocte tegi nostrae patiamur crimina gentis." Renan slightly paraphrases Statius, *Silvae*, book V.2, "Laudes Crispini Vetti Bolani Filii," verses 88–90.

26. In the Crimean War (1853–1856), France joined England and the Kingdom of Sardinia to check Russian encroachment on the territorial integrity of the Ottoman Empire.

27. In 1859, France supported the Kingdom of Sardinia in a campaign against Austria, which ultimately resulted in the unification of Italy. In exchange for its assistance, France obtained Nice and the Savoy from the Kingdom of Sardinia.

28. "Drunk among the sober."

29. "Sister republics" were set up by the French government in territories conquered by the revolutionary armies in the late 1790s.

30. See note 3 in chapter 3.

31. The two ruling families of Milan from the late thirteenth to the early sixteenth century.

32. "The Fates will find their way" (Virgil, *Aeneid*, X.113).

33. Two of the most radicalized working-class neighborhoods in Paris.

34. France's military academy.

35. *Chassepots* were the standard-issue rifles of the French army.

36. See note 33 in chapter 3.

37. Literally, "Lent"; a torture method invented by Galeazzo II Visconti (ca. 1320–1378) designed to keep the victim alive for forty days.

38. The ruling family of the ancient Persian Empire.

39. Three revolutions of the 1860s (Greece, 1862; Mexico, 1867; Spain, 1868), which resulted in the expulsion or execution of monarchs.

40. Governments under the Second Empire customarily indicated a candidate in each constituency in legislative elections as "official," and the local representatives of the central authorities (prefects, subprefects, and so forth) employed different forms of "administrative pressure" in order to facilitate his election.

41. The electoral body of the July Monarchy was selected exclusively on the basis of wealth. One of the key reforms advocated by the Left-wing opposition was the enlargement of the suffrage to certain categories (such as military officers, professors, and so forth) on the basis of their social function—their "capacity"—irrespective of income.

42. Prince Jérôme Napoléon (1822–1891), cousin of Napoleon III, represented the democratic and anticlerical wing of the Napoleonic party under the Second Empire.

43. See note 41 in chapter 2.

## 6. THE WAR BETWEEN FRANCE AND GERMANY
### (*LA GUERRE ENTRE LA FRANCE ET L'ALLEMAGNE*, 1870)

1. The Carolingian emperor Charles the Fat (d. 888) was the great-grandson of Charlemagne.

2. Signed in 843, the Treaty of Verdun settled the succession of Louis the Pious, son of Charlemagne. The Carolingian Empire was divided into three parts: the eastern portion was assigned to Louis the German, the central portion (comprising the Low Countries, Lorraine, Alsace, Burgundy, Provence, and northern Italy) to Lothair, the western portion to Charles the Bald.

3. The Capetian dynasty.

4. See note 32 in chapter 1.

5. The line of the Hohenstaufen emperors became extinguished in 1268.

6. The Thirty Years' War was a devastating religious war in central Europe (1618–1648).

7. Heinrich Friedrich Karl, Baron vom Stein (1757–1831), was a Prussian statesman.

8. The battle of Jena was a decisive victory by Napoleon over Prussia (1806).

9. Or the Battle of the Nations (1813), won by the Sixth Coalition over the French, ending Napoleonic rule in Germany.

10. The Terror (September 1793–July 1794) was a radical phase of mass violence during the French Revolution.

11. An allusion to the conservative, Catholic region of the west of France that rebelled against the revolutionary government in the 1790s.

12. See note 28 in chapter 3.

13. A possible allusion to Alfred de Musset's poem *Le Rhin Allemand* (1841), written in response to Nikolaus Becker's *Die Wacht am Rhein*.

14. The Frankfurt Parliament, which sat from May 1848 to May 1849 as a consequence of the German revolutions of March 1848.

15. The sentence is Bismarck's.

16. See note 27 in chapter 5.

17. A reference to the idea expressed by Vincenzo Gioberti (1801–1852) in his *Primato morale e civile degli italiani* (1843) that Italy enjoyed a primacy among nations.

18. The body established in 1815 to replace the Holy Roman Empire, of which Austria was the leading member.

19. See note 30 in chapter 3.

20. A decisive victory of Prussia over Austria (1866).

21. Meeting between Napoleon III and Bismarck in September 1865 in which the issue of Luxemburg was mooted.

22. See note 15 in chapter 4.

23. The crown prince of Prussia, Frederick (1831–1888), and his wife, Victoria (1840–1901), daughter of the British empress Victoria, were known for their liberal and antimilitarist sympathies.

24. Proverbial expression to denote a prolonged absence leading to bewilderment at the change of conditions: Epimenides the Cretan, a late seventh century BCE philosopher and poet, was said to have slept for fifty-seven years in a cavern.

25. The Ems telegram from the king of Prussia to Bismarck on the crisis concerning the candidature of Leopold of Hohenzollern to the throne of Spain was the incident that precipitated the Franco-Prussian War.

26. See note 20 in chapter 3.

27. The Prussian territorial militia.
28. "Woe to the vanquishers," an inversion of the famous *vae victis* ("woe to the vanquished"), traditionally attributed to the Gaul chief Brennus when dictating the terms of peace with Rome in 390 BCE.

## 7. TWO LETTERS TO MR. STRAUSS
### (*LETTRE & NOUVELLE LETTRE À M. STRAUSS*, 1870-1871)

1. Chapter 6 in this anthology.
2. The empire of Napoleon I (1804–1815).
3. See note 20 in chapter 6.
4. See note 27 in chapter 5.
5. Krak des Chevaliers.
6. "Be you rich, / Be you wise, / Be you handsome; / Pride alone / Besmirches all / If it accompanies it."
7. See note 25 in chapter 6.
8. See note 28 in chapter 3.
9. An allusion to Strauss's book *Voltaire: Sechs Vorträge* (Leipzig: G. Hirzel, 1870).
10. Theodor Mommsen (1817–1903) was a philologist and historian of antiquity.
11. Prussia had insisted that an election be called in France following the fall of Napoleon III to guarantee the legitimacy of the government conducting the peace negotiations.
12. The Lower House of the legislative branch under the constitution of the Second Empire.
13. These two towns were taken from France in the rectification of the border following the Hundred Days (1815).
14. Helmuth von Moltke (1800–1891) was chief of staff of the Prussian army.
15. In the War of the First Coalition against revolutionary France.
16. "We and our works are destined for death," Horace, *Ars poetica*, 63.
17. "Love as though you might hate."
18. Frederick the Great (1712–1786), king of Prussia from 1740, was known for his Enlightenment cosmopolitanism as much as for his military prowess.
19. Victory of Frederick the Great over the French under the prince of Soubise in 1757, during the Seven Years' War.
20. See note 2 in chapter 6.
21. The marriage in 1477 resulted in the incorporation of the Low Countries into the Habsburg domains.
22. Revelation 12:4.
23. The Obotrites and Veleti were medieval Slavic tribes that settled in northern Germany.
24. Modern-day Poznan.
25. The amount of the war indemnity agreed by France in the Treaty of Frankfurt (1871).
26. "There is neither Jew nor Greek" (Galatians 3:28).
27. Saint Boniface (675–754), originally from Wessex in Anglo-Saxon England, was instrumental in the introduction of Christianity in the Germanic part of the empire of the Franks.

28. See note 8 in chapter 6.

29. See note 20 in chapter 3.

30. Following the occupation of Rome by the Kingdom of Italy in September 1870, the governments of Catholic countries were pressured by the papacy to restore its temporal rule.

31. The west of France was traditionally the most staunchly Catholic and conservative area of the country.

32. Georg Herwegh (1817–1875).

33. The verse Renan appears to be referring to is the refrain from Herwegh's "Das Lied vom Hasse" (1841): "Wir haben lang genug geliebt, / Und wollen endlich hassen!" ("We have loved long enough / And finally wish to hate!").

34. Ecclesiastes 3:5.

35. Renan here gives a free rendering of Aeschylus, *Prometheus Bound*, verses 915–927.

## 8. INTELLECTUAL AND MORAL REFORM OF FRANCE
### (*LA RÉFORME INTELLECTUELLE ET MORALE DE LA FRANCE*, 1871)

1. This preface introduced the book version of the *Réforme*, which contained, in addition to the eponymous text, "The War Between France and Germany," the two letters to Strauss, "The Constitutional Monarchy in France," and a slightly edited version of "The Role of the Family and of the State in Education" (chapters 4 through 7 of the present volume), as well as "De la convocation d'une assemblée pendant le siège" (not included in this anthology).

2. The anecdote is drawn from Flavius Josephus (*Bellum Iudaicum*, VI.299–309).

3. The period between the return of the Bourbon monarchs after the defeat of Napoleon and the July Revolution (1814–1830).

4. See note 5 in chapter 5.

5. Chapters 4 and 5 of the present volume.

6. Chapters 6 and 7 of the present volume.

7. Better known as Albrecht von Wallenstein (1583–1634), was a Habsburg general during the Thirty Years' War; his army was infamous for its depredations.

8. "Denying laws exist for him" (Horace, *Ars poetica*, 122).

9. François, duc de la Rochefoucauld (1613–1680), was a writer and politician, notable for his epigrammatic *Maxims*.

10. Louis de Rouvroy, duc de Saint-Simon (1675–1755), was a soldier, diplomat, and courtier; his *Memoirs* were much admired for their tone and scope.

11. Charles de Marguetel de Saint-Denis, seigneur de Saint-Évremond (1613–1703), was an essayist and literary critic.

12. Marie de Rabutin-Chantal, marquise de Sévigné (1626–1696), was an aristocrat famed for her correspondence.

13. Louise de la Vallière (1644–1710) was a favorite of Louis XIV.

14. Anne "Ninon" de l'Enclos (1620–1705) was an author, freethinker, and patron of the arts.

15. Amantine-Lucile-Aurore Dupin (1804–1876) was a novelist writing with the pseudonym George Sand.

16. See note 3 in chapter 3.

17. See note 4 in chapter 3.

18. Émile Littré (1801–1881), lexicographer, philosopher, and physician, wrote the famous *Dictionary of the French Language*. He became one of the chief intellectual supporters of the Third Republic and sat in parliament as a conservative republican in the 1870s.

19. "Nothing under the sun remains unchanged."

20. On September 4, 1870, following the defeat at Sedan, the regime of Napoleon III was overthrown in Paris.

21. In 1792, the French revolutionary army stopped the invasion of the troops of the First Coalition of European Powers at the battle of Valmy.

22. See note 32 in chapter 1.

23. "Be wise now therefore, O ye kings" (Psalms 2:10), quoted by Jacques-Bénigne Bossuet in his *Funeral Oration for Henriette-Marie de France* (1669).

24. See note 6 in chapter 5.

25. See note 27 in chapter 2.

26. See note 24 in chapter 3.

27. See note 29 in chapter 2.

28. Claude Fleury (1640–1723), Cistercian abbot and church historian, was a member of the Académie française and confessor of King Louis XIV.

29. Honoré Gabriel Riqueti, comte de Mirabeau (1749–1791), was an aristocrat, politician, member of the Jacobin club, popular leader in the early stages of the French Revolution, and supporter of a constitutional monarchy on the English model.

30. Refers to the Girondin party.

31. The Merovingian dynasty ruled the Franks from the middle of the fifth to the middle of the eighth century CE. King Clovis I (ca. 466–511) first united all the Frankish tribes under one ruler and converted to Christianity in 496.

32. The successor dynasty to the Merovingians, achieving power in the late eighth century with Charles Martel and Pepin the Short, whose son, Charlemagne, was crowned Holy Roman Emperor in 800.

33. See note 2 in chapter 6.

34. Humbert II de la Tour-du-Pin (1312–1355) was dauphin of the Viennois from 1333 to 1349.

35. See note 28 in chapter 2.

36. Palamède de Forbin (1433–1508) was instrumental in the transferal of the estates of René d'Anjou to Louis XI, who then appointed him governor of Provence in 1481.

37. See note 27 in chapter 3.

38. "One should distrust an interpretation when the speaker could have expressed himself more clearly."

39. See note 26 in chapter 3.

40. See note 5 in chapter 3.

41. The coup d'état of December 2, 1851, which was carried out by President Louis-Napoléon Bonaparte, forcibly dissolved the National Assembly. Under the new constitution (January 14, 1852), the tenure of the president was prolonged for ten years. One year later (December 1852), the Second Empire was proclaimed.

42. Hippolyte Fortoul (1811–1856) was minister of education from 1851 to his death.

43. "Mole, or wart."

44. See note 26 in chapter 5.

45. See note 27 in chapter 5.

46. John II (1319–1364), king of France from 1350 to his death, was taken prisoner at the battle of Poitiers in 1356.

47. Charles VII (1403–1461) became king of France in 1422, during the latter stages of the Hundred Years' War.

48. Francis I (1494–1547), king of France from 1515, was taken prisoner at the battle of Pavia in 1525.

49. See note 8 in chapter 6.

50. See note 28 in chapter 3.

51. See note 34 in chapter 5.

52. Richard Cobden (1804–1865) was an English radical and free-trade liberal politician.

53. William Pitt the Younger (1759–1806) was prime minister of the United Kingdom during the Napoleonic era.

54. Robert Stewart, later 2nd Marquess of Londonderry (1769–1822), was the foreign secretary who represented Britain at the Congress of Vienna in 1815.

55. Arthur Wellesley, 1st Duke of Wellington (1769–1852), was the victor of Waterloo.

56. "The end of France."

57. Lucien-Anatole Prévost-Paradol (1829–1870) was a liberal publicist and member of the Académie française.

58. In the French administrative system, the prefect is the representative of the central government in the various *départements*.

59. This law of April 26, 1855, permitted conscripted Frenchmen to avoid military service by paying a special tax; it amended previous legislation dating back to 1798 (the *loi Jourdan*), which permitted conscripts to avoid the draft by supplying another able-bodied male to replace them on the basis of a private contract stipulating monetary compensation for the replacer.

60. See note 27 in chapter 6.

61. See note 20 in chapter 5.

62. Perhaps an allusion to Prince Jérôme Napoléon.

63. Two of the Grandes Écoles, public establishments of higher learning founded in the late eighteenth century and dedicated, respectively, to engineering and teacher training.

64. "Sheep that have not a shepherd" (1 Kings 22:17).

65. Eugène Rouher (1814–1884), minister of state (1863–1869), was one of the principal leaders of the dominant, conservative wing of the Bonapartist party.

66. See note 13 in chapter 4.

67. See note 20 in chapter 6.

68. The North German Confederation came into being as a result of the 1866 war, in place of the German Confederation of 1815. It was hegemonized by Prussia.

69. This occupation aimed to protect the pope against Garibaldi's designs of annexing Rome to Italy.

70. This foreign venture (1861–1867) of the Second Empire was intended to project France's influence to the Americas (in the context of the U.S. Civil War) by installing Maximilian of Habsburg as emperor of Mexico.

71. The area corresponding to the northern shores of the Black Sea, which for classical antiquity represented the locus of barbarism.

72. See note 12 in chapter 7.

73. Gebhard Leberecht von Blücher (1742–1819) was the Prussian commander at Waterloo.

74. Gerhard von Scharnhorst (1755–1813) led the reorganization of the Prussian military after the battle of Jena.

75. These two texts (Περὶ τῆς Ἀλεξάνδρου τύχης ἢ ἀρετῆς, Περὶ τῆς Ῥωμαίων τύχης) appear in book IV of Plutarch's *Moralia*.

76. The day the Paris Commune was proclaimed.

77. The war indemnity agreed at the Peace of Frankfurt was speedily paid by means of a loan raised by the Thiers government.

78. Alliance treaty between France and Russia (1807) that cost the Kingdom of Prussia about half of its territories.

79. See note 7 in chapter 6.

80. 1 Corinthians 7:31.

81. Types of nineteenth-century firearms, distinguished by their ignition mechanism and effective range.

82. See note 14 in chapter 7.

83. See note 19 in chapter 7.

84. 1848.

85. "Hercules at the Crossroads" is a work on the choice between virtue and vice attributed by Xenophon (*Memor.* II.1.21–34) to the sophist Prodicus of Ceos (ca. 465–395 BCE).

86. Friedrich Carl von Savigny (1779–1861) was a German jurist and historian.

87. At the death of Charles IV (1328), the collateral line of Philippe of Valois was chosen over direct descent through the maternal line (King Edward III of England) on the basis of the Salic law. This was confirmed by a pronouncement of the jurists of the Sorbonne.

88. "Knight."

89. In English in the original.

90. "Art thou also become weak as we? Art thou become like unto us?" (Isaiah 14:10).

91. Probably a reference to the law of May 31, 1850, by which the Second French Republic tightened the prerequisites for inclusion on the electoral roll (lengthening the residency requirements), thereby shrinking the electorate by a third.

92. The Institut de France, which is divided into several classes (Académie française, Académie des inscriptions, etc.).

93. "To rule mankind, and make the world obey" (Virgil, *Aeneid*, VI.851).

94.    "Sacred spring": a religious practice of ancient Italic tribes related to the creation of new colonies by the expulsion of children born in a particular time of the year.

95.    Frédéric Ozanam (1813–1853), a liberal Catholic scholar, was a cofounder of the Society of Saint Vincent de Paul (1833).

96.    Charles Jean Marie Loyson (1827–1912), better known by his religious name Père Hyacinthe, was a French preacher who was excommunicated in 1869 for his opposition to papal infallibility.

97.    The First Vatican Council (1869–1870), which enshrined the doctrine of papal infallibility.

98.    The Western Schism began in 1378 and ended with the Council of Constance in 1417; rival claimants to the papacy reigned in Rome and in Avignon.

99.    The Antipope Benedict XIII, born Pedro Martínez de Luna, had repaired to the fortress of Peñíscola, near Tortosa (Kingdom of Aragon), before being excommunicated by the Council of Constance in 1417; he lived out his days there to 1423.

100.    "Oh, the great goodness of ancient knights!" *Orlando Furioso*, 1:22 (in Ariosto, the expression is ironic).

101.    Generally identified as Septimius Severus (145–211), Roman emperor from 193 CE.

102.    "All was worthless."

103.    "To work!"

## 9. WHAT IS A NATION? (*QU'EST-CE QU'UNE NATION?* 1882)

This chapter reproduces the text of a lecture given at the Sorbonne on March 11, 1882.

1.    The Ancient Persian Empire (550–330 BCE).

2.    The Gallic Empire (260–274 CE) was formed by breakaway provinces of the Roman Empire in the course of the crisis of the third century.

3.    See note 2 in chapter 6.

4.    Saint Gregory (ca. 538–594), bishop of Tours, was a historian of Merovingian France.

5.    Hugh Capet (941–996) was King of the Franks from 987.

6.    The lands belonging to the Habsburgs in virtue of their title as kings of Hungary, comprising parts of modern-day Croatia, Poland, Romania, Serbia, Slovenia, Slovakia, Austria, and Ukraine, as well as Hungary.

7.    A massacre of Protestants throughout France, begun on Saint Bartholomew's Day, August 24, 1572, which caused up to 30,000 casualties.

8.    For instance, the Cathar Crusade (1209–1229).

9.    See note 8 in chapter 4.

10.    See note 23 in chapter 7.

11.    The Ottonian dynasty founded the Holy Roman Empire in the tenth century CE.

12.    Alba Longa was the leading city of the Latin League, founded, according to legend, by Ascanius, son of Aeneas.

13.    A reference to the draft lottery for military service.

14.    Antiochus IV Epiphanes (ca. 215–164 BCE), ruler of the Seleucid Empire from 175 to his death, ordered a persecution of the Jews and defeated the Maccabean revolt.

15. Belgium was formed in 1830 by the secession of the Catholic south from the United Kingdom of the Netherlands that had issued from the Congress of Vienna.

16. A customs union, such as the one established by Prussia in Germany in the 1830s.

17. That is to say along the northern coast of the European continent from the French-Spanish border to the Finnish-Swedish one (which, in Renan's time, was the Russian-Swedish border).

## 10. ISLAM AND SCIENCE
### (*L'ISLAMISME ET LA SCIENCE*, 1883)

This chapter reproduces the text of a lecture given at the Sorbonne on March 29th, 1883.

1. Also known as Gregory Bar Hebraeus (1226–1286), bishop of the Syriac Orthodox Church.

2. Abu Bakr, Umar, Uthman, and Ali guided the Islamic Ummah from the death of Mohammad (632) to the rise of the Umayyad dynasty (661).

3. The Umayyad Caliphate ruled the Islamic world from 661 to 750.

4. The Abbasid dynasty ruled until the Mongol invasion of 1258.

5. The Sassanian Empire ruled Persia and large parts of the Near East from 224 to 651 CE.

6. Khosrow I (501–579) Anushiruwan ("the immortal soul") was "king of kings" of the Sassanian Empire from 531 to his death.

7. The Byzantine Emperor Justinian ordered the Neoplatonic school of Athens closed in 529 CE.

8. The mythological hero of the Persian epic *Shahnameh*.

9. Abu al-'Abbas (721–754).

10. Al-Mansur (714–775) reigned from 754 and founded Baghdad in 762.

11. See note 32 in chapter 8.

12. Harun al-Rashid (763–809) ruled from 786.

13. Al-Ma'mun (786–833) was caliph from 813.

14. Reinhart Dozy (1820–1883) was a Dutch orientalist.

15. Kairouan was a town in central Tunisia famed as a center of Islamic learning.

16. Al-Kindi (ca. 801–873) was a philosopher, mathematician, physician, and polymath born in Basra.

17. Al-Farabi (ca. 872–c. 950) was a philosopher, jurist, cosmologist and mathematician from central Asia.

18. Ibn Sina (ca. 980–1037) was a Persian polymath born in Bukhara.

19. Ibn Bajja, or Avempace (ca. 1085–1138), was an astronomer, philosopher, and physician born in Zaragoza.

20. Ibn Tufail (ca. 1105–1185) was a philosopher, theologian, astronomer, and courtier from Andalusia. He was a pupil of Avempace.

21. Ibn Rushd (1126–1198) was a philosopher, theologian, mathematician, and physician born in Córdoba.

22. Basilios Bessarion (1403–1472), as a member of the Byzantine delegation to the Council of Ferrara, contributed to the revival of classical scholarship in the west.

23. Janus Lascaris (ca. 1445–1535) was a Greek scholar who, after the fall of Constantinople to the Ottomans, helped disseminate the knowledge of ancient Greek authors in Renaissance Italy.

24. See note 11 in chapter 4.

25. A hill on the Left Bank of the Seine, in Paris, where the Latin Quarter is located.

26. The Fourth Crusade (1202–1204), intended to recapture Jerusalem, instead culminated, through a series of events, in the sacking of Constantinople by the Crusaders.

27. Jacques Lefèvre d'Étaples (ca. 1455–1536) was a French humanist.

28. Guillaume Budé (1467–1540), French scholar, was instrumental in the founding of the Collège de France.

29. Gerbert d'Aurillac (ca. 946–1003) was pope under the name Sylvester II from 999.

30. Constantine the African (d. 1098) was a Benedictine monk at the abbey of Monte Cassino and a physician.

31. Francis Raymond de Sauvetât, a French Benedictine monk, was archbishop of Toledo from 1125 to 1152.

32. Ibn Khaldun (1332–1406) was a historiographer born in Tunis.

33. The western region of Arabia containing Mecca and Medina.

34. Al-Battani (ca. 858–929) was an astronomer and mathematician born in Harran.

35. Albertus Magnus (ca. 1200–1280), German Dominican friar, bishop of Regensburg, and teacher of Thomas Aquinas, was canonized and proclaimed Doctor of the Church in 1931.

36. Roger Bacon (ca. 1219–1292) was an English Franciscan friar and philosopher.

37. The dynasties descendant from Ali, the fourth Caliph.

38. Philip II (1527–1598), king of Spain from 1556, fought protracted wars to uphold Catholic orthodoxy.

39. Antonio Ghislieri (1504–1572), Pope Pius V from 1566, presided over the first stages of the Counter-Reformation.

40. Ibn Zuhr (1094–1162) was a physician born in Seville.

41. Rifa'a al-Tahtawi (1801–1873) was one of the forerunners of Islamic modernism.

42. Sir Austen Henry Layard (1817–1894) was the British archaeologist who excavated Nimrud.

43. A traditional Islamic judge.

44. See note 1 in chapter 2.

45. Bede (ca. 673–735) was an English monk and author of the *Historia ecclesiastica gentis Anglorum*.

46. Alcuin of York (ca. 735–804) was one of the chief scholars of the Carolingian Renaissance.

47. See note 4 in chapter 9.


# 11. ORIGINAL UNITY AND GRADUAL SEPARATION OF JUDAISM AND CHRISTIANITY (*IDENTITÉ ORIGINELLE ET SÉPARATION GRADUELLE DU JUDAÏSME ET DU CHRISTIANISME*, 1883)

This chapter reproduces, from a stenographic transcript, a lecture given at the Society for Jewish Studies on May 26, 1883

1. The Mesha Stele, or Moabite Stone, erected around 840 BCE by Mesha, king of Moab, was discovered by Frederick Augustus Klein in Jordan in 1868.
2. Literally, "be the *ger* of."
3. The Jewish revolt against Roman rule precipitated the siege of Jerusalem and the destruction of the Temple in 70 CE.
4. The Gospels of Matthew, Mark, and Luke.
5. Marcion of Sinope (ca. 85–c. 160).
6. Papias (ca. 70–c. 163) was bishop of Hierapolis.
7. A rabbinic text incorporating historical anecdote, moral exhortation, and practical advice.
8. Melito of Sardis (d. ca. 180).
9. Polycarp (69–155), bishop of Smyrna, was a Christian martyr and father of the church.
10. A region and ancient kingdom in central Anatolia.
11. Clement of Alexandria (ca. 150–c. 215) was a Christian theologian and father of the church.
12. Origen (184–253) was a pupil of Clement of Alexandria.
13. See note 10 in chapter 1.
14. See note 16 in chapter 4.
15. This is a reference to a speech entitled "Le judaïsme comme race et comme religion" ("Judaism as race and religion"), given at the Cercle Saint-Simon on January 27, 1883, that is, four months prior to this speech. It has recently been republished in Shlomo Sand (ed.), *On the Nation and the "Jewish People,"* trans. David Fernbach (London: Verso, 2010).
16. The Disputation of Paris (1240) at the court of Louis IX, between a Franciscan convert from Judaism and four prominent rabbis, ended in 1244 with the condemnation and public burning of the Talmud.
17. See note 27 in chapter 2.
18. Adolf Neubauer (1831–1907) was an expert in rabbinical Hebrew who discovered the documents relative to the auto-da-fé of Troyes in the Vatican Library. He is thanked by Renan in the introduction to the *Vie de Jésus* for his assistance on questions of Talmudic interpretation.
19. A Jewish sect that flourished from the second century BCE to the first century CE, devoted to communal life, asceticism, and voluntary poverty.
20. The *Thesaurus philologicus criticus linguae hebraeae et chaldaeae Veteris Testamenti* by Wilhelm Gesenius (1786–1842) appeared in several volumes from 1828 and was left unfinished at the author's death. He had previously (1821) produced a well-known commentary on the Book of Isaiah.

# INDEX